CONFUCIANISM'S PROSPECTS

SUNY series in Chinese Philosophy and Culture

Roger T. Ames, editor

CONFUCIANISM'S PROSPECTS
A REASSESSMENT

SHAUN O'DWYER

Cover images taken by the author.

Published by State University of New York Press, Albany

© 2019 State University of New York

All rights reserved

No part of this book may be used or reproduced in any manner whatsoever without written permission. No part of this book may be stored in a retrieval system or transmitted in any form or by any means including electronic, electrostatic, magnetic tape, mechanical, photocopying, recording, or otherwise without the prior permission in writing of the publisher.

For information, contact State University of New York Press, Albany, NY
www.sunypress.edu

Library of Congress Cataloging-in-Publication Data

Names: O'Dwyer, Shaun, 1969– author.
Title: Confucianism's prospects : a reassessment / Shaun O'Dwyer.
Description: Albany : State University of New York, 2019. | Series: SUNY series in Chinese philosophy and culture | Includes bibliographical references and index.
Identifiers: LCCN 2018040415 | ISBN 9781438475493 (hardcover) | ISBN 9781438475486 (pbk.) | ISBN 9781438475509 (ebook) Subjects: LCSH: Confucianism.
Classification: LCC BL1853 .O39 2019 | DDC 181/.112—dc23
LC record available at https://lccn.loc.gov/2018040415

10 9 8 7 6 5 4 3 2 1

Contents

Preface		vii
Introduction		ix
Chapter 1	The Vicissitudes of Confucianism	1
Chapter 2	Ibsen's Nora and the Confucian Critique of the Unencumbered Self	33
Chapter 3	Confucian Ritual, Hierarchy, and Symmetrical Deference	61
Chapter 4	Filial Piety in East Asia and Beyond	97
Chapter 5	The Unity of Loyalty and Filial Piety: An East Asian Horror Story	131
Chapter 6	Epistemic Elitism, Paternalism, and Confucian Democracy	163
Chapter 7	Perverse Doctrines and One Hundred Schools: Confucianism's Place in Modern Pluralistic Societies	197
Notes		235
Index		265

Preface

This book engages in critical dialogue with a growing English language literature on Confucianism which, at times, has theorized improbable "Confucian" or "communitarian" identities for contemporary East Asian societies. It is also a critical dialogue with my own contributions to that literature over a decade and a half ago.[1] Living in Japan in the intervening years has helped cure me of my earlier communitarian tendencies, and of my previous interest in promoting *Confucian* democracy. For all of its flaws, Japan now strikes me as a consolidated liberal democracy, alongside its neighbors South Korea and Taiwan; and since they democratized, all three nations have provided unprecedented prosperity, civil freedoms, political stability, and peace for their citizens. I doubt that any comprehensive Confucian cultural and moral character can be attributed to East Asian nations today. I do not think a need exists for "Confucian" democracy to arise in them and—taking into account the rest of East Asia—I suspect the possibilities for democracy to take shape in any form, Confucian or otherwise, in North Korea or China in the foreseeable future are rather low. Part of my motivation for writing this book was to explain and justify these doubts; yet a fair consideration of Confucianism's prospects also required me to investigate its contributions to global political and moral philosophy, and to the diverse moral and civic life of East Asian societies today. I hope that readers will see this as a balanced approach, with sufficient tradition-respect for Confucian thought.

I would like to thank a number of people for helping me see this work through to its conclusion. First, I express my gratitude to the editors at State University of New York Press—to Andrew Kenyon, who initially took an interest in the book proposal, and to Christopher Ahn, Chelsea Miller, and Diane Ganeles for shepherding the manuscript through the peer-review and publication process. I am also grateful to two anonymous peer reviewers who took time to read the manuscript and offer both encouraging and constructive comments. Thanks also are due to Raymond Boisvert, Sungmoon Kim, Phillip Ivanhoe, Stephen Angle, and David Elstein, who read and provided helpful comments on drafts of several chapters. Parts of this book were presented at a workshop on Political Theory from East Asia hosted by the Center for East Asian Philosophy at the City University of Hong Kong in August 2016, at a Europe Japan Research Center seminar at Oxford Brookes University in April 2018 and at the Confucianism, Democracy and Comparative Theory conference hosted by the Institute of Glocal Political Thought at Sogang University in May 2018. I would like to thank attendees for questions and comments that helped me during revisions of this book. Finally, I would like to thank Ginny Tapley Takamori, Kanno Reika, and David Groff for their advice with some Japanese translations.

Two chapters in this book are revised versions of previously published papers. Chapter 2 was originally published as "Ibsen's Nora and the Confucian Critique of the Unencumbered Self" in *Hypatia* 31.4 (2016): 890–906; and chapter 7 was first published as "Epistemic Elitism, Paternalism and Confucian Democracy" in *Dao* 14.1 (2015): 33–54. My thanks are due to the editors of these journals for kindly permitting me to incorporate these papers into this book.

Introduction

The Problem of Confucian Heritage

In February 1942, as Japan was consolidating its hold on its newly conquered territories in Malaya, a new military administrator arrived in Singapore. He brought with him an adviser on Chinese affairs who scorned the humanitarian attitude of his predecessor in the military administration, Shinozaki Mamoru. Many years later, Shinozaki described his successor's contrasting administrative philosophy:

> Mr. Takase claimed to be a Confucian, as well as an authority on China and all things Chinese. He based his claim upon his stay in China and Manchuria. He mistakenly assumed that the Chinese community in Singapore behaved like the Chinese in China and observed the same customs. He wanted to rule by force backed by Confucian guidelines. What he failed to understand was that many Chinese in Singapore were born in Singapore, had been educated in English language schools, and could not read or write Chinese characters. They knew little about Confucius.[1]

In accordance with his philosophy of "force backed by Confucian guidelines," Takase proceeded with a scheme to extort fifty million yen from the Singapore Chinese community.

This account must come as a surprise to those who believe that Singapore is a "Confucian Heritage Culture," its ethnic Chinese citizens the often unreflective legatees of primordial Confucian values such as filial piety, harmony, and deference to government authority, passed down to them since their ancestors immigrated from their homelands in China. We know from numerous sociological studies that Singapore's "Confucian" culture has a heritage of recent vintage. It arose out of campaigns in the early 1980s by Singapore's ruling People's Action Party to promote Confucian moral education and a communitarian national identity to legitimize its rule and foster social cohesion.[2]

Yet if the pseudo-scholar Takase ignored the cultural heterogeneity between mainland Chinese and diaspora Malay Chinese in the 1940s, today's new Confucian scholars are sometimes as guilty of ignoring the cultural heterogeneity between contemporary East Asian societies and the profound changes in their ethical and political life since the late nineteenth century. Some have also been naïve about the alacrity with which autocratic rulers have adopted a cultural identity politics of "Confucian values" to foster national unity, and reactive self-definition against "the West."

This book proposes to disentangle philosophically significant discussion of ethical and political concepts in modern Confucian thought from such empirically undetermined assumptions about East Asian cultural identity. There are strong reasons for thinking that East Asian societies are *not* accurately described as Confucian societies. This is not to say that East Asian societies alone have endured the consequences of modernization. Following steep declines in participation in the ritual and communal life of Christianity since the 1960s, Western European nations cannot be meaningfully described today as *Christian* societies either. The respective Confucian and Christian heritages of these societies is not in question—nor is the continued, if diminishing, influence of values derived from those heritages.

Nevertheless, in pluralistic Western Europe and East Asian today, neither Christianity nor Confucianism is ever likely to regain the institutional dominance and cultural legitimacy it enjoyed in the past. Acknowledgment of this fact can provide a more realistic basis for scholarly examination of the value that both ancient and modern Confucian thought, alongside other East Asian intellectual traditions, can have for today's more pluralistic societies. Such acknowledgment can also provide a more realistic basis for political philosophical examination of the kinds of political order within which revived Confucian religious, political, and ethical practices can flourish. In line with that acknowledgment, this book urges a shift in primary ethical focus from the good of associations, including the family, taken by some Confucians to be an ongoing locus of primordial Confucian values, to the good of individuals, attainable through a variety of affiliations, ways of life, and identities.

Introduction

Articulating an Ethical Individualist Standpoint

An ethical individualism will inform the conceptual analyses this book will undertake of Confucian ethical ideas and political philosophical proposals, for which the focus of ethical concern is the good of the individual. Given the antipathy for individualism sometimes evinced in contemporary Confucian scholarship, an empirically based observation will go some way to explaining both the character and pertinence of this ethical individualist standpoint in an East Asian context. That observation is, that for young rural Chinese women in the twenty to thirty-five age bracket, the disintegration of one of the material supports for the practice of conventional filial piety and conjugal obedience—the extended rural patriarchal family and its patrilineal property relations—has likely been a good.

Suicide rates among rural Chinese women under the age of thirty-five were among the highest for this age and gender group in the world up to the late 1990s, at 37.5 per 100,000, according to a *Lancet* study in 2002.[3] A nationwide study of suicide rates conducted in 2014 found this suicide rate had dropped to 3 per 100,000 by 2011;[4] a longitudinal twenty-year survey in Shandong Province also found that suicide rates had decreased by 95 percent for rural women under the age of thirty-five between 1991 and 2010, from 49 per 100,000 to fewer than 5 per 100,000.[5] No improvements in mental health care provision could be cited as an influence on this dramatic decline. But two intriguing correlations suggest a different explanation. One is that this dramatic fall in suicide rates coincided with the movement of tens of millions of young rural women into paid employment, often through immigration to cities far from their rural homes. The other is that as urbanization has reached some 50 percent of the population over the past twenty years, national suicide rates have fallen by 63 percent.

It would be easy to jump to conclusions about this correlation—that after centuries of suicide epidemics occasioned by the oppressions of the "three obediences and the four virtues," young Chinese women have finally been liberated by waged labor and urbanization. However, it cannot be established conclusively whether these suicide rates are only a modern phenomenon, since easily-accessed pesticides in modern rural households have expedited impulsive suicide attempts in ways that would not have been possible in the premodern past.[6] Young working-class Chinese women have also discovered that, much like their Japanese sisters in the early twentieth century and their Korean sisters in the 1960s, they are vulnerable to appalling sweatshop labor conditions, though the associated communal living conditions have also facilitated trade union activism.[7]

Yet certain reliable conclusions can, and have been, drawn. Against those communitarian-minded Confucians who decry the breakup of communal, rural life in East Asia, there is something to be said for the emancipation of young rural women from the bonds of obedience to and financial dependence upon parents, husbands, and in-law families, where, as the authors of one study on rural youth suicide put it, "psychological strain, resulting from conflicting social values between communist gender equalitarianism and Confucian gender discrimination was associated significantly with suicide in young rural Chinese women."[8] There is also something to be said for their movement into urbanized settings and waged labor where they can exercise greater freedom of choice over their lives, and discover a measure of financial self-reliance that buffers them from the arbitrary dictates of families. Geographical separation of young women from the families that would bind them to traditional expectations, and financial independence, have enabled a more voluntaristic attitude to what were once the unchosen life vocations of marriage, childbearing, and care of aged parents-in-law, which subordinated personal interests to those of the family.

Such, I would say, has also been the discovery of young rural women experiencing industrialization the world over. The tragedy of their industrial exploitation, and their struggles against it, are inextricably mixed with their emancipation from patriarchal family relations and economic dependence. Confucian and communitarian philosophers might recoil at the materialistic, individualized way of life many such women have historically embraced, or have felt compelled to adapt to, in conditions of rapid industrialization as once conventional life vocations cease to be viable. But they need to make their case with acknowledgment of the dramatic improvements in life choices, opportunities to earn personal incomes, and life expectancy that rapid industrialization—and social atomization—has also brought for those once subordinated under older, communal ways of living.

This empirical insight lays the ground for the distinctive perspective adopted in this book. While recognizing the value of the philosophical contributions that Confucian thought—and its modern advocates—can make to pressing global moral and political questions today, an important evaluative standpoint of this study is its ethical individualist "capabilities approach" to human flourishing. If not yet universally applicable, I take this standpoint at least to have potential for being made universal. The gist of this standpoint, derived from the thought of Amartya Sen and Martha

Nussbaum, is that moral and political values, principles, and conceptions of the good, as instantiated in practices and institutions, are to be evaluated according to whether they enhance, or inhibit, the fundamental capacities "for truly human flourishing" in individual human beings. These capabilities include health, bodily integrity, educational attainment, practical wisdom and deliberative freedom, and control over one's environment sufficient to provide for one's own and dependents' sustenance.[9] Such capabilities can be understood as "being-able-to's," realized in "functioning" appropriate to the particular ends and goals people value, living within diverse affiliations and associations—*being able to* be healthy, to be in control over what happens to one's body in a variety of interpersonal contexts, to be educated in the skills and knowledge one needs for one's chosen and valued life pursuits, to make decisions meaningfully affecting one's own and one's dependents' goods, to earn an income or be assured of financial support sufficient to fulfill one's needs and interests and those of one's dependents.

While much has been said about the Aristotelian basis of Nussbaum's development of the capabilities approach, in its conception of a distinctive human flourishing realized through exercise of the central capabilities, also lying back of this approach are some fundamental Kantian and Marxian insights into human dignity. Deprivation of capabilities, whether willful or through the diffuse effects of economic deprivation and political marginalization, leaves human beings vulnerable to being used as means to the ends of others, rather than being respected themselves as ends.[10] As the Japanese novelist Natsume Sōseki famously observed over a century ago, it is an insight like this that makes individualism ethical. The *condicio sine qua non* for ethical individualism is not merely "refrain from coercion" but also "refrain from using superior power or status to render another as a mere means to one's ends," thereby obstructing him "from developing his individuality as he pleases for the sake of his own happiness."[11]

This capabilities approach dimension to ethical individualism still requires further explanation, however. Capabilities can be further distinguished into *basic, internal,* and *combined* capabilities. Basic capabilities are innate physical, mental, and emotional powers that naturally differ among individuals. Internal capabilities are personal traits, abilities, and skills acquired through familial health and social nurturance, support and education, including education and training of basic powers and talents. Combined capabilities are the "substantial freedoms" or opportunities people have to exercise, practice, and further cultivate their traits, abilities, and skills in a particular political, economic, or social situation.[12] To suggest an example pertinent to the cases of the sweatshop workers discussed above, an impoverished, rural young woman may have developed sufficient literacy, numeracy, and practical decision-making capabilities to manage her intimate life circumstances and affairs independent of the direction of significant others, and have a desire to do so. A factory job and residence away from her family home enables her to exercise these capabilities as combined capabilities, and *function* in ways that life in a communal, patriarchal community would not permit her to—to earn, spend, and save an income as she pleases; to form relationships, including sexual relationships, with others; to become a trade union activist; and so forth.

Conventional ideals of filial piety and obedience, as embodied in the traditional rural patriarchal family, demonstrably inhibited the development of those capabilities in large numbers of rural Chinese women, and so on this view there is little to regret in the decline of the rural patriarchal family with early twenty-first-century mass migrations of young rural people to urban employment. This conclusion is consonant with the ethical individualist position taken in this book.

The Focus and Plan of this Book

This book will focus primarily on the English language literature on Confucianism. This focus takes into account the efforts of some Anglo-American scholars to recommend Confucian thought as a source of global insight into moral and political philosophical problems beyond East Asia. It also enables light to be shed on the communitarian-liberalism controversy in Anglo-American academia as a background inspiration for some scholars recommending Confucianism as an alternative to liberal individualism and liberal democracy.

Chapter 1, "The Vicissitudes of Confucianism," overviews historical discussion of the dissolution of institutional and discursive Confucianism in the early twentieth century in China and Korea, and the effects of compressed modernization on ethical life in East Asian societies in the second half of the twentieth century. The chapter asks how different contemporary Confucian philosophers have responded to these transformations. It argues for a more eclectic approach to the philosophical heritage of East Asia and its bearing on contemporary ethical and political philosophical problems, and for a more critical review of contemporary Confucian arguments for a primordial "Confucian heritage"–based cultural identity for East Asian societies, differentiated from the "liberal West."

Chapter 2, "Ibsen's Nora and the Confucian Critique of the Unencumbered Self," takes issue with a metaphysical preoccupation in communitarian Confucianism with an "encumbered self" whose embeddedness in unchosen social roles, relations, and obligations is supposedly connected with a richer and more meaningful moral life than that led by the liberal individualist "unencumbered self." Analyzing the global popularity of Ibsen's individualist play *A Doll's House* and the responses to it by Japanese feminists a century ago, the chapter argues for a conception of a "disencumbered self" that *A Doll's House* heroine Nora represents for cross-cultural audiences and readers—a self that unburdens itself of unchosen obligations and roles that impede the development of human capabilities for intellectual and economic independence across different societies.

Chapter 3, "Confucian Ritual, Hierarchy and Symmetrical Deference," takes up a neglected Mohist criticism of Confucian ritual propriety (*li* 禮): that there is an inherent deficit of righteousness (*yi* 義) and humaneness (*ren* 仁) in the extravagance and hypocrisy of Confucian rites, and in their unthinking, customary practice. I reinterpret this criticism in the context of modernized, pluralistic East Asian societies to argue that rites can enact and rigidify status inequalities, exacerbating rather than ameliorating consciousness of inequality, and fueling status conflict; that such enactment infringes upon contemporary, increasingly global values of individual dignity and equality; and that the aesthetic value of socially "thick" rites practices is likely to dissipate in pluralistic social conditions where such conflict occurs. I offer an alternative, socially "thin" and egalitarian conception of rites and deference applicable in both contemporary Eastern and Anglo-American social contexts.

Chapter 4, "Filial Piety in East Asia and Beyond," engages with some dubious arguments made for filial piety (*xiao* 孝) as a distinctly East Asian virtue, or for the rejection of virtue ethics attributions to Confucius's and Mencius's thought, in favor of a distinctive role ethics within which *xiao* represents a "virtuosity" in practice rather than a virtue. Comparatively analyzing conceptions of filial piety in early and modern Confucian thought with eighteenth-century English theological thought and literature, the chapter argues for a more flexible, intercultural interpretation of filial piety as a virtue grounded in universal moral psychological traits associated with profound interhuman dependence.

Chapter 5, "The Unity of Loyalty and Filial Piety: An East Asian Horror Story," occupies the middle ground in this book's assessment of Confucian ethics and political philosophy, investigating projects to moralize the ruler-subject relation in the context of modern nationalism in East Asia, through unifying the Confucian virtues of filial piety and loyalty. Japanese philosopher Inoue Tetsujirō's early twentieth-century modernizing interpretations of Edo period Confucian slogans such as "The National Polity" (*Kokutai* 國體) and "the unity of loyalty and filial piety" (*chūkō ippon* 忠孝一本), and the legitimacy these interpretations gave for Japan's nationalism and militarism in the 1930s, illustrates one troubling political trajectory for this Confucian conceptual relation in East Asian states. This trajectory merits attention in a time of growing nationalist hostilities and geopolitical rivalry in East Asia.

Chapter 6, "Epistemic Elitism, Paternalism, and Confucian Democracy," represents the turn in this study to political philosophical concerns. It adopts a fresh epistemological perspective on the claims, central to the early Confucian tradition, that exemplary persons' moral cultivation and wisdom legitimate their entitlement to rule insofar as they can know the good of those whom they rule and can deliberate and act for that good on their behalf. The chapter accepts that certain Confucian values are compatible with representative democracy today in such countries as South Korea and Taiwan. However, some contemporary philosophical recommendations for a Confucian democracy founder because they hold too closely to Confucian epistemic elitism and paternalism, in the face of increasingly educated and restive East Asian publics. Others founder because they dispense with it or modify such elitism and paternalism, embracing a more participatory conception of democracy associated with Deweyan pragmatism—at the cost of any credible pragmatist or Confucian identification.

Chapter 7, "Perverse Doctrines and One Hundred Schools: Confucianism's Place in Pluralistic Societies," finalizes my challenge to Confucian scholars seeking the establishment of Confucian democracies in East Asia. The chapter argues that the best conditions for the open discussion of Confucian ideas, for the public advocacy of Confucian-inspired policy proposals and for unconstrained pursuit in ethical practice of the conceptions of the good they advocate, are those provided by a liberal democratic order recognizing liberal freedoms and capabilities, as is currently found in Japan, South Korea, and Taiwan. What these conditions also permit is a phenomenon that many modern Confucians implicitly or explicitly resist: a *gesellschaft* of competing ideas, beliefs, and lifestyle practices, tolerant of ways of living that some of its members regard as immoral and depraved. Within this social order, differently reformulated Confucianisms can flourish as reasonable comprehensive doctrines informing civil society activism, Confucian religions, and a conviction-based politics.

CHAPTER 1

The Vicissitudes of Confucianism

A Moral Earthquake and its Aftermath

The nineteenth-century Catholic theologian John Newman once famously mourned the "moral earthquake" of the Reformation, through which the church "lost, and has lost to this day, one-half of Europe."[1] The early modern Catholic church could keep count of its losses as European princes turned to Protestantism, as its churches and monasteries were destroyed or expropriated, and its clergy repudiated their faith or were driven into exile—although the powerful institutional base the Papacy retained enabled it to rally and ultimately to adjust itself to modernization and theological pluralism.

Some contemporary East Asian thinkers also mourn the losses suffered by Confucianism to modernization, civil war, and the iconoclasm of twentieth-century reformers and revolutionaries. Has a similar accounting of losses been possible for Confucianism since the early twentieth-century collapses of the Chinese and Korean monarchical states, and the abandonment of civil service examination systems grounded in knowledge of canonical Confucian texts? Is there good reason to believe that Confucianism has maintained continuity in the ethical lives of East Asians through these changes, rallying and adjusting itself to, even conditioning the industrialization and modernization of East Asia's societies? In order to properly evaluate such claims for continuity, and thus provide a realistic assessment of Confucianism's prospects today, it is important to understand what Confucianism lost as its institutional and intellectual legitimacy gave way during the tumultuous changes that swept over East Asian societies from the late nineteenth century onward.

It might seem questionable to compare the vicissitudes suffered by Confucianism through this era with those suffered by European Catholicism during the Reformation. Convincing arguments have been made to show that a unitary "Confucian religion" and "Confucian philosophy" are inventions of seventeenth-century Jesuit missionaries, eighteenth-century French philosophers, and nineteenth-century Japanese philosophers, and that constructions of Confucianism as a "world religion" are derived from late nineteenth-century European theological scholarship.[2] Doubts over such comparisons between Confucian and Christian "religions" are reflected in ongoing debates over whether to describe premodern state-institutionalized Confucian doctrines as "orthodoxies" evolved to impose uniform belief, or as "orthopraxis" evolved to impose uniform ritual observance. Such doubts also inform debates over whether these state doctrines succeeded in imposing a homogeneous Confucian culture in, say, late imperial China that reached beyond its literate elites to its rural masses.[3] Setting to one side these definitional disputes, it can still be said that Confucian doctrines had institutional bases in the Chinese and Korean monarchical states, which suffered measurable losses in the nineteenth and twentieth centuries: the reform of the premodern education system and the abolition of the civil service examination system (科舉制 *Keju zhi*) that it had served and the decline of state-sponsored temples practicing rites dedicated to Confucius and to other Confucian scholars.

The existential crisis that gripped the Qing Dynasty court in the late nineteenth and early twentieth centuries, under the stresses of rebellions fomented from within and of humiliating military defeats inflicted from without, provided the impetus for far-reaching educational reforms. Regional academies that had once schooled generations of imperial examination candidates in the Confucian canon had their curriculums progressively modernized in the late 1890s, and they were converted into middle schools and high schools in accordance with empire-wide education reforms in 1903. Following the abandonment of the imperial examination system in 1905, Confucian classics became more and more marginal in formal school curriculums, which increasingly used modern humanities and science textbooks translated from Japanese and European languages. With these profound changes, as Gan Chunsong puts it, "Confucian doctrine was no longer the precondition for gaining personal privilege" for aspirants seeking employment within the civil service via the examination system, and it also ceased to be "the sole channel for knowledge propagation" in late imperial China.[4] Civil strife brought further institutional loss: the renowned Hanlin Academy, influential for 1,200 years in formulating authoritative interpretations of the Confucian classics for the imperial examination system, was almost completely incinerated during the Boxer Rebellion in Beijing in 1900, and closed in 1911. In Korea change came at an earlier stage. Hundreds of Confucian academies were closed by order of the Prince Regent in 1871, leaving only forty-seven to continue operating.[5]

Over the course of two millennia there were also temples dedicated to Confucius throughout East Asia and in Vietnam. These temples, alongside Daoist and Buddhist temples, were subject to state patronage and funding. Most Confucian temples were in China and (from the fifteenth century) in Korea, practiced rites for legitimating imperial and monarchical rule, and were also closely associated with the academies. According to Anna Sun, 1,500 such temples spread across China by 1911. Following a brief Nationalist government flirtation with its own Confucian state religion, these temples fell into decay, and their staff dispersed. The Cultural Revolution subsequently wreaked as much havoc on them as the Reformation did on English Catholic monasteries and libraries in the sixteenth century. The Red Guards' desecration of the original Temple of Confucius and of the ancestral graves of the K'ung family in Qufu in 1966 was merely the most prominent of these attacks on China's Confucian heritage. Only a few hundred temples remain today, with thirty-nine now listed as "national cultural heritage sites."[6] Confucian temples were closed in North Korea in the postwar era, while 231 survived the devastation of the Korean War in South Korea and are in use today.[7]

The collapse of institutional Confucianism tells only part of the story of Confucianism's decline in the late nineteenth to early twentieth century. It does not tell us directly how this collapse affected the subjectivity of those who pursued their *dao* through the educational and political institutions that sanctified the Confucian canon, in Korea and China. To get a better grasp of this, we need also to consider the decline of *intellectual* and *discursive* Confucianism as its institutional supports gave away.[8]

Such institutional changes had important effects on the landowning social classes within which examination degree holders and failed-but-learned examination candidates were concentrated—the *Yangban* in Korea and the gentry in China. These landholding elites had performed local government roles and acted as agents for the dissemination and maintenance of Confucian rites among the rural masses. Without examination degrees and academies, they lost the main avenue for accumulating the cultural capital particular to their class. The Yangban finally dispersed following land reforms in the post-1945 era and the upheavals of the Korean War, while the last remnants of the gentry were seen off during persecutions carried out by the Communist Party in China in the 1950s. However, many would reinvent themselves as members of the new, urbanized elites of East Asia's industrializing societies.[9]

Preparation for the local, provincial, and national examinations from the fourteenth to early twentieth centuries required significant investment of finances and energy by Yangban and gentry families in the education of children in the Confucian canon, sometimes informally including girls, who would be expected as mothers to help guide their sons' progress through the examination system. The centrality of success in the examination system for elite social advancement, and the intrinsic value the learning acquired in preparation for it held as cultural capital for the gentry or *yangbang*, ensured that *intellectual* Confucianism occupied a central place in their lives. Benjamin Elman's study of the late Qing examination system shows how elite Chinese youth endured grueling daily regimens of study, beginning at the age of three with the memorization of characters, proceeding through the memorization of the four Confucian books and at least one of the classics by their early teenage years, and finally to the practice of writing composition.[10]

Early in the Qing-era novel *The Dream of the Red Chamber*, one of its heroines, the twelve-year-old Black Jade is asked by her grandmother how far she is advanced with her reading, and replies that she has memorized "the Six Classical books"[11] Yet the aristocratic world depicted in that novel reveals that its young men and women also found time for more edifying or recreational reading and discourse, ranging from the Confucian canon and commentaries to Daoist and Buddhist treatises, popular novels, and poetry. The administrative and security-obsessed system for maintaining the late imperial examination system and policing its candidates are suggestive, as Elman says, of a "coercive technology," a stupendous exercise in coercive "cultural and educational might" that rendered candidates as so many regimented, Foucaultian "docile bodies."[12] Still, it was also one constituent in cultures of shared literary, aesthetic, and ethical interests that extended seamlessly beyond canonical Confucianism to other literary and spiritual traditions. It was willingly participated in by elite youth eager to identify themselves with the erudition of their forbears, and eager to compete for social status that accrued through formal examination success, official appointment, and informal exhibitions of literary refinement. Wu Jingzi's novel *The Scholars* (*Ruilinwaishi* 儒林外史), near contemporary to *The Dream of the Red Chamber*, shows how much the intellectual Confucian world was the subject of intense yearning by those struggling—or failing—to advance in the examination system.

This brings us to *discursive* Confucianism. Discursive Confucianism consisted in the modes or practices of identity derived from popular and elite discourses that were authoritative at any particular time in helping define that identity. Such modes or practices were exhibited in styles of ritual comportment and manners, customs, linguistic and literary cultivation, dress, and so forth. The discourses included the canonical Confucian classics, the (varied) authoritative interpretations of them in circulation, and more popular or folk Confucian texts and traditions. Such discourses also extended to include ritual behaviors and behavioral expectations shared among cohorts of examinees, the families who invested in their education, and office holders in their relations with their former teachers and patrons. The nature of these discourses and the influence they had in shaping people's subjectivities at different times can be inferred not only from the Confucian classics themselves but also from later traditions of scholarly writing, popular texts, poetry, novels, and the diaries of scholars, examinees, and imperial officials.

The dismantling of institutional Confucianism—the abolition of the examination system, the closure or radical reform of schools, the fall of monarchies and of state-sanctioned Confucian cults and ritual—also brought about an eclipse of both intellectual and discursive Confucianism within the space of a few generations. Without the examination system as its rationale for existence, and with the rapid importation of the Western sciences and the humanities, intellectual Confucianism lost most of its status as a means to social advancement, as authoritative cultural knowledge, and as a locus of cultural capital. Discursive Confucianism and the exemplary (or not so exemplary) character types it evoked in Qing China—the teacher, the examination candidate, the literati, and the public servant—also became anachronisms.

Lu Xun's stories are often singled out for their supposedly iconoclastic attacks on Confucianism—with "Diary of a Madman" providing one paradigmatic instance—but in some there are more nuanced depictions of the decline of discursive Confucian self-identification, and of declining respect for Confucian learning in his generation during the first two decades of the twentieth century. The failed examination candidate and titular character of "Kung I-chi," sunk in degrading poverty and petty crime while scraping a living as a scribe, could pass as a character from *The Scholars* of 170 years earlier. In Lu Xun's telling he could just as easily serve as a parable for the fallen state of the literati, or even of the Chinese themselves, under the onslaughts of modernity. In "Soap," the hypocrisy, reactionary conservatism and Confucian sentimentalism of its main character Ssu-min are opened up to subtle ridicule. Ridicule is also subtly expressed for the bizarre antiquarian interests and questionable expertise of the "Seventh Master," a gentry-scholar character presiding over an iniquitous divorce settlement in *The Divorce*.[13]

Yet in Lu Xun's time, staunch defenders of the Confucian canon persisted, such as the philosopher Somerset Maugham interviewed during his travels in China in 1920, who bitterly summed up what had been lost:

> We sought to rule this country not by force, but by wisdom. And for centuries we succeeded. Then why does the White man despise the yellow? . . . Because he has invented the machine gun. That is your superiority. We are a defenceless horde and you can blow us all to eternity. You have shattered the dream of our philosophers that the world could be governed by the power of law and order.[14]

It is tempting to agree with Maugham's interlocutor and blame the collapse of institutional, intellectual, and discursive Confucian on exogenous factors, such as superior European and Japanese gunnery. Yet Gan Chunsong has also drawn attention to the dry rot of corruption within the late Qing examination system and civil service, which damaged their prestige and likely weakened the resolve of their literati defenders when they came under critical scrutiny in the late nineteenth century. Examination oversight was marred by increasing instances of cheating and bribery to examination officials. The sale of civil service positions and titles in the nineteenth century to boost state revenue depleted by the war against the Taiping rebels further undermined the system's legitimacy.[15] Many have criticized the alacrity with which the Qing Court abolished key institutions such as the *Keju*. But in light of the exigencies of the time—the unprecedented crises that had, first of all, overturned the very cosmological basis for the self-imagining of Imperial China's elites—such reforms appear more as the outcome of a not unreasonable desperation.

We should not be so hasty as to proclaim the dissolution of Confucianism only with the collapse of the state institutions that had once been its patrons, such as the Chinese monarchy, the Confucian temples, and the *keju* system. Just as important as the "high" Confucianism associated with the *keju* system, some would argue, was a folk Confucianism diffused through state-sponsored ritual practice and the moral instruction of regional literati into the lives of China's peasant masses. The communal life of rural villages and the patriarchal extended family provided some nonstate institutional basis for continued practice of residual Confucian values, including notably filial piety. Yet, no shortage of Chinese thinkers attest to the weakening of these institutions in the rapid urbanization and industrialization of late twentieth- and early twenty-first-century China, and to the influx of Christianity to fill the spiritual void left by these transformations:

> In mainland China, Confucianism has yet to develop a new organizational structure that is adaptive to a highly mobile modern society. For example, the migration of a large number of farmers into the city is a huge blow to the regulative power of the clan structure and customs that were supported by and supportive to Confucian political structure. A lover of China's traditional cultures cannot help but feel a sense of crisis here. By the sense of crisis, I did not mean to suggest that we resist Christianity and not allow it to be spread in China . . . What worries me and other lovers of the Chinese traditions is that Christianity, with the advantages of being a modernized and "industrialized" religion, of the financial, political, and institutional supports from the West, and of having the halo of being "Western" (read as "advanced"), will further weaken and even destroy the already weakened Chinese traditions.[16]

The Case for a Continued Confucian Identity: "Confucian Heritage Cultures," Confucian Values, and Habits of the Heart

Notwithstanding all the evidence for institutional collapse and social change described above, much English language Confucian literature today works on the presumption of a continuity between the institutional, scriptural, and discursive Confucianism of the past and the political and ethical life of East Asian societies today. They are often categorized as *Confucian* societies, or at least "Confucian Heritage Cultures," since that heritage is still active in shaping those societies' otherwise diverse ethical and political life.

The case for such a continued identity has been built on the concept of culture. Specifically, the argument goes, while the institutional and intellectual supports legitimating the Confucian canon in education and governance undeniably fell away in the early twentieth century, East Asian societies—and some South East Asian outliers—have been able to retain something of their distinct Confucian culture through the persistence of Confucian values and habits ingrained in the quotidian lives of their people—of *ren* (humaneness), *li* (ritual propriety), *xiao* (filial piety), and so forth. This Confucian culture constitutes a bedrock or—for those who prefer more organic metaphors—the cultural matrix or soil for these societies, both underlying, conditioning, and even rejecting subsequent cultural accretions, including foreign philosophies, ideologies, and religions. This underlying cultural matrix is also *unreflective*; its bearers may often be unable to recognize, or articulate, the Confucian origin or character of the values implicitly guiding their *dao*, in contrast to their more consciously professed religious, ethical, or political commitments.

The presumption of unreflectiveness seemingly undermines any singular Confucian identity attribution to these societies. Whatever the deficiencies of placing Middle Eastern or South Asian societies under the respective civilizational or religious-cultural identities of "Muslim" or "Hindu" (and those deficiencies are many), at least a majority of the citizens of those societies do self-consciously adhere to different varieties of Islam or Hinduism. In the case of Confucianism, which today lacks the institutional power bases of present-day Hinduism and Islam, the presumed cultural bedrock or matrix assumption makes up for this lack. Confucianism is what remains fundamental to identifying the ethos and distinctive *dao* of East Asian societies. These attributed characteristics—of an unreflective, culturally foundational Confucian identity—contribute to what I will call the "Confucian Heritage Ethos" (CHE) thesis.

If a normative argument could be associated with this thesis, it would run something like this:

1. There are ethical values and practices that set China and other East Asian peoples apart from the rest of the world, and which have been responsible for their distinct cultural flourishing.

2. Confucianism, as an ethical doctrine, is the chief contributor to these values and practices.

3. To sustain that distinct cultural flourishing in East Asia, Confucianism must be preserved as its central ethical doctrine.

This CHE thesis is an ideal type. The twentieth-century Chinese philosopher Mou Zongsan, often credited as one of the founders of today's New Confucianism, strongly conformed to this type through his close identification of Chinese culture with Confucian learning or *ruxue* (儒学).[17] However, the metonymic association between Confucianism and Chinese culture, or East Asian culture, predates Mou's twentieth-century thought. Some scholars date it to the efforts by Jesuit missionaries writing about China for a European audience to make imperial Confucianism its representative doctrine, in analogy with the role Christianity still held as the "spiritual background" for legitimating temporal political power in seventeenth-century Europe.[18] The "metonymic reduction" of China to Confucianism that appeared at this date was handed down to subsequent generations of European scholars, and was coincidentally taken up by modernizing Chinese intellectuals beginning in the early twentieth century. European "orientalist" imaginings of "Confucian" Asia have at least since the late nineteenth century developed symbiotically with some East Asian intellectuals' Confucian imaginings of their own societies, sometimes in conflict and sometimes in amity. Such imaginings have done duty in a "deficit" understanding of East Asian societies, in which Confucianism bore the blame for China's civilizational backwardness and vulnerability to foreign imperialism. But, as we shall see, they have also done duty in a "surplus" understanding that identifies Confucianism with the cultural and ethical vitality of these societies, and with their successful industrialization.

The "deficit" view of Confucianism is well known and often reiterated; the view of the May the Fourth intellectuals, of Hu Shih and his contemporaries who took the metonymic reduction of China to Confucianism seriously enough to denounce the latter as the one great obstacle to the reform and modernization of China. But what of the surplus view of Confucius? In East Asia, the conventional narrative is that it was the New Confucians such as Mou Zongsan who by the mid–twentieth century were pioneering a "surplus" view, reinvoking the metonymic identification between Confucianism and Chinese culture as a source for cultural nationalism and national renewal. Yet we need to go back earlier than that to grasp the modern development of the Confucian "surplus" view.

Beginning in the late nineteenth century, both Chinese and Japanese scholars grappled with the question of how to translate Western intellectual categories such as "philosophy" and "religion" into their languages, and of how to define their own intellectual and spiritual traditions in relation to these categories. This was not a trivial matter. Domestically, there was an urgent need to evaluate and define these traditions in light of newly encountered philosophical, scientific, and religious traditions from European societies that they saw as superior in technological and military power to their own; this was an acute epistemological as well as existential crisis that needed to be conceptualized, and resolved. Externally, and almost at the same time, the need arose to explain those domestic traditions in a manner that the publics of those same foreign powers would understand sympathetically, in the hope of eliciting "tradition respect," and indeed in eliciting a civilizational recognition that was of existential importance. For at this time, Chinese and Japanese intellectuals were becoming gripped by social Darwinist imaginings of a racial struggle for survival and domination, and it appeared to them that the Great Powers of the West were winning.

A famous instance of such explanation occurred at the 1893 World Council on Religions in Chicago. In a dignified and well-received presentation there on Confucianism, the First Secretary of the Chinese Legation to the United States, Yu Pung Kwang, highlighted the semantic difficulties of translating 教 (*jiao*) as religion and thus rendering 儒教 (*rujiao*) as "Confucian religion." He preferred to describe Confucianism as "ethical systems of thought."[19]

At a slightly earlier date, however, young Japanese scholars had begun the task of translating European philosophical, scientific, and literary works—and concepts—into Japanese, and pondering the conceptualization of East and South Asian intellectual and spiritual traditions in light of these translations. Nishi Amane, one of the first Japanese scholars to study in Europe, began a prodigious career of translating European political, psychological and philosophical thought in the 1870s, yielding a vast vocabulary of Chinese character–based renderings of European philosophical, psychological, and political concepts that subsequently passed into Chinese and Korean usage.[20] Another of these early scholars was the philosopher Inoue Tetsujirō, who compiled an influential dictionary of translated European and Sanskrit philosophical terms in 1881, the *Tetsugaku Jii* (哲學字彙) which he revised in subsequent decades. By the early 1880s it was concluded that "Oriental" thought could be described alongside European thought as philosophy or 哲學 (*tetsugaku*) under the newly minted Japanese translation for that term.[21]

Following his graduation from Tokyo University, Inoue spent 1884 to 1890 studying Kantian and Hegelian philosophy at German universities and traveling through Europe. Prior to his trip to Europe, Inoue had also commenced work on a history of East Asian philosophical thought (東洋哲學史 *Tōyō Tetsugaku Shi*) explaining his motive thus: "Up to now, the splendid history of Western philosophy and religion has been well developed, and its research methods established. However, a history of Buddhist religion (仏教

Bukkyō), Confucian thought (儒學 *Jugaku*) or of *Shintō* has never yet been developed, and its research method has to be established."²²

As Kiri Paramore argues, it was Inoue who gave the first persuasive definition to Confucianism as a mode of philosophical thought, or field of scholarship analogous to European thought and philosophy. He did so by reinterpreting ancient Chinese characters (儒學) that had originally denoted "Confucian learning."²³ He also helped define its status as central to the ethical identity of the Japanese, in distinction from the ethical identity of European civilization, in a newly emerging cultural nationalist discourse. The Preface to his 1900 work on the Japanese Wang Yangming School, *Nihon Yōmei Gakuha no Tetsugaku* (日本陽明學派之哲學) stated that he "felt there was a need for historical research into Japanese philosophy (日本哲學 *Nihon tetsugaku*)" and that his motive for this research lay in eliciting what we might call tradition self-esteem among his fellow Japanese for their own distinctive national morality (国民的道徳 *kokuminteki dōtoku*). For as he saw it, some of his fellow scholars in the Meiji Restoration Era were now "advocating" and "insisting upon" foreign philosophical doctrines such as utilitarianism and egoism; and if the spread of these foreign ideas was not contained, "the likely outcome from all this in the end is the ruination (破壊 *hakai*) of our country's national morality."²⁴ As we shall see in chapter 5, Inoue would give a much more expansive expression to this conception of a national morality in the coming decades.

It is difficult to qualify how directly Japanese scholars such as Inoue influenced contemporary Chinese intellectuals, many of whom received university educations in Japan, and who subsequently sought to revalue Confucianism as philosophy. There are suggestive connections. For instance, during his exile in Japan after 1898 the pioneering Chinese nationalist thinker Liang Qichao interacted with many Japanese scholars, was deeply influenced by Inoue's scholarship on Wang Yangming and his advocacy for a Confucian-centered national morality, attended lectures by Inoue on that topic, and translated a number of Inoue's articles into Chinese.²⁵ In any case, a developing scholarly consensus is that late nineteenth-century Japanese definitions of Confucianism as a philosophy have had longstanding influence in subsequent East Asian and international scholarship on Confucianism.²⁶ By the early 1920s Chinese scholars such as Liang Shuming and Zhang Junmai were beginning to classify Indian and Chinese thought, including Confucianism, alongside Western thought as philosophy. The term *ruxue* (儒學) defined Confucianism as a system of learning or *thought* that fitted within the canons of philosophy, or *zhexue* (哲學),²⁷ much as

Japanese scholars such as Inoue had claimed that it did four decades earlier.

In the long run, with Confucianism redefined as a field of philosphical scholarship, its advocates could find a means to ensure it outlived the death of its premodern institutionalized, scriptural varieties. Decades of excellent scholarship have been put into making a persuasive case for the legitimacy, and intellectual worthiness, of East Asian philosophical traditions against Eurocentric definitions of philosophy. With such status, Confucian thought can be understood as a set of ethical and political philosophies that can yield insight into contemporary ethical and political problems, in the way that scholars such as Stephen Angle argue that it should, when he writes that Confucianism seeks to "articulate truths about how people should best organize their societies" *anywhere*.[28]

There are, however, somewhat more ambivalent consequences to this redefinition of Confucianism. These arise from the uses Confucianism has been put to in defining a distinctive cultural and ethical identity for East Asian nations (as described above), and which Inoue sought to do with his studies in Neo-Confucianism. This was for the purposes of ethnocultural nationalist or pan-Asian self-definition against the West, and against the culturally corrosive intellectual and economic forces attributed to it at different times; atomistic individualism, egoism, materialism, and neoliberalism. In this instance Confucianism could again be defined independently of the vanished political and educational institutions within which it had held canonical status.

In Japan, Confucian virtues, including especially filial piety (孝 *kō*) and loyalty (忠 *chū*), came instead to be seen as constituents of a national and ethnic spirit, or *volksgeist* (国民精神 *kokumin seishin* / 民族精神 *minzoku seishin*), that together comprised a national morality distinct from that of China or of Western nations. Translations of these latter Hegelian and post-Kantian concepts into Chinese characters can be found in the 1912 revised edition of Inoue's *Philosophical Dictionary*, and they helped retool Confucian virtues for a cultural as well as statist nationalism in Japan that claimed an unbroken heritage extending into the premodern past.[29] Chinese thinkers such as Mou Zongsan later used a similar conceptual template, employing the same post-Kantian and Hegelian concepts of national and ethnic spirit and national culture (民族文化 *minzu wenhua*) to argue for the centrality of Confucianism to Chinese culture. However, unlike Inoue's Confucian nationalism, Mou's cultural nationalism remained solidly connected to advocacy for a liberal democracy within which Confucianism could attain its true character.[30]

In today's "surplus" interpretation in contemporary Confucian thought and its impact on modern East Asian societies, the CHE thesis manifests itself in two ways. The first makes Confucianism the equivalent of the Protestant ethic in the economic rise of East Asia's dragon economies. This branch of the thesis arguably took inspiration from Robert Bellah's pioneering 1960 study of incipient modernization in late premodern Japan, *Tokugawa Religion*. Bellah's study argued that indigenous value systems—in Japan's case, *Shintō*, Buddhism, and Confucianism—could provide a Weberian "functional analogue" to Protestantism in the West, in driving economic, educational, and political reforms that prepared Japanese society for more wide-ranging modernization in the late nineteenth century.[31]

Developed at a time when Japan was on its way to establishing its status as a postwar economic power, this thesis later took hold among Asian studies scholars as other East Asian countries embarked on their own successful industrialization projects. Confucianism, the ethical tradition most easily identified as indigenous to East Asia, could now become a source of cultural pride through being correlated in a positive manner with East Asia's successful industrialization. This neatly reversed the "deficit" correlation it had previously labored under.

It was Western-based Asian studies scholars including Tu Weiming and Peter Berger who adapted the CHE thesis to explain the rapid development of East Asian economies.[32] Other scholars such as Ezra Vogel and Morishima Michio have also been its advocates, though with some reservations.[33] They concur that while state support for Confucianism did collapse, Confucian values have persisted as often unconsciously held "habits of the heart" among elite and ordinary East Asians. Values such as filial piety, harmony, loyalty of ordinary citizens to governing elites and those elites' benevolent paternalism have, on this argument, helped drive the remarkable economic development of the East Asian tigers of Japan, South Korea, Taiwan, and (more latterly) China in the postwar era. Tu Weiming sums up this view in a way that also bears witness to the enduring influence of Robert Bellah's thought in the CHE thesis, this time in the concept of Confucianism as a "civil religion" analogous to the civil religion Bellah attributed to the United States:

> . . . more than a century of western domination has not totally undermined the moral fabric of the Confucian discourse . . . the

Confucian discourse remains the "civil religion" of East Asia, including Mainland China, North Korea and Vietnam. By "civil religion" is here meant the value system that guides ordinary behavior as well as gives ultimate meaning to life in society.[34]

But Tu goes on to admit that East Asian societies, dominated for a century by "western ideas rooted in the Enlightenment mentality which glorifies science and democracy" are no longer traditionally Confucian. To get over this hurdle, Tu avails himself of another of Bellah's coinages, arguing that what persists today, informing and shaping the industrialization of East Asia's tiger economies, is a "bourgeoise Confucianism" at once distinguished from the "high Confucianism" of China's premodern "Mandarin elites" but also in continuity with it.[35] If institutional Confucianism no longer holds sway, Confucianism retains its dominion in the hearts (or the "heart-mind") of East Asians.

The second main branch of the CHE thesis is in some ways a continuation of the first, and some of its scholarly advocates are adherents of the first branch as well, but it looks forward to a substantive Confucian role in the future ethical and political life of East Asian societies. As we have already noted, for the CHE thesis, Confucianism is the foundational cultural matrix or native soil of East Asian societies, and this conditions, and limits, the types of ethical life or political institutions and practices that can stably settle or take root in those societies. There are subtle differences to how these conditions and limits are stated, however. In one sense they are shown to be obdurate, resisting certain nonindigenous ethical and political traditions, or strongly conditioning their actualization in those societies. In another sense they are vulnerable to a deracination in the face of influxes of nonindigenous ethical and political traditions, and this deracination will constitute a grievous loss to East Asian cultural heritage, as well as leading to social anomie, spiritual decay, and political disunity in East Asian societies. In light of this latter sense, some scholars will claim that there is an imperative to preserve Confucianism as the distinct ethical and political inheritance of East Asian societies against such deracination. The erosive, nonindigenous traditions most referenced in discussions of this second branch of the CHE thesis are those of political liberalism, economic neoliberalism, and, in ethics, liberal individualism.

This branch of the CHE thesis has an interesting genealogy. The self-destruction Europe brought on itself in World War I encouraged disillusionment about Western civilization among Japanese and Chinese intellectuals[36] and coincided with a growing cultural nationalism that sought self-definition from the West through the articulation of distinctive national and ethnic characters. The economic instability of the 1930s and the growth of hypernationalism and fascism also saw the enlistment of Confucianism into a Japanese national identity sharply distinguished from the supposed materialism and individualism of the West, as we shall see in chapter 5.

The 1958 "Manifesto for a Re-Appraisal of Sinology and Reconstruction of Chinese Culture" (为中国文化敬告世界人士宣言 *Wei Zhongguo Wenua Jinggao Shijie Renshi Xuanyan*) by Zhang Junmai, Tang Junyi, and Mou Zongsan is regarded as a landmark statement of this branch of the CHE thesis in the postwar era,[37] but it was not until the 1970s that this thesis began to gain a wider audience, including in the Anglophone world of Sinology and comparative philosophy. At the same time—in the 1970s through the 1980s with the ending of the Cold War—the lights of universalist political ideologies such as Marxism were fading in Western academic and radical political circles, and among elites in communist nations who had witnessed its economic and political failings firsthand. The subsequent market-based reforms in numerous postcommunist societies, and in China, seemed to provide proof of a growing economic globalization dominated by Western liberal ideology. The post–Cold War era saw the birth of arguments for a coming intercivilizational struggle, exemplified in Samuel Huntingdon's influential "Clash of civilizations" thesis, which had a profound impact on many Chinese scholars and political leaders. This thesis heightened their sense of cultural difference from "the West" and gave them renewed confidence to identify the cultural resources—namely, in Confucianism—with which they could articulate a counternarrative for their societies' successful modernization, in the face of "liberal Western" assertions of global economic and cultural hegemony.[38] The self-confident aspects of this cultural pride were intermingled with a more fragile self-regard, which provided a defensive motivation for the ideal of reasserting distinctive national cultures: to ward off the globally homogenizing forces of globalization and liberalization.

It is easy enough to denounce the reactionary nativism and self-serving character in the "Asian values" rhetoric that reached its height in the 1990s. More worthy of note are the not always reactionary intellectual currents also informing these reactions, often in Anglophone university humanities departments, including postcolonial theory,[39] comparative cultural studies, and communitarianism, revaluing and asserting what are construed to be premodern or ethically and culturally particular indigenous traditions ignored or threatened by Westernization. Today the pressing issue is not the danger of conquest by Western powers, but of "cultural survival," cultural self-determination, and the demand for recognition of cultural specificity in the face of a seemingly Western-imposed globalization.

Some of the more ardent defenders of the idea of a Confucian and communitarian East Asia manifesting cultural difference from the West are scholars writing in English in North American and East Asian humanities departments. Since this book will be engaging with the thought of these scholars, it would be useful to dwell on the motivations for the sometimes rather sharp assertions of cultural difference between Eastern thought and Western philosophy sometimes found in their scholarship. One more frequently stated motivation arises from a disenchantment among both progressive and conservative Anglo-American intellectuals with the ills of neoliberalism and atomistic, rights-based individualism in their own societies. There is sometimes manifested an attitude of what the Japanese call *akogare* (憧れ), or yearning, for the supposed *gemeinschaft*-like communitarian values of Confucian societies, which provide an alternative to the alienating egoism and inequality of American society today. Beginning with Josiah Royce, American moral philosophers have from time to time looked to an idealized East in search of remedies to a perceived excess of individualism in their own societies.[40]

Yet just as important is an attitude of what sociologist Aamir Mufti has called "anthropological philanthropy."[41] While Mufti coined this term to characterize a recent trend of valorizing orientalism about political Islam in postsecularist anthropology, I believe it applies in some Anglo-American comparative philosophy on Confucianism as well. At the heart of this anthropological philanthropy is a concerted scholarly effort to atone for and remedy past Eurocentric dismissals of non-Western intellectual and spiritual traditions, which often were integrated with colonialist economic and military strategies pursued by the Great Powers against East Asian, African, and Middle Eastern societies. This postcolonialist sensibility is laudable when based on rigorous, dispassionate comparative studies that have the *result* of eliciting the intercultural tradition respect discussed earlier. In the case of East Asian studies, it lurches into more perilous territory when it merely reverses the terms of older, Confucian *deficit* imaginings of East Asian societies with a Confucian *surplus* imagining that replicates the same reductive "Western" and "Eastern" tropes for articulating the cultural differences between them: the deficient "individualism" and "rationalism" of Western thought, opposed to the praiseworthy "communitarianism" and "aestheticism" of Confucian thought. A mode of analysis committed to locating and valorizing these tropes for East Asian cultural difference cannot help but find what it is looking for.

Such scholars are participating in a tradition of criticism on behalf of cultural difference and independence extending back to Johann Herder, who first popularized the concept of "culture" itself in the eighteenth century. Herder was deeply sensitive to the plights of European folk cultures and of non-Western societies threatened by the homogenizing influences of French Enlightenment thought and European colonialism. So when, for instance, Roger Ames and Henry Rosemont complain of an "unfortunate asymmetry" in comparative philosophy that makes Anglo-American thought the universal, default norm against which Chinese thought is defined and assimilated, losing its distinctiveness,[42] they would have found a sympathetic ear in Herder. For he railed against the universalist, homogenizing aspirations of an Enlightenment thought and science carried by the "threatening hands of the Europeans," and defended the right of the Chinese and other non-European peoples to hold to their own intellectual traditions and despise "even the most beautiful rose brought to (them) by a serpent."[43]

The political and ethical theoretical implications of this application of the CHE thesis I want to draw attention to are these, assuming that a Confucian ethic has had the beneficial influences claimed for it in East Asia's industrialization and economic development, and that Confucian values, habits of the heart, and civil religion are continuous with the institutionalized Confucian cultures of East Asia's premodern societies. First of all, then, it can be (and has been) argued that Confucianism has a special claim to preeminence in generating distinctive political and ethical theories suited to the cultural and political conditions of contemporary East Asia. Confucianism can claim to have been an enduring intellectual influence in China and then East Asia over two millennia, to have been central to the elite educational cultures and political orders of Korea, China, and Vietnam from the fourteenth to fifteenth centuries onward, and to the ritual and ethical lives of regional elites and masses in the same time period. In having played such a central political and ethical role in the premodern past, and in continuing to exert a beneficial influence in East Asia's modernization, Confucianism can thus be argued to have a special legitimacy as a source of political and ethical philosophical ideas for conceptualizing the ideal political order and conditions for human flourishing for East Asian societies today.

Second, and relatedly, Confucianism can claim to have such preeminence on the basis of its long, enduring cultural presence in the ethical lives of East Asians themselves. It can be said to be the outcome of an *organic* transmission within and between their cultures, in one of the senses Johann Herder meant by organic—as a receiving of a tradition transmitted by others, in which the recipient absorbs it and converts it "into his own nature, as the food by means of which he lives."[44] As such an organic transmitted tradition, Confucianism can be shown to have gradually became adapted to and domesticated within the particular intellectual, ritual, ethical and political life of East Asian societies. It can then be contrasted with *external or alien* political ideas and ideologies imposed from without, or from the top down through domestic reforming zeal within in a much shorter time span. Modern Western ideas of Enlightenment rationalism, individualism, economic liberalism, liberal democracy, and human rights are prime candidates for such designation, either forced on East Asian societies from the late nineteenth century up to today by the colonialist or economically hegemonic policies of Western nations, or imposed internally by local elites scrambling to modernize and industrialize their societies. The ethical individualism at the heart of the present study can also be rejected on these same terms, as something inimical to the organic Confucian inheritance of East Asians.

Taken seriously, these claims not only purport to position Confucianism as a key philosophical resource in political and ethical philosophical theorizing for East Asian societies; they also establish its *preeminence* over claims made on behalf of originally non–East Asian political philosophies, including, say, Marxism, liberalism, or different varieties of ethical individualism to a say in theorizing East Asian political order and ethical life. One strong implication of a distinction between organically transmitted cultures and traditions, and alien ideologies and doctrines abruptly introduced from without, is that the latter, by definition, are less likely to be assimilated or "digested," to become domesticated. As "alien transplants" suddenly introduced to native cultural soils, these ideologies are likely to be rejected, to be misunderstood and misapplied, or they insinuate themselves in such a manner as to cause widespread anomie, cultural confusion, and conflict in their clash with indigenous values. The apparent lack of support for Western ideas of liberal freedoms even in democratized East Asian countries and the apparent growing cultural dislocation of East Asians torn between globalizing influences of neoliberalism, materialism, and individualism on the one hand and indigenous Confucian values on the other may all be cited as evidence for the difficulties of introducing and normalizing Western liberalism in Confucian East Asia.

So it is also common in Anglophone Confucian ethical thought today that the focus for moral reflection in Western moral philosophy—in both its utilitarian and deontological guises—is the rational, autonomous rights-bearing individual and that this individualism, so conceived, cannot be properly realized in Confucian societies, having developed in the culturally specific circumstances of Western liberal societies. Thus according to Henry Rosemont, in cultures—such as Confucian cultures—in which there is no concept of human rights, how can, or should "the members of those cultures imagine what it is like to have rights, or that it would be right or good or proper for them to so imagine?"[45] Supposing that they do have some idea, Bhikhu Parekh asserts that "some will find the language of rights individualistic, legalist, statist and aggressive, ideally suited to their idea of an atomized Western society but not to one as cohesive as theirs."[46] Indeed, according to Ruiping Fan, "Confucianism is not compatible with the liberal version of human rights because Confucianism cannot accept the absolutist principlism and individualism that characterize the liberal version of human rights."[47]

For political philosophers such as Tan Sor-hoon, "Confucian societies are capable of an alternative future as Confucian democracies, different perhaps from Western liberal democracies."[48] For other theorists such as Daniel Bell, Confucianism, alongside legalism, has "shaped and continues to shape understandings informing political practices and ways of dealing with social problems" in East Asia, and so "If human rights, democracy, and capitalism are to take root and produce beneficial outcomes in East Asia, they must be adjusted to" these political traditions.[49] For David Hall and Roger Ames, John Dewey's pragmatist democratic ideals are suited for such adjustment, and can help develop a "viable and humane democracy that remains true to the communitarian sensibilities of traditional China while avoiding many of the defects of rights based liberalism."[50]

From the 1990s down to today, such conceptions of a distinctly Confucian political, ethical, and Confucian cultural identity (or narrative) for East Asian societies have been assailed by critics for being analytically imprecise, empirically underdetermined, and even question-begging. Critics have pointed to the diversity of religious and political values and identities within and between modern East Asian societies, to the internal diversity within so-called Confucian doctrines themselves and to the self- or reverse-orientalizing character of present-day "Confucian values" talk, to call into question the search for a distinctive, modern East Asian Confucian culture.[51]

Still, the efforts by the late nineteenth-century Japanese state and of post-1945 industrializing East Asian governments to legitimate their modernization through appeals to "tradition," and by inculcating what they deemed to be traditional (and often recognizably Confucian) virtues through mass education, are real enough. Equally real is a recent cultural efflorescence in China as both intellectuals and the public have developed a renewed interest in the folk- and high cultural practices of Buddhism, Confucianism, and Daoism, finding in them an antidote to the alienation provoked by modernization, and an inspirational source for spiritual meaning and renewed cultural identity. This efflorescence involves genuine bottom-up participation by a growing public of readers and practitioners, largely free of top-down direction by the Chinese Communist Party.[52] In the past decade the Chinese Communist Party has attempted—with hesitation—to harness the popularization of Confucianism for its own legitimacy, laying claim to its credentials as both steward and promoter of Chinese culture.[53] Behind this efflorescence is a growing cultural self-confidence buoyed by China's tremendous economic advances since the 1980s, and, from the Chinese government's point of view, an eagerness to project that cultural self-confidence on an international stage.

So I do not want to dismiss out of hand attributions of Confucian identities to East Asian society, nor to belittle claims about the continuance of Confucian values in the lives of twenty-first-century East Asians. But these attributions do merit closer philosophical scrutiny, and this will be the subject of the rest of this chapter.

The Philosophical Cases for East Asian Confucian Identity and their Challenges

I will accept on principle that Confucian values, virtues, or habits of the heart are candidates for consideration as "thick ethical concepts"—concepts that carry, and entangle, both descriptive and evaluative content, such that, as Hillary Putnam once put it, "to use them with any discrimination one has to be able to identify imaginatively with an *evaluative point of view*."[54] This mutual entanglement of descriptive and evaluative content is aptly put in Bernard Williams's characterization of a thick concept being both "guided by the world" and "action-guiding . . . guided around the world by its descriptive content, but it has a prescriptive flag attached to it"[55] The meaningful application of such a thick concept requires first that it make sense in its application to states of affairs, or to individuals, from the point of view of a community within which that thick concept is customarily used. If the concept does indeed make sense when used in an ethical judgment of conduct, this gives the person uttering it and those hearing it and consenting to it reason for action. Thus, saying that defrauding one's elderly parents of their income is an unfilial act must correspond in some way to the descriptive content of what filial piety is for a community in which the terms *filial* and *unfilial* are meaningful, and apply meaningfully to what are understood to be permissible and impermissible ways in which children become involved (or not) in their parents' financial affairs. If meaningful, such judgment gives reason for moral condemnation and actions to intervene to stop it, punish it, and secure relief for the victims of that unfilial conduct.

So to be able to pick out the extension and intension of such a concept, one must be competent in understanding how that concept is a value that is action guiding within the practices of a particular community or society, even if one personally rejects it as an evaluative, action-guiding standard. Insofar as such concepts, at any one time, stably hold this intertwined descriptive and evaluative content for the community or society whose practices they are instantiated in, they can be described in Emile Durkheim's terms as *social facts*. That is to say, they hold their descriptive and evaluative content independently of any individual whim or desire that this content be other than what it stably is for a specifiable community. They are also experienced as having a "compelling, compulsive power" insofar as they are embodied in ethical codes that are themselves independent of individual whim.[56] These values stably hold this content as an outcome of unreflective customary observance, or as the settled and widely acknowledged outcomes of inquiry and reflective criticism, which finds that they are justifiably valued. Either way, the content of such concepts is independent of individual will and (with a few exceptions) cannot be altered by it.

I will set out here three criteria by which we can, or cannot, say that there are today *Confucian* values that fall under this definition of "ethically thick concepts" and that are social facts in the manner just described:

1. That they are the subject of a minimal common specification to the communities or societies within which they are (or were) instantiated

2. That they are (or were) demonstrably instantiated as action-guiding values in the communities and societies to which they are attributed

3. That they are the subject of a noncontested attribution as *Confucian* for the communities and societies within which they are (or were) instantiated

Some explanation is called for. Criterion 1 points to the need for a fine-grained analysis of how an ethically thick concept may be specified relative to particular linguistic, ethical, or religious communities, on the understanding that specifications may vary at different times, or between different communities in the same society. Across both Christian communities and secular organizational and social life in Western European societies, for instance, *charity* can be specified as the practice of benevolent giving to the needy. But for Roman Catholic communities, charity has a richer intension as *caritas*, incorporating love for God and for fellow human beings. These different descriptive contents for charity are complementary, but a more finely grained analysis will delve into the different communities for which these senses have differing social facticity.

Criterion 2 draws attention to the difficult matter of value instantiation. Assuming a finely grained, specifiable value content as outlined by criterion 1 above, there is still the need to demonstrate that it is instantiated as a social fact, which is to say that it is both "guided by the world" and "action guiding" because it is embedded in the life of both individuals and associations, establishing (1) the ideals or exemplars toward which the conduct of individuals and associations is aimed in fulfilling a way of life or enterprise particular to an individual or association and (2) the ideals and exemplars that provide standards for evaluating when conduct falls short of or satisfies the ends of some way of life or enterprise. Attribution of such values requires rigorous study grounded in philosophical anthropology and psychology, both through inferring a particular value instantiation from studies of the characteristic habits, practices and evaluative judgments of individual, associational, and institutional life, and through studies of the self-reported value commitments of individuals and representatives of associational life. Robert Bellah's investigation of individualist values in middle-class American life in *Habits of the Heart* provides one example of such a study.

Criterion 2 thus requires a fine balancing of emic and etic perspectives in determining whether such values are correctly attributed to a particular way of individual and community life. It takes into account both that values (or deficiencies in their realization) may be mistakenly attributed and not instantiated, or that they were once instantiated, but have become obsolete, no longer "guided by the world," thus rendering their application anachronistic.

So it is the case that with cultural change, certain values can cease to be instantiated in a community's life, retaining their social facticity only in a historical sense. The seventeenth- through nineteenth-century European concept of honor, enacted in the last resort in dueling rituals, and the concept of chastity, applied mostly but not exclusively to the sexual conduct of women, are now obsolete. It is of course possible retrospectively to "identify imaginatively with (the) evaluative point of view" implied by honor and chastity and thereby grasp both the descriptive and evaluative content of such concepts, but they are no longer social facts in contemporary ethical life.

Supposing that a particular "ethically thick concept" is minimally specifiable in relation to the ethical life of a particular community, and is instantiated in the ways of life and practices of both individuals and associations, there is the further question of whether the concept is to be defined as *Confucian*, which brings us to criterion 3. The retort will be that obviously some values are iconically Confucian, such as filial piety, for instance. The reply to this retort is that, first, this does not establish an exclusive Confucian claim on this value (if this claim is being made), as other religious and philosophical traditions, such as Judaism or Christianity, may make a claim on it. Second, some contemporary Confucians are, as we shall see shortly, inclined to cast their net beyond "iconic" ethical concepts as filial piety to incorporate a much wider range of values. The question to ask is whether this Confucian attribution is contested or not—whether it is the subject of a conflicting claim from another tradition within the same society, or indeed whether, from an emic perspective, it is even acknowledged to be Confucian at all. In this respect we need to be on our guard against a tendency to reduce Confucianism to an open cultural identity canvas, abstracted from historically specific social practices and institutions, so that as Kiri Paramore puts it, "any theory or value that could be related" to a canonical Confucian text "could also be claimed for Confucianism."[57]

The Dream of the Red Chamber gives us a vivid presentation of the specification and uncontested instantiation of such an ethically thick concept, albeit at the rarefied level of the highest class of nobility in the lives of the fictional Jia clan in Qing era China. At one point the households of the Jia estate are abuzz with news of a forthcoming "visit of filial reverence" by Jia Yuanchun, a daughter of the family who has become an imperial consort. A nurse asks for an explanation of the meaning of this visit, which provides the occasion for Jia Lien, one of the men of the household, to expound upon filial reverence and the emperor's fervent embrace of it:

> Our present Son of Heaven is a great advocate of filial reverence. He regards the respectful attitude of children to their parents as a universal law of nature which is binding upon the whole

human race regardless of difference of class; and he considers that the maintenance of filial reverence is the most important duty of a wise government, because by it human society can be kept in order in the simplest, most natural way. Our reigning monarch himself shines forth with good example in this respect by surrounding his aged parents, their former Majesties, with every conceivable sign of filial love, day and night.

In his effort to further promote filial reverence, the emperor notes that his consorts rarely have the chance to meet their parents and express their filial devotion to them, "and that the divinely appointed harmony that should rein in human society is severely injured by this." Moved by these thoughts, he proposes that his wives be able to meet their parents in the imperial palace twice a month. His still living, retired parents respect his attentions but fear the inconvenience and indignities to the court that might come with such visitations, and issue an alternate ruling that the imperial wives be allowed, on request, to visit their parents on the condition that their parents have accommodation appropriate for an imperial consort.[58]

This passage provides us with an instance of a thick ethical concept that is specified and subject to a common understanding as a social fact for the aristocratic community depicted in *Dream of the Red Chamber*. The emperor's conviction that filial reverence is binding for all classes and for all human beings also illustrates a universalist ideal for filial piety which comported with the interethnic unity promoted by China's eighteenth-century Manchu rulers, sensitive to perceptions of their own foreignness in the eyes of their elite Chinese subjects. Second, it is shown to be instantiated as an action-guiding norm at a number of levels of social practice—at the level of imperial decree itself, by the emperor and his parents who seek a more harmonious expression of filial reverence in their court and among their subjects in the rituals and ceremonials of the visit of filial reverence, which Confucians will tell us are intended to regulate and dignify the human passions and affections particular to filiality, and in the filial intent and affections of Jia Yuanchun herself for her family.

For the Anglophone Confucian thought at the focus of this study, it is clear that conceptual blind spots and biases may sometimes compromise its ability to meet these three standards for social facticity of thick ethical concepts. Consider the fine-grained conceptual analysis needed to address criterion 1, that a thick ethical concept be specifiable as holding its evaluative and descriptive content for a specifiable community. One notable problem in light of this criterion is what feminist philosopher Uma Narayan has described as a cultural essentialist habit that "equates the values, worldviews and practices of some socially dominant groups with those of 'all members of the culture.'"[59] In the present case, the danger is that, given a prior assumption that a given society is *Confucian*, some thick ethical concept deemed to be Confucian in nature will be held to be a value for an entire national community, and will be held to have primordial instantiation in habits and practices extending back to the premodern past.

For instance, into the twentieth century, certain specifiable values have been the subject of elite and popular consensus *as well* as contestation in the development of modern East Asian nation-states—particularly, of filial piety and loyalty, as we have seen. Such value specifications are to be found, for instance, in the work of influential moralists and education officials promoting Confucian education for their citizens, as well as in more popular discourse. Take for example the 1890 *Imperial Rescript on Education* (教育ニ関スル勅語 *Kyōiku ni kan suru Chokugo*), one of the foundational documents of the new Japanese nation-state and written by government officials Inoue Kowashi and Motoda Nagazane. It set forth a conception of filial piety and loyalty that was to be profoundly influential in Japan's pre-1945 education system. It incorporated filial piety and loyalty into a famialist conception of the state (家族国家 *kazoku kokka*) with the paternal figure of the emperor and his unbroken ancestral lineage at its center.[60] It would be easy to assume that these modern, *statist* conceptions of filial piety and loyalty were specifiable as *the* Confucian thick ethical concepts for the entire Japanese state of that period.

Yet, in the early twentieth century, anti-statist, popular conceptions of filial piety circulated and anchored themselves in more localized traditions. One example is Yosano Akiko's antiwar poem "Thou Shalt Not Die" (君死にたもうこと勿れ *Kimi Shinitamō Koto Nakare*) written for her brother, who was engaged in the siege of Lushan in the Russo-Japanese War in 1904. Her verses explicitly give priority to the familial and filial obligations he has to their Osaka merchant family, with its inherited "laws of a merchant house" (家のおきて *ie no okite*), *against* the state requirement that her brother offer up his life in loyalty to the emperor.[61] This poem was immensely popular at its publication, and also attracted accusations of being unpatriotic and treasonous.[62] Both the *Imperial Rescript* and Yosano's texts provide snapshots into the rival varieties of statist and antistatist conceptions of filial piety instantiated in early twentieth-century Japanese popular and elite discourse.

Criterion 2 requires us to delve deeper into both emic and etic understandings of the instantiation of Confucian values in East Asian life today. Two questions need to be more seriously considered in the Anglophone Confucian literature in light of this criterion. The first concerns whether the Confucian thick ethical concepts are indeed instantiated according to the (highly diverse!) emic self-assessments of East Asians, and according to the etic based sociological studies of the behaviors and practices in which those values are found to be instantiated or not. The second question concerns the claimed *primordial* status of those values—whether their presumed instantiation in, say, the "heart-mind" of contemporary East and South-East Asians represents an unbroken continuity with those same values as they were instantiated in premodern Asian states. The legitimacy and persuasiveness of many contemporary Confucian arguments for a distinct Confucian ethics, for a distinct Confucian democracy or other form of illiberal political order, depend directly or indirectly on this primordialist thesis. If the primordialist argument holds, Confucianism can stake its claim to a level of historically prior importance and value as an indigenous, organic ethical tradition over more recent "Western" imports such as political liberalism, individualism, and Christianity, which might also have a claim on the heart-minds of contemporary East Asians.

There are reasons for doubt over both of these questions. Much of the current New Confucian literature asserting the ubiquity of *unreflective* Confucian values and habits of the heart in the quotidian lives of today's Chinese, and of East Asians in general, suffers from two potential disadvantages in light of criterion 2. First of all, the attribution of such values and habits may not be the outcome of careful, fine-grained qualitative as well as quantitative research into the value orientations of contemporary East Asians. It is noteworthy in this respect that Robert Bellah's *Habits of the Heart* study investigated the values of middle-class Americans, balanced self-reported insights of respondents with the etic perspective of an anthropologist, and revealed not one, but four varieties of individualism in middle-class American life: of older biblical, republican individualisms gradually ceding influence to the newer utilitarian and expressive individualisms of a modern, urbanized American society.[63] By contrast, efforts to attribute a deep matrix of Confucian habits of the heart or values to 1.5 billion East Asians of diverse creeds and social classes, living under markedly different political regimes, must be greeted with great scholarly caution unless they are grounded in the sort of analysis that Bellah and his colleagues pioneered.[64]

The conclusions Doh Chull Shin drew from his analyses of the Asian Barometer Survey and World Value surveys of East Asian's ethical value commitments should also give political philosophers pause before they commit themselves to the notion of a singular, deep Confucian value or habit attribution to the citizens of East Asian societies:

> In historically Confucian East Asia today, popular attachment to Confucianism is miles wide but only inches deep: most of the population report attachment, but a shallow attachment, to Confucian legacies . . . (the region) is no longer a single cultural zone in regard to the public's attachment to the legacies of Confucian social and political ethics. The region is divided into two subregions: in one, there is broad, but not deep support for Confucian legacies; in the other, support is neither broad nor deep.[65]

Second, taking seriously the notion that ethically thick concepts *are* action guiding, such analysis must probe beyond culture identity–attributing platitudes about Confucian values and look for evidence to show that they retain their authority to be action-guiding in actual conduct—or whether they are in the process of losing it. For instance, South Korea, supposedly the most Confucian of East Asian societies, had by far the highest elderly poverty rates in the OECD in 2013,[66] elderly suicide rates in East Asian nations are double or even triple those in Western European and North American nations,[67] and cohabitation between parents and married children—one of the bases for everyday practice of filial piety in the past—is in steep decline across the region. These factors *may* be taken as indirect evidence that with the shrinkage, geographical dispersal, and economic insecurity of families and the growth of single-person households in historically low welfare societies in East Asia, filial piety is less of an action-guiding value than it was in the past. This conclusion is compatible with the understanding that filial piety may be an object of nostalgic yearning in people whose lives have been shaken by rapid cultural and technological change.

Finally, even granting that there is such instantiation, advocates of a Confucian ethic thesis must also come to grips with and refute arguments by East Asian sociologists and political scientists that even if today's Confucian values are still observed, they have a shallow rather than primordial historical horizon, as products of a twentieth-century modernization that is *discontinuous* with the institutional Confucian life of premodern East Asian states. Thus, contemporary instances of filial practice are sometimes argued to be an artifact of a twentieth-century universalization of a previously elite Confucian famialism, and of famialist welfare policies by East Asian developmentalist states in the twentieth century that encouraged co-residency with elderly family members, which rationalized filial piety ideologies to motivate citizens to undertake elderly care.[68]

Supposing that an "ethically thick concept" is minimally specifiable in relation to the current ethical life of a particular community, and is demonstrably instantiated in the ways of life and practices of both individuals and associations, there is the further question of whether the concept is to be defined securely as *Confucian*, which brings us to criterion 3. The question to ask is whether this Confucian attribution is contested or not—whether it is the subject of a conflicting claim from another tradition within the same society, or indeed whether, from an emic perspective, it is even acknowledged to be Confucian at all.

An instance of arbitrariness in attributions of Confucian identity to certain value concepts can be found in the editorial introduction to a collection of papers on affective relations in East Asian societies. The editors recognize the importance of avoiding cultural essentialism and orientalism in comparative philosophical discussion of a value such as *guanxi* (关系) and call for "more fine-grained philosophical analysis of what Confucianism says regarding the importance of affective relations for the self . . . (and) fine-grained historical analysis to specify the transmission of affective relations over the years." However, they go on to make the following statement: "To the extent that *guanxi* is rooted in Confucian culture, it is also important to study its manifestations in other East Asian societies that have been influenced by Confucianism."[69]

Apart from the rather static, ahistorical concept of "Confucian culture" evident in this description, such rootedness cannot be assumed; it must be the outcome of the very fine-grained philosophical and historical analyses the editors advocate. One task of such analysis is to interpret the manner in which members of China's political elites in different eras have negotiated the tension between their respect for ideals of moral cultivation within long-term, affective familial and familial-like relations of gift giving and exchange that could be compared (without anachronism) to the types of relations that constitute *guanxi, and* their respect for an ideal of meritocracy that militates against official appointments influenced by obligations incurred in those same affective-based connections. From such interpretations it would be possible to infer whether or to what extent *guanxi*-like behavior is a trait that is, or was, valued by Confucianism at different times. Failure to undertake such analysis can lead to crude, question-begging assumptions that if behavioral trait *x* is an East Asian trait, it must also be Confucian, because East Asia is a Confucian culture.[70]

A good deal hangs on the outcome of inquiries into these three conditions for identifying Confucian thick ethical concepts. Suppose that specifiable Confucian values or habits of the heart are weakly instantiated or no longer instantiated, failing to meet these standards, or lack organic continuity with Confucian practices of the premodern past, or that even though certain values are claimed for Confucianism that attribution is disputed, for instance by rival, non-Confucian traditions. Suppose that Confucian habits of the heart, even if still held to or still the objects of nostalgic longing, no longer constitute a deep moral-psychological and cultural matrix in the ethical lives of most East Asians. If this is so, "Confucian Heritage Ethos" justifications for giving Confucian philosophical doctrines (in all their diverse contemporary formulations) precedence over other political philosophical theories such as liberalism in proposals for new or reformed political constitutions in East Asia are less convincing. So also might justifications fail for drawing a line between Confucianism as a live, organically inherited intellectual tradition more suited to the polities of East Asia and the external intellectual traditions supposedly lacking such organic grounding, because they are less able to be transplanted into East Asian cultural soil. Incompatibilities and difficulties in application there may well be, but these could also be explained by more historically proximate factors than an organic Confucian cultural heritage. One such factor is the twentieth-century statist, developmentalist, or Communist heritage of East Asian societies, which may leave some of their citizens and political elites inhospitable to liberal conceptions of individual and civil rights.

Avoiding the Cultural Identity Politics Trap in East Asian Philosophy

In a recently published book, Joseph Chan addresses the question of why he should not develop a distinctive political philosophy of his own, without relying on Confucian ideas or a Confucian self-identification. His answer is instructive:

> [M]y interest in Confucianism is cultural as well as philosophical . . . (my) interest reflects my cultural commitment as a Chinese scholar, and my desire to see this traditional school of thought-one that has influenced China and other societies for more than two thousand years-remain alive and vital, and develop and flourish into an attractive vision for modern life and society.

For this reason he identifies himself as a "Confucian-inspired scholar." Chan states further that his interest in the Confucian classics is a continuation of his immersion in ancient moral thought, East and West, which shared a common perfectionist orientation to "ethics, society and politics."[71]

The question I would like to ask Chan and other philosophers who identify themselves as "reconstructive" and "progressive" Confucianists, or as "Confucian inspired" philosophers is this: why only Confucius? Why *must* Confucianism be identified as the paradigmatic East Asian philosophy, from which insights into the modern world's moral and political problems are to be mined, often with considerable exegetical ingenuity and selectiveness?

I have of course already supplied some of the explanation why. Confucianism, still remembered as the scriptural basis for educational and governing institutions in premodern Chinese and Korean states, and as the foremost canon of ethical thought in East Asia, has become central for some cultural nationalist self-definitions in the face of a feared Western political as well as cultural hegemony. Anglophone comparative philosophy eager to atone for past (or not so past) colonialisms and cultural imperialisms from the West, and in search for ethical alternatives to an alienating liberal individualism, has also contributed to the continued articulation of such self-definitions.

More important are the empirical and conceptual problems in identifying East Asian societies as "Confucian" societies, or as societies still influenced in their ethical and political life by a primordial Confucian heritage culture. That there are enduring values that enjoy social facticity as thick ethical concepts still active in the quotidian lives of East Asians and that are demonstrably *Confucian* needs to be demonstrated through conceptual and empirical study, rather than just assumed, especially in the face of social science scholarship that Confucianism today is neither so continuous with the past nor so active in the ethical and political life of the present. Yet even if that hurdle should be cleared, political problems remain to be considered for scholars who want to build a case for an enduring Confucian political and ethical culture in East Asian societies.

These problems center on whether such scholarship will become complicit with a cultural or statist nationalism that takes Confucianism as one of its central self-identifications. In chapter 5 I will outline the catastrophic trajectory of one such statist nationalism in early mid-twentieth-century Japan. In the meantime, I will conclude with an outline of three orientations that this study will take toward the question of "Confucian Cultural Identity" from chapter 3 onward, as providing an alternative approach to the study of Confucianism in Anglophone comparative philosophy.

First of all, the task of explaining and justifying the worth of Confucian ethical and political ideas for global ethical and political problems should be detached from the projects of articulating distinctive Confucian ethical and political identities for East Asia, on the basis of assumptions about enduring Confucian habits of the heart, values, civil religions, and so forth. The latter projects, I would argue, should be the object of caution until or unless better social scientific groundings can be found for their presuppositions of enduring Confucian identities in East Asian life. The following chapters of this book will embody this cautious, critical approach.

Second, it is time to heed Chad Hansen's neglected call to go beyond a "ruling interpretative theory" that identifies "Chinese philosophy with Confucianism," which discusses other Chinese, non-Confucian philosophies "from the perspective of Confucianism" and "dismisses obvious philosophical objections to Confucianism as Western or modern anachronisms and hints that critics who raise these objections have an unfair analytic bias."[72] The following chapters will draw freely from Mohist as well as modern non-Confucian philosophical perspectives on ancient Confucian thought and its modernizing reinterpretations. Not only do these perspectives yield fresh criticisms of ancient and modern Confucianisms by contemporaries well versed in their weaknesses, they also testify to a diversity in East Asian philosophical traditions that advocates of the "ruling interpretative theory," for all of their own wider scholarship in East Asian intellectual traditions have rather perversely contributed to undervaluing. The "surplus" view of Confucianism as *the* paradigmatic Eastern philosophy, central to the distinctive political and ethical identity and civilizational flourishing of East Asia—is but the mirror image of Confucianism as *the* paradigmatic basis for East Asia's centuries-long civilizational stagnation, generating a distinctive, backward ethical and political culture that also made it vulnerable to colonization and Western-defined modernization. In different ways, both views do an injustice to the traditions of Confucianism.

Last, the following chapters will repeatedly draw attention to the inevitable cultural hybridity that frames, and entangles the hermeneutics of intercultural "East-West" dialogue, of cultural self-presentation and of representation of other societies' traditions and creeds as "culturally different." Somerset Maugham's Chinese philosophical interlocutor, who spoke so eloquently to him of a Chinese Confucian civilization threatened by Western gunnery, is a good example to start with. His name was Gu Hongming, and he was born in colonial British Malaya, of mixed ethnic Chinese and European ancestry, raised as a multilingual British subject, and educated not in the *keju* system but at Scottish boarding schools and at the University of Edinburgh. He did not begin learning the Chinese language, nor study the classical Chinese and the Confucian classics themselves, until he was in his mid-twenties, when he became an early convert to the cause of Chinese cultural nationalism.[73] His early twentieth-century writings on behalf of Chinese civilization and culture, which found much more favor with European and Japanese than with Chinese readers, are as reflective of his romantic nationalist ideals and his deep European literary knowledge as they are of his deep knowledge of the Confucian classics and Chinese literary heritage. He turned to Matthew Arnold in order to explain to his readers the "imaginative reason" that revealed the "spirit of the Chinese," as seen in the "best of their art and literature," and Wordsworth's poem "Tintern Abbey" provided him with the language to explain what was distinctive about that spirit.[74] This is not to say that Gu's self-presentation as a Chinese scholar and his scholarly presentations of Chinese culture and civilization were therefore fake. It is rather that such presentations—the elaboration of cultural and civilizational identities different from the "West" and deserving of equal respect with it—are, in their very invocations of distinct "culture" and "civilization," shot through with concepts, ideals, and yearnings spliced from the multiple, internally diverse cultural heritages of China and of Europe. In such hybridity there is reason for optimism, rather than pessimism, about bridging "cultural divides" in philosophy.

CHAPTER 2

Ibsen's Nora and the Confucian Critique of the Unencumbered Self

The Confucian Dimension to the Liberal-Communitarian Debate

In chapter 1 I argued that some doubt hangs over the notion that Confucianism provides material for the modern-day construction of a Confucian ethical and democratic political life in East Asia different from that of the liberal West. I called attention as well to the yearning for a culturally different "other" in East Asian societies. This finds expression in a valorizing orientalism in some Anglophone Confucian philosophy, in the conviction that there is in the "communitarian" life and Confucian philosophy of East Asian societies an alternative vision of the good ethical life that does not prize the "autonomous, rights-bearing individual." My concerns about this valorizing orientalism have been drawn in broad brush strokes so far, however. It is time to go into more detail about these reservations, beginning with the very conception of ethical personhood offered by communitarian and communitarian Confucian philosophers today, set up in contrast against the liberal individualist "unencumbered self." The theorizing of this contrast is a major thematic preoccupation for today's communitarian Confucians. In making the case for the ethical value of the *disencumbered* individualist self against these communitarian philosophers, this chapter will also provide me with the pretext to further explain the ethical individualism that underlies the normative vision for this book.

Like many philosophical controversies, the Anglo-American liberal-communitarian debate ran out of steam without a decisive conclusion. Communitarian philosophers highlighted deficiencies in a liberal individualist conception of the "unencumbered," "freely choosing" self "unencumbered by antecedent moral . . . or civic ties,"[1] an "individual prior to and apart from all roles."[2] They also criticized a moral universalism that ignored its own cultural and historical contingencies and a liberal morality which, in prioritizing "the right" over "the good," undermined the community life needed for its sustenance. Yet, whether they invoked an earlier era of Republican liberalism or of premodern community life, communitarians could not offer a compelling alternative to pluralistic liberal institutions and practices.

Still, this debate lives on in other forms, behind arguments about the universal application of liberal conceptions of rights and the individual in non-Western societies with supposedly more communitarian cultures, such as in East Asia. One point of contention is whether there is (or could be) an ethically universal basis for criticism of patriarchal marital practices and for women's right to exit from them, which trumps the culturally particular role-expectations placed upon married women within nonliberal societies or communities. Is the solution to these problems only found in an ideal conceptualization of women's identities as unencumbered, rights-bearing selves, free to choose their social roles? Or do reformed nonliberal moral traditions offer more ethically particularist and culturally appropriate internal criticism of unjust practices? Some contemporary thinkers inspired by Confucian thought believe that they can, and their arguments merit scrutiny.

A late nineteenth-century literary work might not be expected to foster insight into these debates. Yet Henrik Ibsen's play *A Doll's House* has had such enduring influence in international argument over women's rights, including first of all their right to exit from unjust roles and relationships, that its implications for the controversies described above should not be ignored. Some twenty-five years ago Jeremy Waldron argued that a bedrock of guaranteed individual rights remains vital to securing individual welfare even in affective relations such as marriage, and that communitarians underestimate the prospects "for things to go wrong" in such relations whenever they rail against invocations of such rights.[3] This chapter uses the international reception to Ibsen's *A Doll's House* to develop Waldron's original thesis in a more explicitly intercultural direction, adopting a broader capabilities approach to frame the individual freedom to exit from iniquitous affective relations.

The two arguments advanced here, drawing inspiration from this play and the international arguments over gender and justice it has provoked, are as follows: First, that the closing pages of Ibsen's play offer one compelling version of the *ethical* individualist self as a *disencumbered* rather than *unencumbered self*, a self detached by conscientious reflection from roles it finds to be unjust. Second, and against ethically particularist Confucian objections, the global influence of this play—illustrated in its first non-Western performances in Japan at the beginning of the twentieth century—points to the potential for cross-cultural standards for the criticism and principled rejection of marriage practices that impede women's human capabilities. These standards are embodied in the conduct of Nora's disencumbered self. Early Japanese bluestockings' responses to Nora's individualism provide evidence for the intercultural articulation of those standards.

Ethical Individualism in *A Doll's House*

In 1908 Edmund Gosse recalled the first Norwegian performances, in 1879, of Henrik Ibsen's play *A Doll's House*; a play that climaxes with its housewife protagonist, Nora Helmer, deserting her paternalistic, selfish husband and her family to pursue her own self-education. Gosse claimed that "all Scandinavia rang with Nora's 'declaration of independence.'"[4] Gosse probably had the following exchange from the play's last scene in mind. Nora's husband, Torvold, shocked at Nora's announcement that she will leave him, reminds her of her "most sacred duties" to her husband and children, that "before all else" she is "a wife and a mother." She replies:

> I don't believe that any longer. I believe that before all else I am a reasonable human being, just as you are—or, at all events, that I must try and become one. I know quite well, Torvald, that most people would think you right, and that views of that kind are to be found in books; but I can no longer content myself with what most people say, or with what is found in books. I must think over things for myself and get to understand them.[5]

At the time of the first performances of *A Doll's House*, Nora's declaration was understood by her detractors and sympathizers to be revolutionary. But for contemporary communitarian thinkers such as Alasdair Macintyre, Charles Taylor, and Michael Sandel, and for communitarian Confucians such as Henry Rosemont, it would express a shopworn metaphysical *idée fixe*. It expresses the problematic ideal of an *unencumbered, liberal individualist* self, a substantial, rational self separate from and able to define itself outside of traditional roles and responsibilities, "unencumbered and unconstrained . . . altogether independent of others in deciding what to do."[6]

What Nora's individualism expresses is not just a repudiation of her marriage and parental responsibilities to pursue her own good. It also articulates for itself an ideal of *authentic selfhood* counterposed to the social roles that she repudiates for its sake. Moreover—as Charles Taylor states in his partially sympathetic appraisal of the ideal of authenticity—such a person "feels called to do this";[7] Nora feels that she would be untrue to the better, more authentic self she could become if she does not desert her family.

The question arises of what individualism is in question here, and I think *A Doll's House* points toward *ethical* individualism. I want to highlight two not automatically compatible facets of this individualism in the philosophical literature devoted to it:

1. *Objective/Normative*: the focus for moral concern is the individual and the individual's capabilities for human flourishing; the moral worth of institutions and practices in any society is to be measured by whether they hinder or promote fulfillment of those capabilities.[8]

2. *Subjective/agentic*: the source of moral principles and values, of moral evaluation, and of final authority in moral evaluation is the individual.[9]

Number 1 specifies the capabilities approach to ethical theory that has already been outlined in the introduction to this book, according to which capabilities are what human beings "are able to be and to do" if they are to be fully-functioning human beings leading dignified lives.[10]

A sympathetic reader of *A Doll's House* may be inclined to the objective/normative position of ethical individualism. Nineteenth-century marriage as depicted in *A Doll's House*, and the norms that made an economically and mentally dependent state in marriage the only viable vocation for middle-class women, stand condemned for hindering their capabilities for full human functioning. Nora complains that she only ever had the same opinions and tastes as her father and husband; maintained by them in a state of immaturity, she is never able to fulfill even her roles as a wife and mother.[11]

Most likely, the sympathetic reader will also lean toward the subjective/agentic perspective on ethical individualism that Nora herself adopts at the end of the play, that she can no longer be in a state of mental dependence, which means that *she* is to be the ultimate moral authority for evaluating her marital state and her place in the world as a woman.

A little reflection reveals an incompatibility. On the objective normative/evaluative view presented in human capabilities theory, there are moral facts about institutions and practices that can be arrived at through appropriately conducted inquiry, facts about whether those institutions and practices enhance or obstruct human capabilities. Yet on the subjective/agentic view, since the individual is the ultimate source of moral principles and values and the ultimate authority in moral judgments, there are no moral facts that hold independent of the individual's judgments or preferences, and "no empirical description of the world compels us to adopt any set of moral evaluations or principles, or even limits the range of our value choices."[12]

We can imagine, then, an objective/normative perspective establishing that certain practices within a community or society do hinder certain women's fundamental capacities, and so are to be judged sexist and unjust. However, we can at least conceive of the subjective/agentic position of someone, let's say "individual A," engaged in those practices who will protest that, according to her reflectively chosen principles and values these practices are not sexist or unjust at all, but rather are integral to the fulfillment of her own self-chosen *telos* in life. Since the individual is the ultimate authority in moral evaluation, she will also feel justified in rejecting the supposedly empirically grounded conclusions of the objective/normative analysis as offensive or culturally imperialistic. Even worse, if someone else, "individual B," similarly but unwillingly engaged in those practices, disputes A, claiming that they *are* sexist and unjust, that the full realization of her own capacities requires the reform/elimination of those practices or her exit from them, there are no objective moral facts or criteria allowed by the subjective/agentic view for adjudicating the arguments of the two parties.

An additional possible objection arises from feminist epistemologists regarding the individualist framing of the objective/normative and subjective/agentic positions. Suppose that the objective/normative position is occupied by institutionally powerful agents, in relation to women who (unlike Nora, say) are members of "hermeneutically marginalized" ethnic and racial communities. Policymakers and experts occupying the objective/normative position may conclude that women in these communities have had their chances for human flourishing impeded by patriarchal institutions and practices specific to those communities. The women in those communities who protest otherwise are exhibiting their epistemically compromised "adaptive preferences"—the "adaptation of desires and preferences to existing inequalities viewed in terms of perceived legitimacy," where those preferences are the result of unreflective habituation and deeply "conditioned perceptions" of what constitutes such legitimacy. Their own perspectives on their lives may then be dismissively relegated to a "subjective" position, though one acquired through unreflective habituation rather than reflective choice.[13] Epistemic injustice can take two forms in such conclusions. One is what Miranda Fricker terms testimonial injustice, when women in those positions are denied epistemic credibility and silenced through having an *a priori* "oppressed minority women" status ascribed to them.[14] The other is *contributory injustice*. Suppose that those same women *do* reflectively value their own, community-, and tradition-specific hermeneutical resources for conceptualizing their human flourishing, yet the institutionally powerful agents evaluating their life situation willfully refuse on *a priori* grounds to acknowledge these hermeneutical resources as holding epistemic value. The latter will thus not engage those women's expertise in formulating, and evaluating, their own conclusions, that will in consequence be biased and distorted.[15]

One way around these incompatibilities and potentials for epistemic injustice is to assert conditionally the priority of the objective/normative view for ethical individualism, but to maintain important insights from the subjective/agentic view for criticism and modification of the former view—namely, that the individual participating in institutions and practices is not only the *focus* of moral concern in evaluating those institutions' and practices' hindrance or enhancement of individual capabilities, but is also one of the most important agents for articulating such concern, on the assumption that firsthand experience lends epistemic credibility (if not finality) to her insights into life within those institutions and practices.

This does not appear to eliminate the potential conflict between Individual A and Individual B or between the subjective/agentic and objective/normative perspectives discussed above, but it is not intended to. I will merely assume that subjective/agentic perspectives can in principle yield epistemic insight, and that objective/normative and subjective/agentic perspectives can *both* be internally diverse and fallible, so therefore likely to benefit from being exposed to dissenting insights. There is potential here for concerns about epistemic injustice to be allayed, so long as stipulations are made for women from marginalized communities to become meaningful participants into inquiry regarding the obstacles, and facilitators of their human flourishing within their communities (and outside of them). However, the compromise I suggest between these perspectives does stipulate that meaningfully free participation in patriarchal institutions and practices rests on unrestricted capabilities of practical reasoning and freedom of association.

This attempted balancing of objective/normative and subjective/agentic perspectives can also neutralize the problem of "adaptive preferences." My perspective, in not preempting valuation of certain exercises of individual agency, opens up a space for at least contentious tolerance between divergent assessments of practices that are arrived at reflectively, and leaves the door open for continued argumentation over their ethical worth. It accepts that women can reflectively embrace patriarchal gender roles, and can have a reflective (and not just "conditioned") preference for living in patriarchal associations or communities.

A final feature of this balancing is that it enables an expansive domain for ethical perfectionism and ethical pluralism, but it is incompatible with political perfectionism. A political perfectionist doctrine through which the state promotes the good of its citizens—a perfectionism that many Confucians advocate for—will potentially clash with the capabilities approach outlined above. If the subjective/agentic approach commits a person to an exercise of capabilities—of *functioning*—incompatible with that conception of the good(s) the state promotes in accordance with political perfectionism, prima facie grounds arise for the state to discourage that person from doing so, through coercive or noncoercive means. Yet, at least where coercion is concerned, this would amount to the state impeding the exercise of certain important capabilities, such as the capability for practical wisdom and reflective choice, through which individuals can assess, revise, and change their conceptions of the good on their own through trial-and-error experience or inquiry. Political perfectionists, including Confucian political perfectionists, may have a rejoinder to this objection, and I will take up this issue again at the end of the chapter, and in chapter 6. Suffice it to say that for ethical individualism, the permissible, nonperfectionist justification for coercively curtailing exercise of capabilities arises whenever such exercise unjustly interferes with others' exercise of their capabilities, with the realization of *their* human flourishing. It does this either through coercion (as classical liberals understand it) or through a failure to observe special obligations the agent is already bound to observe in assisting those others to realize their capabilities.

Communitarians, Confucians, and the Disencumbered Self

There is a strong communitarian Confucian objection to the analysis developed above. The objection is that for people reared in traditionalist communities, the most valuable social roles and relationships are often those they *have not* chosen but have been born into and/or unreflectively accepted. To suggest as the objective/normative perspective does that an institution's or practice's respect for individual freedom of choice be a primary criterion in evaluating its moral worth is already to yield to an individualist bias. This is not to say that Confucians' own perspectives forbid criticism or exit from unjust social practices and institutions. Rather, they will argue that criticism proceeding from an individualist, rights-based position imposes Western values on non-Western societies and is unlikely to be persuasive in those contexts. There are metaphysical and ethical aspects of their perspectives that need to be disentangled, however, to get to a deeper understanding of what they mean by "encumbered" and "unencumbered" selves.

It is relevant here to quote Henry Rosemont's Confucian conception of a selfhood realized through its ethical cultivation in social roles:

> . . . the Confucian self is not a free, autonomous individual, but is to be seen relationally: I am a son, husband, father, grandfather, teacher, student, friend, colleague, neighbor, and more. I live, rather than "play" these roles, and when all of them have been specified, and their interrelationships made manifest, then I have been fairly thoroughly individuated . . .[16]

Rosemont argues for a role-ethical interpretation of Confucian ethics, alongside other communitarian Confucian thinkers such as David Hall and Roger Ames.[17] Unlike communitarian thinkers such as Alasdair Macintyre, these role-ethicists reject background metaphysical interpretations that invoke a substance-property-virtue attribution in their own understanding of encumbered, role-bearing selves.

Henry Rosemont and Roger Ames will agree with communitarians that unchosen roles can be constitutive of the self, rather than being attributes voluntarily taken on by it. But for them, assuming as Alasdair Macintyre does that there is a substantial self to which roles are attributed that define "partially at least and sometimes wholly my obligations and my duties"[18] is to commit to an individualist metaphysics that is alien to the thought of Confucius and Mencius.[19] They would also object to analytic moral philosophies that interpret roles as relational properties (such as "being a mother") or membership properties (such as "being a Christian" in a protestant congregation).[20] Rosemont, Hall, and Ames would argue that talk of roles as properties of substantial selves, and of *virtues* through which those roles are exercised well, leads to their reifying abstraction from the self and the contextual situations in which they are practiced. For neither Confucius nor Mencius, they say, developed the notion of the individual as a "separate, indivisible thing" that, through having attributed to it "some essential property or properties," qualifies as a member of a social class or morally significant category.[21]

So the primary categories lying behind a Confucian role-ethics are not Western ontological concepts; they are social roles such as mothering or teaching and the selves constituted by such roles, and these roles have no existence beyond the selves and the relations in which they are exercised. While in contemporary analytic philosophy "being a father" counts as a relational property, for these Confucian thinkers it is no more than the undertaking of a socially recognized and ethically valuable role, one of a number which, in establishing ever-expanding relationships with others, is constitutive of rather than being attributable to that self. The successful practice of fathering requires not the exercise of virtues defined in abstraction from role-exercising contexts but a nonreified *virtuosity* (*de*), an aesthetic, rites-governed performance of actions[22] that facilitates the ethical, emotional, and physical well-being of children.

There are ethical perspectives that track changes in the undertaking or divestment of roles by persons in this implicit Confucian metaphysics, and for those perspectives something has usually gone wrong when divestment occurs.

For Confucian role-ethicists, evaluative utterances attach themselves to the exercise of roles and the establishment of relations with others through them. Personhood is achieved through the fulfillment of roles, and successful personhood is achieved through the quality of the relationships established in the fulfillment of those roles. By living up to rites-based standards that ethically exemplary persons (君子 *junzi*) set in contextually sensitive ways, and by relating to others as fathers, mothers, siblings, work colleagues, and so forth, the self establishes itself "authoritatively" as the focus of those relationships. The person who voluntarily divests herself of these roles thus loses some or many means by which to establish her own self, and in most circumstances (excepting those that are oppressive) is to be criticized for also renouncing the relationships through which that self is established and renders itself capable of benefitting others.

This is not to say that advocates of Confucian role-ethics believe in blind submission to social role expectations. In Confucian thought, responsible fulfillment of a role includes remonstrating with those whom we are connected with in different social relationships, if they should exercise their own roles unlovingly or unjustly. As Rosemont and Ames point out, the early Confucian texts forcefully make the case for remonstrance in preventing parents, officials, and princes from sinking into improper conduct to the detriment of those whom they are responsible for.[23] Here there is the basis of a particularist, internal criticism of oppression in practices and institutions. Remonstrance proceeds from the point of view of shared but also reformable standards of behavior internal to traditional practices, which are appealed to when fellow practitioners fail to live up to them.

A criticism Confucians might level at Ibsen's Nora, then, is that she does not give remonstrance a chance with her husband, and appeals to external standards of intellectual and moral self-realization that are incompatible with her being a wife and mother in her marriage. She appeals to a seemingly extra-traditional, individualist "view from no-where" to criticize her marital practice, and justifies exit on the basis of that criticism. Yet Torvold admits near the end of the play that he has "strength to become a better man."[24] For modern Confucians who also support gender equality, such as Rosemont, this admission could be taken as proof of the persuasive power of remonstrance to reform traditional gender relations. Acting individually and collectively, women like Nora have the power, they would say, to compel recognition of their changed status as equals with their own capacity to earn incomes, while also recognizing—together with men—the ethical priority of family interests over individual aspirations wherever they are in conflict. Nora refuses to recognize that priority when she sheds her own roles. Only if Torvold behaves like a tyrant would these modern Confucians concede that she should flee.

In contrast to the Confucian relational perspective are the metaphysical commitments implicit in "liberal" individualism. Michael Sandel describes a self-parodying conception of such individualism, culled from 1970s pop psychology.[25] Society is an association of individuals, each with their own preferences and conceptions of the good, bonded together in mostly contractual associations, within which individuals choose to assume social roles and responsibilities. Such selves are substantive and possessed of the capacity for choice independent of the social roles and responsibilities they undertake. The self expresses itself through the choices it exercises within its social roles. But there is also a second-order level of choice exercised by a substantive self "behind the scenes" of its roles, which can appeal to seemingly nontraditional criteria of individual rights and preferences when choosing whether or not to remain bound by its roles. Through voluntary, contractual association with others, individuals come into possession of certain relational and membership properties within the practices and organizations constituted out of their mutual association, and they divest themselves of those properties when they "contract out" of those same practices and organizations.

For an ontological individualism compatible with this liberal individualism, possession of relational and membership properties depends on the individualistic properties of "the population as a whole."[26] Being a husband will depend on the individual volition, expressed through relevant preferences and consenting speech acts, of myself *and* my prospective spouse in the marriage contract, the assent of a celebrant, the tacit recognition of state officials, and of individuals constituting a wider society within which my act of marrying and practice of marriage has legal validity.

The notion of a substantive self exercising volition and choice independently of social roles or properties has consequences for how those roles or properties are conceptualized. Whether involuntarily inherited or acquired, many properties may be divested without loss to this substantive self as various associations are voluntarily terminated and new associations contracted into, accordingly as the individual's life plans change. From "being a wife" to "being a divorcee" or from "being a Christian" to "being an atheist" are relatively simple transitions achieved through the exercise of individual preference and appropriately sanctioned speech acts. A voluntaristic conception of attachment to both initially unchosen and chosen social roles and obligations suggests a more fluid metaphysics of the self, allowing for more frequent changes of roles, of lightly worn relational and membership "baggage" than Confucians would allow for. So the metaphor of the "unencumbered" self seems appropriate.

There is diversity in the content of moral judgments tracking changes in attribution of relational and membership properties to individuals within this ontological individualism. A society of individuals allowed to pursue diverse conceptions of the good while itself giving no preference to which is the good for all will tolerate a wide variety of judgments on such changes. Nora's renunciation of her roles as wife and mother and her quest for a true self will not command universal approval. But no customary or legal power is admitted to prevent her from slamming the door and walking out. Only where Nora's actions also constitute coercion, or injustice against others, would state coercion against her be acceptable. On a conventionally liberal interpretation, if Nora were a sole parent who makes no legal provision for the care of her children before departing to pursue her preferred way of life, she would be violating their rights to care and physical and financial support, and would accordingly face both legal punishment and moral opprobrium.

The difficulty is whether the Confucians' or communitarians' conception of a self constituted through and encumbered by its roles is *truer* than the metaphysics of the individualist self as outlined above. On this point there is ambivalence in the communitarian and modern Confucian literature. Henry Rosemont argues that the notion of selves as "autonomous individuals" distorts "badly what actual human beings are like"[27]—the liberal individualist conception of the self gets wrong the kinds of selves we all in fact are.

Michael Sandel represents a more moderate view, in which the implicit metaphysics of liberal individualism and the jurisprudence based upon it fails to respect those people who still understand themselves as "encumbered selves." For these persons, most often found in traditional, religious communities, "the observance of religious duties is a constitutive end, essential to their good and indispensable to their identity," and they are "claimed by religious duties they cannot renounce."[28] Thus different kinds of self may be possible in different kinds of social conditions, to which a metaphysics of "encumbered" and "unencumbered" selves are respectively faithful. Yet Sandel believes that contemporary liberal society is not so hospitable to "encumbered" selves, and also that encumbered selves are able to live a more morally desirable form of the good life.[29]

What weakens the case against "the liberal individualist self" as a metaphysically unfaithful conception of the self is that most communitarians and contemporary Confucians favor a constructivist understanding of selfhood. Thus, they recognize that in modernizing societies, the self and its relationship to its roles does change accordingly as, to use Macintyre's words, there are changes in the moral "language which the self specifies and through which the roles are given expression."[30] In a liberal society, the liberal individualist conception of the self is what selfhood for a majority *really* is experienced as. Thus Rosemont himself admits that, in "a consumptive, property- and thing-oriented society such as our own" the notion that we are autonomous individuals "becomes a self-fulfilling prophecy."[31]

The Unencumbered and Disencumbered Self

Irrespective of the arguments Confucians and communitarians marshal against the "unencumbered self," Ibsen's Nora does not fit that type well. She is not a volitional agent through and through, and certainly we are not invited to see her from the outset as an individual possessed of the freedom to choose prior to her being a wife or mother (as we can tell by her remarks to Torvold that she was merely "passed" to him by her father). Her ultimate conclusion is that she *can no longer believe* that she is wholly constituted by, or wholly identified with, her roles as wife and mother, and this change of belief is forced on her by the dual revelations of her husband's selfishness and of her own infantilized state. Her altered doxaistic commitment becomes, as Sandel himself would recognize, an issue for conscience, since she confronts social roles and obligations that have become intolerable in light of her altered beliefs.[32] Still, her new state of belief is not governed by her will. In this way Nora is on the cusp of the conscientious freedom that Sandel approves of.

Under another description, however, choice is vital to Nora's full exercise of conscience. She can choose to stay with Torvold and her family, and end up being false to the newfound belief she has in herself as a human being independent from her husband's fickle tutelage. Or she can leave her marriage and family, educate herself, and work to become true to this idea of an independent self. So what Sandel, or Rosemont, understand to be a liberal concept of freedom of choice needs to be retained to give full characterization to Nora's moral agency.

Nora's conduct points to a notion of a *disencumbered* self, a self at first unreflectively immersed in variously unchosen social roles and the functions associated with those roles, a self whose identity is in large part constituted out of them, who subsequently feels called by a compulsive change of belief to renounce them. This much we can grant to the Confucian role-ethicists discussed above—that our social roles are not necessarily lightly worn, may be unchosen, and can indeed be in some sense constitutive of who we are.

Choice, however, intrudes at the level of the decision to act for or against the conscience that arises from this change of belief, to remain in or exit from the roles that are no longer considered worthy of commitment. Sandel writes of those persons who see themselves as "claimed by religious duties they cannot renounce," but this is not the only position that conscientious persons may adopt in relation to religious belief—or to social roles. For as William James once observed, counterconversion from religious faith to atheism is an important aspect of religious experience, and such renunciation can be undergone as a painfully unchosen alteration in belief.[33] Indeed, we could imagine a person whose identity is more integrated with her roles and responsibilities than Nora's is undergoing an even more agonizing, involuntary process of conscientious detachment from those roles than Nora. However, in the end, there is still the momentous choice to depart from or remain within the actual community that still holds to those beliefs. Nora's rejection of her "sacred duties" as wife and mother is at least partly misrepresented by Sandel's or Confucian thinkers' notions of a wholly volitional, autonomous "unencumbered self." But this much can be retained from the implicit individualist metaphysics outlined above: that for a self engaged in a process of critical evaluation of once tacitly consented to roles and relationships, certain properties can at the conclusion of that evaluation cease to be integral to that self, and may be divested.

The Japanese Bluestockings and Ibsen's Nora

Now this notion of a disencumbered self may still be indistinguishable from the "emotivist" self dissected by Alasdair Macintyre, a self devoid of any substantive identity because (potentially) so easily divested of identity-constituting roles, duties, and its overall telos, but whose choices to do so can only be egocentrically preference-based, without rational justification. This leaves us with the *subjective/agentic* conception of ethical individualism intact, but also adrift, cleaved from any possible mooring with an *objective/normative* conception that ties it to an objectively principled rejection of those roles and duties.

In answer to this, I will propose the following thesis. When Nora views her married state as being so abject that she is driven to believe that her own humanity can only be found outside of it, this is, from the point of view of the objective/normative perspective of ethical individualism, a predicament for women in *any* society who come to realize that the practice of marriage within their society inhibits their capabilities to be fully human beings. This brings me to the second question I want to address here. Is the sense that her situation is morally intolerable, is unjust in denying to her what she conceives as her due, a conviction that is sufficiently intelligible across different cultural contexts to ground cross-cultural justifications for ethical individualist criticism of the practices that impede such individual realization? Does it ground cross-cultural justifications for individuals to *disencumber* themselves of their roles and obligations in those practices through exit?

I argue that it is intelligible across different societies, to the extent that modernization, including the modernization of gender roles, and the cultural crises it engenders is itself an interculturally intelligible process of social change, and to the extent that Ibsen's play was itself, historically, an instigator for debates within such crises, in European, American, and East Asian societies.

In the decades following its inaugural Norwegian performances *A Doll's House* traced a meteoric path across nations, detonating explosions of controversy in its wake. Writing of its first Norwegian performances, Edmund Gosse remarked: "People left the theatre, night after night, pale with excitement, arguing, quarrelling, challenging. . . . The disputes were at one time so violent as to threaten the peace of households."[34] Similar scenes ensued with the first performance of *A Doll's House* in London a decade later. In *fin de siècle* France, initial dismissals of Nora and the closely associated character type of "The New Woman" as representative of "Nordic" and "Anglo-Saxon" fashions gave way to cultural panic when these alien fashions took hold, threatening what many intellectuals regarded as French marital tradition and the natural order governing relations between the sexes.[35] In late nineteenth-century India, a rising young writer reacted with disdain to *A Doll's House*, allegedly declaring that "No Bengali woman would behave as Nora did." Decades later, Rabindranath Tagore changed his mind. His 1914 short story "Letter from a Wife" imagines his heroine Mrinal's liberation more lyrically and emphatically than the freedom Ibsen envisaged for Nora at the end of *A Doll's House*. Tagore's story set off a minor cultural panic among conservative Indian critics at the time.[36]

Cultural panics also set in some time after the first performance of *A Doll's House* in Japan, at Tokyo University in 1912. Academics and the press initially praised the play's technical aspects, while disavowing the relevance of the European "Women Problem" to Japanese culture, and the Japanese version of the "new woman" (新しい女 *atarashii onna*), became a subject of media curiosity. A nonconformist group of intellectual women associated with the new literary journal *Seitō* (青鞜 *Bluestocking*) who emerged to prominence at the same time, however, quickly turned public sentiment against the *atarashii onna*, for such women personified a threat to the natural gender order as it was characterized in modernizing Japan. Over the next few years, some of *Seitō*'s leading writers radicalized and began to focus their critical attention on a state-sanctioned gender doctrine that corralled a newly-emerging class of educated women into a narrow new gender role: *ryōsai kenbo* (良妻賢母), or "good wife and wise mother."

This controversy cannot be accurately portrayed as a confrontation between a "Westernized" individualist feminism and a traditional Confucian gender role ethos. *Ryōsai kenbo* was not an originally Japanese or Confucian way of thinking about gender roles. It was a doctrine that a modernizing elite developed to rationalize gender roles in the interests of building a powerful nation-state, and it borrowed heavily from contemporary Western ideologies for the sexual division of labor and women's education during the period of nineteenth-century industrialization.[37] As historian Koyama Shizuko put it, "*ryōsai kenbo* is . . . a modern mode of thought, discontinuous with the Edo period that resembles views of women in postwar Japan and in the west."[38] In contrast with the limited, Neo-Confucian education given to upper-class and wealthier merchant-class women in premodern Japan, *ryōsai kenbo* required the mass education of Japanese women so that they could morally educate children and manage households in an industrializing nation-state.

This is not to say that traditional Confucian beliefs were irrelevant to this process of rationalization. Advocates of *ryōsai kenbo* in the late nineteenth and early twentieth centuries found themselves having to accommodate teachers and parents who insisted that young women be schooled in traditional Confucian female virtues (婦徳 *futoku*) of obedience, faithfulness, and submissiveness.[39] *Ryōsai kenbo* doctrine was therefore modified to permit a continuation of these traditional virtues through the mass education system, at a time of deep anxiety among conservatives about the pace of social change.

Such concessions papered over a major transformation in gender roles. However, they contributed to Japanese elite's ability to frame the argument over *ryōsai kenbo* as a dispute between those wanting to uphold traditional, culturally particular Japanese women's virtues and roles, and those wanting to overthrow them through appeal to "Western" ideologies. So in 1913 authorities issued a wave of warnings or outright bans on women's magazines, including *Seitō*, which criticized *ryōsai kenbo*. Officials deemed these publications to be "harmful to the time-honoured virtues of Japanese women" and "destructive to the family system and disruptive of social mores," providing evidence of "Japanese women being unduly swayed by distorted Western ideas about women."[40]

While it is tempting to develop an historical-based argument against the Confucian credentials of *ryōsai kenbo*, I prefer here to consider the philosophical insights that can be drawn from the Japanese bluestockings' response to Nora's exit from her marriage, and from their criticisms of *ryōsai kenbo*. In her summary of a special supplement to the January 1912 issue of *Seitō* dedicated to reviews of the first Japanese performance of *A Doll's House*, historian Tomida Hiroko notes that reviewers' "responses to Nora's leaving her husband and children were like those of western female readers and audiences."[41] One reviewer, Kato Midori, touched on Nora's abandonment of her children and the "miracle" she hopes for from Torvold before remarking, "Thinking at last how much time there was left for her life and about the coming of the 'miracle'; when she understood that, the buds of her self-awakening grew, the outer surface of her character (性格 *seikaku*) was torn away and her naked, inner character came to be revealed."[42] Kato sympathetically identified a "quest for authenticity" in Nora's rejection of her marriage; other reviewers were inspired by Nora to call for revolt and for a disencumbering of old traditions and practices. "The woman problem for this century is women's revolution (革命 *kakumei*) against men";[43] "we will work constantly to break with the old moralities and customs that have been troubling us."[44] *Seitō* editor Hiratsuka Raichō submitted the one dissenting review, castigating Nora for her naivety.

Ibsen's Nora provided an initial point of identification for the Japanese bluestockings who went on to condemn the gender order of their time as an obstacle to women's self-realization and freedom of choice; and who condemned invocations of women's virtues as a cloak for the instrumentalizing of women's bodies to men's interests. They saw in this play the thwarted aspirations and the resentments that Joan Templeton in her analysis of *A Doll's House* described as a "compendium of everything that early modern feminism denounced about women's state."[45] "Amidst we Japanese possibly there are many who are like Nora but haven't realized it," Kato Midori wrote. "Still, there are many who have tasted the bitter anguish of her awakening."[46]

Hiratsuka Raichō, once so dismissive of Nora, soon came to her own awakening. In 1913, radicalized and provoked by public censure of *Seitō*, she composed a polemic titled "To the Women of the World" that assailed *ryōsai kenbo* doctrine. She wrote:

> Do women's entire lives have to be sacrificed to the necessity of preserving the Japanese race? Are women to have no other business besides the business of reproduction? As far as women are concerned, is marriage the sole, the absolute door to their lives? Is being a wife and a mother to be the only calling for women? We can no longer believe such things. Besides marriage, why shouldn't there be limitless doors to women's lives, open to each and every individual (各人個々別々に *kakujin koko betsubetsu ni*)? Besides being a "good wife and wise mother," why shouldn't there be limitless callings for women, for every individual? Why shouldn't freedom of choice (選択の自由 *sentaku no jiyū*) be within the grasp of each individual?[47]

Turning to the "so-called female virtues" of obedience, loyalty, and the rest, Hiratsuka wondered why they have been required of women, why they should be considered *women's* virtues. Her answer: because they existed "for the sake of men's lives." Arranged marriage, which was then the norm for middle-class men and women, was for Hiratsuka an inherently corrupt practice within which women's bodies and labor were instrumentalized for men's interests; "I wonder how many women have, for the sake of financial security in their lives, entered into loveless marriages to become one man's lifelong servant and prostitute."[48]

In *Cities of Words* Stanley Cavell grants a measure of Kantian insight into Nora's plight, when her husband reminds her that she has duties to others before her duty to herself. Up to the play's ending, her material and intellectual dependence on Torvold deprives her of being a "sovereign and subject of the kingdom of ends" existing in reciprocity with others legislating moral laws for themselves and for humanity as a whole. Rather, she finds, "everyone else legislates for her, but in such a way as to deny reciprocity with her own powers of legislation."[49]

There is the common element that fictional and living exemplars of the "new woman" rebelled against in diverse cultural circumstances in the late nineteenth and early twentieth centuries, and found in the state of being instrumentalized and of being deprived of their capacity for full humanity the justification for repudiating patriarchal gender roles.

And so we come back in the end to the ethical individualist perspectives outlined at the beginning. We have considered the insights of fictional and living critics into the middle-class practice of marriage in Western and non-Western societies in the late nineteenth and early twentieth centuries. These insights coincide with the objective/normative perspective on marriage advocated by the capabilities approach. For, as Martha Nussbaum puts it, in patriarchal practices of marriage, wherever they are found, "women are not treated as ends in their own right, persons with a dignity that deserves respect from laws and institutions. Instead, they are treated as mere instruments of the ends of others—reproducers, caregivers, sexual outlets, agents of a family's general prosperity."[50]

In being treated as instruments, they are denied the exercise of capabilities by which they can fully function as human beings: for bodily integrity, for thought and practical wisdom grounded in adequate education, and for material control over their environment, provided by ownership of property and freedom of choice in vocation and employment.[51] Meanwhile, in the metaphor of "awakening," a metaphor used by Western and Japanese feminists for their realization of the injustice of unchosen roles that thwarted their desires for a more fully human life, and of the possibility of emancipation from them, the subjective/agentic perspective also comes into its own.

So Hiratsuka wrote in "To the Women of the World": "Once awakened (一度目覚めた *ichitabi me zameta*) we cannot sleep again. We are alive; we are awake."[52] So Kato Midori could associate Nora with "awakened women" (覚醒した女 *kakusei shita onna*),[53] and the poet Yosano Akiko could proclaim in verses especially written for *Seitō* that "All the sleeping women are now awake, and moving."[54] With such awakenings, the burdens of the encumbered self could no longer claim unreflective allegiance.

The Confucian Alternatives?

Can Confucian role-ethicists present a compelling, ethically particularist alternative to these ethical individualist criticisms and rejections of patriarchal gender roles? One potentially promising avenue for a Confucianism alternative to my discussion of the *disencumbered* individual lies in early Confucian discussions of exit from unjust relationships. The classical Confucian literature admits exit as a correct response by ministers to the egregious moral and ritual failures of the rulers who employ them. Both Mencius and Confucius are said to have resigned from ministerial posts when princes failed to heed their remonstrances or acted in ritually inappropriate ways. No such exit option is admitted in family relations, however, even in the face of grave injustice or inhumanity. As the ancient Confucian text *The Book of Rites* puts it, "If (a minister) have thrice remonstrated and is still not listened to, he should leave (his prince's service). In the service of his parents by a son, if he has thrice remonstrated and is still not listened to, he should follow (his remonstrance) with loud crying and tears."[55] The legendary emperor Shun is an exemplar for such filial forbearance, patiently enduring his father's filicidal hatred.

The likely (though unstated) reasons for this uneven approach to exit are that, for Confucians, family relationships are the irreplaceable nursery for central ethical qualities such as humaneness, justice, and ritual propriety, and the relations in which those qualities are cultivated are paradigmatically nonvoluntaristic—we cannot choose, or replace, our parents and siblings as we can the princes we serve. Wives, however, are absent from early Confucian discussions of remonstrance and exit. Their entry into marriage was hardly voluntary, and they were expected to be obedient and docile toward their husbands and in-law families.[56] We can infer that wives, bound by customary role expectations to obey husbands and parents-in-law, to care for children and also to help fulfill their husbands' filial commitments by caring for his parents, were allowed little in the way of powers of exit. On the other hand, bound by those same expectations they had to exercise love and forbearance even in the face of injustice or inhumanity from their families. Feminist-minded Confucian role-ethicists, and communitarians, will argue that women are right to flee tyrannical and abusive relationships, but it is not clear how much the early Confucian literature from which they draw inspiration gives principled support for that position.

Other modern Confucian thinkers have a more generous and nuanced understanding of the autonomy that underlies the agency of the disencumbered individual, and are less willing to denounce it *tout court* as the incorrigible offspring of Western liberal individualism. Thus Joseph Chan presents an intriguing modern Confucian perspective on the concepts of moral autonomy, a version that he believes classical Confucianism did embrace, and on personal autonomy, which he thinks it did not, but which he believes modern Confucianism should try and incorporate.[57] This distinction between the moral and personal concepts of autonomy is worth revisiting, because this chapter has defended a version of the personal autonomy thesis, and because it provides an opportunity to explore in some more detail classical Confucian discussions of exit from unjust relationships. The question, then, is whether Chan's reformed Confucian perspective incorporating both moral and personal autonomy will be more accommodating of Nora's exit from her family, and of a capabilities approach to ethical individualism.

For Chan, the Confucian approach to what we would call moral autonomy is shaped by classical Confucianism's understanding of voluntary endorsement of and reflective engagement with ethical standards of conduct. It would not be enough, as some communitarians argue, to say that people are born into a morality rather than freely choosing it; for it to be morality (and not, say, a coerced or customarily reflexive habit or way of acting) it must be something we are properly motivated to do, for the right reasons, through active cultivation of our moral sensibility.[58] Moreover, *ren*, or humaneness, requires reflective engagement with and endorsement of morality, ranging from reflection on one's own conduct through to reflection on one's caring relations for others, which militates against an unthinking and potentially inhumane acceptance of ritual proprieties and customary behavioral norms. Mencius, for instance, ridiculed the notion that certain ritual prohibitions on physical contact between the sexes could prevail even in a situation where one's sister-in-law's life is in danger and she needs to be pulled to safety.⁵⁹

Both of these attitudes, of voluntary endorsement of and reflective engagement with morality, could condition Confucian understandings of exit from unjust social relationships in interesting ways. Though Chan only touches on this question of exit, I think it possible to reconstruct a plausible early Confucian justification for exit, as Chan might develop it. Confucius sometimes left the service of a prince in haste, "after the rice had been emptied from the steamer,"⁶⁰ but sometimes he did not; while another sage, Po Yi, would "only serve the right prince and the right people," avoided the company of those who did not practice the rites properly, and departed from service to a prince quickly "when there was disorder."⁶¹ Such sages or humane men were prepared to remonstrate with princes, or in worse cases to resign from their service and immigrate to other states. From an attitude of voluntary endorsement of morality and reflective engagement with it, through which the sages or humane persons "takes control of (their) moral life" and "form(s) an independent will" it follows that they are disposed "to stand firm on the moral position that they reflectively endorse"⁶² even when this disagrees with the opinions of their masters or of the multitude, and even when this stand could lead to loss of employment, status, or even life.

Thus when Mencius wrote that it was the business of a humane man "to set his mind on high principles," he had principles like this in mind—the humane man should hold that "it is contrary to *ren* to kill one innocent man; it is contrary to rightness to take what one is not entitled to."⁶³ In the application of these principles there is a steadfastness in conduct, and a resolution about the triggers for exit that takes us a fair distance from the more prevaricating contextualism of a Confucian role-ethics. If any ruler were to order the killing of people he knows to be innocent as a means to his ends, or to drive his subjects into poverty by extracting from them more than is his due in taxes and *corvee* labor, the way of a sage or *junzi* minister is clear. He should refuse to serve such a ruler in the first place, or resign and depart if in his service, or in the most extreme cases foment a rebellion against his master.

But does this understanding of moral autonomy bring us any closer to a Confucian endorsement of Nora's exit from an unjust marriage? As Chan himself would likely point out, the answer is no. For, first, Confucian moral autonomy is compatible with a society in which there are otherwise restricted life and vocational choices, which constrain exit options, and this provides one domain where modern concepts of *personal* autonomy diverge from

Confucian *moral* autonomy. For personal autonomy, a key component of the good life is the availability of choices in a range of relationships and vocations that the agent can freely enter into or exit from. For moral autonomy, it is sufficient that the agent be able to "make moral decisions that he can reflectively endorse and be able to act on this basis,"[64] but otherwise that he accepts a prevailing regime of social relations in which his options are limited by customary expectations. As we have seen, for Confucians there are compelling reasons for sons not to desert their parents, even in the face of gross injustice from them, and as Chan points out, in an example that is more relevant to our consideration of Nora's exit from her marriage, in traditional China "arranged marriage was the norm" and children accepted the choices of mate made for them by their parents. The morally autonomous person reflectively accepted and worked with the cards she had been dealt in her life. So even a refined understanding of the Confucian notion of moral autonomy does not give much room for Confucian forbearance for, let alone endorsement of, Nora's exit from her family.

Second, from their moral autonomy perspective Confucians would reject the subjective/agentic understanding of ethical individualism, and this provides a second source for the distinction between moral and personal autonomy. The Confucian sage or *junzi* strives, through reflective endorsement, to make morality his own morality, but it is not his morality because he has chosen it. This morality is in the first place a tradition of ethical norms and rites that he is inheriting from the past, which in broad outline he does not question but still seeks to interpret, to question in some details and to adapt creatively (and aesthetically) to his own life circumstances. He makes it his own by cultivating his moral sensibility within and through it. In situations of moral stress and dilemma, according to Chan, it follows that it is not the *junzi*'s choices or preferences that are paramount, but rather what he wills, given the constraints of the moral principles he has inherited, cultivated, and identified with, and given the exigencies of the situation he faces. It is not simply a matter of choice that a humane person resigns in protest from employment by an unjust prince and leaves his state; instead, given the ethical life he endorses and has reflectively cultivated, he cannot help but resign from government service if he is to live up to the ideal of a *junzi*. The Confucian is thus closer in his reasoning and conduct to a Thomas More, encumbered in his conscience by his commitment to natural law and to papal authority in interpreting that law, than to the autonomous Sartrean hero, for whom "free choice and individuality (are) the sources of morality,"[65] and who owes allegiance only to moral principles he has freely chosen as an individual. I have already argued that there is more to Nora's rejection of her marriage than an exercise of choice based on her unique, subjective embrace of expressivist moral principles, that she also wills her exit under compulsion of her newfound insights into the moral value of her marriage. However, there is in her reasoning a rejection of conventional morality, of what books, other people, and indeed exemplarily moral people would teach her or model for her, and this would trouble the Confucian advocate of moral autonomy.

Finally, and most critically, Chan highlights one important difference between Confucian and liberal theories of freedom. The liberal concept of personal autonomy contains within it what Chan calls a *context-independent* justification of freedom; freedom in conduct is not defensible on the grounds of the content of that conduct—whether, for instance, it is ethically right conduct—but on the grounds of its being the autonomous choice of the ethical agent.[66] Another way of putting this is that freedom has intrinsic value for the advocate of personal autonomy; it is to be prized, and protected, irrespective of whether it is exercised for morally praiseworthy or blameworthy ends. For the Confucian advocate of moral autonomy, however, support for freedom is content-dependent. To the extent that freely chosen conduct realizes some ethically praiseworthy aim, it is to be prized and protected.

The implication, then, is that whereas a liberal conception of autonomy will only support coercive interference in freely chosen conduct—no matter how unethical—if (and only if) it is itself coercive or illegal, the Confucian advocate of moral autonomy *may* see reason for using coercion to prevent or to stop even noncoercive conduct it deems to be unethical. Someone's conduct being unethical is a necessary but not sufficient reason for coercive efforts to curb it, for a Confucian of this sort may still regard the costs of coercion as too excessive, in negating an autonomy that would still enable an agent to achieve good. With this argument Confucians may be able to defuse capability theorists' objections that political perfectionism potentially interferes with the exercise of capabilities through which individuals can revise and improve their conceptions of the good on their own. Classical Confucians considered moral persuasion and example to be preferable to force when a person goes ethically astray, given their own support of the idea that ethical conduct should be voluntarily endorsed, not forced.

Yet, as Chan points out, Confucians may, while preserving moral autonomy, resort to indirect coercion. They may curtail someone's conduct not in order to improve her, but to prevent her from corruptly influencing others. They may also ban certain expressions or literature that they deem have a similarly corrupting influence on ethical conduct. The basis for such an approach to coercion lies first in the aspiration of Confucianism to be a comprehensive morality for society, ranking and prescribing the ethical goods of all its members, and indeed making ethical goods the paramount goods of the life for all in society. It lies secondly in Confucianism being a politically perfectionist doctrine of the sort described above, which sees the state as a primary agency in promoting ethical conduct and virtue.[67]

So far it does not seem that Chan's sympathetic Confucian treatment of autonomy will lead to endorsement of the exit of a Nora Helmer, given the manner in which Confucian ethical autonomy accepts customary constraints on freedom within family life. Modern Confucians would not countenance the idea of forcibly returning someone like Nora to her family, even if to prevent her from corruptly influencing other women. But they might consider banning certain feminist literature (and even a play like *A Doll's House*!) to prevent the spread of ideas harmful to ethical life and harmony in the family. It is indeed possible to envisage a Confucian perfectionist endorsement of the bans the Japanese police placed on *Seitō* and Hiratsuka Raichō's writing.

Chan ultimately does not think the classical Confucians' conception of moral autonomy is sufficient for a Confucian ethics in postindustrial, pluralistic societies, for which freedoms in choice of vocation and lifestyle have themselves become customary. Thus, he wants to see Confucian ethics integrate some degree of personal autonomy—in a striking contrast with Confucian role-ethicists such as Henry Rosemont, who reject it. But there are limits to how much personal autonomy can be assimilated to Confucianism. This is because, for Chan, the political perfectionism of Confucianism is "a major feature of Confucian political theory." Political perfectionism would have to be abandoned if a more absolutist concept of personal autonomy as *personal sovereignty* were adopted, the sort that gives ethical priority to the "subjective/agentic" standpoint over political perfectionism, which in principle supports "moralistic and paternalistic interference in other people's lives."[68]

I would agree with Chan that personal autonomy is not an absolute moral value. It can compete with "and sometimes be outweighed by" other values such as "ethical ideals and well-being." From an ethical individualist point of view, this makes sense. As I have already argued, the objective/normative perspective on ethical individualism does allow for criticism of choices made autonomously if they arguably lead to self-defeating inhibitions of capabilities, or if they focus too narrowly on one's own good to the exclusion of others' goods. It also places no barrier in the way of individuals committed to those choices arguing back. Remonstrance with and criticism of such individuals would count as noncoercive "moralistic interference with other people's lives." Indeed, the objective/normative position accommodates those critics of Nora, such as Hiratsuka Raichō, who thought that her decision to leave her family would threaten to inhibit exercise of her capabilities, since she has no means in view of financially supporting herself.

It is the political perfectionism Chan holds to that provides grounds for concern. In seeing the state as a major agent in promoting ethical conduct, political perfectionism can still allow for a strong defense of personal autonomy and civil liberties, on the grounds that coercively interfering with people's personal autonomy to prevent them from doing the wrong thing can have counterproductive effects on their ability reflectively to endorse and achieve their moral good. It could, as Chan thinks, thereby incorporate a context-independent justification for personal autonomy; people's right to do morally questionable or wrong things would be accepted, since it is better that they learn by themselves from their mistakes and reflectively come to endorse a better *dao* than that they be coerced into doing the right thing.

Still, there is an important question over how much this moderated political perfectionism constitutes an advance over the more conservative political perfectionism described earlier, which would mandate coercion not to correct people in their own moral lives, but to prevent morally questionable literature or actions from corrupting *other* people's lives. A Confucian political perfectionism, or other political perfectionism similarly interested in protecting the sanctity and stability of family life as the nursery of the virtues, might still call for paternalistic state interference where it deems that personally autonomous conduct is endangering the stability of family life. And this does seem to have been the attitude of the late Meiji- and early Taisho-period police authorities overseeing the activities of the young *Seitō* writers. In many ways they were tolerant of those authors' writing and conduct, which extended to Nora-like desertions of husbands and families. And yet, when their writings and other women's magazines began to question some central tenets of state familist ideology, police censors intervened—not to prevent Hiratsuka Raichō and her peers from morally harming themselves, but to prevent them from morally harming other women.

Chan might ultimately oppose such police censorial powers in the present on prudential grounds; today, as expressive, pluralistic values have taken hold in society, it makes sense for Confucianism to broaden its appeal by, for instance, rejecting more authoritarian ideals of filial piety, and thus ensuring that a modern Confucian political perfectionism does not come down on the side of authoritarian, patriarchal power in family life. But ultimately this prudential argument is not as strong as it looks. From a politically perfectionist point of view, the idea that personal autonomy can "sometimes be outweighed by" other values such as "ethical ideals and well-being" still contains within it the possibility of censorship of literature that undermines support for such ideals and well-being, or coercive attempts to rein in the corrupting, wayward actions of women like Nora and her bluestocking supporters. It is not unimaginable that one goal of a politically perfectionist Confucian regime, if such a regime were to exist, would be indirectly to hem in personal autonomy when it comes into conflict with its own comprehensive ethical vision for the good life in the family.

Ultimately, the difference with an ethical individualist endorsement of personal autonomy comes down to this. The individual, with her capacities, including her power of choice over how to live her life, is the ultimate focus of concern, not the good of the family or other institutions, including the state itself. Unethical, but otherwise minimally reasonable and noncoercive functioning that leads to individual failure, or that encourages others to do likewise, provides neither sufficient nor necessary conditions for direct or indirect political perfectionist interference. A political perfectionism can go some way to accommodating this ethical standpoint with its endorsement of personal autonomy, but not all the way. For ethical individualism, even if it is correct that Nora is selfish in leaving her family, or that she will end up destitute on a park bench, there is no reasonable justification to coercively interfere with or penalize her decision to exit. Only if Nora leaves her children with no other parent or carer, so that they might themselves starve or suffer neglect, destitution, and loss of education, does an injustice arise that requires coercive remedy. *Confucian* political perfectionism may set the bar for coercive state intervention lower, on the basis of (1) a comprehensive doctrine of, or (2) on more loosely articulated and less rigidly ranked conceptions of, the good and welfare of the family, and of the centrality of those goods for the good of the state itself.[69]

However, this chapter has been more concerned with competing conceptions of the ethical self than with arguments over political perfectionism and autonomy. I believe I have done what I could to defend an ethical individualist conception of the disencumbered self, embodied in Henrik Ibsen's Nora, from Confucian advocates of a more relational concept of the self that provides inadequate protection for the individual against being coercively instrumentalized for the good of the family and of the state. A fuller critical assessment of Confucianism's political perfectionism, considered in a political philosophical light, can wait until chapters 6 and 7 of this study. A more immediate consideration to reflect upon is this: that it is not just roles and their relational ethical dispositions that constitute the encumbrances of Confucian selves. Just as important is cultivation of the ritual proprieties that both symbolize and enact the qualitative character of relations between those selves. Confucian understandings of ritual have also long been the subject of controversy, especially in traditionally hierarchical social relations, such as those between women and men in families. The question of whether there is ethical value in Confucian interpretations of ritual that can survive feminist or egalitarian criticism will be the subject of the next chapter.

CHAPTER 3

Confucian Ritual, Hierarchy, and Symmetrical Deference

A Courtroom Encounter

A man approaches a courtroom, handcuffed, his head bowed, flanked by police; he is a convict serving a prison sentence, suffering the further ignominy of bankruptcy proceedings. His original crime is that he had sexual relations with other men. Salacious details about those relations have already been splashed across the newspapers and have animated high-society gossip, so that his reputation is in tatters and his life as a public figure ruined. All around he can hear the din of contemptuous chatter from an onlooking crowd. He looks up to see his friend and ex-lover waiting for him; as he passes, the friend gravely raises his hat to him, and as if by magic, the crowd is hushed.

This is what transpired the day in December 1895 when Robbie Ross greeted his friend Oscar Wilde outside the London Bankruptcy Court. Ross's dignified gesture of acknowledgment made a deep impression on Wilde, who later wrote in *De Profundis* that "Men have gone to heaven for smaller things than that."[1] It was a courageous act when the safer, socially approved ritual option would have been to turn away from Wilde, and in the language of the time, to "cut him dead."

I want to use this story as the starting point for a fresh approach to contemporary Confucian scholars' interpretations of ritual propriety (禮 *li*), and the contribution Confucianism can make to developing it as a topic for contemporary philosophical discussion. I agree with a number of scholars interested in Confucian *li*, beginning with Herbert Fingarette, that Confucius did yield highly important insights into the moral, aesthetic, and indeed magical dimensions of ritual that later Confucians such as Xunzi systematized. I part company with these scholars in taking more seriously the objections that ancient critics of *li* such as Mozi and more modern critics have leveled against it. The danger the Mohists highlighted is of an intrinsic failure in *li,* through its becoming an ingrained, customary practice that works against both righteousness, or justice (*yi* 義), and *ren*. A modern criticism of hierarchy-respecting ritual that I will also consider is that it may serve as an instrument for enacting and rigidifying status differences that often (though not always) track political and economic inequalities, normalizing relations of exploitation and subordination between the more and the less powerful. Modern *li* can thus perpetuate itself without either *ren* or *yi*.

The second part of my argument, acknowledging both the value of Confucian scholars' insights and the insights of the critics of *li* develops a different conceptual approach to the value of ritual. Confucian scholars have often insisted on the centrality of hierarchy-respecting deference in explaining the character of the relations enacted through li. However, in today's more pluralistic and fluid social orders, there is a rather strong justificatory burden on defenders of *li* to dissociate hierarchy-respecting, or asymmetrical deference2 from ritual postures lacking in *yi* and *ren*, which enact now unacceptable status differences to the detriment of individual dignity.

On the other hand, I intend to show that symmetrical deferential gestures—such as the one Robbie Ross paid to his convicted friend Oscar Wilde—hold greater significance than a mere mutual acknowledgment of humanity. While taking inspiration from Confucian insights into the ethical and political value of ritual practice, in this chapter I propose to shift emphasis from asymmetrical, hierarchy-respecting deference ritual to provide an account of the role that symmetrical deferential ritual relations can play in ameliorating agonistic political and ethical interaction in more liberal social orders.

The Confucians and Mohists on Ritual Failure

The question I want to begin with is an ancient one in Chinese philosophy: In what circumstances can we say that ritual (*li*) has gone wrong, has departed from righteousness (*yi*) and benevolence or humaneness (*ren*)? Michael Kualana Ing has written an intriguing study on dysfunction and failure in early Confucian ritual, and he provides an interesting distinction on types of ritual failure inferred from early Confucian interpretations of ritual: failures in *competency* and failures in *efficacy*. Failures in competency occur when practitioners improperly enact a ritual through lack of skill, practice, motivation, or knowledge of its "script," in situations where they (or witnesses) believe that they should have followed that script. Failures in efficacy occur when the script of the ritual itself, even when followed punctiliously, is not sufficiently adapted to or is in some more intractable way inappropriate for the political, economic, cultural, or interpersonal aspect of the context in which it is performed, or when some accident intervenes such that it fails to "come off," to have its intended effects for its participants and audience.[3] Ing notes that it can sometimes be difficult to distinguish between these two types of failure, and to ascertain whether the ritual performers are at fault for it. In the Confucian literature, disputes sometimes occur between Confucius and his followers over whether or not a particular ritual practice failed, and whether it failed due to personal incompetence or to a contextual problem in the ritual setting that thwarted its performance.[4]

Both the Confucians and their Mohist critics had very interesting things to say about ritual failure, which have some bearing on contemporary Confucian defenses of ritual. So, excluding cases of unpreventable failure in ritual, I think it worth clarifying in what other ways ritual practice can fail through lacking *yi* or *ren*, according to both early Confucians and Mohists.

In the *Analects* Confucius gives us one example concerning the Chi family, upstart vassals within the sixth-century BCE state of Lu. At a lavish festival in celebration of their family ancestors, they held an elaborate dance involving eight rows of eight dancers. However, this dance with sixty-four performers was traditionally the prerogative of the Chou royal family, held in celebration of their royal ancestors. Confucius, disgusted at the effrontery of the Duke of Chi, spluttered: "Having eight rows of dancers in his hall! He who does not shame to do this would not be ashamed of anything."[5]

My second example, though not from the classical Confucian literature, was related by the fourteenth-century CE Japanese writer and priest Yoshida Kenkō:

> Once, when the holy man Shoku of Koya was on his way to the capital, at the narrow part of the road he ran into a woman riding on a horse. Her groom failed to rein in the horse, with the result that the holy man's horse was pushed into a ditch. The

holy man rebuked the man: "what incredible disrespect! Among the four classes of disciples of Buddha, a nun (比丘尼 *bikuni*) is inferior to a priest (比丘 *biku*), a layman (優婆塞 *ubasoku*) to a nun, and a laywoman (優婆夷 *ubai*) to a layman. This is an unheard of outrage—for a laywoman like you to kick me, a priest, into a ditch.

The groom replied, "What do you mean sir? I can't make sense of what you say." The holy man, more annoyed than ever, cried "What's that you say, you infidel, you ignoramus!" Having pronounced these harsh words, he looked as if he regretted his intemperate abuse and, turning his horse in the direction from which he had come, fled the scene. It sounds as if it was a most elevated quarrel.[6]

Both of these examples involve violations of *ren* and *yi* in tokens of ritual practice, on the Confucian understanding of those virtues. And both allude to the ways in which social rank is inappropriately and inhumanely enacted through ritual proprieties—or enacted in expectation of their performance. The Chi family's performance of the dance with eight rows of eight dancers is a clear instance of *inefficacy* in ritual practice. However punctilious they are in observance of that ceremony, they are without *yi* for performing a ceremony that is the prerogative of a royal family, and without *ren* in upending and endangering the stability of a social hierarchy mandated by heaven, within which certain ritual practices are aligned with particular social ranks.

The case of the holy man Shoku is different. An expected ritual gesture, that the groom would deferentially rein in the horse of his mistress and let a man of superior rank pass, does not occur, most likely because the groom is just too surprised to act quickly enough. The holy man commits a category mistake in treating this accident situation as an act of effrontery against his rank. There is a failure here to understand the correct, context-responsive performance of rites; Shoku grossly misreads the situation he falls into, and insists on a ritual posture utterly inappropriate to it, thereby manifesting a deficient understanding of *yi*. The groomsman's bewildered response to Shoku's verbose self-assertion, and the latter's undignified departure, underscore the lack of gravitas in this situation.

In losing his self-control and succumbing to prideful anger, the priest Shoku is also acting without *ren*. In the interaction between the failed *ren* and *yi* of this encounter, we can also sense an injustice. Shoku bullies a man and woman of inferior social rank, expecting ritual proprieties that could not reasonably be expected in the situation at hand. In this failure we see very clearly what a number of Confucian scholars have been insisting on in their own criticisms of ritual when it becomes a blindly followed practice: the importance of reflexively individual creativity in appropriate enactments of *li*, in the right manner and circumstances, with due, humane respect for others. Such a capacity for appropriateness and creativity is the hallmark of the *junzi*'s morally authoritative personality.

Therefore these judgments on particular instances of ritual failure or misguided ritual expectation do not lead us into negative judgement of what Confucians understand to be appropriate enactments of the ancestral dance, or of the appropriate ritual deference that is due to persons of superior rank.

Things are different with the Mohist criticisms of Confucian ritual. Using Ing's terminology, we could summarize those criticisms as stating that Confucian ritual is always inefficacious because its scripts are incorrigibly inappropriate for the economic, social, and ethical dimensions of the contexts in which it is performed. So Mohists famously attacked the wastefulness of certain types of ritual performance such as aristocratic dance, music entertainments, and elaborate funerary rites. Mozi held that extravagant funerary rites and "lengthy mourning periods" "are contrary to righteousness (*yi*) and benevolence (*ren*) and "should not be practiced by filial sons."[7] Mozi's criticisms of elaborate funerary rituals depend for their force on the assumption that those rites are observed punctiliously and inflexibly, and therefore without regard to *yi*—that they violate *ren* by beggaring the families of the dead who must pay for elaborate coffins and grave goods, and empty the coffers of states that must pay for burial ceremonies for their ministers and princes, leading to neglect of the needs of their living subjects. Moreover, lengthy mourning periods and fasting distract ministers from their duties or simply incapacitate them, damaging their ability to serve the state, while farmers are distracted from their duties to tend their fields. Since in Mozi's state consequentialism the good of the state, conceived as its wealth, order, and population, is the end against which practices such as rites are evaluated, Mozi believed that rites must be condemned for failing to serve that end.[8]

However, Mohist criticisms of Confucian ritual did not end there, and opened up into a general criticism of customary acceptance of rites, whether Confucian or not. So Mozi asked, "can we actually say that they represent the way of benevolence and righteousness? This is what it means to accept what is habitual as proper, and what is customary as right."[9] For the Mohists, certain ritual practices violate *ren* and *yi* in all their possible instantiations, such as those of barbarian peoples that mutilate the corpses of the dead or involve cannibalizing first-born infants. These obviously were not the same as the Zhou Dynasty rites that Confucians sought to conserve and codify. Mohists had one more argument against those Confucian rites, however—that they were inefficacious because they failed to have their intended effect on their audiences, in part because of audience suspicions over the intent behind the Confucians' performance of rites. Confucians professed that ritual conduct was intended to convey an impression of self-cultivation, dignity, and finely adjusted regard for others, but this was not how the Mohists saw it.

Chapter 10 of the *Analects* provides examples of Confucius's fastidious attention to deportment in dress and ritual manner, and of the subtle adjustments he made to his demeanor in response to the different social ranks and circumstances of the persons he encountered. These stories convey a picture of highly disciplined, dignified, and reflexive responsiveness to other persons and situations. Confucius harmonizes his dress, speech, gestures, and manner to others and to their situations, tacitly and masterfully enacting a complex code of behavior expressed in gesture, dress, and deportment which, to observers and participants, marks him out as an exemplary person who has made that code his own. His conduct thus answers to Fingarette's invocation of the "magical" in ritual, involving "great efforts produced effortlessly, marvelously, with an irresistible power that is itself intangible, invisible, unmanifest."[10] One example will suffice:

> In bed, he did not lie like a corpse. At home, he did not put on any formal deportment. When he saw any one in a mourning dress, though it might be an acquaintance, he would change countenance; when he saw any one wearing the cap of full dress, or a blind person, though he might be in his undress, he would salute him in a ceremonious manner. To any person in mourning he bowed forward to the crossbar of his carriage; he bowed in the same way to any one bearing the tables of population. When he was at an entertainment where there was an abundance of provisions set before him, he would change countenance and rise up.[11]

Compare that passage, however, with Mozi's assessment of the Confucians' ritual demeanor and deportment:

> ... the Confucians corrupt men with their elaborate and showy rites and music and deceive parents with lengthy mournings and hypocritical grief. They propound fatalism, ignore poverty, and behave with the greatest arrogance. They turn their backs on what is important, abandon their tasks, and find contentment in idleness and pride. They are greedy for food and drink and too lazy to work, but though they find themselves threatened by hunger and cold, they refuse to change their ways. They behave like beggars, stuff away food like hamsters, stare like he-goats, and walk around like castrated pigs.[12]

Confucians complain that these accusations are absurd and—like so many other of Mozi's accusations—slanderous. But it is easy to overlook their more serious import. They remind us that Confucius and his immediate successors lived in ethically diverse societies in which their own moral and ritual injunctions were not universally upheld, and their ritually coded behavior not always recognized and acknowledged in the way they hoped it would be. They had therefore to fight for recognition and acknowledgment. And the effect among those who disagreed with their precepts and manners was the opposite of harmonizing. Their emphasis on "showy rites" and carefully expressed deportment and gesture, their elaborate shows of grief, and their alleged idleness and sponging off social betters provoked accusations of arrogance and hypocrisy. Here, in the space between failed *ren* and *yi*, lies a sense of injustice. In the Mohists' eyes the Confucians insincerely gamed rites for their personal advantage, flattering social superiors, and marketed themselves as "ritual experts" to the gullible in order to gain more than was their due in free food, income, and status.

The negative Mohist reaction to rites is also, however, aesthetic, responding to the supposed magic qualities of the rites themselves. The reflexive, ritually coded harmonizing of demeanor, gesture, and voice to situations and persons is supposed to convey an impression of gravity, dignity, and beauty. In the picture of Confucius's conduct when passing "the vacant place of the prince," we can see the conjuring up of a subjunctive reality, the "as if"[13] of dignified respect and deference to a social superior that draws us away from the potential for brute, coerced submission in this hierarchical political relation, and also magically "makes real" that as if:

When he was passing the vacant place of the prince, his countenance appeared to change, and his legs to bend under him, and his words came as if he hardly had breath to utter them. He ascended the reception hall, holding up his robe with both his hands, and his body bent; holding in his breath also, as if he dared not breathe.[14]

Yet, for the Mohist observer, unmoved by "showy rites," this same scene will appear repugnant and ludicrous, a display of hypocritical self-abasement intended to curry favor with social superiors—with bent legs and bent body, the Confucian "walks around like a castrated pig." The sense of magic associated with Confucian rites, of "the power of a particular person to accomplish his will directly and effortlessly through ritual, gesture and incantation,"[15] dissipates in a welter of derision. Fingarette remarks that rituals can fail to "come off" either by being performed in a clumsy, underskilled manner, or be mechanical and dull through "lack of serious purpose and commitment." But the Mohist reaction to Confucian rites underlines a third source of failure in ritual efficacy that Fingarette seems to be aware of.[16] Rites performed skillfully and with serious commitment may fail when their audience does not share in the "thick" or "high context" cultural mores that render such performance meaningful and accomplished in the way that it is intended to be. So both the audience and the overall setting are inappropriate for its successful enactment.

The Mohists show us that the funerary rites of barbarian peoples misfire by not having their intended effect on us, if we happen to observe them; they provoke disgust and horror rather than a magical sense of awe and piety. Insofar as we regard our repugnance as being grounded in justified moral judgments, we will also condemn the barbarians for accepting "what is habitual as proper, and what is customary as right." In the society within which the followers of Confucius and Mozi dwelled and competed with each other for official patronage, Confucian rites themselves were for some observers also ugly and undignified, in addition to being irredeemably bereft of *yi* and *ren*.

What reply can Confucians make to these criticisms? They may take up Xunzi's justifications for ritual practice, written with Mozi and other critics in mind, at a time when Ruists were struggling to gain state patronage for their doctrines. Xunzi's justification invoked three interlocking sets of reasons for explaining and justifying ritual and music: that they regulate and moderate basic human emotions and desires; enable fulfillment of piety toward heaven, earth, and fellow human beings; and both enact and harmonize socially necessary hierarchies in rank. While all three justifications require some explanation, the third could be taken as the most decisive response to Mozi, who also insisted on the importance of hierarchy in ranks for social order.

At a fundamental level, Xunzi stated that ritual provides for the appropriate fulfillment of human desires, educating them and ordering them into preestablished, flexible patterns of conduct and practice. The unconstrained seeking after satisfaction of desires is a source of social disorder, so the sage kings of old established rites "to train men's desires and provide for their satisfaction."[17] This civilizing function of rites has often been pointed to by other commentators. The *Book of Rites* emphasizes that by restraining and schooling desires, rites enable human beings to distinguish themselves from animals: for "if (men were as) beasts, and without (the principle) of propriety, father and son would have the same mate. Therefore, when the sages arose, they framed the rules of propriety in order to teach men, and cause them, by their possession of them, to make a distinction between themselves and beasts."[18] Herbert Fingarette provides a modern formulation of this conviction: "Men become truly human as their raw impulse is shaped by *li*. And *li* is the fulfillment of human impulse, the civilized expression of it."[19]

The ritual rationale for funeral rites provides one example for Xunzi's thesis. The death of loved ones, beginning with parents, is the occasion both of extreme grief and of the search for means to express it; yet this can lead to extreme gestures such as prolonged health-endangering periods of mourning and fasting and extravagant expenditure on funerals—as Mozi himself pointed out. However, the passing of loved ones can also provoke less estimable emotions and desires in surviving children, including resentment against the dead for the inconvenience their passing causes, indifference, poorly concealed (or unconcealed) satisfaction in instances where relations with them had soured, and miserliness in preparing their burial out of the belief that resources are better expended on the living, beginning with oneself, rather than on the dead.

Funerary rite patterns, with well-defined, time-honored procedures dictating the length of mourning, the dressing of corpses, the nature of the burial ceremony and funerary feast, all calibrated to the rank of the deceased as well as to the material circumstances of the living, provide the means for appropriately regulating, expressing, or restraining the emotions and desires of the living in relation to the dead, and for striking a mean between extravagance and miserliness. This can be read as a rejoinder to Mohist accusations of ruinous extravagance in funerary rites:

> Rites trim what is too long and stretch out what is too short, eliminate surplus and repair deficiency, extend the forms of love and reverence, and step by step bring to fulfillment the beauties of proper conduct. Beauty and ugliness, music and weeping, joy and sorrow are opposites, and yet rites make use of them all, bringing forth and employing each in its turn.[20]

Yet the education and regulation of emotions and desires still does not tell us much about what Emile Durkheim and other sociologists might call the *functionality* in rites—about what purpose or ends they are seen to serve; though regulated and moderated expressions of reverence and longing are better than those that are unconstrained, what end is served by expressing piety and reverence for the dead? Here we arrive at what Xunzi called the "three bases" for the rites: understanding "Heaven and Earth as the basis of life, the ancestors (as) the basis of family and rulers and teachers (as) the basis of order." Rites provide for the appropriate expression of piety and reverence toward these bases, for what they give: for "if there were no heaven and earth, how could man be born? If there were no ancestors, how could the family come into being? If there were no rulers and teachers, how could order be brought about?"[21] And so from the fulfillment of duties of piety arise various types of rites. There are the sacrifices to heaven and to the soil performed by emperors, and funerary and ancestral rites performed by all, adjusted to the social ranks of the departed, which establish and maintain a continuity of respect and piety between the living and the dead, of both families and of communities. Finally, there are the more quotidian expressions of ritual deference and piety social inferiors express to superiors, such as parents, elder siblings, and rulers.

And so we come to the more contentious of Xunzi's justifications for rites, at least from a modern, egalitarian point of view. Social hierarchy is necessary, and ritual provides the means for articulating and maintaining that hierarchy in a noncoercive, orderly, and harmonious fashion. Equality of rank can lead only to chaos, Xunzi thought, and with his pessimistic insight into human nature he provided a compelling picture of unconstrained egalitarian social relations would look like, reminiscent of Hobbes's conception of unconstrained social relations in the state of nature. Goods will be insufficient to satisfy all since presumably all, with the same desires, will strive in uncontrolled fashion and in contention with each other to acquire the same types of goods, but cannot command each other to produce more. There will be no social unity, and no one can claim the power to govern or employ others. Moreover, such a state of affairs is not in conformity with the cosmic order, for "[t]he very existence of Heaven and Earth exemplifies the principle of higher and lower." A society lacking distinctions in ranks will also suffer from quarrelling, leading to fragmentation and loss of security as people are unable to live safely, since no one will take leadership roles to manage social order. So the sage kings of old "regulated the principles of ritual in order to set up ranks" distinguishing the rich and the poor, the eminent and the humble, seeing to it that the former governed and employed the latter, while they also benevolently "watched over those below."[22] Through such an order of ranks, goods could be produced to satisfy all.

Here Xunzi appeared to steal a march on Mozi. For his thought experiment of a society lacking in social hierarchy has a strong resemblance to Mozi's historical reconstruction of an early egalitarian stage in human society. According to Mozi, since human society at this time lacked leaders and hierarchy it suffered from an intolerable diversity and conflict of opinions, leading to disharmony in the family and social disorder. Moreover, in this early society the strong refrained from helping the weak, and the wealthy let their stored-up goods rot rather than sharing them with others.[23] As we have seen, Mozi prized social order and the efficient production and distribution of resources to all as ends against which social practices, including rites, were to be evaluated. But while Mohists castigated rites for being obstacles to the fulfillment of these ends, Xunzi regarded rites as serving social order and prosperity.

So for Xunzi, unlike Mozi, ritual principles are essential for enacting hierarchical ranks and for ensuring orderly observance of their associated duties—filiality to parents, respect for older brothers, obedience to superiors, and (in rulers) the organization and prosperity of society through the correct employment of subordinates.[24] The Mohists were at one with Xunzi in upholding social hierarchy, but for Xunzi they lacked the insight to understand how such an order can be maintained through ritual, and the emotions and needs of its participants regulated with a minimum of legal coercion. Xunzi's genius was to explain how ritual fulfills these requirements. For ritual transforms human emotions and needs, fitting them into traditional patterns of conduct that allow for their fulfillment, rather than leaving them untrained and therefore controllable only by legal coercion. This point would not have been lost on princes on the lookout for ways to maintain social cohesion and order in the insecure conditions of the Warring States period.

Xunzi's depiction of a community drinking party provides a microcosm for this ordered and just regulation of human desire and need (no mean achievement when the consumption of alcohol is involved). It enables for the distribution of goods in a communal setting in which the needs of all are met, in which the different ranks and value of participants are encoded and enacted through ritual etiquette and also harmonized in an aesthetically pleasing manner. After describing the elaborate proceedings of the party, with the offerings and libations of drink, the seating arrangements of guests, the ceremonies and music performance, the order of drinking decided by age and rank, and the ending of formal ceremonies after which the party is given over to free drinking, Xunzi enthused:

> When the distinction between eminent and humble is made clear, when the complexity or simplicity of the ritual is adjusted to distinctions of rank, when there is harmonious pleasure without abandoned behavior, drinking according to distinctions of age but with no one left out, and drinking and feasting without disorder—when these five types of conduct are achieved, they will be sufficient to insure moral training to the individual and peace to the state, and when the state is peaceful, the world will be peaceful.[25]

Ethical Individualism, Progressive Confucianism and the Problem of Oppressive Ritual

So much, then, for the disputes over ritual between the Mohists and the Confucians. For the Mohists, a state consequentialist perspective provided the main thrust of their criticism of Confucian ritual. As we have seen, they also believed Confucian ritual was inefficacious in failing to have its intended effects on its audience, making Confucians appear hypocritical, unjust, and undignified. Confucians such as Xunzi could most successfully reply to the Mohists by affirming the contribution of rites to the very same ends that Mohists prized: the maintenance of a stable social hierarchy that guaranteed both peaceful interpersonal relations and a just distribution of goods.

From a modern, ethically individualist perspective, there may be other reasons, however, for thinking something is wrong in accepting that "what is habitual as proper, and what is customary as right" in the matter of ritual, and these reasons also point to the injustice that arises in the space where failure in *ren* and *yi* interact. These reasons focus on rites that enact status inequalities in relations of political subordination and economic exploitation. In such contexts, rituals of hierarchy-respecting deference work to enable those relations of subordination and exploitation; the rituals *normalize* these relations for their participants, habituating them (more or less consciously, more or less willingly) to their roles in these relations, and sacrificing their ability to actualize their own capabilities to the interests of powerful institutions and groups.

The stories of the eight teams of eight dancers and of the priest Shoko's encounter with a horsewoman have sufficed in discussing the challenges ancient Confucians faced in justifying right ritual, and in criticizing ritual that had gone bad through lack of competence or efficacy. Some more up-to-date twentieth-century descriptions of "bad" ritual, normalizing the just-described relations of subordination and exploitation, can serve as a challenge and provocation to contemporary Confucian defenders of rites. The "bad" rituals I describe can be classed as instances of what Erving Goffman called "status rituals," in which a coded gesture, address, salutation, or more complex repertoire of ceremonial actions functions as "a symbolic means" to communicate to a recipient appreciation of that recipient—where appreciation can be understood more specifically as "regard." They are also *asymmetrical* status rituals insofar as the regard one person is obliged to pay to another, and is expected to render, is not returned in the same form, though some reciprocal response may be expected (such as gratitude, or a protective gesture).[26] Asymmetrical ritual relations do not always track differences in social hierarchy position or wealth, though the "bad rituals" I want to consider mostly do so.

The first instance of such ritual practices is taken from anthropologist Bertram Doyles's 1937 study of racial hierarchy rituals in the Jim Crow American South, *The Etiquette of Race Relations in the South: A Study in Social Control*:

> Negroes normally greet white men with the title "Mister." When we stopped at a crossroads store for information, my guide was quick to doff his hat and preface his every sentence with "Mister" and to end his every interrogation with "Sir." . . . When persons of the two (racial) groups meet, varying with locality, the Negro is expected to speak first and, perhaps, "bow with the greatest deference" . . . The rule is that shaking hands, walking together, and otherwise associating in public, except on terms of superior

and inferior, are not done. The rule is, however, honored in the breach occasionally.²⁷

The second concerns a ritual of twentieth-century Japanese workplaces, centering on female workers' ceremonial serving of tea (お茶くみ *ochakumi*) to male colleagues and superiors:

> It is a long-established tradition in Japanese offices that employees, even if their wages are low or the work unsatisfactory, are supplied with as much tea as they wish to drink. The central reality about this ritual is that all the activities relating to it except the drinking—heating the water, assembling the employees' personal cups, pouring and serving the tea (and remembering which cup belongs to whom), afterward gathering, washing, and arranging cups and cleaning the counter where the tea was made, and buying the tea or making sure that it is bought—are the assigned domain of women employees.... [and] In an office, tea is served not in a random fashion or on the basis of physical proximity to the server, but precisely according to status, from the highest-ranking person first right down to the lowest-ranking person last.²⁸

On the face of it, some Confucians may think it unjust to equate the racialized rituals of the postbellum American South, associated as they were with overtly violent practices of white supremacy such as lynching, with the nonviolent but hierarchical gender norms of late twentieth-century Japanese workplaces. On deeper inspection, however, they share some affinities, if we consider them in light of the rationales for ritual practice reconstructed from Xunzi above.

First of all, in both instances rites serve(d) to moderate and school human desires into established codes and patterns of conduct, "civilizing human impulse." The human impulses to assert status and secure recognition from economic and social subordinates can be enforced through extreme measures such as violence, and human needs for sustenance can also be attained by similar means, by the stronger forcing the weaker to service their bodily needs.

There is a way in which it can be said that ritualizing status differences associated with skin color or gender difference both enacted *and* "civilized" those differences, and the same applies to the ritualizing of activities in which one person sees to another's sustenance. Oral history studies of life in rural postbellum Georgia indicate that interracial relations there were characterized by a higher degree of ritualization than in other parts of the South. Coincidentally, public terrorism and other collective violence against black people, including lynchings, were rare in comparison to other wealthier or more urbanized regions of the American South. Segregation was also less enforced, and violence against black people when it occurred was more personal and centered on perceived infractions of deference ritual.[29] In the decorous image of tea service in the Japanese workplace there is also a replication of an idealized domestic sphere in which women compliantly and perceptively see to the needs of men without being forced or intimidated into doing so.

Second, both of these status rituals involve due reverence for one of what Xunzi called the "three bases of the rites—that of "rulers and teachers (as) the basis of order." Regard is more precisely expressed here as a form of esteem toward a superordinate, who individually or as representative of a class of social superiors has the welfare of the subordinate in their power. As Susan Pharr puts it in her analysis of tea service, "in the status ritual of pouring tea, the social inferior expresses deference and dependence and is rewarded by the superior's protection."[30] It is harder to grasp what reciprocity was expected in black people's deferential ritual to white people, but Bertram Doyle perhaps identified it as a state of affairs in which the black person "is able to gain an income without constant disharmony."[31] The expectation is for a reciprocating "protection," including continued waged employment by white employers, then, or that the superordinate refrain from verbal abuse or physical violence.

Last, by enacting and normalizing status differences that constituted a racial-economic hierarchy on the one hand and a gendered hierarchy on the other, such status rituals enable an orderly state of affairs in which social obligations and expectations and goods are distributed, (largely) without coercion. "The comparatively little friction between races" living in close proximity and economic interdependence with each other in the post-bellum South, Doyle opined, was "perhaps due to the fact that there was a code of etiquette in race relations."[32] The Japanese workplace tea service could be argued to function in a similar manner to Xunzi's drinking party. It harmoniously enacts status differences between the servers and their recipients, as well as differences in rank between recipients of the tea, while at the same time decorously opening up "lines of communication" between similarly or differently ranked participants in this communal rite.[33] More prosaically, it ensures the orderly and equitable fulfilment of their bodily needs.

Many Confucians would object to such a rationalization of ritualized racial and gender hierarchy. For instance, Stephen Angle's progressive Confucianism makes the case for nonoppressive social hierarchy and deference, and identifies six "defeaters" whose presence in social relations would justify them being labeled "oppressive."[34] These defeaters could be used to show how the Jim Crow South's racial etiquette and possibly even the Japanese tea service rituals are oppressive. The first defeater, rigidity, refers to the establishment of superordinate and subordinate identities that are resistant to variation in context or capability. A superior status that is conferred by membership in an identity group that exercises expectations for deference from inferior groups across different social contexts, without regard for differences in capacities or other social roles that would normally justify reciprocating deference, approximates this defeater. The racial etiquette of the Jim Crow South, which required blacks to express asymmetrical deference to whites in a wide range of private and public settings, irrespective of the other social roles and capabilities they respectively possessed, surely provides one instance of this. The requirement of Japanese female workers to replicate a gendered family domestic role in serving tea to male peers, irrespective of their own workplace rank and capabilities, provides another instance.

The second defeater, coercion, is obviously represented in the ever-present threat of violence facing black people who, accidentally or not, failed to show due deference to white people. In his autobiographical story "The Ethics of Living Jim Crow" about the observance of "racial etiquette" in the South in the 1930s, Richard Wright casually remarked that he had seen "Negroes take a blow in the mouth" from white men for the most subtle infractions of that etiquette.[35] In her study of a Kyoto city government office in the 1970s, Susan Pharr found that women interviewed for a position at the office were asked about their willingness to make tea for their male colleagues (though it was not a formally contracted duty), and those who expressed a reluctance to do so were unlikely to be hired.[36] This could be said to constitute an indirect form of coercion.

The third defeater, sacrifice, refers to deferential relations in which one value is forfeited "without thereby realizing some other end that one also endorses."[37] Though Angle's phrasing of this condition is somewhat vague, one would assume that for black people acutely aware of civil rights and racial equality discourse in the immediate aftermath of the Civil War, and again with growing conviction in the twentieth century leading up to the Civil Rights Movement era, the constant sacrifice of personal dignity and humanity in race-based deference was a hard bargain to accept when the only return was an economically and politically subordinate life free of violence. Both Susan Pharr's and Ogasawara Yuko's sociological studies of Japanese female office workers found that their subjects often regarded tea service as "demeaning" "because it called attention to their subservient role."[38] There is in these reactions a similar resentment about the forfeiting of dignity and recognition in such rituals, even if Japanese women's workplace relations are not fraught with the threat of violent coercion.

The next defeater, omnivalence, follows from the first, rigidity, in inflexibly requiring a deferential race- or gender-based posture across different social contexts, overriding other grounds for reciprocating deference based on criteria such as expertise, occupational status, or age. The fifth defeater, indefeasibility, identifies the characteristic of intransigence in status superiors in response to questions or challenges. The personal, and sometimes public, collective violence that greeted black challenges to racial etiquette, and the outraged but largely silent affront among male workers that greeted a famous 1963 "tea service rebellion" by Kyoto City office female workers studied by Susan Pharr, reflect this characteristic to a greater or lesser degree.[39] Finally, the sixth defeater is emptiness, in which deferred-to superordinates do not live up to the virtues or responsibilities associated with their role. For black people, compelled to express ritual deference to whites as tokens of a superior racial caste rather than in light of their individual merits, this was one of the most galling aspects of Southern racial etiquette. For the female city office workers Susan Pharr observed, lack of reciprocating gratitude and grace by male superiors receiving their tea "drained deference behavior of its emotional rewards," making this ritual both onerous and demeaning.[40]

As Angle points out, these defeaters can be instantiated to greater or lesser degrees in deferential social relations, rendering them more or less oppressive, or perhaps not oppressive at all, but onerous or insulting. For progressive Confucians such as Angle, the trait that would most incline a hierarchical, asymmetrical status ritual toward oppression is its rigid privileging of a singular, overriding attribute such as race, class, or gender as grounds for the expectation of deferential regard across different contexts, excluding other traits in subordinates that would justify reciprocating deference. The "entanglement" of such asymmetrical status ritual with differences in political power and wealth reinforce its oppressiveness.[41] In such instances, the expectation for *categorical*-based esteem for persons representative of a socially and legally recognized superior class, gender, or race may override any expectation for reciprocating deference to others belonging to a subordinated categorical identity. That is, those subordinates may not reasonably expect reciprocating *role*-esteem for holding a particular office or title, nor *capacity*-esteem for demonstrating a particular skill or intellectual or moral excellence.[42]

It is worth asking how this entanglement would be so oppressive. Perhaps the model for such entanglement is the head of the Weberian "patrimonial household," who held a socially and legally sanctioned categorical identity as an aristocrat or, more commonly, as a male head of household. Such a person combined in himself control over the household's economic resources and labor, legally sanctioned political power to distribute or withhold those resources and to command the obedience and labor of household members, and customary entitlement to expect ritual tokens of submission and deference in return for his patronage and protection. In such households, relations were highly ritualized, the rituals asymmetrical,[43] and the potential for oppression lay in the holder of patrimonial power abusively and exploitatively extracting a maximum of labor (or sexual gratification), income, obedience, and deference for a minimal or dubious return of gratitude or protection, with relative impunity under the law.

Asymmetrical status ritual can thus symbolize and affirm differences in political power and economic wealth, and through constant practice habituate one party to accepting a subordinate status that is also political and economic in character.

Going beyond progressive Confucians' rejections of rituals that affirm racial and gender hierarchies, the following could be added. The symbolic offering and accepting of, or expectation of appreciation and regard, in status ritual becomes a means for affirming one's face, in the sense of face meant by Erving Goffman. Face is a positive self-valuation held in terms of "approved social attributes" sustained by a "line" or repertoire of verbal and nonverbal, often ritual acts through which a person affirms that self-valuation and valuation of others in social interaction.[44] The repertoires associated with a line are institutionalized, in accordance with "known or visible attributes" that go with that person's appearance, status, role, competences, and skills.

Consider how these lines are maintained in situations where categorical differences in identity are affirmed—those involving members of one status or caste group, with a shared cultural life, publically recognized social identity, and conventionally (or legally) recognized honor and rank such as that held by the head of a patrimonial household, in their encounters with members of a socially inferior status group.[45] The "line" available to the former in relations with status subordinates are all in the way of affirming their value and eliciting (or demanding) regard for it in more or less subtle ways from subordinates. They incorporate subtle expressions of gratitude, downwardly expressed acknowledgment through unspoken gestures or expressions communicating contempt, exclusion, and even the threat of violence when deference is not forthcoming.

Members of the status-inferior group, on the other hand, have a far more limited "line" available for self-expression. It is almost all in the way of expressing regard for the other, for sustaining *his* face as status superior, and this other-regarding conduct is the means by which one's own face is allowed to be maintained. Outside of this repertoire, gestures are limited through which the status inferior can preserve a self-valuation independent of the subordinated valuation placed on herself in this status ritual exchange, and acting out such a gesture is fraught with risk if it is perceived to threaten the status superior's face. Richard Wright described one such fraught encounter in a Southern department store elevator in the 1930s, where the ritual expectation for him to remove his hat in the presence of two white men was thwarted by his hands being full with parcels:

> One [of the white men] very kindly lifted my hat and placed it upon my handful of packages. Now the most acceptable response for a Negro to make under such circumstances is to look at the white man out of the corner of his eye and grin. To have said "Thank you!" would have made the white man *think* that you *thought* you were receiving from him a personal service. For such an act I have seen Negroes take a blow in the mouth. Finding the first alternative distasteful, and the second dangerous . . . I immediately—no sooner than my hat was lifted—pretended that my packages were about to spill, and appeared deeply distressed with keeping them in my hands.

So Wright avoided responses that might have provoked violence or which would have endangered his own sense of face, and thus was able to salvage "a slender shred of personal pride."[46] In this way we can say that, irrespective of whether they are entangled with wealth and political inequalities or not, certain status rituals—most typically, those affirming categorical differences in social hierarchy—in themselves can violate ethical individualist principles. They do so by inhibiting capabilities for self-expression in the interests of affirming and enacting the status of members of a superior status group, where the submission of the status inferior is a means for the status superior's self-affirmation, *without* reciprocating compensation or benefit. This type of inhibition is conceivable in situations where the status difference does not track differences in economic or political power[47] but it is amplified when it is (as Stephen Angle puts it) entangled with status-group-defined differences in wealth and political power.

Finally, and briefly, there is the negative aesthetic component to such unethical status rituals, through which they lose their efficacy, and legitimacy, much like the Confucian rites the Mohists criticized. For observers who do not share in the hierarchical status group ideology that both legitimates and is acted out through such rituals, a profound ugliness is manifested in their practice. It signifies the dehumanization both of those who, by a mere accident of birth, inherit a sense of face that must be affirmed by eliciting deferential regard from others, and those who, by a mere accident of birth, have no other role in ritual exchange than to affirm that face in status superiors, and who face loss of livelihood and violent retaliation if they refuse. Lilian Smith's 1949 memoir *Killers of the Dream* famously testified to this ugliness in the socialization of black and white children in early twentieth-century rural Georgia:

> From the time little southern children take their first step they learn their ritual, for Southern Tradition leads them through its intricate movements. And some, if their faces are dark, learn to bend, hat in hand; and some, if their faces are white, learn to hold their heads up high. Some step off the sidewalk while others pass by in arrogance. Bending, shoving, genuflecting, ignoring, stepping off, demanding, giving in, avoiding. . . . So we learned the dance that cripples the human spirit, step by step by step, we who were white and we who were colored, day by day, hour by hour, year by year until the movements were reflexes and made for the rest of our lives without thinking.[48]

Modern Confucian Justifications for Hierarchy-Enacting Ritual

The argument offered so far is very far from rejecting all enactments of hierarchy-respecting status ritual as oppressive. Progressive Confucians can still find ways of justifying such rituals when they are shown not to be ethically compromised by the defeaters described earlier. Other Confucians may seek to decouple hierarchy-respecting status ritual from affirmations of categorical identities, and focus on rituals that enact esteem for more situationally specific identities such as occupational statuses, or for people who demonstrate moral and intellectual excellence. I will briefly consider two such arguments for hierarchy-respecting status ritual in the Anglo-American Confucian philosophical literature, by Daniel Bell and Aaron Stalnaker.[49]

Bell argues that the relative economic equality of East Asian societies is connected to the social inequality expressed in their various codes of ritual conduct. These codes generate a strong sense of community cohesion and obligation of the sort Xunzi describes, constraining the impulses of the more socially powerful to enhance their power by expanding their control over resources at the expense of the weak. Bell begins his argument with the observation that "Korea and Japan have relatively equal distributions of wealth compared to most industrialized countries in the world" and yet that they are also "perhaps the most hierarchical societies in East Asia." The point of his argument is to show that "social inequality can actually contribute to economic equality in contemporary East Asian societies."[50] In these societies, where ritual enactments of status difference rather than the conspicuous displays of wealth and power are preferred markers for status superiority, "the powerful need not rely on superior wealth to show their 'superiority' to the same extent."[51]

So while rituals exemplified in the drinking parties celebrated by Xunzi and in the drinking parties of office workers today "involve the powerful and the powerless," the powerful are "less likely to seek other means of domination such as material wealth."[52] This state of affairs is to be contrasted with the rather more lamentable sort of economic inequalities that correspond with the practice of Western-style "handshaking rituals" in other East Asian and South-East Asian societies such as Hong Kong, China, and Singapore. These are the sorts of clubbish rituals "which will take place largely among members of the same class," perpetuating a separation between the powerful and the weak, preventing the kind of communal solidarity between them that presumably would keep in check the acquisitive inclinations and conspicuous consumption patterns of the powerful. From this separation, and from the unconstrained acquisitiveness of the powerful, the need arises for coercive efforts by the state to redistribute income to protect the poor and vulnerable. In Japanese workplaces on the other hand, bosses share in ritual activities with their workers, including group exercise, karaoke singing, after-hours dinners, and also participation as guests of honor at their weddings. These activities generate a sense of solidarity with workers and encourage more benevolent conduct toward them, Bell avers, and they presumably limit any propensity for executives to bid more competitively for the enormous salaries and other exclusive perks their Western counterparts enjoy.[53]

If correct, this argument provides an instance of hierarchy-respecting deference rituals uncompromised by the six defeaters. Company bosses, executives, and managers hold more occupationally defined social roles rather than categorical identities, and thus the defeaters of rigidity and omnivalence associated with such identities do not apply in this case. Nor does the sacrifice defeater apply, for job security and lack of inequality in wealth are valuable compensations for the sacrifices to personal face sometimes required by hierarchy-respecting, asymmetrical ritual conduct. However, Bell's arguments founder on certain inconvenient facts about economic inequality in Japan and South Korea today. The claim that "Korea and Japan have relatively equal distributions of wealth compared to most industrialized countries in the world" has been untrue at least since the economic crisis in East Asia in the late 1990s. According to 2014 data, out of forty OECD countries listed on the Gini income inequality index, Japan was ranked fifteenth and South Korea nineteenth. The United States was third, Australia thirteenth, France twenty-first, Germany twenty-third, and Sweden twenty-seventh. For relative poverty (or share of the population holding less than 50 percent of median wealth), Japan ranked sixth with 16.1 percent and South Korea eighth with 14.4 percent out of the same number of OECD countries, well ahead of the United Kingdom, Australia, Germany, France, and the Scandinavian countries.[54] South Korea and Japan are in a high to middling position in unequal wealth distribution relative to "most" industrialized countries, with more socially egalitarian countries in Western and Northern Europe and Oceania further down the Gini and relative poverty indexes for economic inequality. On this data, and assuming that hierarchy-respecting ritual is more frequently practiced in Japan and Korea in comparison to more socially egalitarian European and Oceanic societies, it is questionable whether there is a virtuous correlation between the frequency of hierarchy-respecting ritual in workplaces and more egalitarian distributions of wealth.

A moderated defense of Bell's argument could point out that the virtuous correlation between ritual-based social hierarchy and relative income equality *once* held in Japan and South Korea, before the economic crisis of the 1990s and the subsequent embrace of more neoliberal economic policy by South Korean and Japanese governments. But this argument is vulnerable to the correlation fallacy. Institutional arrangements worked out as part of the social contract between employees and companies in Japan's and

Korea's postwar developmental states, mandating both seniority-based wage differentials and restraint in such wage differentials in return for loyalty and compliant workplace relations, may provide more fundamental explanations for the relative lack of wage differentials between bosses, managers, and their employees. Still, this interpretation could admit a role for communal ritual practices in providing the social glue for day-to-day solidarity in the developmental state's social contract between employers and employees.

Most importantly, however, Bell does not consider the effects of gender difference in his assessment of these countries' "relative economic equality." South Korea tops the gender wage gap in OECD countries with a gap of 36.60 percent, with Japan in third place at 26.59 (by comparison, the United States is in thirteenth place and Germany fifteenth).[55] These income disparities are due to a still-rigid sexual division of labor in family life and ongoing sexual segregation in employment patterns. Bell has focused on occupational-based status differences as they are enacted in workplace social rituals between superiors and subordinates, and so his argument seems to avoid the ethical pitfalls of affirming deference status rituals in relation to categorical identities. But we have seen how tea service rituals enact more categorical, gender-based differences, with women workers replicating traditional domestic roles in servicing the needs of male co-workers, in ways that they can find demeaning. Such rituals render women as an instrumentalized means to the affirmation of male solidarity across social hierarchical lines, uniting men in their shared enjoyment of female labor, in a shared sense of face, even while substantial income differences between the genders persist. Thus, the rather idealized correlation between ritualized social hierarchy and economic egalitarianism that Bell upholds is empirically underdetermined, and vulnerable to both progressive Confucian and ethical individualist criticism.

Aaron Stalnaker provides a more analytically rigorous justification for hierarchy-respecting asymmetrical deference ritual in modern democratic societies, both Western and Eastern. Against the notion that deference is a "feudalistic cultural holdover" and an "anti-democratic vice," Stalnaker argues that early Confucian treatments of deference as a virtue "have important things to tell contemporary Western thinkers about the culture of democracy."[56] Rejecting a simplistic interpretation of deference as "toadying" to the powerful, Stalnaker works in part from a distinction present in Mencius between ritual respect for superior moral and intellectual authority ("honoring the excellent" *zūn xián* 尊賢), which requires due acknowledgment and attentiveness to such authority and ritually "treating the eminent as eminent" (*guì guì* 貴貴), which requires due recognition of office holders of higher institutional rank (such as dukes or kings).[57]

It may seem that a roughly modern equivalent for the distinction between "honoring the excellent" and "treating the eminent as eminent" is the aforementioned distinction between capacity-esteem and role-esteem in deference ritual. However, Stalnaker would insist that it is not enough to "salute the uniform and not the man" in role-esteem deference, to honor merely the role in separation from its bearer. Special esteem or "appraisal respect" is due both to the virtuous and also to the eminent as office holders, though the justifications for such appraisal differ. With regard to the eminent, Stalnaker seems to be saying that we ritually defer to the eminent in the expectation that they *will* live up to the high standards of competence and virtue that we associate with fulfilment of their office, that they will be just and benevolent—"the premise of the deferential respect for superiors is that those superiors have special responsibilities by virtue of their position."[58] The ritual posture of status subordinates is compatible with and even mandates remonstrance, or sometimes revolt, by persons of moral and intellectual authority when office holders fail to exercise appropriately such authority and humanity.[59]

Much like Bell, Stalnaker argues that hierarchy-respecting status ritual practice ideally serves to moralize and humanize status superiors, whether they are parents, teachers, or rulers of a state. Ritualized performance of deference not only marks recognition of status difference; it also reminds the holders of higher status of the responsibilities that go with their rank or their moral and intellectual excellence, to act up to the obligations that go with their status, so that they are worthy of the deference bestowed upon them. Ritual legitimizes office holders' authority, and serves as an internalized code of self-disciplining conduct[60] through performance of patterned modes of conduct that are believed (at least tacitly) to hold office holders to this self-discipline.

What of the contemporary relevance of these insights, valuable as they are for comprehending the importance of status difference–enacting ritual in moderating and humanizing political authority in pre-Qin Confucian thought? Stalnaker reminds us that moral and institutional elites are an undeniable presence even in modern democratic states, and indeed those states require such elites to "function, even to flourish." What early Confucian theories provide us with is a set of insights into how "elite restraint and responsibility" can be maintained. All persons have a certain minimal moral value according to early Confucian thinkers such as Mencius, perhaps compatible with modern liberal ideals of the equal dignity of all persons. But persons of demonstrated moral and intellectual excellence are *more* valuable and should therefore be treated accordingly, given greater privileges to go along with (and to remind them of) their greater duties and responsibilities.[61]

Hierarchy-respecting ritual conduct can also serve to humanize otherwise agonistic and confrontational stances in pluralistic societies with different groups attempting to resolve social injustices and inequalities. So a ritualized, dignified performance of deference to authority holders is compatible with, even essential to, the successful conduct of nonviolent protest, requiring law-abiding restraint and order in the face of violent provocation from authority holders, even as protestors defy the law in other ways, thereby powerfully reminding elites of their responsibilities to rectify injustices.[62]

Now Stalnaker's thesis could be questioned by those who accept that ritual has an important part to play in contemporary, pluralistic, and democratic societies, but that its expression should be egalitarian rather than status-difference enacting, and consist in a Kantian acknowledgment of the humanity of others as members of the kingdom of ends (an argument I will turn to again later). Stalnaker responds to this by drawing a further distinction between more generalized expressions of respect, which are minimally due to all other members of a modern democratic society, and "special respect" that is more "agent relative and recipient relative."[63] General respect is compatible with acknowledgment of the humanity in others. But differentiated "special respect" for holders of superior office or rank, and for the morally and intellectually virtuous, has its place in modern democracies even if we are inclined, in somewhat bad egalitarian faith, to undervalue its importance. We express deference to both because, on the one hand, we esteem those of high moral and intellectual authority for their superior achievement and their ability to instruct and advise us, such as teachers or mentors. On the other hand, we use ritualized gestures to express esteem for the office held by office holders, ranging from police through to judges and politicians, thereby implicitly reminding of their own responsibility to live up to the obligations of their offices. Critical to this thesis is that office holders should also defer appropriately to persons of inferior rank possessed of superior moral and intellectual authority, who advise and remonstrate with them.

Even egalitarians could sympathize with this thesis, with its intimations of morally upright dissenters "speaking truth to power," and of the powerful feeling compelled to listen and display ritually appropriate humility in response. Stalnaker is thus opposed to advocating deference to rigid, categorical identities. On his interpretation, Confucians would go further in imposing on the powerful the obligation to *seek out* and receive the advice of such morally upright people, with due respect and humility. In this sense, the ritual hierarchy enacted by Confucian deference does not track economic or political inequality in the way that deference to more categorical identities often has. The morally upright person may indeed be of substantially lower income, educational attainment, and political status.

Particular, hierarchy-respecting deference, and not just the mutual forms of deference holding between equals, are important, then, in noncoercively driving us, powerful and weak alike, into "more mutually responsible relationships." The habits learned and cultivated in these relationships can influence and shape people's behavior, generating co-operativeness among the general public for office holders, beginning with legitimately elected heads of state (while making allowance for ritually appropriate expressions of discontent and remonstrance). Deferential rituals can also elicit responsible behavior from office holders, maintaining a social order in which there is legitimacy for office holders who obtain and occupy their offices uprightly, and who care benevolently for the less fortunate.

Stalnaker acknowledges that instituting a Confucian deference "would require a dramatic expansion of respectful behavior towards others" in today's pluralistic democracies.[64] However, "contemporary democracies can and should be conceived as containing a variety of justly hierarchical relationships," he writes, and "deference is a substantive, if complex, virtue for the people in those relationships; in other words, appropriate deference contributes to and is indeed part of the good of agents and the whole society."[65]

Stalnaker's argument for the continued importance of hierarchy-respecting deference rituals in contemporary, pluralistic democracies is a powerful one, and one to which I can find no substantial objections. There are, however, some reservations that I want to put forward, in the spirit of testing and probing his arguments, with the purpose of encouraging their refinement, or of uncovering problems that merit closer scrutiny.

The first reservation arises from the concern that Stalnaker appears to replicate the early Confucians' optimistic moral psychology regarding the capacity for appropriately enacted ritual to (1) civilize status superiors and constrain them from abusing the deference and obedience status inferiors pay to them for personal gain or (2) constrain status inferiors from acts of duplicitous deference or uncivil disrespect and disobedience that can impair the office holders' exercise of their duties. In other words, we might find unrealistic the expectation that ritual will both be sustained by and encourage the cultivation of virtues central to furthering the goods of status inferiors and superiors, and of the institutions that they work together to sustain. A person of *ren* and *li* petitions a powerful office holder with appropriate deference, implicitly communicating the expectation that the office holder will live up to her expectations of benevolence and justice. But how are we to gainsay that the office holder will not take for granted this deference as a "perk of office" and respond arbitrarily or even abusively, willfully refusing to live up to such expectations?

Consider Alasdair Macintyre's conception in *After Virtue* of the internal and external goods of practices, such as families, arts and crafts, scholarly communities, or sports teams.[66] Deference is central to realizing internal goods such as fairness, love, and constancy in family life: "its goods can only be achieved by subordinating ourselves within the practice in our relationship to other practitioners."[67] So deference is offered to others in their roles as parents and for their moral qualities, in return for their physical, emotional, and moral assistance in realizing these goods. Deference enacts the childrens' acknowledgment of dependence on and acceptance of their parents' care and moral guidance. But where practices are corrupted, deference will be made to serve external goods such as wealth, political power, and personal status at the expense of internal goods. Macintyre speaks of the "restricted households of Highbury and Mansfield Park"[68] as the domains for a limited realization of a teleological pursuit of the good life in the early modern settings of Jane Austen's novels.

But the Harlowe Estate of Samuel Richardson's *Clarissa*, or the Jia Estate of Cao Xueqin's *Dream of the Red Chamber*, provide a near-contemporary counterpoint to this idealized conception of deference and the realization of the good life in families. In these households we see deference instrumentalized by the powerful to maintain and aggrandize external goods of status, wealth, sexual gratification, and political power in order to "raise a family," as Clarissa Harlowe ironically puts it, often with little of value by way of compensation to status inferiors, including their servants or their adult children. The latter can be crushed in the result (as Clarissa certainly is, in spite of her constancy and deference), or they may game deferential esteem for status superiors in their own pursuit of wealth, income, and influence. The prominence of legal constraint on the conduct of authority-wielding persons ranging from parents to political leaders, and a keener awareness of the rights of children in modern liberal democratic societies arises, in part, from a pessimism that people can be trusted enough to live up to the expectations of virtue in the roles they occupy as bearers of authority. The suspicion is that they will abusively take advantage of the deferential conduct of status inferiors rather than respond to it with benevolence and justice.

Stalnaker will probably agree that in modern, rule-of-law mass societies where the categorical identities of the past have faded (if not completely disappeared), there is less scope for such oppressive abuses of hierarchy-respecting status rituals. All the more reason, then, he might argue, to encourage their practice, knowing that powerful legal backup exists to protect the rights of social subordinates when deference fails to elicit virtuous conduct from social superiors. This is a good reply, but it also connects to a question concerning the overall plausibility of Stalnaker's thesis in the very democratic societies in which he thinks deference for office and for estimable moral and intellectual qualities has a useful place. That question is, whether such societies, marked by *deritualization* of social relations, could conceivably enable his envisaged "dramatic expansion of respectful behavior towards others," at least if that means hierarchy-respecting deference ritual.

This question concerns the weakening of deferential ritual as either capacity- or role-esteem, or some combination of the two. As sociologists of ritual point out, the highly personalized relations of patrimonial institutions, and the categorical identities they sustained, have been in decline for centuries as societies have become more bureaucratized, more impersonal in their institutional relations, and in which social stratification has gradually given way to "functional specialization." Japanese political scientist Maruyama Masao came to a similar conclusion sixty years ago. Changes in deference ritual are rooted in a (always incomplete) transition from what he called a "being" society in which esteem is paid in accordance with identity-constituting attributes (属性 *zokusei*) a person holds in a comprehensive social hierarchy, to a division of labor "doing society," in which esteem is paid to more institution- or workplace-specific functions (役割 *yakuwari*) people exercise as managers or employees, and which command little esteem outside of the settings in which they are exercised.[69] The pace of the "decline of deference" quickened in the twentieth century. Stalnaker regards esteem for office holders and for the morally and intellectually upright as important qualities for pursuing the good in contemporary societies. However, in modern mass societies, contact with office holders ranging from police and bureaucratic functionaries to judges and politicians tends to be intermittent and characterized by more perfunctory expressions of deference.[70] Indeed, in the context of education, since 1960 even countries such as the United Kingdom have seen declines in deferential authority orientations in students toward teachers.[71] This state of affairs stands in contrast to the more highly pressured deferential rituals of patrimonially based social relations, in which social superiors concentrated in their persons extensive political and economic power, and patronage capacities, over their subordinates.[72]

Cross-contextual, particular esteem for moral and intellectual excellence has also shrunk in modern societies, perhaps in part because fewer criteria are agreed on across the diverse settings of those societies for what constitutes a generally acclaimable intellectually or morally estimable character.[73] It is telling, as sociologist Randall Collins remarks, that entertainment and sports stars have become "contemporary sacred objects" in today's societies, and objects of cross-contextual, indeed international, capacity-respecting deference.[74]

Ritual in Socially Egalitarian Settings

In their different ways, Stalnaker, Bell, and Angle testify to the importance of hierarchy and of hierarchy-respecting deference rituals to well-lived ethical lives and to peaceful, cohesive social order. However, Confucians can respond to this state of affairs in ways different from recommending an expansion of hierarchy-respecting deference. I have conceded that the arguments in favor of this expansion are in principle strong. On the other hand, I want to pursue a revaluation of ritual activity in the more socially egalitarian public spheres of today's liberal democracies, in which I think it less likely that hierarchy-respecting Confucian ideals of "treating the eminent as eminent" and "honoring the excellent" can be realized in the way Confucians such as Stalnaker or Angle hope. My standpoint finds some affinities in contemporary Confucian scholarship. Sungmoon Kim thinks there is a way of revising the Confucian concept of *li* to allow for what he terms "Confucian incivility," including disharmonious disagreement and argument in the forthright addressing of ethical and political differences. Confucian conceptions of ritual can, on this account, provide a way of revaluing the range of ritual practices currently extant in the communal practices of debate and conflict resolution in liberal democratic civil societies. They can do so while avoiding an aesthetic preoccupation with harmonious, "non-dialogic, ritualistically orchestrated 'tacit' consensus," which can provide a particularly insidious, because ostensibly nonadversarial cover for an oppressive conformism and exclusion of dissent.[75] These latter "bloodless" understandings of ritual in any case overlook the conflictual, homicidal ritual expressions that early Confucian texts such as the *Book of Rites* also allow for, such as in the pursuit of blood feuds against the murderers of one's kin,[76] though this is obviously not the kind of Confucian "incivility" that Kim and I have in mind.

We can also find much to agree with in Tan Sor-hoon's hybrid Confucian and Deweyan account of ritual as a means for fostering harmonious co-operation and character cultivation in even conflictual situations. In itself, the inculcation of such practices allows for cultivation of "sensitivity and understanding toward other participants" in many sorts of co-operative endeavors. In more conflictual argumentation, "the predisposition toward a harmonious solution and the avoidance of an adversarial stance can have a significant impact on the outcome." Indeed, in the best cases where ritual practices foster mutual respect and understanding and noncoercive community building between representatives of different argumentative positions, they are a "powerful means of increasing the chances of an outcome acceptable to all."[77]

Finally, we can see in Erving Goffman's studies of status ritual a rich variety of deference rituals that do not conform to the *status difference*-enacting archetype of deference ritual. *Symmetrical* deference can take many forms, including highly-scripted ritual greetings and gestures betokening mutual, respectful acknowledgment between status equals. Also, deferential behavior can be based in sentiments other than esteem, such as trust, directed toward strangers as guests.[78] These can provide material for elaborating a defense of ritual acknowledgment for the dignity and humanity of others, for particular esteem and for trust in more egalitarian, public sphere exchanges.

I return now to the incident related at the beginning of this chapter, in which Robbie Ross raised his hat to his convicted friend Oscar Wilde. I want to give a more detailed illustration of how Ross's simple, conventionalized ritual of acknowledgment and respect can have magical effects as profound as any Albert Fingarette finds in ritual, but in a symmetrical social interaction.

The first thing to note is that the *conventionality* of this gesture, appropriately enacted through *yi*, enables restraint and meaningfulness in expressing a range of emotions that other gestures would not achieve. A tearful embrace would have violated late Victorian norms of emotional restraint between middle-class men and perhaps called too much suspicious attention among observers to the proclivities of Ross himself, to the detriment of his intended acknowledgment of Wilde. A verbal outburst or denunciation would have made a similarly negative, detrimental impression, violating tacit ritual norms for conduct in a hallowed public place such as a court of law. On the other hand, a more economical nod of respect or a locking of eyes could have been easily missed by observers, and failed to qualify as the sort of publically recognizable gesture Ross was intending. And so it too would be susceptible to misfire as a failed ritual gesture, and not accord with *yi*.

Second, what Ross achieved so economically (at least for the audience who were progressive minded, in his day and in our own) with this gravely dignified raising of his hat to Wilde was the signaling, and enactment, of unbroken friendship and loyalty. It was an acknowledgment not only that this man Wilde was still, to him, deserving of the respect due to a fellow man and moral peer, but also that he still deserved the loyalty due to a friend. Ross therefore also implicitly rebuked the injustice of those others, whether strangers or former friends, who had judged that he could no longer be such a person. In this gesture there is also *ren*, or humanitarian regard, for Ross was bravely calling attention in his gesture to a grave injustice—that a man had been deprived of his freedom and dignity, and cast out of society for doing something that should not be a crime. In according to Wilde the deference due to someone *as if* he were still a member of that society, Ross was defying that judgment. Ross's gesture incorporated a more generalized respect for Wilde as a fellow member of the kingdom of ends who had been wronged, as Stalnaker would point out. But here there is also a more particular respect, and esteem for Wilde as a friend.

Finally, something can be said, too, regarding the "magic" and aesthetic quality of Ross's gesture. Such a quality would by no means have been universally appreciated; to those observers who believed Wilde to be guilty, it may have come across as a duplicitous gesture. But its subtle, dignified performance stood less chance of provoking a more open, angry response from those repulsed by Wilde's conduct than a more open expression of affection or protest would have, and that too must be factored into the appropriateness, the *yi* of Ross's choice of gesture. Indeed, according to Wilde's testimony in *De Profundis*, it took place "before [a] whole crowd, whom an action so simple and sweet hushed into silence."[79] Here we can get some insight into how, in the terms communicated by contemporary Confucian scholars, Ross authoritatively established both himself and Wilde through his self-disciplined, graceful performance of a highly conventionalized, coded ritual gesture and thereby achieved something magical. For a very short time, for those observers who were sympathetic or even ambivalent, Ross would have seemed to have transformed Wilde from a shamed, convicted sodomite back into what he once was, or ought to have been—an esteemed, equal member of a moral community, and a person deserving the loyalty of a friend. It moreover established Ross's own character as someone who had the courage, and grace, to acknowledge Wilde in this manner.

It is possible, then, to provide a rich account of symmetrical deference ritual that goes beyond the generalized esteem expressed in others as civic equals, to incorporate more particular regard and esteem for them. But I wish to apply these insights in considering how such deference ritual can play a role in civilizing and moderating a more agonistic aspect of social exchange in modern pluralistic societies.

The Mohists and Confucians of old would see some of their fears of a leaderless, chaotically opinionated society realized in the often unruly, confrontational civil society relations of present-day liberal democracies, in the West and in the East. Today we are also in the midst of an international revolt against political and intellectual elites, increasingly held responsible for the ills of globalization, including widening and increasingly intergenerational inequalities in wealth, status, and educational attainment. Many less-educated people see their status and income security threatened in conditions of social and economic change; often residing in rural districts far from the secular, cosmopolitan lives of those elites, they have taken their resentments out on them at the ballot box, fueling the resurgence of nationalist, nativist, and xenophobic political movements across Europe, South Asia, and America. What Isaiah Berlin described as the "bent twig" consciousness he found in European nationalism and global anticolonial nationalisms, the snapping-back by those who feel humiliated by the economically powerful and the intellectually sophisticated, is once again regnant.[80]

In these polarized economic and political environments, the "markers of hierarchy,"[81] the ritually affirmed signs and symbols of higher and lower social rank and of lesser or greater moral and intellectual merit are heavily contested. The Confucians knew something of this, as we have seen; in the intellectually and politically diverse life of the Warring States, those who claimed sagedom for Confucius could find their claims opposed and even ridiculed by Mohists, Daoists, and Legalists. In the vast and far more diverse, socially egalitarian public spheres of today's mass societies, such contestation is even more intense. Fingers are often pointed at the internet, and especially at social media platforms, as communicative media that have further intensified this contestation.

Social media provides the acme of the socially egalitarian marketplace of opinion and information, in which any participant can claim the expertise or authority to create, disseminate, criticize, and reject information, and to esteem or denounce its communicators. This is a sphere in which publically accredited experts participate too. However, they are as vulnerable as any other participants (and sometimes more so) to criticism and denunciation when they invoke their expertise to question information that has acquired currency among ideologically polarized online factions and coalitions. Short-term political power can be quickly mobilized and concentrated on social media to influence the policy and practices of institutions, as well as of political authorities, who can quickly find themselves barraged with online denunciations. It can also cross "the fourth wall" to aid in the rapid mobilization of mass political movements and activism. Today political office holders can find their authority to act limited—and the deference they believe is due to their office dissipate rapidly—in the face of such coordinated online and offline mobilization.

It is interesting to ask whether social media interaction can itself become ritualized. The lack of bodily, ceremonial gesture and expression in such interaction would incline some to say that it cannot. On the other hand, social media is not just a medium for communicating information; it is also a medium for enacting community—often of an ephemeral, short-term variety—around the objects that community forms to sacralize, or to deem sacrilegious, such as opinions and opinion holders. There is a rich menu of actions for symbolizing such enactment—for expressing "likes" and for "following" esteemed opinions or opinion holders, and icons, memes, and formulaic expressions for expressing approbation and agreement, sometimes as simulacra for esteem-based deferential gesture. But there is also a battery of symbolic actions for expressing offense, contempt, or exclusion, and for "performative shaming" directed, often behind the veil of pseudonyms, at others irrespective of their attributed expertise or office. This virtual public sphere brings together vast numbers of opinion holders and information bearers, most often as strangers to one another, without the mediating (and potentially ameliorating) influences of bodily gesture or ceremonial eye contact and voice intonation. In doing so it can serve for the enactment of spectacularly vehement denunciation, contempt, and exclusion against whatever or whomever its temporary online communities deem to be sacrilegious.

How, then, does the above-mentioned schema for ritual acknowledgment and enactment of esteem for a social peer, and friend, apply to the sometimes rancorous, often anonymous, exchanges and argumentation taking place in today's public spheres, offline and online?

Contemporary East Asian, European, and American societies have ritual gestures and patterns for ordering formal and informal argumentative discourse, minimizing the risks of more vehement, even violent, confrontation taking place, cultivating in all participants a restraint on self-centered assertiveness and providing conventionalized patterns of conduct to express that assertiveness with civility. These conventional ritual behaviors include coded speech patterns and formulaic statements for acknowledging the status of other participants (e.g., forms of address such as "Ms.," "Professor," and the like), or for refusing such status recognition in the interests of more informal, egalitarian discussion; nonverbal cues and gestures and formulaic expressions for formally or informally opening and closing discussion, for acknowledging turn-taking in argument and for acknowledging disagreement; civil gestures such as bowing and handshakes to acknowledge those representing a different point of view from one's own; and so forth. Equivalent visual cues and symbols as well as formulaic expressions do much of the same work for online discussion.

For those of an ethically universalist bent, these ritual practices would provide the living tissue and muscle to (for example) the universal presuppositions of discourse ethics in argumentation, ideally signifying and enacting tacit, harmonious and noncoercive assent to guarantees to all participants for "freedom of access, equal rights to participate, truthfulness on the part of participants (and) absence of coercion in adopting positions" and in which the only force permitted is "the force of the better argument."[82] As far as the present argument goes, the reader need not subscribe to Jürgen Habermas's version of this universalism, to an understanding of such presuppositions as "transcendental constraints" or regulative ideals deduced from argumentative practice as such, which "make possible" the very practice that any participants understand as argumentation. A more Deweyan understanding of such principles, as idealizations of tacit norms evolved in more historically contingent practices of inquiry that are themselves subject to periodic evaluation, will also suffice. In that Deweyan capacity, those norms can still specify counterfactual conditions of ideal argumentative exchange, constituting principles for observing and criticizing the often imperfect, distorted, and even repressive conditions in which deliberation over norms and values takes place. The appropriate ritual enactment of these presuppositions in argumentation constitutes, I would add, additional reason for thinking that argumentative discourse is (more or less) approximating these ideal presuppositions.

I turn now to the aforementioned criteria of the conventionality, economy, and aesthetic quality of symmetrical ritual deference to see how they apply to argumentative discourse. Formulaic, patterned expressions for addressing interlocutors in an agreed-upon formal or informal manner, the shaking of hands and nodded acknowledgments at the commencement and conclusion of argument, and their more iconically cued online discussion equivalents constitute a code for acknowledging others as equal participants in argument. They also signal acknowledgment of those others as reasonable agents capable of presenting arguments that can persuade others, irrespective of how divergent their opinions and reasoning are, and of how persuasive they are subsequently deemed to be. Such conventional expressions and gestures steer a moderating course between excessive gestures of regard for interlocutors, which can be misinterpreted as ironic or sarcastic disregard, and expressions or gestures that express the desire to humiliate, dominate, and exclude interlocutors (for instance, by refusing to address them in an appropriate manner).

Second, the economy of such deferential gestures and expressions lies in their capacity, in a few words, gestures, and expressions to convey a wide range of other-regarding moral attitudes such as acknowledgment of interlocutors' reasonableness and dignity, expectations that they will live up to the standards for competent participation in argumentation, and trust in their willingness to participate in good faith in it. Thus they incorporate more generalized role-respect and civility for other participants as reasonable dialogical partners, and more role- and agent-relative special respect for interlocutors, communicating mutual expectations for participation with competence and honesty in the practice of argumentation.

Finally, there is the aesthetic and "magical" dimension to the deferential ritual element in argumentation. Through their conventionality and economy of expression, they enact equal status inclusion. Interlocutors in informal arguments over values, formal debating partners, participants in formal problem-solving meetings and debates, citizens and politicians engaged in discussion over policy evaluation and formulation online and off—through more or less rigorously coded, scripted ritual conduct intended to communicate mutual regard, all relate to each other *as if* they are equals (though their expertise and the quality and persuasiveness of their arguments may in fact be found to diverge). In appropriately ritualized communication, gesture and posture, interlocutors establish themselves and each other as bearers of equal dignity, humanity, and dialogical competence in spite of potentially profound disagreement. They also acknowledge by acceding to participate that they are open to the possibility of changing their minds by the compulsion of evidence and better argument, or at least to respecting the integrity of an argumentative position that they might previously have rejected and regarded with contempt. The more this enactment of mutually acknowledged inclusivity, equality, and respect is carried off with seeming effortlessness in the teeth of (and possibly with an ameliorating effect upon) profound disagreement over values and norms and the profound interpersonal dislikes they can give rise to, the more we can say the ritual performance has "magically" succeeded.

It would be wise, in view of the present-day, polarized conditions of ethical and political argumentation, to conclude on a pessimistic note. There is little prospect for a "massive expansion" of mutually regarding deference ritual in today's ethical and political argumentation and controversy, and even less prospect for expansion of the sort of hierarchy-respecting deference ritual Aaron Stalnaker has advocated. If the presuppositions of argumentation with their "rigorous idealizing content" are, as Habermas argues, "islands in a sea of practice" that seldom lives up to them,[83] so too the ritual conduct in argumentation outlined above is an ideal that is not often lived up to in practice. Sometimes the issues at stake are perceived to be of such importance that it is difficult to restrain the urge to denounce other's arguments with polemics, and to try to shame them into silence. Sometimes a position or opinion being defended is so morally repugnant that it is reasonable to refuse to engage with it. Withdrawal from dialogue and mobilization for protest or civil disobedience then seems inevitable, though this form of political action need not be devoid of its own deference ritual. Finally, the entrenchment of growing income inequalities in some liberal democracies is also facilitating an outsized influence for the wealthiest citizens and institutions in political discourse, potentially nullifying the equalizing influence of symmetrical deference ritual in civil society argumentation. I have merely argued that different Confucian conceptions of ritual can provide insight into understanding why symmetrical deference ritual conduct is something more than mere superfluous ornamentation to the practices of argument and persuasion when norms and values come into conflict. Such conduct can civilize those practices and ameliorate the more combative tendencies in argumentation—to dominate, dehumanize, humiliate, and exclude interlocutors.

CHAPTER 4

Filial Piety in East Asia and Beyond

Filial Piety and "Asian Culture"

In contemporary Confucian scholarship, filial piety (*xiao* 孝) is sometimes identified as a key value or virtue for demarcating cultural difference between China or East Asia and the West. In the English language scholarship, an intriguing coalition of interests has transpired between those scholars who wish to explain to an English-speaking readership a virtue that affords clear differentiation of "familial" East Asian social life from the "individualistic" social relations of the West and those Anglophone scholars who look to East Asian filial piety for a compelling ethical alternative to these same individualistic relations.

Hsieh Yuwei wrote fifty years ago that filial piety has been involved in all aspects of Chinese life for "several thousand years" and that the "Chinese emphasis upon filial piety" "is one of the outstanding characteristics which have marked the difference between China and Western countries."[1] Li Chenyang cites scholars such as Hsieh to describe Chinese culture "as the culture of filial morality," and describes filial piety as one of the moral precepts that deeply divides "traditional China from the contemporary West."[2] Doh Chull Shin writes in his survey of contemporary East Asian attitudes to democracy and Confucian values, that "In the west, there is no equivalent to the Confucian concept of filial piety."[3] Ruiping Fan represents a more moderate view, insisting that while "the Confucian moral values of *ren* (humanity), *yi* (appropriateness), and *xiao* (filial piety) have been rooted in the Chinese mind for thousands of years, transcending various types of economic forces and institutions," filial piety is also a universal human sentiment.[4]

In their philosophical translation of the *Xiào Jīng* (孝經), "The Classic of Family Reverence," Roger Ames and Henry Rosemont acknowledge the importance of "family values and structures" in all societies, but they claim on the basis of archaeological evidence of ancestral sacrifices extending back five millennia that "family values are discernable, and discernable as fundamental, throughout (Chinese) culture" and that "family reverence was one of the most basic and defining values of the Chinese people."[5] They do not deny that filial piety has some importance for Western societies. However, they reject the usual translation of *xiao* as filial piety in favor of "family reverence," arguing that "piety" is associated with deference to transcendental religious figures "associated with the Abrahamic traditions."[6] Thus, family *reverence* as they interpret it is an ethical *dao* particular to Chinese culture.

Finally the editors of a book on *Filial Piety in Chinese Thought and History* observe, rightly, that "Today, in the face of the forces of modernization and globalization, *xiao* has been singled out as a key to preserving Chinese tradition and identity" before adding, in somewhat mystical language, that "it remains integral to the Chinese heart-mind, and, given the impact of Chinese tradition on Korea and Japan, to the larger East Asian cultural environment."[7]

In contrast with much of this scholarship, this chapter aims for a more universalist understanding of *xiao* or filial piety, looking to its potential to provide a more inclusive ethical perspective on family life in all its forms in postindustrial societies today, a perspective that is also in accordance with the ethical individualism supported throughout this book. I will argue that a fuller, deeper discussion of the ethical import of filial affection in contemporary postindustrial societies must take into account not only what legitimate expectations parents may place on children, both to fulfill their emotional and physical needs as their parents and to fulfill the goods of family life as a whole, but also what legitimate expectations parents may have for their children's forbearance (or respect) as they pursue their own life interests and projects, sometimes beyond the family. Achieving these aims, however, requires first confronting the above-mentioned culturalist trends in scholarship on Confucian *xiao*,[8] to argue that filial piety in its diverse forms and practices is a virtue, which, far from being distinctive to Chinese or East Asian "culture," has at different times been valued and disputed in both Eastern and Western societies.

Filial Piety as a Virtue

Henry Rosemont and Roger Ames have, as we saw in chapter 2, argued against the virtue-ethics interpretation of filial piety and of other ethically valuable qualities such as *ren*. They claim instead that early Confucian thought includes a role-ethics that is "*sui generis* in both philosophy and religion, both east and west" embodying a "specific vision of human beings as relational persons constituted by the roles they live rather than as individual selves" and that this vision further embodies "a specific vision of the moral life that takes family feeling as the starting point for developing a consummate moral competence *and* a religious sensibility grounded in *this* world."[9] They provide a number of reasons to show why *xiao* or *ren* are not rightly construed as virtues. These reasons cluster around metaphysical and moral-psychological assumptions about what is unique to selves construed in a Confucian, relational way, in contrast to the conceptualizations of the self and the virtues in the Western philosophical tradition.

We also saw in chapter 1 that Ames and Rosemont do have one intriguing reason for being so insistent that this role-ethics is "*sui generis* in both philosophy and religion, both east and west" and is *not* a virtue ethics. This reason is connected to a methodological criticism of much comparative philosophy—that it expressly, or more often tacitly, favors the "Western side." Such bias can be expressed in a reliance on Western philosophical terms as the de facto standards of evaluation or identification. In refusing to identify filial reverence as a virtue, or indeed as the "filial *piety*" of the Abrahamic religious tradition, Rosemont and Ames are attempting to avoid the "unfortunate asymmetry" in comparative philosophy with its tacitly assumed premise that "Chinese philosophy's encounter with Western philosophy has been its defining moment" and in terms that reflect more favorably on and perpetuate the intellectual dominance of Western philosophy. On the face of it, this appears to be a more political—one might say, "postcolonial"—than philosophical criticism of comparative philosophy. But the criticism does have philosophical import, for Ames and Rosemont believe that this asymmetry also distorts our understanding of Chinese philosophies by assimilating them to Western philosophical categories.

In contrast, Phillip Ivanhoe argues that we cannot distinguish between "authentic and inauthentic fulfillment of roles" nor establish an ethical ideal that realizes itself in multiple social roles—much as the *junzi* is said to do without an account of virtues that specify how well those roles and the ideal personhood itself are cultivated and performed.[10] Seen in this light, ethical qualities such as *xiao* and *ren* are best understood as virtues, and Ivanhoe argues we should interpret the early Confucians as advocating a virtue ethics. In this, Ivanhoe echoes an argument made by Alasdair Macintyre of the need for functional concepts for specifying the *telos* of particular social roles through which we can evaluate that they are being performed well, and also of the need to specify the good or *telos* of a whole, unified human life, fulfilled by relevant exercise of virtues across different roles and practices.[11] Indeed, filial piety would be paradigmatic of those virtues that can be performed in multiple roles, and in fulfillment of the goals of a whole life. While it initially appears "tied to a particular role" as a son or daughter, filial piety is also "the source of virtuous dispositions in general" and "an expression of other virtues," such as *ren*. Finally, filial piety can be expressed in other roles to parent-like individuals, including teachers or mentors.[12] Ivanhoe concedes that room remains for acknowledging the more salient position of social roles in the Confucian exercise of virtues, such as Mencius's six fundamental human social roles, or *wulun*, in comparison with Aristotelian virtue ethics. It could also be said—though I will not press the point—that for Greek philosophers like Plato (in the *Critias*) and Aristotle, the laws and the constitution of the city state play a more primary role in the moral education of youth than does the cultivation of filial piety within the family.

Other scholars have looked into the potential for symmetrical translations of virtue concepts between English and Chinese, without prejudicing culturally distinct understandings of those concepts in early Confucian thought. Thus, for Liu Liangjian, a comparative analysis of the term 德 (*de*) in the classical Confucian corpus and ἀρετή (*arête*) in Aristotle's ethics allows us to claim that the ancient Chinese 善德 (*shande*) or modern Chinese 美德 (*meide*) can function as equivalents for a generalized conception of virtue in both; and so "there are some good grounds for comparison, and further, dialogue between virtue ethics and Confucianism." He goes further to argue that there is something distinct in the way that *de* conceptually unifies virtuous character and virtuous conduct, while also recognizing the difference between "the virtue of human behavior" and "the virtue of human nature," whereas Western moral theories have often tended to split between action-oriented and agent-oriented theorizing about ethical conduct. Thus, there is room for arguing that Confucian virtue ethics, far from standing in an inferior relation to Western virtue ethics, has distinctively valuable philosophical insights of its own for virtue ethics.[13]

Here is not the place to debate whether these arguments amount to a refutation of the role-ethical understanding of filial reverence. For my purposes in this chapter, it is sufficient that cogent arguments exist for identifying Confucian ethics as a virtue ethics, or at least for identifying in it equivalent ethical concepts to European virtue ethics, and for conceptualizing Confucian accounts of virtues such as filial piety in a way that does not assimilate them in distorting fashion to classical Greek or Anglo-American philosophical concepts of virtue. My more universalist approach to filial piety will in any case avail itself of these arguments for filial piety as a virtue.

Yet some might object to my drawing on Anglo-American philosophical perspectives and arguments over filial piety to develop my own interpretation of filial piety. Some might suggest that Western philosophers, moralists, and theologians have not inquired very deeply into filial piety, if it all, and that if they have, it has been from a "rights-based perspective."[14] Some contemporary philosophers have indeed adopted a rights-based justification for filial piety, and I will consider one such argument by Christine Hoff-Sommers later. On the other hand, some European philosophers, theologians, and novelists *have* given detailed consideration to filial piety, from a theological, virtue-based perspective. Indeed, as I intend to show shortly, for much of the eighteenth century, English theology, literature, and polite conversation gave it very detailed consideration indeed. It is worth considering modern, rights-based theorizing about filial piety in Anglo-American philosophy, as well as the older, more theologically based understandings of filial piety in eighteenth-century thought, in light of what modern commentators on the Confucian virtue of filial piety have to say about it. Such a comparativist perspective, pursued without any "unfortunate asymmetry," may yield fresh insight into the problems facing the practice of filial piety in aging postindustrial societies today.

Indeed, it must also be said that rights-based liberal conceptions of the family that we take for granted today were once strongly disputed. In fact, the antipatriarchal, Lockean conception of the family had no easy victory against its theological, patriarchalist opponents in eighteenth-century England. Thus, the influential sermons of the early eighteenth-century bishop William Fleetwood and of the mid-eighteenth-century Irish theologian Patrick Delaney provide an understanding of filial love and responsibility that is still grounded in preliberal conceptions of the virtues, and so, to some extent, is the ideal of filial piety upheld in Samuel Richardson's 1748 novel *Clarissa*. These controversies are worth dwelling on from the comparativist perspective mentioned above. For while they tell of a crisis for patriarchal famialism that saw it succumb to more liberal, conjugal conceptions of family life, they may also yield moral psychological insights into filial piety that have some affinities with modern Confucian concepts of filial piety. And I shall argue that these concepts are not to be lightly dismissed in comparison to rights-based perspectives.

I will first summarize the modern interpretations of Confucian filial piety put forward by Li Chenyang and Phillip Ivanhoe, which can provide criteria for identifying these affinities.

In the *Analects*, Confucius famously distinguished the highest practice of filial piety from lesser varieties of care for parents, observing that "filial piety nowadays means the support of one's parents. But dogs and horses likewise are able to do something in the way of support;—without reverence, what is there to distinguish the one support given from the other?"[15] But why should there be such reverence? What justifies it, and what is its content? One possible problem for Western thinkers, as Phillip Ivanhoe points out, is that when they do treat filial piety as a subject for philosophical inquiry, they tend to focus either on gratitude for life and parental sacrifice, or on friendship as its bases. While such a focus can provide some material for defending filial piety as a worthy virtue, it fails to grasp some important aspects of parent-child relations, misconstruing "the true source and foundation of filial piety."[16]

Ivanhoe notes that both early Confucians and other thinkers do emphasize "gratitude for the gift of existence" as one justification for filial piety—children "owe it" to their parents for having brought them into existence. This debt-based argument presents a number of problems in itself, such as its conflation of *causal* owing in the sense of "owing one's having been born to one's parents" with moral debt or contract-based obligation, where the latter is inappropriate given that children do not exist when the "debt" is "contracted." Moreover, where gratefulness for the "good" of life is concerned, problems arise with assuming that parents intend the good of their children through the act of procreation, and whether existence by itself is a good for which children should be grateful for.

So Ivanhoe concludes—and this also finds support in the Confucian literature—that "[g]ratitude must be supplemented with feelings of reverence and love that are seen as the natural response to the sustained, particular, and characteristic nurture and love that good parents bestow upon their children." Filial piety is grounded in acknowledgment of the abjectly dependent condition that children begin their lives in need of parents' "protection, nurturance and material support"[17] and in acknowledgment of the critical role parents play in their children's early education, in shaping their character and capabilities, which in Confucian thought means "introducing them into the humane social life described by Confucian rituals and norms."[18] So long as these myriad goods are bestowed out of love and consideration for the good of children, gratitude, love, and reverence are appropriate responses to these activities, which typically involve great sacrifice from parents. Reverence in particular is a justified emotion, out of recognition of the fact that all the sacrifice and effort behind parental love, education, and concern cannot ever be reciprocated. From a slightly different but complementary perspective, Li Chenyang states that filial piety is a duty arising from the roles we undertake in familial and wider social relations as alternately benefactors and beneficiaries, as persons in need of care and as carers. An essential part of what it means to cultivate *ren* is for children, as children, to care for, love, and revere their parents, just as their parents cared for and loved them when they were dependent and needed care.[19]

As a virtue, filial piety is "a cultivated disposition to attend to the needs and desires of one's parents and to work to satisfy and please them"[20] and is an appropriate response to parental love and care. Now it must be said that a good deal of Ivanhoe's discussion of the myriad goods and love bestowed by good parents on children is largely inferred from the early Confucian literature, rather than stated there explicitly. As Li Chenyang notes, the lack of explicit justification may be owing to the fact that, "in the old days there was such overwhelming support for filial piety that it did not need philosophical argument to support it."[21] And so also the content of children's filial behavior toward their parents is sketchily stated in the *Analects*: "Meng-sun asked me what filial piety was, and I answered him,— 'not being disobedient.'" Fan Chi said, "What did you mean?" The Master replied, "That parents, when alive, be served according to propriety; that, when dead, they should be buried according to propriety; and that they should be sacrificed to according to propriety."[22]

Beyond being loving and being solicitous of parental needs, filial children also honor, revere, and obey their parents. However, obedience must be tempered with a willingness to remonstrate with parents in an appropriate and restrained manner when they do wrong, and this should be counted also as an expression of filial love and solicitude.

Finally, behind the formalized rituals of grieving and annual sacrifice for dead parents we can also discern the love and gratitude to parents who had sacrificed so much and bestowed so many goods on their children.

Reverence and love for parents after their deaths is justified in the sense that parents' deaths do not constitute an arbitrary end point for filial love. Rather, children should continue to acknowledge all that their parents have done for them, keep them in their minds, and honor them in their own conduct.[23]

In addition to filial piety being an appropriate response to parental love and care, a further justification for filial piety lies in its being the first training ground for self-cultivation in social roles that are constitutive of our identities, and in the cultivation of the cardinal virtue of *ren*. As Ivanhoe observes, from their position of relative neediness and dependence, children (ideally!) learn how powerful individuals like their parents sacrifice much in order to provide love and care for their children, powerfully showing that "acts of parental love express the priority of care and sacrifice over power and prerogative."[24]

A Filial Piety Controversy in Georgian England

In eighteenth-century England a debate unfolded about filial piety in which established, patriarchalist, famialist understandings of filial piety came under strong challenge. Both middle- and upper-class parents at the time had to confront a weakening of their own power over their children. Not only was the patriarchal absolutism of previous centuries questioned in the political and educational treatises of John Locke, but its economic basis had been slowly undermined in the development of a market society and the weakening of feudal norms in the preceding centuries. This generated conflict with traditional parental prerogatives over young adult children's choices of vocation and marriage partner, as increasingly financially independent young people exploited loopholes in existing legislation and canon law, to solemnize clandestine marriages outside of consecrated venues.[25] Here there were openings for a growing moral educational literature to advise parents and children on parental and filial duties, and for novelists to dramatize the consequences of conflicts over those duties.

In William Fleetwood's 1705 *Relative Duties of Parents to Children, Husbands and Wives, Master and Servant* and Patrick Delaney's 1738 *Fifteen Sermons Upon Social Duties* we find a conception of filial piety that goes well beyond the birth-debt and gratitude-based justifications for filial piety that Phillip Ivanhoe and Li Chenyang find to be inadequate in Anglo-American philosophical treatments of filial piety. Both of these divines emphasized the moral emotions of love, honor, and reverence as fundamental, much as the early Confucians did. Fleetwood understood the biblical injunction for children to "honor their father and mother" as meaning that "we are commanded to *love* them, to *respect* them, to *obey* them, and to *succour* and *support* them all we can."[26] And there is theological justification for regarding filial piety as *not* being grounded simply on acknowledgment of indebtedness for existence. For just as love of God is founded not just on His giving us existence but also in fitting us to seek our own good, so love for parents is not just founded on them giving existence to children, but also on their having made their children "capable of receiving and enjoying other good," which includes goods of the body, mind, religious instruction, and the inculcation of moral character, through "endless Labors, Watchings and Solicitudes."[27] In addition to love and honor, children also owe to their parents "Respect . . . all external Honor and Civility. As love comprises all internal honor and Esteem, all their behavior is to be submissive, dutiful and mannerly."[28] Filial obedience is justified on account of the undoubted good will, superior wisdom earned with age and experience, and sacrifices parents make that they command "out of love and design our Good thereby."[29] However, and this is an important caveat, Fleetwood felt it unrealistic that a duty to love can be imposed upon the will, for we can only love those we have apprehended to be loveable. So "it will depend much upon the parents' Management, whether the children shall love with the Affection of the Heart."[30]

Delaney expressed similar sentiments. There is a theological basis for filial piety in that parents are, next to God, "the authors of our being," God being properly our father, but we are to honor our parents as "his substitutes on earth."[31] However, Delaney was also not content with this birth-debt justification for filial piety alone. We owe our duty to honor our parents not just on the basis of our existence, but also from the support given to us by their "care and affection," and all those who can take the place of our parents and "eminently contribute to our well-being," such as teachers and spiritual pastors, are also owed "paternal honor."[32] Much like the Confucians, then, Delaney emphasized the capacity for filial love and reverence to expand beyond family relations to other relations characterized by paternalistic benevolence and subordinate need.

Delaney, more than Fleetwood, provided detailed moral psychological explanation for the basis of filial love in parental self-sacrifice and care and in children's own initial helplessness and neediness, and supplied a sentimentalist justification for filial love missing from more austere, patriarchalist justifications for filial obedience advanced in the previous century by Robert Filmer. So he wrote, "GOD knows, the pious returns due from children to parents are at once the strongest dictates of gratitude and justice, and are but a poor re-tribution for all the care and expence of education, for all the anxious hours, and sleepless nights . . . in solicitude for our welfare, and in distress for our ill health, and ill conduct."[33] Children cannot fully reciprocate such care and sacrifice, yet they can return love, as much as it is "in (their) power to make."[34]

Yet Delaney emphasized the need for filial honor and obedience to parents with greater asperity than did Fleetwood a generation earlier. In addition to the love due to parents in return for the diverse physical, emotional, and moral goods they help their children to realize, parents are to be honored "in reverence" and in "obedience." Honoring parents involves "a filial and affectionate awe" filled with "veneration and esteem" conforming to parents' wishes and abstaining "religiously" from conduct that might cause them trouble or disquiet." Though he admitted the anachronism in this admonition, Delaney insisted that veneration for parents should ideally also show itself in ritual conduct of the sort practiced in the patrimonial households described in the last chapter—"in demeanor, in lowliness and submission of gesture, bowing the head, and bending the knee."[35] Children must also obey parents, as this is an injunction founded on "the law of God" but also "by the dictates of reason" since parents are naturally the superiors of children, having the advantage of "years and experience."[36]

Delaney appealed to biblical precedents as well as the precedents set by the "wiser heathens" such as the Romans and the Chinese to justify such obedience. Referring to the death penalty and other exemplary punishments handed out in Qing Dynasty China to unfilial children and to the families and communities that fail to prevent their impiety, Delaney wrote, "it is the noblest monument of that wisdom, and virtue, by which the Chinese think themselves distinguished above the rest of the world at this day; the mighty veneration to parents injoined by their laws, and the severe and exemplary punishment of undutifulness and disobedience."[37] Delaney's admiring references to Chinese morality and to Confucius, which provided him with salutary illustrations of filial conduct and of exemplary punishment for the unfilial[38] are exhibits of that cultural hybridity in moral thought that I described at the end of chapter 1. They provide further attestation for the high esteem European moralists and philosophes held for Confucian thought in the first half of the eighteenth century.

Like the early Confucians, Fleetwood and Delaney believed that remonstrance, appropriately and reverentially exercised, was integral to filial love. According to Fleetwood, when the commands of God and parents conflict, children are to obey God and disobey their parents.[39] Moreover, when parents direct their children to break the "laws of the land," children must also disobey, given the indisputable precedence of the public over private good and the importance of law in sustaining the former. Nevertheless, children must remonstrate with their parents and persuade them to forgo such commands.[40] In thus subordinating filial piety to temporal and divine law, Fleetwood's conception of filial piety evaded some of the dilemmas of Confucian conceptions that placed filial reverence on a more equal footing in ethical value to loyalty to rulers.

In Delaney, too, we find importance given to remonstrance, but with one startling difference. While Fleetwood unambiguously required that children submit themselves to both divine and temporal law when it conflicts with parental command, Delaney was less clear about the priority of temporal law, for he took more literally the *New Testament* injunction in the Book of Colossians, "obey your parents in all things," as founded in both the law of God and reason. So "unless (parents) should injoin something contrary to the commands of GOD; in that case (and in that alone) your disobedience must be excused from the prior obligation you owe to your Creator," leaving open the interpretation that children may, in compliance with filial obedience, break temporal law.[41] Delaney, so impressed by the austere filial morality of the Chinese, would likely have held Honest Gong—the sheep stealer's son—in the same contempt as Confucius did.

So far, then, we have seen some interesting parallels with the early Confucian tradition in the importance it gave to the reverence, honor, and love that children ought to pay to their parents, compatible with a remonstrative attitude toward wrongful parental conduct, while going beyond mere gratitude for the debt of existence. We also find parallels with the rich moral psychological insights that Phillip Ivanhoe develops into the "true foundations of filial love." If differences exist, they are found in the lack of consideration given to the practice of mourning and sacrificial rites for parents after their deaths—practices that would have struck these Protestant divines as idolatry.

Also like the early Confucians, Fleetwood and Delaney regarded filial piety as the nursery for other virtues. For Fleetwood, filial love is the "Foundation of all other Love, and the true Cement of all Relations and that which truly obliges to the Performance of all Duties, and makes them to become Duties, antecedently to all Commands, Whether of God or Man."[42] Delaney pursued this argument with stronger emphasis. For him—as much as for Li Chenyang—filial duty was of such importance because "all our other duties to mankind begin and are founded here. It is from a right deference to the authority and institutions of parents, that we learn to become good men, good neighbors, good friends, and good subjects, as well as good sons."[43] In practicing filial piety, children learn also to respect all those who can take the place of parents "and "eminently contribute to our well-being" and who are therefore owed "paternal honor," be they teachers, pastors, or indeed the governors of the nation in which children are subjects. Reciprocally, regarding the duties of governors, "the wellbeing of the community hath the same dependance, upon their paternal care and vigilance, that particular houses have upon the prudence and affection of the masters of families." Government is to be regarded both as "originally derived from paternal authority" and also as "an enlargement upon that authority."[44]

So here as well are parallels with interpretations of early Confucian ethics that regard filial piety as foundational to the practice of virtues in social roles and relations radiating out from the family toward others, and to the "great family" of society itself. Indeed, it is striking to see Delaney uphold a familist patriarchalism that Locke had argued against in the *Two Treatises of Government* half a century earlier.

Both Fleetwood and Delaney found themselves grappling with the problem of adult children's filial obligations in their choice of marriage partners. Both tried to reconcile, somewhat unsuccessfully, acknowledgment of the rationality of adult children in their capacity to decide prudently for their own marriage choices—much as Locke had argued—with the conception of divinely sanctioned parental authority and filial obedience that they still held to. They did so in light of facts that they could not disavow, and which was to become a central theme in Samuel Richardson's novel *Clarissa*—that parents may be unreasonable, even vicious rather than virtuous, and dictate their children's marriages on the basis of their own desire for financial gain and status, making their children the nonconsenting means to their ends. They had, in other words, to factor into their casuistry the problem of virtue failure, in a justification for filial love and obedience grounded on a default assumption of parental love and benevolence as the norm in family life. The crux of the matter, as put to Samuel Richardson soon after the publication of *Clarissa* in 1748 by one of his correspondents, the bluestocking Hester

Chapone, was this: must children "then pay the same obedience to cruel tyrants as they would do to kind and indulgent parents?"[45]

Fleetwood noted that obedience to parental dictate in the choice of marriage partners is not explicitly identified as a filial duty in the Scriptures, but is implied in the direction for children to honor and obey their parents, and canon law restricted marriage to those aged over twenty-one who had the consent of their parents. Yet Fleetwood adduced a number of reasons why children should not be forced against their will to marry the partner of their parents' choice. First of all, love and affection cannot be dictated, and on this ground alone parents should be "very careful and considering, that they urge their authority too far, in constraining their Children to Marry" where there is no mutual affection.[46] Since Christian practice also forbids divorce or extramarital sexual relations, this consideration makes it even more important that people be allowed to marry "none but whom they love, and still intend to love."[47] Moreover, in then contemporary English custom, women were allowed sufficient personal freedom to "make it somewhat more reasonable for them to choose their partners, with whom they are to live, not in Confinement, but at Liberty."[48] Finally, and most critically, "Parents are not to let the Consideration of Fortune and Estate so preponderate and over-weigh over all other Considerations," such as virtue and good qualities in the choice of a mate for their children.

These and other factors, including the maturity of the children and whether they are embarking on a second marriage, limit parental authority over their choice of mates. In these constraints room remains for a significant degree of filial disobedience, even if, as Fleetwood recommended, it be exercised only with reluctance and in the worst cases.[49] To resolve the potential deadlock this concession to filial disobedience might produce, Fleetwood recommended a resort to a forerunner of Adam Smith's "impartial spectator," the judgments of "fair and equal, wise and understanding People." So if parents seek for their children a marriage the children cannot consent to, the children voice their objections with sufficient humility, and "the whole neighbourhood also condemn the proposal after thorough acquaintance with it," filial disobedience in such cases is not sinful. On the other hand, when nothing is objectionable in the character of the parents' choice for a marriage partner, and the proposed union is "such as would satisfy a wise and sober, and impartial man," children "must obey in these cases."[50]

Fleetwood at least could avail himself of the authority of hypothetical impartial spectators and sympathetic neighbors as courts of last resort.

Delaney instead invoked an older patriarchal conception of parental power over children in constraining their filial disobedience in matrimonial choice: "as long as children continue a part of their parents' family (which must be till they think fit to dispose otherwise of them) they are absolutely in their parents' power, and have no more right to dispose of themselves, than they have to dispose of the parents' fortune, or inheritance, or any of their goods."[51] Unlike Fleetwood, Delaney thought it acceptable to appeal to the practices of "wiser heathens" such as the Romans or the Chinese in justifying absolute parental authority in marital choice, even in the cases of "exalted" adult sons. In addition to the theological justifications for such authority, Delaney claimed that when judging prospective marital partners for their children, parents are too wise and prudent to be distracted by finery and outward form, which is so often incompatible with virtue or modesty. Nonetheless, Delaney also declared that "parents must not force "children to marry against their will."[52]

In the second of his *Two Treatises of Government*, Locke argued that parents (and not only fathers) "have a sort of rule and jurisdiction over (children) when they come into the world, and for some time after, but it is but a temporary one," with "age and reason" loosening the bonds of obedience and dependence, so that eventually "man is left at his free disposal." For Locke held that human beings were free under all natural and civil law, once they had acquired sufficient powers to understand the law and the limitations it put on their freedom. If this applied already to Adam in his created state, in full power of his reason, it also held for his descendants, born into a state of dependence but capable of growing into the full possession of their reason under parental guidance. The freedoms permitted by English law—"to have the liberty to dispose of his actions and possessions, according to his own will, within the permission of that law"—were given to persons who had turned twenty-one, "and in some cases sooner."[53]

Yet it is this right that Delaney expressly denied over fifty years after the publication of *The Two Treatises of Government*. So long as children remain a part of their parents' family and until their parents decided otherwise, adult children had no more right to dispose of themselves or their possessions than they did of their parents' possessions. Delaney thus opposed the possessive individualism Locke advocated, which bestowed ownership rights on bodily "actions and possessions" once the age of majority was reached.

Let's sum up what has been discussed so far. In the work of eighteenth-century British divines Fleetwood and Delaney we find the working out of a relational conception of moral and civil duties, in which duty to God is fulfilled in part through the fulfillment of divinely sanctioned duties to other persons, beginning in family relations and radiating out to all other morally and civically important relations, including those of subjects to their rulers. For these divines, as for the early Confucians, filial piety is a virtue that is foundational in the cultivation of other virtues needed to fulfill all other relational duties.

Fleetwood and Delaney, however, had to respond to multiple challenges to this conception of filial duty that neither the early Confucians nor contemporary moralists in Qing Dynasty China had to face. There was (1) the creeping delegitimation of feudal control and patriarchal authority over children, quickened by Locke's attacks on patriarchal government in states and in families, and by his stress on parental responsibility for the moral upbringing of children; (2) a growing sentimentalist notion of marriage and family life that emphasized mutual love and affection over external goods of property consolidation and of social status as the overall *telos* of upper-class family life; and (3) a growing conviction in the rational self-command of young adult children and the rights to individual self-expression that this self-command bestowed, which placed limits upon the exercise of parental authority.

The limitations in Fleetwood and Delaney's equivocal responses to these challenges were exposed in dramatic form in Richardson's 1748 novel *Clarissa*, which tried through the multiple perspectives of the novel's correspondents to combine Christian, patriarchalist, and sentimentalist understandings of filial love and duty. In his failure to harmonize these perspectives, and in his failure to give adequate weight to the effects of parental virtue in harming the religious and moral lives of children, Richardson gave reason for his many otherwise sympathetic readers, and critics, to excise the requirement for obedience in affairs of the heart from the duties of love, honor, and reverence in filial piety.

Samuel Richardson knew the works of Fleetwood and Delaney well, and had published the sermons of the latter through his printery. It has been claimed, with justification, that the ethical thought of both is invoked in his novel *Clarissa*.[54] Richardson took seriously Fleetwood's claims that "there is no relation in the world, either natural, or civil and agreed upon, but there is a reciprocal duty obliging each party," with the family being the training ground for the cultivation of such dutifulness, and providing a model for wider reciprocal duties in the rest of society. For Richardson there were two corollaries to this axiom, as he stated to one of his many correspondents in 1749—first, that "[t]he want of duty on one side justifies not the non-performance of it on the other, where there is reciprocal duty," and second, that where there is such want of duty on one side, continued performance of duty "enhances the merit on the other, when it is performed."[55] If for early Confucians the sage king Shun's forbearance illustrates the merits of his own constant filial reverence in the face of his father's murderous impulses, so too is Clarissa's constancy and desire for forgiveness from her father a token of her exemplary fulfillment of her filial feeling, even if his tyranny represents a dreadful "want of duty" on his own part.

From the contrasting points of view of its many correspondents, Richardson's *Clarissa* lays out to his readers the dreadful train of consequences for Clarissa Harlowe that follow from her family's efforts to force an unwanted marriage partner upon her, and from her naïve and desperate decision to trust in her former suitor, the libertine Lovelace, to assist her flight following her family's enraged reaction to her refusal. Her father's tyrannical intransigence, goaded by his son and supported by the duplicitous motivations of the rest of her family, and their schemes to accumulate wealth, property, and status using Clarissa as a means to these ends represent the antithesis of her steadfast adherence to filial duty.

Clarissa's disastrous decision to trust Lovelace to help her flee from her family's power, her father's terrifying curse on her, and Lovelace's cruel betrayal of her trust set the scene for the gradual unraveling of her life through the ten volumes of the novel. In depicting Clarissa's Christian forbearance, constancy, and desire for forgiveness throughout her suffering—and in the face of terrible provocations from Lovelace and her family—Richardson hoped to deliver a lesson in theodicy to his readers. In her constant filial devotion, her enduring faith through affliction and the grace in her forgiveness of those who are afflicting her, Clarissa is also an exemplary Christian. In what Richardson called "the triumphant death of Clarissa," the continual expression of her virtues in the midst of such suffering is something "HEAVEN *only* could reward."[56]

Yet it was Clarissa's steadfast filial devotion that proved Richardson's Achilles heel with many otherwise admiring readers and correspondents, some of whom were horrified at the cruelty of the Harlowe patriarch and the conniving of the Harlowe family against Clarissa. For correspondents with Richardson, such as the bluestocking Hester Chapone, who looked to Locke's thought for moral guidance in reading *Clarissa*, surely she and other women in her situation had a "natural right to refuse her obedience" against tyrannical parents and even, where the threat of force intervened, to resort to every prudent measure "to get herself out of their power"?[57]

For such readers, Richardson's theodicy and the promise of rewards of the hereafter as a reward for Clarissa's constancy and faith seemed weak compensation for the injustice and suffering she is made to endure. The arguments over the justification for Clarissa's filial obedience to her father seems to have been settled by around 1800, and at the time of its settlement understandings of filial piety had also been transformed. In the 1790s, Mary Wollstonecraft, no friend to Richardson's austere theodicy, insisted that parental affection and patient instruction, not severe authority, were the instigators of filial reverence in children.[58] The early nineteenth-century editors of a collection of Hester Chapone's works criticized Richardson for "carrying . . . to the most rigid extreme" the by then outmoded belief that parental authority "extended to a right to control the affections" of children.[59] Of course, this was no full victory over patriarchal power in family relations. Feminist theorists such as Carole Pateman argue that the scene was set not for the end of that patriarchy with the defeat of status-based patriarchal power, but for its transformation in a conjugal sexual contract in which men maintained power of access over women's labor and bodies.[60] In the more contractual and also sentimentalist conception of the family, filial piety—once bound so strongly to patriarchalist ideals of paternal power—gradually lost its status as the focus of the family's moral life, and ceased to be referred to as a virtue in common language by the beginning of the twentieth century.

The Revolt against Patriarchy in East Asia and the Predicament of Filial Piety in Postindustrial Societies

A revolt against familial patriarchy eventually occurred in twentieth-century East Asia, though here it would be more accurate to speak of a rapid collapse in traditional patriarchal authority as much as a revolt. While eighteenth-century England had the leisure of a century of debate to resolve the problem of filial obedience and virtue failure in the family, time was limited for such conversation in the breakneck modernization of family life in East Asian societies. Twentieth-century Japanese, Korean, Chinese, and Taiwanese governments encouraged a rapid if not complete shift in emphasis from the extended patrilineal family to the conjugal family unit as the basis for a new sexual division of labor, in a new private sphere for their industrializing societies. They also promoted urbanization policies that ultimately weakened the material basis for traditional filial obedience to parents. The migration of rural youth to industrializing urban centers for employment produced an economic independence that undermined patriarchal familial authority more completely than did the literary expressions of revolt against patriarchal parental authority in the works of Chinese May the Fourth–era intellectuals.

Modernizing Japan also played a crucial role in transforming East Asian understandings of filial piety, and in pursuing industrial and urbanization policies that transformed its practice. A seventeenth-century moral instruction manual for upper-class Japanese women that remained a mainstay for their education until the late nineteenth century, the *Book of Women's Learning* (女大学 *Onna Daigaku*)—translated into English in 1905 as *Women and Wisdom of Japan*—set out straightforward prescriptions for women's filial behavior:

> It is the chief duty of a girl living in the parental house to practise filial piety towards her father and mother. But after marriage her duty is to honour her father-in-law and mother-in-law, to honour them beyond her father and mother, to love and reverence them with all ardour, and to tend them with practice of every filial piety.[61]

The early twentieth-century Japanese translator of this work into English noted that it was seldom read by the young Japanese women of his time, even though certain of its precepts were being absorbed into the new, modernized mass education system.[62] Change was not long in coming. Mid-eighteenth-century British bluestockings like Hestor Chapone were content to advocate a mere right for young women to refuse parental choices of marital partner, and to escape only in the worst cases of parental tyranny. However, some early twentieth-century educated Japanese women went considerably further in flouting their parents' wishes, sometimes exceeding the examples of contemporary "new women" in Europe and America. As I argued in chapter 2, their actions provide a more emphatic exemplification of the "disencumbered self."

Thus, when in 1914, at the age of twenty-seven, Hiratsuka Raichō decided against her parents' wishes to elope with her younger, lower-class, and unemployed lover, refusing to marry and eventually having children with him out of wedlock, and indeed refusing "unnatural obligations such as to treat (my) husband's parents as (my) own" she was violating practically every precept on feminine chastity and filial piety set forth in the *Onna Daigaku*. She suffered no legal sanctions for doing so.[63]

Though such principled defiance of parental authority was rare, the strong-willed independent woman able to finance a life in defiance of parental authority became a trope for widespread social anxiety over the march of modernity. Tanizaki Junichirō's novel *The Makioka Sisters* (細雪 *Sasame Yuki*) illustrates such anxiety with ambivalence. The novel portrays the predicament of a declining merchant family in late 1930s Osaka whose patriarch is already dead, and whose eldest son-in-law, the head of the family, is not able or willing to impose his authority on the most wayward of the unmarried Makioka sisters, the artistically talented and entrepreneurial Taeko. She reveals in her financial independence and in her love affairs with lower-class men a flouting of the ideal of the filial daughter, which the family has limited means to stop. Her subsequent prostration with dysentery and the loss of a newborn child near the novel's conclusion seem to be punishment for her dissolute, unfilial behavior and excessive modernity.[64] Yet her more traditional older sister, Yukiko, who tacitly consents to an arranged marriage with a middle-aged, indolent playboy aristocrat, seems resigned to an uncertain fate at the novel's end, and is plagued by diarrhea on a long train journey to her marriage in Tokyo.[65]

Eighty years on, the practice of filial piety faces numerous challenges in contemporary aging, postindustrial societies. In Japan and in the rest of East Asia, the Confucian cosmological basis for filial piety—the hierarchies of Heaven and Earth, of the monarchy's rulers and the ancestors they cultivated reverence for, and of the families of subjects who were bound likewise in this order of filial reverence—collapsed long ago with the fall or radical political transformation of those monarchical states and the dethronement of Confucian learning. It is difficult to say whether the filial piety ideals and practices of today are continuous with the practices of the premodern past, as noted in chapter 1. In any case the evaluative vocabulary associated with filial piety—*xiao* (孝), *hyodo* (효도), or *oya kōkō* (親孝行)—remains intact in quotidian ethical discourse, but rapidly changing demographic, economic, and social conditions have made adherence to many of its norms and expectations increasingly difficult.

In Western European, North American, and oceanic societies, some of these same demographic and cultural pressures on filial practice are also present, though more developed elderly welfare safety nets and pensions have (so far) prevented the upsurge in elderly poverty striking East Asian societies. Yet unlike in East Asian societies, the moral vocabulary of filial piety has, as we have seen, fallen into disuse in Western European and North American societies since the late nineteenth century.

Moreover, eighteenth-century writers such as William Fleetwood, Patrick Delaney, and Samuel Richardson all took natural law for granted as the moral foundation for their understandings of filial duty, and for Richardson, Clarissa's filial piety is preeminent in enabling her to attain her *telos*—in her death and in her afterlife. Their understanding of children's duty to their parents are at variance with how it is understood in secularized Western European and American societies today, where, as Elizabeth Anscombe once claimed, the idea of a divine lawgiver has largely been given up, but the language of a law-based conception of ethics remains, with its emphasis on duties and obligations.[66]

As things stand, in English-speaking countries, we could say that moral vocabulary is impoverished in not supplying terminology to evaluate how children are already doing well, or badly, in their relations with parents—but probably no more well or badly than what their ancestors were doing two or three hundred years ago. To tell someone to "respect the freedom of choice of your parents" regarding elderly parents' reasonable decisions over how to dispose of their affections to other persons, or how to manage their own assets, might capture something valuable about how adult children should relate to their parents. But it seems defective in not picking out why such respect is morally significant in being expressed by children for *their* parents, and so it only halfway approximates what is meant when we say, in the ethical vocabulary of another time, that such children should "be filial."

On the other hand, while in East Asia such an ethical vocabulary for filial piety still exists, demographic and cultural transformations in family life, including decreased fertility and shrinking family sizes, are placing increasing burdens on expectations for its practice. I think it is clear that for somewhat different reasons, the existing ethical vocabularies in East Asian, Western European, and North American societies are inadequate to the task of evaluating what we get right as well as wrong in our relations with parents *as parents* today.

Contrasting Modern Rights-Based and Virtue Ethical Approaches to Filial Piety

It is important to ask whether a virtue-based concept of filial love and duty remains justifiable, in light of the changes to ethical vocabulary and the demographic and cultural changes described above. Like Phillip Ivanhoe and Li Chenyang, I believe that the Confucian-inspired virtue ethical approaches to filial piety are less prone to fall into difficulties than are the rights-based approaches found more often in the analytic philosophical literature, though the latter can supplement the former by supplying justifications for protection of elderly welfare in cases of virtue failure, abuse, and neglect. Perhaps the most notable example of such a rights-based philosophical treatment of filial piety is Christina Hoff Sommers's 1986 essay "Filial Morality," which I will consider here.

Sommers's moral criterion for evaluating children's fulfillment of parental expectation of filial duty is the principle of noninterference: the right of "every moral patient" "not to be interfered with in the pursuit of his or her noninvasive interests."[67] The derivation of filial duty from this right is through analogy with promise keeping. By promising another person an object or a performance of an action, I am giving over to that person ownership of the object or performance. On the assumptions of (1) the legitimacy of transferred ownership of both goods and performance of actions through promise and contract and (2) the equal entitlement the transferee has both to the unimpeded use and performance of his or her own possessions and actions and to the promised use and performance of another's transferred possessions and actions, the breaking of that promise amounts to interference with another's right to pursue his or her own noninvasive interests.

This may seem too generic a deontological schema for filial duty; after all, contract-based obligations for the keeping of promises for the transfer of goods and services appear more suited to commercial transactions. Sommers produces a more nuanced interpretation of this schema by proposing a thesis she calls "differential (ethical) pull": the "pull," or felt compulsiveness of moral duties, is stronger toward some moral agents than toward others, and that compulsiveness depends on circumstantial factors such as how moral patients and agents are related to each other in particular associations.[68] From the undertaking of long-term, demanding, and intimate affective relations such as those of nurturer to nurtured in a family, Hoff-Sommers argues that especially strong expectations upon the beneficiaries of such nurturance arise in analogy to those of promiser to promise. They arise even if no explicit promise is made by the nurtured party to fulfill those expectations, and they are nonvoluntarily entered into by children from the time of their birth. In fulfilling their nurturing role, parents inevitably acquire these expectations of filial performance by children, and the latter's failure to perform counts as interference with the parents' right not to be interfered with in the pursuit of their own noninvasive interests. Even worse than the case of the violated promisee, the parent faced with filial impiety suffers a diminishment in his or her identity, through suffering an affront to what is often a highly significant role in adult human life, as a parent. The list of duties and feelings that parents have such a right to are extensive, including "being grateful, loyal, attentive, respectful and deferential."[69]

Hoff Sommers's approach satisfies a common-sense moral intuition, found as we have seen in both early and contemporary Confucian and eighteenth-century English theological understandings of filial piety, that parents do have legitimate expectations of filial feeling and duty from their children in return for the nurturance and the sacrifices they have made for them. Her deontological perspective also universalizes these expectations and the corresponding obligations to meet them, implicitly repudiating the more culturally particularist notion that filial piety is less important today in "Western" societies than in "Confucian" societies.

Against these advantages, her rights-based approach appears at once to perform too much and too little on behalf of its intended purpose. Li Chenyang has briefly criticized some deficiencies in her approach, but there are others.[70] Any number of onerous duties and feelings could be implied by the parental expectations Sommers lists, that children be "grateful, loyal, attentive, respectful and deferential." Among these we could class James Harlowe's expectations for Clarissa's deference and submission to his will, the justification being that "he has the right of a father in his child, is absolutely determin'd not to be bully'd out of that right."[71] And we see in this assertion the impact Clarissa's disobedience and initial alliance with the rake Lovelace is having on her father's dignity and status as her father.

Sommers is not interested in protecting the privileges of domestic tyrants; she argues that she is merely concerned with "the wishes of the average parent who is neglected or whose wishes are disregarded when they could at some reasonable cost be respected."[72] Obviously we need stipulations on what counts as "reasonably legitimate expectations by average parents" that are derived from moral common sense, and sensitive to generational changes in such moral common sense since the time of Georgian England or Qing Era China. The difficulty is to articulate such stipulations in a way that does not water down significantly the differential pull dimension to Hoff-Summer's principle of noninterference. James Harlowe's expectations of filial obedience from Clarissa were excessive even to some of Richardson's contemporaries. Yet (for example) an impoverished, lonely elderly widower living in a Seoul slum who expects a monthly phone call from his salaried children may be exercising diminished filial expectations, arising from "adaptive preferences," which could still also satisfy Hoff Sommers's designation of "reasonably legitimate expectations."

At the same time, the principle of noninterference may deliver too little, for its conventional meaning gravitates in a different direction to the one Sommers intends for it with her concept of differential pull. This principle, often connected with the classical liberal conception of self-ownership in our bodies and our labor, more intuitively establishes the right of adult children *not* to be interfered with by their parents in the disposal of their own selves, their labor, and their assets. Sommers cites with some approval the existence of laws in some states requiring children to perform some minimal filial care and income support for their parents. Yet the strongest objection to such laws must surely come *from* invocations of the principle of noninterference—that adult children not be coerced into parting with income, goods, or labor that they have not promised to provide to their parents.

I conclude, then, that a deontological, rights-based perspective is not up to the task of justifying the differential pull-based moral obligations that Sommers associates with filial piety. Sommers's differential pull thesis will still be useful in explaining why certain rights violations, such as physical abuse or financial fraud, are especially egregious when committed by children against their parents. However, I propose from this point to give preeminence to the virtue concept of filial piety itself, and to sketch the conditions for exercising this virtue in relation to the *need-based* goods and goods of *deliberative freedom* (including autonomy) of parents. Culturally or even family-particular filial goods may be secondarily derived from the context-sensitive elaboration of this virtue concept.

Under filial "need-based goods" we can place the satisfaction of the conditions for parents, including elderly parents, to be able to "fulfill (their) human functions in a fully human way" *as* parents of their children in their co-operative living of family life—and these conditions are "needs-based" because parents need and depend on co-operation from their children for their fulfillment. Need-based goods fulfilled through filial virtue are those connected with the capabilities of emotion and affiliation, maintained through children and their own families having regular, loving contact with their parents; meaningful participation and sharing in their children's lives; respect paid in recognition for parent's rearing, moral guidance, and education of their children, in their formative years and beyond; and of self-respect by being recognized as such a participant, in the manner that is due to parents, by children. For frailer, physically or mentally impaired parents, need-based goods include the fulfillment of capabilities such as bodily health and integrity, when they need assistance to fulfill them; and in the provision of adequate nutrition, hygiene, transportation, medical care, and shelter, in a manner respectful of their human dignity and emotional needs.

These needs-based goods are often (but not always) instances of what Simon Keller calls *special* goods, goods that can be meaningfully satisfied only because they are realized through the co-operation of the parents' children. Meaningful human contact and meaningful participation in other's lives are *generic* goods for any healthily sociable human being; but parents ordinarily derive particular value from continued contact with and involvement in their children's lives because it is their children's lives, the lives of those who they spent much of their own lives rearing and cohabiting with.[73] To put it another way, the capability of affiliation in any reasonably sociable adult can be flexibly exercised in a range of environments, in the building of new acquaintanceships and friendships, or in the revival of old ones. But for that same person as a parent, capability deprivation occurs when he is unable to have meaningful contact with and involvement in the lives of his children and their families.

Challenges to this distinction between *generic* and *special* needs–based goods, and to the healthy functioning of affiliation, arise in relations with physically or mentally impaired elderly parents. Frail elderly parents may expect the provision by their children of physical and emotional care as *special* filial goods, the value of which will decline if that care is outsourced to people outside of the family. Yet it may be beyond the financial, physical, and emotional capacities of adult children to accommodate such expectations on their own. Historically (especially but not exclusively in East Asia), it is women, as daughters or daughters-in-law, who have been burdened with such expectations, to the point where their own life and career aspirations, or even their ability to earn much-needed income to support their families, are compromised to fulfill the needs of elderly family members. The question then arises of how needs-based goods are adequately met when children outsource some or all of this care labor to people or institutions outside of their family.

Mentally impaired parents may also become increasingly unable to participate actively in the lives of their children and their families, or to derive meaningful satisfaction from such participation, to the point where they can no longer recognize themselves in the role their family continues to recognize and acknowledge them in. People in an advanced state of dementia no longer have a sense of their own dignity and of their distinctly human needs, rendering them vulnerable to neglectful and abusive treatment by carers. The satisfaction of needs-based goods must in such circumstances be adjusted to attentive understanding of declining parental capabilities.

There are, however, diverse problems in conceptualizing a virtuous disposition in children to fulfill parental needs-based goods, even where they can be fairly described as special goods, and even if we can invoke the concept of "differential pull" to explain why children are especially at fault in not attending to those needs. Take for example the good of "filial obedience," satisfied in the ritualized gestures set out in *The Book of Rites*, or in Patrick Delaney's prescriptions for filial adult children. Such a good can be plausibly attached to a need for recognition, grounded in a traditional sense of parental *dignitas* and *amour-propre*; it is also a special good that no one other than children are meaningfully positioned to fulfill. Yet as we have already seen, parents in urbanized East Asian, European, and North American societies are no longer in an economic or legal position to expect such obedience from their adult children, and few contemporary Confucian or Anglo-American theorists of filial piety recognize a moral duty or virtuous filial disposition to render such obedience.

Even the fulfillment of needs-based goods such as affiliation, bodily health, and integrity in, for example, infirm elderly people raise special challenges. Amartya Sen has observed significant differences in how persons can convert resources into capabilities, depending on their own bodily and mental states, social and physical environments, status, and so forth.[74] Significant investments of resources including income, physical and emotional labor, medical expertise, and medical treatment are needed, for instance, in helping infirm and frail elderly people remain healthy, maintain some deliberative control over their bodily circumstances, and sustain personally enriching social lives.

The cultivation of such capabilities and their realization in the sort of functioning that is needed for a dignified, flourishing life can sometimes give rise to potentially demanding filial duties and demanding expectations for filial virtue, when need-based goods are recognized as special goods. Yet, as has been well noted in contemporary scholarship on filial responsibility, expectations on adult children (or adult in-law children) to fulfill these duties or cultivate such virtues can be onerous and unjust. Three commonly cited intuitions can be used to invoke the defeasibility in designations of such goods as special goods in filial relations. These are (1) prior parental dereliction, when a history of physical and emotional abuse and neglect by parents gives children reason to minimize or terminate relations with parents; (2) deliberative freedom infringement, where filial expectations would unreasonably deprive adult children of their ability to reflectively choose or will activities central to their good, including careers, choices of places to live, and financial support for their own children's education[75] and relatedly; (3) injustice, in infringements of deliberative freedoms that prevent the attainment of life opportunities to which adult children have a reasonable claim, including when, for instance, traditional, gender-biased expectations for intimate personal care for aged and infirm parents unfairly deprive their female adult children or daughters-in-law of such opportunities[76]

However, a rigid insistence on the defeasibility of special goods in filial relations in light of these intuitions may deprive our concepts of filial duty and virtuous disposition of meaningful normative content. Not only expectations for filial obedience, but also expectations for physical and emotional care, or love and companionship may also be dispensed with if they run aground on these intuitions. In protecting the capabilities of adult children so assiduously, a line of argument such as this may end up endorsing capability deprivation of vulnerable, elderly parents. In an era of shrinking and geographically dispersed families, declining birthrates, and increasingly difficult, costly, and complex care needs for growing cohorts of the "oldest old," there is no denying that acute moral problems and dilemmas can arise for adult children and their parents when children are not ideally positioned to fulfill need-based goods that they recognize as special goods—or which only their parents insist are special goods, for that matter.

Nevertheless, to state that particular designations of needs-based goods as special goods are defeasible in light of the intuitions mentioned above is not to say that those goods will thereby be neglected. This is not the case. Where it is unjust as well as impractical to expect families to attend directly to all of the needs-based goods of elders, it is acceptable in light of the special good theory outlined above for families to rely on professional carers, residential care facilities, or, in conditions of poverty, to rely on direct government welfare agency assistance to take many of those care responsibilities on. If there are special goods children have a duty to fulfill in such circumstances, they are the goods of filial solicitude, of children attentively overseeing the professional care of parents, and providing companionship and emotional care through regular visits. On the other hand, a person who deliberately takes on the care of a physically or mentally incapacitated parent as a vocation, and is capable of reflectively justifying it as his vocation, has no reason to invoke such intuitions and describe the burdens of such care as unjust. In such circumstances, filial piety finds better definition as unforced virtuous conduct rather than as a duty.

Needs-based special goods have been the traditional focus of filial piety, and for sound reasons. If there is one insight we can take from Confucian or eighteenth-century English conceptions of filial piety, it is that enduring love, respect, and solicitude for parents are appropriate, cultivated ethical responses for the investment of time, resources, and love at least competent parents put into raising their children from a state of helpless dependency into physically, mentally, and emotionally capable young adults. This uniquely intimate, involuntary relationship is, in its healthy varieties, also the basis of special emotional goods that cannot be satisfied so easily (if at all) by non–family members. Moreover, in periods before the appearance of universal pensions and welfare for retirees in developed nations, and in many developing nations today, the family was (or still is) the major provider for the care of physically or mentally impaired and frail elderly.

Yet today, with increased self-images of personal independence, and of increased physical health, fitness, and disposable incomes at least among wealthier retirees in North America, Western Europe, and Japan, and with growing expectations for elderly autonomy in residential care and hospital settings in North America and Western Europe, there is another set of goods that filial virtue can serve. These are the goods of parents' deliberative freedoms, including autonomy. These goods do not always require critical emotional, physical, or financial input from children in co-operation with parents for their fulfillment, such as the love, respect, care, and physical, emotional, and financial support that it can be a child's part at different times of life to give to a parent. Rather, deliberative freedoms cover the capability to evaluate, reflectively possess, and put into effect preferences and goods that an agent finds reason to value—and, alternatively, the capability to reflectively divest herself of preferences or goods that she finds reason to disvalue. These may include goods of affiliation: new connections, friendships, loves, and associations; of project realization, in planning for and working toward life pursuits, careers, or enterprises in accordance with their own worked-out preferences or values; of ownership—of holding property assets and disposing of them freely; and of bodily integrity in making decisions related to bodily health and medical care. It might seem that the prima facie filial duty for adult children is that they *not* unreasonably interfere with, and at least minimally tolerate their parents' freedom to deliberate over these goods and preferences. However, part of the exercise of a modern, filial disposition might extend to promoting parents' ability to exercise deliberative freedoms in more personally vulnerable circumstances.

This latter consideration complicates our picture of the goods of deliberative freedom. There is the better-known and now socially approved autonomy of the active elderly, of usually wealthy European, American, or Japanese retirement-aged people engaged in business, volunteering, travel, higher education, and elite-level sports, and receiving widespread social approval for doing so. Yet less prominent in public view is the plight of poorer, lonely, and frail elderly, more often female, facing critical financial or medical decisions after a lifetime of being dependent on others to make those decisions on their own behalf, and lacking a self-image of themselves as competent to make such decisions on their own. An attitude of filial forbearance is reasonable in the case of more active, autonomous elderly parents, and I will consider this attitude again at the end of this chapter. But what filial expectations can reasonably bind adult children to assist vulnerable elderly parents when they seem to lack the capability of deliberative freedom?

Borrowing from the philosophical literature on autonomy, two benchmark conditions are to be met for deliberative freedoms to be actuated in conduct. First is the condition of *authenticity*, realized in the agent's ability, and desire, to reflectively accept as her own—or reject as not her own—preferences, values, and conceptions of the good, in contrast to being committed to them unreflectively, or having them coercively imposed on her.[77] Second is the condition of *competence*, that the agent is capable of such rational reflection and self-control, and is not subject to mental disabilities, self-delusions, interpersonal or political constraints on abilities to exercise such reflection, and so forth.[78]

For feminist and other critics of standard concepts of autonomy, the ability to satisfy these two benchmarks will differ along lines of class, educational attainment, and gender. The question arises of how to remedy these discrepancies. Suppose that autonomy is a valuable good to possess, especially because of the abilities it confers to deliberate over life situations and plans in conditions where others cannot be relied on to deliberate competently or trustworthily on an agent's own behalf—because they lack insight into that agents' needs, or because they may exploit her vulnerabilities for their own advantage. If this is so, some sort of duty or responsibility arises to promote this capability, be it through the agent's own self-cultivation, through the efforts of individuals connected to the agent as carers or educators, or through state policy. Autonomy promotion could thus become a goal of moral and political perfectionism. This is the position of advocates of *relational* autonomy such as Catriona Mackenzie.[79]

Advocates of relational autonomy will go further, however, by stating normative standards on the content of what may be authentically and competently claimed by an autonomous agent. Theirs is both a relational and substantivist concept of autonomy.[80] For a feminist substantivist approach to autonomy, for instance, a woman's preferences for a patriarchal or paternalistically governed way of life would likely fail to be autonomous in light of such standards, because her life conditions and the institutional settings within which they unfold suppress women's autonomy and normalize "adaptive preferences." Suppose that a mentally competent widowed elderly woman habitually defers to the judgment of her male adult children concerning decisions about her medical care and financial affairs, out of her own conviction that, as a woman and lifelong housewife once dependent on her husband's authority, she is not personally competent to make such decisions. A woman in this situation is not autonomous because her preference for such a way of life is not cultivated in social and institutional conditions conducive to autonomy. Patriarchal family relations and restrictive gendered divisions of labor deprive women like her of the material and psychological means for autonomy, and, through systematically misrecognizing her as someone not deserving of respect as an autonomous agent, habituate her to a self-image that normalizes the lack of self-determination in her life.[81] Considering the vulnerabilities of autonomy deprivation in agents such as this woman, it becomes a matter of justice that "the state and other social institutions have duties to foster the kinds of social conditions that are conducive to realizing citizens' autonomy" in the family, care and medical institutions, and so forth.[82]

There might seem little to distinguish this perfectionist position from the argument that I favor, that there are good reasons to promote the capability of deliberative freedom in people whose life circumstances and relationships have deprived them of the means, or opportunities, to cultivate that capacity. But it is another thing entirely for the state or medical authorities to encourage a person to cultivate autonomy competence and authenticity in alignment with a *substantivist* understanding of authenticity and competence. Supposing a person already is in possession of a self-image that is authoritatively and competently self-determining, or has (with the assistance of significant others) latterly been cultivated to that level, and so is in a position to exercise "combined capabilities." It is entirely conceivable that such a person may still *reflectively* prefer submitting to the paternalistic control of others, including family members and medical professionals in deliberations over important medical decisions. She may satisfy broad competence and authenticity standards for autonomy in justifying such a way of living even as she insists on continuing to delegate control over her living conditions to such paternalistic control.

It is not always clear that perfectionist advocates of a more substantive conception of autonomy will accept these assertions as reasonable grounds for desisting from efforts to promote autonomy, particularly when the individual subject to that suasion insists on holding to values, goods, or preferences that do not satisfy a substantivist (i.e., a feminist or Millian liberal) conception of what values, goods, and preferences can be authentically and competently had as the outcome of autonomous reflection.[83] Arguing for a continued duty to promote autonomy beyond the point where commitment to paternalistic, patriarchal goods and values has been reflectively flagged invites what I would call a paternalist paradox. The paternalism in question here is what Jonathon Quong calls *judgemental* paternalism, in which an agent is motivated to try and improve the "welfare, good, happiness, needs, interests or values" of another agent by a "negative judgement" about the latter's ability to decide competently on those matters in a deliberative problem she faces.[84] Suppose Agent A evaluates the content of Agent B's preferences, values, and goods and infers from that content that her rationale for holding them is wanting in authenticity and competence, in light of a substantivist, antipaternalist doctrine of autonomy X, inasmuch as A prefers to delegate important decisions about her welfare to paternalistic authority figures in her life. Suppose that B reflectively justifies her preferences and values to A. Nevertheless A, believing that she knows better than B what her good should be, is motivated to promote B's autonomy, so that she becomes capable of self-determinedly identifying with a different set of preferences, values, and goods that align with X. The paradox is that A is motivated *paternalistically* to ignore or discount reasons B offers for holding to her goods, preferences, and values of her paternalistically governed life. The consequences of such paternalistic autonomy promotion in elderly health care, for instance, can be both oppressive and alienating, given the sometimes intimidating differences in status and power between medical professionals and patients.[85]

Perfectionist advocates for relational autonomy may well be underestimating the capacity of bureaucratic medical authorities to paternalistically impose their will on patients even as they are attempting to promote their capacity for autonomous consent. These advocates also tend to presuppose a dyadic relation between patient and professional carers in medical care decision making that sidelines wider family participation—an aspect of autonomy approaches to medical care that irritates Confucian bioethicists.[86] But if we move outside this dyadic relation, is there a filial expectation that could hold for children to help promote the autonomy of parents who are such patients?

Adult children can in theory play a mediating role between health care professionals concerned to obtain authentically voluntary, informed consent to care and treatment options, and elderly patients who may be too exhausted by illness, too unconfident of their own decision-making capacities, or too impaired by declining cognitive abilities to meet such expectations.[87] If the bureaucratic, institutional setting of medical and elderly care practice risks fostering a misguided paternalistic motivation to encourage autonomy, adult children may be better positioned, through a lifetime of intimacy and insight into parental character, to find a way of talking their parents into a positive, self-affirming self-image consonant with more active, self-assertive participation in decision making over their own welfare. Alternatively, drawing on the same insight, they may be best positioned to act on behalf of parents no longer willing or able to exercise deliberative capabilities over medical treatment or care decisions. In such circumstances, where adult children possess such insight, the solicitude they exercise on behalf of vulnerable parents in such circumstances counts as an important filial virtue, and as a special good. I admit that the persuasiveness of this argument is contingent on a depth of intimacy and knowledge between adult children and parents that is not always present. More context-dependent casuistry is needed to specify how adult children can be positioned to promote autonomy as a filial duty.

Feminist relational autonomy theorists tend to focus on the vulnerabilities of women whose deliberative capabilities have been suppressed by patriarchal institutions and relations. However, a full consideration of filial duty and virtue in light of parental deliberative freedom should also extend to cases where parents are capable, in nonoppressive social conditions, of authentically and competently deliberating over and acting for their good. An ancient Korean folk tale provides an interesting avenue for considering this question, especially because it touches on an issue that long troubled Confucians—the sexual conduct of widowed mothers. "The Bridge in Gyeoungju" tells of a widowed mother living with her seven sons during the time of the Kingdom of Silla, who nightly takes a boat across a nearby river to visit her lover, after she thinks her sons have fallen asleep. Worried for their mother's safety and knowing the reason for her night-time excursions, the sons build a stone bridge for her to cross the river more safely. In one documented version of the story, the mother, ashamed at what her behavior has led her sons to do for her, stops visiting her lover. This provides a conventional Confucian subtext to the story, in which the sons' filial behavior is rewarded by their mother desisting from her sexually deviant behavior, to conform to the ideal of a chaste widow. But in oral versions of the story, the mother does not desist, and continues visiting her lover until she dies. In these non-Confucian variants of the tale, the reward for the son's filial behavior is the knowledge that their mother can now more safely fulfill her human desires—desires that they have implicitly acknowledged and respected by building the bridge for her.[88]

In this story, the widow places an unspoken expectation on her sons: that as she pursues her love affair discretely, they be forbearing and not voice any suspicion they may have about her night-time forays, nor try to stop her if they find out what she is doing. In this case the expectation for filial piety is not conceived so much on an understanding of parental neediness—for love, care, and support from children. Rather, it is conceived around the notion that children, having had their parents invest so much of their lives in raising, educating, and guiding them, owe it to their parents to be at least forbearing, and at most respectful and supportive, as they pursue *their* own interests, and desires. Such forbearance is not simply a generic good. Parents who embark on eccentric, expensive, or personally risky life pursuits can take for granted forbearance from the rest of society. But what can be especially valuable for them is that their children, as *their* children, express that forbearance. There is good reason, then, to regard filial forbearance as a virtue and as a special good that children can be well placed to fulfill as a duty toward their parents.

Yet this folk tale admits a role for a relational conception of autonomy as well. The sons' construction of the bridge for their mother promotes her autonomy. It does so literally in making her nightly forays to her lover's village less dangerous, but it is also a very public gesture that tacitly legitimates a self-image for herself as someone entitled to act on her emotional and sexual desires as she sees fit, rather than being left to indulge them in a more precarious, furtive manner, out of a sense of shame toward, and on behalf of, her sons. The sons' gesture can be seen more naturally as the spontaneous expression of a virtuous filial disposition than as a duty. Of course not all filial children are well positioned through, say, the possession of the requisite skills or resources to carry out such elaborate undertakings as duties to their parents.

I hope that I have shown the benefits of the more universalist perspective on filial piety developed in this chapter. This perspective proceeds from common moral psychological insights into the physical and emotional dependencies, interdependencies, and vulnerabilities of family life as the basis for filial practice, past and present. It also develops new insights into the difficulties of practicing different varieties of filial piety in aging postindustrial societies in Asia, Europe, and America. It can do all these things while according "tradition-respect" and, indeed, acknowledging its intellectual debt to Confucian thought on filial piety.

More needs to be said about filial piety and cultural identity, however. One element that many modern advocates of a culturally particular concept of filial piety in East Asia (such as those quoted at the beginning of this chapter) share is a progressive political vision. They are, for the most part, eager to hitch their modernized conception of filial piety to a vision of a democratic social order that respects women's equal rights and the claims of social justice, inside of the family and in society at large. However, they are often naïve about other, deeply illiberal variants of cultural and national particularism in East Asia, for which famialism and filial piety are also central. One such particularism is the topic of the next chapter.

CHAPTER 5

The Unity of Loyalty and Filial Piety: An East Asian Horror Story*

The Parable of the Upturned "Japanese" Moustache

In his 1924 satirical essay *My Moustache*, Lu Xun identified the moustache as a signifier for national identity, remarking on how often his own, which once pointed upward, had led people to think he was Japanese. On visiting a temple of Confucius, he even overheard a fellow visitor, a Confucian scholar, inspect the turned-up moustache on one of the portraits of Confucian scholars and emperors on the walls, and say—"this was faked by the Japanese! Look at that moustache! Japanese style!" But recently excavated ancient statuary from the Han and Northern Wei Dynasties also featured upturned moustaches; was everyone really to believe that these were also fakes planted by the Japanese? Yet, Lu Xun added slyly, the turned-up moustache was after all not an immutable Japanese national characteristic. The Japanese only began to wear their moustaches like that after the Meiji Restoration in 1868, presumably under German influence, following the fashion of the Kaiser himself.[1]

Lu Xun's story could serve as a bleak, ironic parable for the national morality (国民道徳 *kokumin dōtoku*) elaborated for the new Japanese nation-

---

*I owe inspiration for the title of this chapter to "Idealism: A Victorian Horror Story," a chapter in Australian philosopher David Stove's book *The Plato Cult and other Philosophical Follies* (London: Wiley Blackwell, 1991).

state in the early twentieth century under the influence of European (and specifically, German) nationalist thought. By the 1930s, this morality had become implicated in Japanese imperialism and hypernationalism, justifying Japan's cultural and moral hegemony in East Asia, and its war against China. A modernized interpretation of Confucianism played a major role in this morality. In this morality Confucianism became "Japanized," like the "Japanized" moustaches in the Confucian temple portraits and ancient Chinese statuary, in order to generate a moral self-image for Japan unique and distinct from that of other nations, including China. This Confucianism was held to be superior to China's, and served to legitimate putting China in a position of moral tutelage under Japan. The ideal of the "unity of loyalty and filial piety" (忠孝一本 *chūkō ippon*) particular to the Japanese polity is central to these assumptions of uniqueness and superiority. The Tokyo University professor of philosophy, Inoue Tetsujirō, was a central player in the modern formulation of this "Japanized" Confucian ideal.

In this chapter I will sketch some of the philosophical waystations in which premodern and modern thinkers grappled with the problem of harmonizing two highly valued, and potentially conflicting, ethical ideals of filial piety and loyalty. These waystations include early Classical Confucian formulations of this problem, the protonationalist efforts of Japanese Mito School thinkers to harmonize these ideals in the early nineteenth century, and finally Inoue Tetsujirō's harmonization and (Weberian) rationalization of these ideals in his own variety of Confucian statist nationalism.

My aim in this sketch is, alongside other scholars who have investigated the Japanese historical background to today's "New Confucianism,"[2] to issue a warning. Among New Confucian scholars writing for both English and Chinese audiences are those who see the elaboration of a Confucian civil religion as an effective bulwark against the effects of liberal individualism and globalization, which is at the same time faithful to, and continuous with, the Confucian cultural heritage of East Asia. Whether they envisage such civil religions as providing the ethical bedrock for a democratic or undemocratic state, it would be better for them to attend to the Japanese historical precedents for these ideas. The project of affirming a nonsectarian, organic Confucian religiosity in East Asian society is, in the end, difficult to disentangle from more exclusivist, statist projects for a comprehensive quasi-Confucian doctrine fusing filiality and loyalty to the state that arose with the first flourishing of nationalism in East Asia around the turn of the twentieth century.

Instability in the Conceptual Relation between Filial Piety and Loyalty

From the Late Warring States period through the Han Dynasty and beyond many Chinese scholars, officials, and rulers debated the balance of obligations within what Norman Kutcher has described as the "parallel conception of society," in which devotion to parents was supposed to harmonize with devotion to rulers.[3] Other scholars, notably the legalists, disputed whether such a harmonization between these obligations was possible.

This parallel conception could be conceptualized in two ways. The first emphasizes the *complementarity* of loyalty to state with filiality and fraternity in the family. There are two grounds for this complementarity. First, family bonds are nurseries for the ethical qualities that later secure devotion to rulers as well as competent rule over the state. The son who learns to practice filial piety to parents and fraternal devotion to brothers will grow up to be an obedient, loyal subject of the state, and the *junzi* who cultivates such virtues and orders his household well will also acquire the ethical qualities for governing states well. The second ground for complementarity is established through exemplary ethical conduct. When a *junzi* who is a minister or prince cultivates filial piety and fraternity within his family, he models ethical qualities for his subjects to follow and also fosters their loyalty through their knowledge of his selfless devotion to his parents (the sage king Shun being the oft-cited model).

The second, more ambitious conceptualization asserts some sort of identity between filial piety and loyalty. The ruler of a state is a father to that state—and so loyalty and filial piety merge in subjects' devotion to the father-like figure of the ruler. Filiality toward parents is in this sense preparatory for loyalty to the ruler, who is the father of all, and that loyalty is itself an expression of filial piety, carried over from the family and converted into an equivalent devotion to rulers.

This latter conceptualization is a potentially powerful formulation, but there are limits to how far the identity in fathering roles between rulers and the paterfamilias can be conceived, and thus how far the analogy between filial piety and loyalty can be carried. According to Mencius, and perhaps the *Book of Rites*, devotion to rulers is moderated and made defeasible by a voluntaristic component, as discussed in chapter 2. Rulers and fathers can both be remonstrated with in the service of loyalty and filiality. Yet ministers may also choose to leave the employment of a prince who does not heed their remonstrances. For Mencius at least, they may also choose to see the worst such princes as criminals who have forfeited the mandate of heaven, and who may then be legitimately overthrown. A son cannot conceivably take this voluntaristic, or in the last resort punitive, approach to his relationship with his father. He may not reject his father and seek a better one, and he may not choose to see him as a criminal who must be handed over to justice for his crimes. Unlike the role of biological father, the ruler's role as father to his people was conditional, first of all upon the mandate of Heaven and then upon the virtuous self-cultivation he needed to engage in to hold on to that mandate.

There are also problems with the thesis of the complementarity of filial piety and loyalty. Mencius's discussion of Emperor Shun as an exemplarily filial ruler is, as noted in chapter 2, contentious, both for ancient Chinese and modern readers. Mencius cited the *Book of Odes* verse "He was always filial / And, being filial, he was a model to others"[4] to point out that Shun, as ruler, had a special responsibility to model filial piety and fraternal love to his subjects, for seeing it, they would be more loyal to him and take his behavior as a model to emulate appropriately in their families, in accordance with their material means and rank.

Yet on another argument not unfamiliar to the scholarly discourse during the Late Warring States era, what Shun also appears to exemplify in his conduct is a partiality for family members at the potential expense of both his own and his subjects' welfare. There is the matter of his hypothetical treatment of his father, already discussed in chapter 2. There is also a matter that troubles one of Mencius's followers, Wan Chung, concerning Shun's treatment of his younger brother, Hsiang. Hsiang is described as having "devoted himself every day" to plots to take Shun's life. Yet Shun enfeoffs Hsiang with the distant province of Yu Pi. What troubles Wan Chung is the apparent inconsistency in Shun's conduct as emperor. He is recorded as having banished three other men who had committed crimes, and having executed one—yet he gave his own brother, "the most wicked of them all," a fiefdom instead of punishing him, and as Wan Chung adds pointedly, we may wonder what the people of Yu Pi had done to deserve such a governor.[5]

For someone like Wan Chung, Shun's conduct arguably models not only filiality and fraternity, but also partiality, in a way that sets humaneness and filial piety against justice or *yi*. What he models can also be easily imagined as the sort of conduct that is a source of disloyalty of subjects to the state—though the intent of his exemplary filiality is to encourage such loyalty. Officials and other rank-holding individuals might see such behavior as an example for them to engage in partial conduct, seeking rewards and sinecures for undeserving, even criminal family members, or aiding and abetting the escape of family members from justice when they commit serious crimes such as homicide (rather than say, stealing a sheep).

This exchange between Wan Chung and Mencius gives us a taste of the conceptual instability that plagues efforts to harmonize filial piety and loyalty to state. We know Mencius's view was hardly a majority position—that even in the Han Dynasties, the first era in which Confucianism became a state dogma, there was considerable argument over how to avoid conflict in meeting both commitments, and emperors themselves faced serious criticism if they displayed partiality toward family members in the manner of someone like Shun.[6]

Legalists such as Han Feizi emphatically rejected any causally beneficial connection between moral cultivation and filial piety in the family on the one hand, and loyalty to the state on the other. Rather, they construed the former as merely private interest (私 *si*), potentially antagonistic to and sometimes ruinous to the public interests of state (公 *gong*) if it is not completely subordinated to them. In part this is because of an ethical pessimism about the capacity of virtuous exemplars to model successfully ethical behavior to those (many) people who are less ethically capable than the exemplar. But this is not the only criticism Han Feizi brought to his rejection of the complementarity of private and public interest. Han revisited some famous Confucian moral fables to show that the powers Confucian officials exercise in promoting filial piety are also ruinous for loyalty to state. Honest Gong, the peasant who, on Confucius's recounting, self-righteously and without filiality surrenders his father to the law for stealing a sheep is, according to Han Feizi, put to death by a presumably upright Confucian magistrate for "being an infamous son to his father." The damage the magistrate thereby does to the state is twofold, according to Han Feizi—not only does he execute a man who is "an honest subject of his sovereign," in executing him and closing the case there the magistrate does not report "the felonies of state" (meaning the original theft of the sheep) to the authorities, and is therefore disloyal.[7]

I will briefly consider one early Confucian potential response to such criticisms, since it has some bearing on later Japanese elaborations of the unity of filial piety and loyalty. *The Classic of Filial Piety* (孝經 *Xiao Jing*), attributed to Confucius but likely composed around the beginning of the Han Dynasty, was probably written late enough for the author(s) to have in mind the criticisms of the legalists. The first chapter of this brief work contains an answer to their challenges by itself: filial piety is the "root" of all virtue and the basis of all moral teaching—this merely adumbrates earlier Confucian discussions. But the introductory chapter goes further to trace the course of filial piety through a *junzi's* life career, in a way that harmonizes it seamlessly with loyalty to the ruler. The beginning of filial piety is not to damage or destroy our bodies, which are received from our parents. But the *end* of filial piety is the cultivating of our character so that we can "make our name famous in future generations and thus glorify our parents," and the way to do that is by virtuous, loyal service to the ruler.[8]

This passage establishes the complementarity of filial piety and loyalty without necessarily merging the two. Glorifying the name of one's family through virtuous, loyal service to the ruler is the end of filial piety, but no transfer of filial affection to the ruler need be implied by this complementarity. By itself, this chapter offers one possible reply to Han Feizi's denunciation of the Confucian's attempts to fuse "private" cultivation of filial piety with the public interest of service to rulers.

The other plank in the *Classic*'s response to critics of the complementarity thesis is indeed to assert the *identity* of filial piety and loyalty; loyalty itself is an expression of filial piety, transferred from father to ruler. This at least is the case for the filial piety of inferior officers in their service to their superiors, including ministers and princes. Love is given equally to filial service to mothers and fathers, while in service to fathers and to rulers, reverence is also the common affection. This identity in reverence appears to transfer filial affection to the ruler as well, for "when they serve their ruler with filial piety, they are loyal" though this filial piety is reserved for rulers and fathers only, for in reverent service to other superiors, inferior officers are "obedient." This identification of the ruler as a surrogate parent is reinforced later on with a quotation from the Book of Odes, where the ruler in his capacity as an ethical exemplar and teacher to all his subjects makes him "the parent of his people."[9]

Japan's Response to Western Encroachment: Aizawa Seishisai's Protonationalism and the Oneness of Loyalty and Filial Piety

Doctrines of the complementarity of filial piety and loyalty, though unsatisfactory in some respects and lending themselves to sometimes socially destabilizing interpretation, otherwise served well to rationalize the loyalty of ministers and officials to rulers during the centuries when Confucianism was an institutionalized dogma of state. In early nineteenth-century Japan, at a time when Confucian scholarship was flourishing in a number of academies, scholars turned to the question of the complementarity and identity of filial piety and loyalty with new urgency. The Mito Academy in particular made the first moves in reinterpreting their parallelism, its scholars mindful of an unprecedented need to bind all of Japan's subjects into a protonational consciousness capable of resisting the European powers.

Aizawa Seishisai 会沢正志斎, a leading scholar of the Mito School, completed his *New Theses* (新論 *Shinron*) in 1825, at a time of growing European naval and mercantile encroachment on Japan's maritime borders, and in awareness of information from abroad about European colonial expansion in South East Asia. He was able to infer that part of the strength of these Western nations lay in the unity of their people behind their rulers. Aizawa believed that it was Christianity that provided this unity, and that, like the Confucian sage kings of old who cultivated the kingly way (王道 *ōdō*), using moral example, ritual, and music to bind their subjects to their will without the need for force, European rulers were able to use Christianity to similar effect on their subjects.[10] Aizawa sought to elaborate an equivalent religiosity that could be fostered among the Japanese people.

In reflecting on this equivalent, Aizawa hit upon the idea of the national polity, or *Kokutai*, which would be much used and developed by later nineteenth- and twentieth-century scholars and propagandists. Aizawa also further developed the Mito School's synthesis of nativist *Shintō* and neo-Confucian ideas that later, modernizing thinkers would also embellish. The gist of the *Kokutai* as Aizawa understood it was this: an order of ritual-based, noncoercive rule initiated at the dawn of time by The Sun Goddess Amaterasu and continued by her imperial descendants in an unbroken imperial line up to the present day. It was Amaterasu who established "the norms of human conduct," of loyalty to ruler and filial piety, which "constitute the ultimate way of Heaven."[11] In the *Daijō* (大嘗) ceremony, each succeeding emperor ritually gives filial reverence to Amaterasu and her successors, his ancestors. The noble families participating in this ceremony are also brought into a communion with it, so that they also worship their divine ancestors with filial reverence, who had in the past loyally served Amaterasu and the imperial ancestors.[12]

In this way, Aizawa reiterated and embellished the earlier classical Confucian doctrines of the parallelism of filial piety and loyalty discussed earlier in this chapter. Through ritual reverence for their ancestors, the emperors exemplify filial conduct for their subjects. Through ritual reverence for their own ancestors who loyally served the imperial ancestors, the noble families practice filial piety after the example of the emperor. But they also practice loyalty—for, Aizawa pointed out, in knowing how our own ancestors loyally served the imperial ancestors of the present emperor, "How can we ignore ancestral will? How can we turn against the ruler?" Thus the oneness of filial piety and loyalty is revealed: "Loyalty and filial piety have always been one and the same: Filial devotion is transformed into loyalty to ruler, and loyalty is demonstrated by respecting the wishes of the forbears."[13] And this is what the *Kokutai* also amounts to for Aizawa—a national identity founded on a noncoercive political rule achieved through ritual, cultivated first of all in the exemplary filial conduct of the emperor, which brings together the hearts of the people behind him in a unified filial piety and loyalty. Subsequent generations of scholars in the late nineteenth and twentieth centuries would interpret the *Kokutai* concept differently, but Aizawa's original definition remained at the heart of these later interpretations.

Aizawa's was a restorationist doctrine, however. He saw in his own day a falling from the exemplary ritual conduct of the past, and denounced the Buddhist, Christian and vulgar Confucianism that stood in the way of its revival. It was also protonationalist in that it envisaged a unification of the populace in a common national identity—formulated around the rituals of filiality and loyalty that secured allegiance to the emperor and the divinely sanctioned imperial line—and formulated for the purposes of more effective self-defense from the military and doctrinal encroachments of the European powers. It therefore goes too far to describe the national morality that Inoue Tetsujirō and his intellectual peers developed less than a century later as an "invented tradition" in a radical break with the traditions of the past, or even to describe what Aizawa himself advocated in such terms.[14] For at least some aspects of late nineteenth- and twentieth-century national morality and *Kokutai* ideology had conceptual continuities with premodern concepts, including late Tokugawa conceptualizations of the Kokutai itself, and of virtues such as filial piety and loyalty. The same holds for Aizawa's protonationalism, synthesizing older *Shintō* traditions and Classical Confucian concepts to conjure up a sense of a national consciousness that had a convincing appearance of continuity with the ways of the sage kings in antiquity.

Inoue Tetsujirō and the Political Philosophical Status of the *National Morality*

There were, then, continuities with the past. Still, the conceptualization of Confucian and nativist *Shintō* ideas by a European educated scholar such as Inoue Tetsujirō in the rapidly industrializing conditions of late nineteenth- and early twentieth-century Japan could not help but also diverge from what scholars in a dynastic, agrarian society made of them even two generations before. Inoue *rationalized* the classical and Japanese Confucian ideas of filial piety and loyalty in the service of a statist conception of the "national idea," in ways that Aizawa Seishisai could not have imagined. Though there were plenty of competing nationalisms in late nineteenth- and early twentieth-century Japan, statist and antistatist, liberal and illiberal, cultural and ethnic, it was Inoue's statist nationalism, combining European, Confucian, and nativist Japanese doctrines that enjoyed the endorsement of powerful institutions such as the Ministry of Education.

Despite his immense influence as professor of philosophy at Tokyo University, and as a scholar working with the Japan Education Ministry in developing moral education for Japanese schoolchildren, Inoue is not an obvious choice for discussion as a political philosopher. In the introduction to the 1974 English translation of his work *Studies in Intellectual History of Tokugawa Japan*, Maruyama Masao remarked that Inoue's "numerous books and articles on the National Morality, strident as they were in their exhortatory tone, had little scholarly value" and this comment sums up the post-1945 Japanese scholarly consensus on Inoue. Yet in the same work Maruyama also paid tribute to Inoue's immense contribution as a scholar to studies of Tokugawa Confucianism. Using the categories of Western philosophy, Inoue was the first East Asian scholar to treat Japanese Confucianism as "thought," Maruyama wrote.[15]

To put it simply, though what Inoue wrote about filial piety and loyalty in works such as *Outline of a National Morality* lacks philosophical value, it is worth understanding how Inoue adapted his considerable European philosophical and Confucian learning for nationalist purposes. A sense of threat from the European powers, followed later by a sense of mission for Japan as the leading colonial power of Asia, framed the elaboration of a "Japanized" Confucianism[16] that reinterpreted the virtues of filial piety and loyalty as central values of a uniquely Japanese national morality, distinct from the moralities of China and the West. In putting his considerable knowledge of classical Chinese and Tokugawa Confucianism at the service of this national morality, distorted and sophistical though it was, Inoue did something that was of political philosophical interest. He provided a means by which Confucian ideas could be rationalized in the construction of a modern, nationalist civil religion or state religion.

A second problem for our interpretation arises in how to treat the influence of Inoue's key Confucian ideas in the construction of this national morality. How important were such ideas in constructing the ideal subjectivities of loyal Japanese subjects in the key decades of Japan's progress through early industrialization in the late nineteenth century to the development of hypernationalism and militarism in the 1930s and 1940s? In *Nationalism*,[17] Elie Kedourie attributed tremendous influence to German intellectuals, beginning with Kant and the post-Kantian thinkers such as Fichte, for generating the idea of individual and national self-determination. As a "dynamic doctrine," this idea "encouraged and fostered habits and attitudes" in which nationalism found for itself "the great source of its vitality."[18] Are we then to attribute to Inoue, himself a student of post-Kantian philosophy, the same mediating influence? That the "great source of vitality" for Japanese hypernationalism during the critical decades of the 1930s and 1940s lay in Inoue's hybrid *Shintō*-Confucianism, which swallowed the individual up as a loyal, filial subject in a famialist conception of the state not unlike other varieties of statist famialism being advocated in Europe, the Middle East, and South East Asia at that time?[19]

However, Ernest Gellner famously criticized Kedourie's theory that nationalism was originally an idea hatched and incubated by German intellectuals such as Kant.[20] The nationalist idea is rather, he argued, a product of an industrialization process unfolding since the eighteenth century, accompanied by the culturally homogenizing forces of urbanization and mass literacy that arose to accommodate the need for new divisions of labor in an industrializing economy. The idea of the nation, and of nationalism, developed to make sense of these developments already underway in eighteenth- and nineteenth-century Europe. If this is so, Inoue and other Japanese scholars deserve less credit—or blame—for the direction that Japanese nationalism took, from its more defensive, conservative variety in the late nineteenth century through to the anti-Western hypernationalism and militarism of the 1940s.

I hope to show, however, that Inoue's conceptualizing of filial piety and loyalty testifies to some extent to the independence of ideas—ideas ultimately drawn from a protonational consciousness among the Neo-Confucian scholars of late Tokugawa (and preindustrial) Japan, themselves dimly aware of and reacting to a powerfully unifying national consciousness among the European powers. These ideas, of (1) the unity of loyalty and filial piety, (2) a single, unbroken imperial line with divine ancestry that was the focus of that filial piety and loyalty, which (3) was connected by ethnic blood ties to the Japanese people to constitute one great family would become influential as recurring themes in Inoue's work on public morality, and ultimately in the hypernationalist propaganda tracts that recycled these ideas in the 1930s and 1940s. Though these ideas could not have arisen in the form they did without the prior material development of industrialization and a transformed division of labor in late nineteenth-century Japan, we can still agree with Weber's often-quoted maxim that "not ideas, but material and ideal interests directly govern men's conduct. But very frequently the 'world images' which have been created by ideas have, like switchmen, determined the tracks along which action has been pushed by the dynamic of interests."[21]

Our next waystation in the development of the unified concept of filial piety and loyalty should begin with the *Imperial Rescript on Education* discussed in chapter 1, one of the foundational documents of the new Japanese nation-state. As Nishibe Susumu, one of its present-day philosophical advocates put it, its "fundamental spirit . . . begins with Confucianism."[22] Its coauthors Motoda Nagazane and Inoue Kowashi had both received a traditional Confucian academy-based education in their youth. The *Rescript* is a document that amalgamated Confucian virtues with a national *Shintō* cult centered on reverence for the emperor and his ancestors. It exhorted Japan's subjects to fulfill their duties in the five primary Confucian relations, to cultivate their intellectual and moral powers, and to devote themselves to protecting the nation. This way (道 *dō*) was represented as being the "teaching of the imperial ancestors to be observed alike by Their Descendents and the subjects, infallible for all ages and true in all places." Yet the *national Shintō* cult it expressed was *sui generis* in Japanese society. Here was a potent instance of a new, modern ideology synthesizing premodern concepts to generate a powerful sense of unbroken continuity with the primeval past, represented by the fiction of an unbroken imperial family line descended from the Sun Goddess Amaterasu. The stark modernity of the document is displayed in the following exhortation to the emperor's subjects, irrespective of their class or status: "should emergency arise, offer yourselves courageously to the State."[23]

The *Rescript* aimed to foster the ideal of a family state (家族国家 *Kazoku Kokka*) in which filial piety and loyalty merged in reverence for the emperor and his ancestors, as the paternal heads of the state. "Our subjects ever united in filial piety and loyalty"—these two Confucian virtues stand out at the beginning of the Rescript as the chief qualities that bind Japanese subjects in their allegiance to the state, and to the Imperial Household that represents it. From 1890 the *Rescript* was read before assembled students and teachers in schools throughout Japan. Inoue Tetsujirō was commissioned in 1891 by the Ministry of Education to produce a textbook, the "Commentary on the Rescript" (勅語衍義 *Chokugo Engi*) to explain the *Rescript*'s somewhat obscure text to the pupils who had to learn it by heart.

As has been pointed out elsewhere,[24] the *Commentary* provides a decidedly conservative interpretation of the *Rescript*. Of interest is the progress Inoue made toward a focus on the unity of loyalty and filial piety, which would become the key Japanese virtues in the National Morality he would elaborate in later decades. Early on in the *Commentary*, Inoue summed up what the purposes of the *Rescript* were: "solidifying the nation's foundations by cultivating filial piety, fraternal respect, faithfulness and sincerity (孝悌忠信 *kōteichūshin*), and cultivating a co-operative love of country (共同愛國 *kyōdō aikoku*) in readiness for unexpected emergencies."[25]

In this passage we can also clearly see the recruitment of ancient virtue categories into a modern nationalist sensibility. The compound noun for filial piety, fraternal respect, faithfulness, and sincerity is first attested in the *Mencius*, but in the *Commentary* it is reinterpreted on behalf of a modern, unified national consciousness.[26] Later in the *Commentary*, Inoue also singled out for especial notice "serving the way of loyalty and filial piety" (忠孝ノ道ヲ盡クス *chūkō no dō wo sukusu*), linking it to the "exploits of the imperial ancestors over several thousand years" in which "our nation's subjects (臣民 *shinmin*) give loyalty to rulers and filial piety to parents" and "serve the ruler of one nation with a gentle spirit." Inoue added: "[L]oyalty and filial piety to the lord and father is an extremely important matter for morality."[27] At this point Inoue evoked the identity of filial piety and loyalty in a similar manner to the way it is evoked in the ancient Classic of Filial Piety.

In the second edition of the *Commentary*, published in 1899, Inoue would go further in articulating this unity thesis, reinterpreting the Mito School's early nineteenth-century Japanese Confucian understanding of the oneness of filial piety and loyalty as a unity. He explained its rationale thus:

> The principle of the unity of filial piety and loyalty (忠孝一本ノ主義 *chūkō ippon no shugi*) is the reason for our nation's continuous flourishing unto eternity; if we do not follow the faith of our ancestors, filial piety and loyalty lose whatever important, central meaning they have . . . filial piety and loyalty are truly of profound, central import for the establishment of our nation as a state having its foundation in the faith of our ancestors.[28]

Commenting on the growing importance of this doctrine of unified filial piety and loyalty in Inoue's thought at this time, historian Eshima

Kenichi states that for Inoue "the establishing of 'the essential unity of filial piety and loyalty' is indispensable for the observation of ancestor worship," and that this conception of ancestor worship is the foundation "for realizing our country's national polity (*Kokutai*)." Moreover, Eshima adds that in the revised edition of the *Commentary* Inoue insisted on something that is less emphasized in the first edition: that there is peculiar to our country a "family system" (家族制度 *kazoku seido*) that the form of the state and the spirituality of ancestor worship derive from, and both of these aspects finally come together to be referred to as "the unity of loyalty and filial piety."[29] Inoue was finding the language to express what he thought was distinctive to Japan's national morality alone.

In Inoue's conception of a unified loyalty and filial piety integral to a family system that is unique to Japan, there emerges a Weberian "world image" subtly different from that of the early editions of the *Commentary on the Rescript*. The threat of invasion and domination by foreign great powers exercised the imaginations of late Tokugawa reformers, Meiji-era statesmen, and intellectuals such as Inoue up to the 1890s—and this threatened sensibility was not without justification. But with ample proof of success in modernization and a military victory over China in 1895, a new world image started to take hold, even if it did not wholly supplant the older sense of threat. It was of a Japan able to hold its own in a world of modern great powers, as a rising power itself, and of a Japan that was also *different* morally and in the particulars of its national polity and national spirit (国民精神 *kokumin seishin*), not only from the West but also from China. In the elaboration of this difference Inoue gave subtle articulation to a moral superiority, which would receive explicit formulation in the coming decades. This assertion of difference and superiority defined a trackline that led to a later moral legitimation of hegemony *over* China and East Asia.

In the preface to his *Outline of a National Morality* (国民道徳概論 *Kokumin Dōtoku Gairon*) first published in 1912, Inoue wrote that in December 1910 the Minister of Education, Komatsu Eitaro, requested him to lecture on national morality for the ethical training of students at teacher training colleges, and this was followed up by lectures at a number of other colleges and universities,[30] out of which the *Outline* was developed. Inoue was appointed by the Ministry of Education, alongside other leading scholars and intellectuals, to head a Movement for National Morality (国民道徳運動 *Kokumin Dōtoku Undō*), and we have already seen in chapter 1 that the concept of a national morality had already emerged in Inoue's studies of Japanese Confucianism in 1900. In 1912, unease over public loyalty to the emperor had grown following the sensational 1911 trials of anarchists who had plotted to assassinate the Meiji emperor, and over the continued influx of foreign ideas and ideologies that had already been a matter of concern for Inoue over a decade earlier.[31]

The description of the National Morality as *morality* (道徳 *dōtoku*) rather than as religion (宗教 *shukyō*) was significant. It reflected the commitment of leading Meiji-era politicians and intellectuals to a modernizing relegation of religion into a private sphere, where religious freedom was protected by Article 28 of the 1890 Meiji Constitution, and the elevation of morality to the public sphere, where it could be defined around ideals of loyalty to the emperor.[32] A national morality could then be presented as a secular, rational discourse superior to religion, and also as binding on all subjects, irrespective of their private religious devotion. How this morality is to be defined in contemporary terms—as a national or civil religion, or as a "civil theology"—is a question I will consider at the end of the chapter.

One secular objective for Inoue in the *Outline* was to articulate in the national morality what was unique about Japan's national spirit, in distinction from that of other nations. In doing so he availed himself of Hegelian-influenced understandings of national spirit, or *volksgeist* (国民精神 *kokumin seishin*/民族精神 *minzoku seishin*), which he had first translated in his *Philosophical Dictionary*, and which were becoming prominent in early twentieth-century Japanese discussion over national identity. He stated that "the national morality is the manifestation (顯現 *kengen*) of the *volksgeist*,"[33] and that this spirit is peculiar (固有 *koyū*) to Japan.[34] There is indeed some affinity with what Hegel in *Lectures on the Philosophy of History* described as the "national spirit"—a nation's "self-consciousness in relation to its own truth and being" which, as self-conscious, is "the nation's culture."[35] The ethical life of the national spirit constitutes the "lived reality of the state," embodied in its citizens' possession of its distinctive patrimony, different from that of other nations—its lands, laws, institutions and customs, history, and remembered heritage.[36] Inoue shared with Hegel a state-centered conception of the national spirit, though he diverged from Hegel in his increasingly illiberal understanding of that conception.

Yet Inoue's elaboration of this national spirit peculiar to Japan acknowledged that important components of its patrimony were once imported from outside. Historian Kenjō Teiji points to four doctrinal components in Inoue's national morality: an original Japanese volksgeist, and also doctrines introduced from foreign nations—Confucianism, Buddhism, and the ideas of Western civilization, which had all helped develop Japan's national morality into modern times.[37] The original or unalloyed (純粋 *juniki*) Japanese volksgeist was, for Inoue, largely comprised of *Shintō* and *Bushidō*, with the latter described as "the principle for the foundation of the nation."[38] *Bushidō* provided Inoue with the nativist bedrock for his national morality, though in keeping with his syncretic approach to its constituents, he stated that both Buddhism and Confucianism subsequently "enriched" (豊富 *hōfu*) the development of Japan's volksgeist.[39]

Nevertheless, certain factors made Confucianism more important to the development of *Bushidō* and of a national morality than Buddhism or Western civilization. Both Buddhism and Confucianism had been "assimilated (同化 *dōka*) into the Japanese national spirit," it is true. However, there were some deficiencies in Buddhism that ensured that it never fully conformed with the "time-honored customs" (古来風俗 *korai fuzoku*) of Japan as Confucianism had. Unlike Confucianism, Inoue averred, Buddhism lacks a doctrine of moral education in the family system, and it also does not incorporate ancestor worship.[40] Meanwhile, in spite of the benefits Western ideas had brought to Japan, "one outcome of the introduction of Western civilization (西洋文明 *Seiyō Bunmei*) . . . is the forceful intrusion of unsound, dangerous and poisonous ideas"—a statement that highlights Inoue's deep ambivalence about the incorporation of Western ideas into the national morality.[41]

A *rationalized* Confucianism, reconfigured to accommodate the modern demands for popular allegiance to the nation-state, thus gained the leading role in Inoue's exposition of a national morality incorporating filial piety, ancestor worship, *Bushidō*, and reverence for the emperor and imperial household. Some idea of what this rationalization means can be had from revisiting some of Ernest Gellner's remarks on protonationalist consciousness in premodern "clerisies" or cultured elites, of which Aizawa Seishisai was a member. In the main, those clerisies historically sought to maintain their exclusionary status rather than to universalize their skills, ritual practices, and doctrines to lower social strata. Referring to those rarer members of the clerisy who did in some way seek such a universalization, Gellner insisted that it "simply cannot be done." Such universalization could not be put into effect without industrialization, radical changes in the division of labor, urbanization, and the introduction of a culturally homogenizing system of mass education.[42]

Aizawa's own policy proposals bear Gellner's argument out. Aizawa was in favor of some limited mobilization of the nonsamurai classes as auxiliaries for the defense of Japan,[43] but in no way did he subscribe to a program of mass education and a *levee en masse* for all available manpower to defend the realm. He could not imagine such a mass mobilization in a society in which the means for bringing such innovations about were not yet available. He also remained committed to the social rank prerogatives and division of labor of Japan's agrarian society. Inoue, on the other hand, wrote under the guidance of a modernizing educational bureaucracy in dedication to its mass educational goals, which included eliminating from collective consciousness any of the old caste divisions and sentiments that stood in their way. In the *Imperial Rescript on Education*'s exhortation in times of emergency for subjects to "offer yourselves courageously to the state, and thus guard and maintain the prosperity of our Imperial Throne coeval with heaven and earth," Inoue saw the "quintessence" of the unalloyed *volksgeist* of *Bushidō*.[44] Yet Inoue's nationalist reinvention and rationalization of *Bushidō*, assimilating into its code of loyalty and self-sacrifice all Japanese men of fighting age, is alien to Aizawa's own status-defined limitation of full military participation to men of the samurai class.

Yet Inoue faced two formidable tasks in his discussion of *chūkō ippon*. First, he had to convincingly differentiate this concept from Chinese Confucian concepts of filial piety and loyalty, for the very notion of a distinct, as opposed to culturally derivative, national morality depended on success in this task. Second, he had to show that the historical support for this distinctive concept of a unified loyalty and filial piety—a single, unbroken imperial line extending all the way back to its founder, the Sun Goddess Amaterasu—was not a myth contradicted by historical evidence.

However, Inoue's brief survey of the historical development of *chūkō ippon* required some acknowledgment of the Chinese as well as Japanese Neo-Confucian contribution to the evolution of this concept, though he also contrived to show how this same concept remained underdeveloped in China. Inoue admitted the contributions of Chinese Confucian ideas of filial piety and loyalty to the Japanese formulation of *chūkō ippon*, with quotes from *The Classic of Filial Piety*: "As they serve their fathers, so they serve their rulers and "when they serve their ruler with filial piety, they are loyal." On the Japanese side, he found the ancestral concept of *chūkō ippon*, the oneness of filial piety (忠孝一致 *chūkō icchi*) in the early nineteenth-century writings of the Mito School, and in the writing of the mid-nineteenth-century modernizing samurai intellectual Yoshida Shōin.[45]

I will now outline some of the retooled Confucian doctrines that together constitute Inoue's concept of *chūkō ippon* that also made it distinctive from concepts of loyalty and filial piety found in China or in the West.

I. The harmony of "individual" and "integrated" family systems. Within the Japanese social order, Inoue argued, there is a system of individual family units (個別家族制度 *kobestu kazoku seido*) and an integrated family system (総合家族制度 *sōgō kazoku seido*) comprising the entire nation under the emperor. These systems are harmonized, or "absolutely co-exist," making the unity of loyalty and filial piety possible in the following way. In separate families members serve the male family head (家族長 *kazokuchō*) with filial obedience, and in the same manner, subjects serve the emperor as the head of the one, integrated family, and with the same heartful sincerity (眞心 *magokoro*): the "serving of the family head with filial piety is a contracted form of the subjects' relation to the emperor in the nation" and this, for Inoue, constitutes a "great homogeneous" system through which the unity of filial loyalty and piety come into being.[46]

However, this integrated family system is not to be understood merely by analogy with the individual family, as a reading of early Confucian texts such as *The Classic of Filial Piety* might suggest. The integrated family system is *also* connected by a common ancestry that unifies the Japanese people through blood: "for the most part, the Japanese people are nothing less than the latest children in the lineage of the race descended from the Sun Goddess"[47]; and so there is between ruler and ruled a "connection of blood" (血族的関係 *ketsuzokuteki kankei*).[48] Therefore, literally, just as under one family head individual families are established, so under the emperor the great family of the nation as a horizontal and lateral system of ethnically related families is established. Serving the emperor with loyalty, then, is an extension of the "great filial piety." In this way filial piety and loyalty are one, there is no incompatibility (扞格 *fusekaku*) between them, and together they establish the Confucian "Great Principle of Duty" between subjects and rulers (大義名分 *taigi meibun*).[49]

II. The unity of loyalty and filial piety is also secured through filial piety being an expression of obedience to the will of parents and ancestors, who themselves were loyal to a single, eternal, unbroken imperial line (萬世一系の皇統 *bansei ikkei no kōtō*), an argument originally put forward by Aizawa, as we have seen.

Of course, Inoue could not easily dismiss the problem that so exercised previous generations of Confucian scholars, and their legalist opponents: the problem of what filial children should do when parents act in a manner contrary to loyalty to rulers, or directed their children to act disloyally. How can filial piety and loyalty to ruler be preserved in such circumstances? Inoue's solution to this problem is rather glib. While he argued that there is no incompatibility between filial piety and loyalty, in the case of parental will or conduct that is unjust and disloyal, the son must, "for the sake of his ruler and nation (君国 *kunkoku*) throw away his filiality and hold onto loyalty." "Loyalty is a weightier thing than filial piety; giving up the smaller thing is to recognize that Japan's ethnic community (日本といふ民族団體 *Nihon to ifu Minzoku Dantai*) is the most important thing," and this is truly what the Great Principle of Duty is. Still, in the ordinary way of things, there is a "noncontradiction between filial piety and loyalty."[50] Unlike past generations of Confucian scholars, Inoue could throw onto the scales the weight of modern concepts of national allegiance and ethnonational belonging, in order, when necessary, to tip them in favor of loyalty, and greater filial piety to the emperor, against filial piety to parents.

These, then, are some of the main innovations that Inoue introduced to refine the doctrine of *chūkō ippon*. He had, as noted earlier, a number of concerns and objections to attend to. First was the problem of demonstrating how *chūkō ippon* is unique and distinct from the filial piety and loyalty of the national moralities of other nations—for, he insisted, *chūkō ippon* is not practiced in China, the West, or anywhere else.[51]

Inoue drew on his extensive knowledge of Chinese history and Confucian scholarship to construct his case for distinguishing the distinctly Japanese unity of filial piety with loyalty from Chinese national morality. Perhaps the simplest argument he advanced was that there was no social organizational basis, no integrated family system, to support that system in China as there was in Japan. This is for the simple reason that there have been frequent dynastic changes and conquests that have brought China under the power of different—even ethnically different—ruling families. Thus there was no single, unified imperial line stretching back into the immemorial past as there had been in Japan, and at times no ethnic kinship between rulers and ruled. So the will of ancestors could be thwarted, and filial piety and loyalty set at odds with each other by dynastic changes that required subjects to transfer their allegiances to a new imperial court. For instance, with the Manchu conquest and the establishment of the Qing Dynasty, subjects' filial compliance with the will of their ancestors, loyal to the previous Ming Court, put them at odds with loyalty to the Qing court.[52]

The brute facts of dynastic change, foreign conquest, ancient practices of abdication in favor of virtuous successors who have no blood relation to the ruler (禪讓放伐 *zenjyō hōbatsu*), and the overthrow by righteous ministers of vicious rulers (革命 *kakumei*) ensured that even the greatest Chinese Confucians could not ensure continuity in the observance of their doctrines beyond the termination of their dynasties. Inoue held up for special praise Song Dynasty Confucians and scholars such as Cheng Hao 程顥 and Sima Guang 司馬光 for helping develop the idea of the loyal subject and for "greatly illuminating the Great principle of duty" between subjects and rulers.[53] But the process of moral development they contributed to within their own realm was terminated with the fall of the Song Dynasty to the Mongol invasion. Thus, "[t]he foundations (根柢 *kontei*) for the idea of rendering devotion/loyalty (忠義 *chugi*) to the court were demolished," and a different idea of loyalty to sovereign had to be developed in relation to the new Yuan Court. Japan, with its continuous, unbroken imperial line, had avoided this fate.[54]

While trying to differentiate the affective and ethical content of the relation between rulers and ruled in Japan from that in China, Inoue also had to concede that Song Confucians such as Zhu Xi 朱熹 developed very profound teachings on loyalty between subject and ruler,[55] and there is naturally such loyalty between Japanese subjects and their ruler. However, in the Japanese case there is something more. In the testaments of ancient Japanese emperors and also in the *Imperial Rescript on Education*, there is proof of reciprocal parent-child love between ruler and subject in Japan, and Japanese rulers and ruled are also bound by a tie of common blood, which provides "natural preparation" for this affectional tie.[56]

So these were the arguments that Inoue marshaled to demonstrate the distinctiveness of the Confucian ideal of unified loyalty and filial piety in Japan as opposed to the ideals of loyalty and filial piety found in the Chinese Confucians. Though poor and contrived, these arguments would be recruited in later decades in more vehement assertions of the superiority of Japan's national morality over that of China.

Still, Inoue knew that some would try to point to weaknesses in his thesis. Scholars trained in "Western ethics," influenced by "Western religion" or practicing as Western-trained historians, were apt to be highly skeptical about notions of an unbroken imperial line descended from the Sun

Goddess. Yet for Inoue the historical veracity of these notions was absolutely foundational to the integrity and distinctiveness of Japan's National Morality, to the integrity of the *Kokutai*, and to the plausibility of the unity of filial piety and loyalty thesis itself. So Inoue felt compelled to address the Nanbuko-cho Problem (南北朝問題 *Nanbokuchō mondai*), which did pose some acute difficulties for the historical postulates of the national morality. It was a fourteenth-century political crisis that saw the Japanese imperial family divided from itself into warring northern and southern factions, each represented by its own emperor, for a period of nearly sixty years. For proponents of the National Morality such as Inoue, it was vital not only to demonstrate which was the legitimate line, but also to show that this fifty-six-year factional rift within the imperial family did not undermine the thesis of a single, uninterrupted imperial line.

Inoue admitted the importance of this problem but deferred a solution for it to a special appendix on the problem at the end of *Outline for a National Morality*. Inoue proposed a number of conditions for ascertaining the legitimacy or illegitimacy of rulers of the Northern and Southern Courts, including most importantly that they be affiliated with the imperial family, that they be in a position of legitimate succession, and that they be attached to the three sacred treasures or regalia of the imperial throne.[57] There were other conditions, too, that seem oddly anachronistic for a fourteenth-century setting, such as that the ruler "be of sound mind and body" and that he enjoy the support of the masses. In accordance with these conditions, Inoue determined that Go-Daigo, the incumbent emperor before the onset of the Northern and Southern Courts period, who subsequently set up the Southern court following defeat in civil war, was the legitimate sovereign. He was, Inoue concluded, in the direct line of succession from the first Japanese emperor, Jimmu, was naturally affiliated as emperor with the imperial family, and was in possession of the three imperial treasures when he fled Kyoto to found the Southern Court. There was in the end no difficulty, Inoue stated, for delivering a verdict—from the point of view "of the Fundamental Doctrine for the foundation of our country," The Northern Court was illegitimate."[58]

However, Inoue's inquiry was merely an exercise in *post-hoc* rationalization. After a bitter controversy over the Northern and Southern Court problem, which had embroiled the government, historians, and leading scholars such as Inoue, the Ministry of Education had declared in 1911 (prior to the publication of Inoue's *Outline*) that the Southern Court was the legitimate court, from which the present emperor was descended. This was a conclusion that Inoue enthusiastically agreed with. And he took a leading role in warning historians not to wade into public controversies about the past such as the *Nanbokuchō* Problem, where their published conclusions could impact on public perceptions of the national morality and the *Kokutai*—for "historians are prone to survey this problem just from a historical point of view, and thus it is extremely difficult for them to see the alternative."[59] The quality of Inoue's argumentation, and his preference for a mythologized national past over an evidence-based historical past, should not concern us overmuch. What is important is that his contrived arguments were intended to overcome doubts over whether Japan's imperial line, unlike that of China, was single and unbroken, for this was the foundation for the distinctly Japanese morality of *chūkō ippon*.

Japan's National Morality and the "China Incident"

It is time to return to the earlier Weberian discussion of the ideas, as "world images" that define the tracks along which material and ideal interests have moved. In what ways did the Confucian-influenced National Morality and concept of *chūkō ippon* act as tracklines for such conveyance? At this juncture it is worthwhile remembering a point Eshima Kenichi makes about Inoue's work on the National Morality: that in it the Confucian principals (本義 *hongi*) of loyalty and filial piety were exclusively "Japanized" through being adapted to the ideal of a single, eternal Japanese imperial line.[60] The powerful "world image" this particularism generated had domestic and external orientations, as we have seen. Domestically, it helped generate a modernized nativism flexible enough to admit and catalyze foreign doctrines as its own (Buddhism, Confucianism, and certain imports from "Western Civilization") while also drawing a line against more "poisonous" Western ideas. Externally, in its ideal of a perfected, Japanized Confucianism distinct from that of China, there was both inspiration and *post-hoc* justification for Japan assuming a position of regional hegemony that imperial China had once held. Japan's colonialism and militarism, motivated by a quest for geopolitical influence, status, and economic resources, could be ennobled, and justified, in moral language in which it presented itself as the leader of an Asian civilization different from the individualistic, capitalist West. In this there was a superficial harmonization of material and ideal interests.

We have to go forward to the late 1930s and 1940s to see the endgame for this world image. By 1937, the ideological atmosphere in Japanese politics was far more conflictual than it had been two decades earlier. The political system and the armed forces were heavily factionalized. The authority of civilian government was steadily undermined by the terroristic activities mid-ranking military officers directed at elected officials at home, and by military campaigns initiated by the armed forces in an as yet undeclared conflict in China, often beyond the control of civilian government. Rival nationalist ideologies also revealed themselves in doctrinal conflicts over the meaning of *Kokutai*. Finally, the idea of a national morality grounded on an ethnic nationalist famialism was proving difficult to align with newer ideas of a multiethnic empire and cultural community of Asian nations, with Japan at its head.

Inoue Tetsujirō no longer had a leading influence in these events and controversies, and in the more febrile atmosphere of that era's hypernationalism he had himself been targeted for censure over a minor typographical error in the spelling of an ancient emperor's name, which extreme nationalists interpreted as a lack of respect for the imperial line.[61] A younger generation of Confucian scholars, such as the Wang Yangming specialist Yasuoka Masahiro, were theorizing a modernized concept of the Kingly Way as an ideal for moralized governance in Japan, and as an ideal for a pan-Asian moral order governed by Japan. Like Inoue before him, Yasuoka had numerous patrons in government ministry and indeed military circles.[62] Yet Inoue's interpretation of the Confucian component of Japan's national morality and *Kokutai* had become the common sense of this new generation of propagandists and government officials. In March 1937, a panel of leading scholars and educators, including the Buddhist philosopher Watsuji Tetsujirō, Inoue's former student, produced for the Ministry of Education a book titled *Principles of the National Polity* (國體の本義 *Kokutai no Hongi*). With more intensified anti-Western and nativist rhetoric, this book reiterated some Confucian concepts Inoue had been instrumental in modifying and promoting, including *chūkō ippon*.

Not far from the beginning of the *Principles of the National Polity* is a statement of its definition of the national polity that makes clear the importance of loyalty and filial piety:

> The Great Japanese Empire (大日本帝 *Dai Nippon Teikoku*) obeys the decrees of the Founder of the unbroken imperial line, which will reign forever. This is our eternal and immutable national polity. This moral law is the basis for the people single-mindedly carrying out the imperial will as one great family state, manifest-

ing well the virtue (美徳 *bitoku*) of loyalty and filial piety. This is the essence of our national polity.⁶³

This looks more like a modernizing gloss on Mito School ideology than something that might have been adapted from Inoue Tetsujirō in particular, but two further passages seem to bear Inoue's stamp. One is dedicated to an explanation of *chūkō ippon*, a virtue "founded on our national polity (that) shines forth beautifully." It cites the same statement from the mid-nineteenth-century samurai intellectual Yoshida Shoin that Inoue had used in *Outline* to explain the antecedents of *chūkō ippon*: "the unity of ruler and subject, the oneness of loyalty and filial piety (君臣一本、忠孝一致 *kunshin ippon, chūkō icchi*); this is so only in my country."⁶⁴ This statement, the authors of the *Principles* claimed, is "extremely pertinent to a discussion of the way of the unity of loyalty and filial piety." The authors then went on to make the same point that Inoue had made about the distinctiveness of this way to Japan: that the being one of loyalty and filial piety is a morality distinctive to Japan (我が国の道徳の特色があり *waga kuni no dōtoku no tokushoku ga ari*), and no similar instance of it is to be found elsewhere in the world.⁶⁵

The second passage, from the conclusion of the *Principles*, concerns the rationale for differentiating Chinese from Japanese Confucianism, including, in particular, their respective conceptualizations of loyalty and filial piety. Like Inoue, the authors of the *Principles* emphasized that in China the Confucian-sanctioned practices of righteous revolution, and of abdication in favor of virtuous successors unrelated by blood to the sovereign, ensured that the unity of loyalty and filial piety could never be established in China. Yet they went further than Inoue in attributing to Chinese Confucianism an "individualist tendency" (個人主義的傾向 *kojinshugiteki keikō*). Once Confucianism had been "purified" (醇化 *junka*) of these tendencies and elements by the *Kokutai*, it was able to serve in the development of Japan's "National Morality."⁶⁶

This is sufficient, I think, to demonstrate how Inoue's Confucianized national morality had become absorbed into the hypernationalist propaganda of the 1930s. Yet the usefulness of Inoue's Japanese Confucian doctrine did not stop there. With the setting up of a puppet regime in Machukuo in 1932, the onset of the second Sino-Japanese War in 1937, and the occupation of much of Northern China there arose a need to better articulate the ideal interests motivating Japan's involvement in Manchuria and China. In this respect the world image of Japan as the guardian of East Asia's cultural development, in differentiation from the capitalist, individualistic West came into play. Inoue's thought helped express the Confucian component of that self-image, even if he was no longer so influential in propagating it.

The 1941 propaganda treatise *The Way of Subjects* (臣民の道 *Shinmin no Michi*), issued by the Ministry of Education to schools to instruct Japanese children on their duties as subjects to the emperor and *Kokutai* in wartime, explained the by now familiar ideology of the unbroken lineage of the imperial house from the Goddess Amaterasu, and the familiar platitudes about the unity of loyalty and filial piety particular to Japan's *Kokutai* being "without peer" in other nations (他國に比類なき特色が存する *takoku ni hirui naki tokushoku ga son suru*).[67] Yet this treatise also had to justify, in suitably moral language, the recent military adventurism in China. The following passage captures the tenor of this justification:

> the purpose of the "China Affair" is to enlighten China (支那の蒙を啓き *Shina no mō wo hiraki*), to strengthen Sino-Japanese co-operation, to foster co-existence and co-prosperity, to set up a new East Asian order and to contribute to establishing world peace.[68]

This justification is striking for its omission of material interests (such as the quest for enhanced geopolitical status and demand for territory and resources), but the ideal interests it states should not be disparaged as cynical propaganda. There were Japanese administrators, intellectuals, and political leaders who sincerely believed in the "moral case" for a benevolent Japanese leadership over China and other Asian nations, embodied in the ideal of a "Kingly Way." Such Kingly Way advocates were not only numerous but also ideologically diverse, including conservative Confucian scholars such as Inoue and Yasuoka Masahiro, and also men like the progressive journalist and sinologist Tachibana Shiraki, who saw in Manchukuo the potential for a Kingly Way as an egalitarian, anticapitalist democracy.[69]

Inoue took up the topic of the Kingly Way in his 1939 book *Eastern Culture and China's Future* (東洋文化と支那の将来 *Tōyō Bunka to Shina no Shōrai*). Inoue was now in retirement and no longer so influential with the Education Ministry. Even if the book itself reiterated extant moral justifications for Japan's military and colonial presence in China, he could at least demonstrate that Japan's ideology for cultural leadership in East Asia was in accord with his vision of a renewed Confucianism in China's national morality.

Inoue's arguments for this renewal, such as they are, do not require detailed exposition. He observed that while in China's past "Confucius, Mencius, Song Learning, Wang Yangming and other supremely excellent scholars had been preeminent," in present-day China, "Confucianism has—contrary to expectations—fallen into vulgarity" and "the traditional spirit of worshipping Confucius . . . has been broken."[70] The remedy for this degraded state was a policy he rather grandiosely claimed to have stated himself in an article for the magazine *Japan Critique* late in 1937: that China abandon Sun Yat Sen's republican political philosophy of the "Three Principles of the People" and found itself instead on its traditional national morality—namely, Confucianism.[71] This was in accordance with a principle of "Luminous Virtue and New People" (明徳新民 *meitoku shinmin*) that appears to be a variation on the "New People's Principles" (新民主義 *shinminshugi/hsin-min chu-i*) ideology, an ideology proclaimed by Japanese administrators and collaborating Chinese officials for the Japan-controlled administration in Northern China, to counter the influence of Sen's Three Principles.[72] This ideology took its name and inspiration from the first lines of the Confucian classic *The Great Learning*. It was also "no less than what was established in Manchukuo as the spirit of the national founding of the Kingly Way" (王道 *ōdō*).[73]

Inoue believed that if a "New China" purified of republicanism and communism sought to accomplish its cultural development through the "Luminous Virtue and New People" principle, it would achieve the same perfect results as Manchuko already had.[74] Yet China could not achieve its Kingly Way and the "'Luminous Virtue and New People" principle in complete independence from Japan. If China abandoned Sun Yat-sen's Three Principles and adopted the Kingly Way, Inoue suggested that "our nation Japan should serve as its model" (範を我が日本に取るべきである *Han wo waga Nippon ni toru beki de aru*). What this actually meant was that China should follow Manchukuo in moving to adopt a "Japanized Kingly Way" (日本風の「王道」 *Nippon fū no "ōdō"*). This was the Japanese "Imperial Way" (皇道 *kōdō*) also advocated by scholars such as Yasuoka Masahiro, which unlike the older Chinese Kingly Way, rejected the politically destabilizing Mencian doctrine of righteous revolution. If the "New China" could achieve this reformation, a "common cultural flourishing" between Manchukuo, Japan, and China could also be accomplished.[75]

Of course the campaign for a re-Confucianized China under the tutelage of a Japanese "Kingly Way" failed long before 1945, though it bore out, in blackly comic fashion, the paranoia Lu Xun attributed to his compatriots, who believed that their cultural heritage was being "Japanized." Historian John Boyle observed that the "New People's Principles" mass moral educational campaigns may have been comprehensible to those older Chinese who had been educated under the institutional Confucianism of the late Qing Empire, but they bewildered younger Chinese who had not, but who had to endure an alienating regime of Confucian ethics education supplemented with Japanese propaganda and language instruction. Ultimately, however, the legitimacy of diverse Kingly Way discourses was undermined by the heavy-handed control Japanese officials exercised over the occupation administration, by the everyday humiliations and violence meted out to the Chinese by racist Japanese officials and soldiers,[76] and most of all, by the atrocities and destruction perpetrated by Japan's armed forces in the Second Sino-Japanese War. The ideal interests of reenculturating and re-Confucianizing China under Japanese tutelage, morally compromised as they were, were pushed aside by brute material interests to acquire control over land, resources, and pacified populations in China. That great Pan-Asianist Rabindranath Tagore recognized these compromised ideal interests clearly in 1938, in an accusing letter to his fellow poet Noguchi Yone: "You are building your conception of an Asia which would be raised on a tower of skulls."[77] In this final waystation for the "Japanized" Confucianism of the "unity of filial piety and loyalty" in our analysis, we have also reached the conclusion of our East Asian horror story.

Confucianism, National Morality, and Civil Religion Today

What then is the reader to make of the career of the moral-political concept of *chūkō ippon*, from its supposed incipient statements in the *Classic of Filial Piety* through its incorporation in the statist nationalism of a modernizing Japan, to its catastrophic denouement—in a conflict in China that took between fifteen and twenty million lives, and in the crushing military defeat of Japan? Some readers will respond that Inoue's national morality was based on a highly distorted and corrupted variety of Confucianism—that it hardly even deserves to be called a "Confucianism." It sacralized the Japanese imperial house, rendering its incumbents and institutions impervious to the ultimate transcendental and temporal sanctions recognized by classical Confucians: the withdrawal of the Mandate of Heaven, and the overthrow of vicious rulers by righteous ministers. The Confucian faith that rulers are ethically perfectible and are capable, through exemplary ritual practice and self-cultivation, of rectifying themselves and their subjects had a complementary insight: that rulers can also be incompetent or vicious, and that virtuous ministers may appropriately respond to such failures through remonstrance, resignations, or revolt. This central Confucian insight could not be incorporated into an ideology that founded its distinctiveness on the inviolability of the Japanese imperial line, and that sacralized its representatives so that, as descendants of the Sun Goddess, they could only be conceived as ruling through an infallible paternal solicitude for their subjects.

This is a just criticism of Inoue's Confucianism. But that is no reason to dismiss Inoue's ideology as irrelevant to present-day discussion of Confucianism in political philosophy. What Confucians today need to confront is not only the later twentieth-century appropriation and retooling of Confucianism as an ideology for legitimating illiberal developmental states in East Asia, but also the appropriation and incorporation of Confucianism into the statist ideologies and imperialism of pre-1945 Japan. That Confucianism was in this instance distorted by statist nationalism and imperialism is, as I said, beyond doubt. The more difficult question to confront is how vulnerable Confucianism still is to being retooled by an autocratic statism today in East Asia.

For if historical precedents and the current troubled state of East Asian geopolitics are any guide, if Confucianism is ever going to be institutionalized as the ruling ideology in East Asia's political orders, it is *not* likely to be in some partnership with communitarianism, Deweyan pragmatism, liberal democracy, or other varieties of progressive democratic institutions. Its more likely embodiment is in a legitimating nexus with an illiberal nationalism that would, in present-day geopolitical conditions, be self-defined in cultural antagonism against both "the West" *and* against other East Asian states. A revived "national morality" grounded in Japan's particularist *Shintō*, Confucian, and Buddhist traditions is on the agenda of illiberal nationalist Japanese scholars such as Nishibe Susumu, as an antidote to postwar American-imposed values and education that had dragged its morality "into the swamp."[78] And as we shall see in the next chapter, there are also advocates of an illiberal Chinese Confucian state religion, such as Jiang Qing.

With this history, and in light of the present-day antagonistic nationalisms in East Asia, rich in mutual perceptions of threat and grievances over past victimhood, the prospects of Confucianism—slim as they are—may yet again be realized in a manner that thwarts the intentions of those Confucians committed to a more progressive, just, and equitable political order in East Asia. A measure of intellectual foresight is called for in these circumstances. Ideas may define their tracklines with the intent or approval of their authors—such as Inoue Tetsujirō—but they also may not, if they are appropriated for political causes and ideologies that their authors abhor. This latter possibility is what today's Confucians must guard against, and I suggest one political philosophical concept that needs more careful scrutiny in light of the discussion in this chapter: the idea of a Confucian civil religion, derived from Robert Bellah's concept of civil religion as "a collection of beliefs, symbols, and rituals with respect to sacred things and institutionalized in a collectivity," such as a nation.[79]

As noted in chapter 1, a number of Confucian scholars have claimed that Confucian habits of the heart constitute or are central components in the civil religion(s) of East Asian societies. Obviously, if Inoue Tetsujirō's national morality is an instance of civil religion with a strong (if distorted) Confucian component, there is a Japanese precedent for a Confucian civil religion in East Asia that is largely unacknowledged by its latter-day proponents. This gives reason for disquiet over present-day advocacy for this concept in East Asia. Scholars familiar with Inoue's thought have taken this view.[80]

However, other scholars have tried to insulate the concept of civil religion from assimilation to concepts of state or national religions, and thus preserve it for a more democratic and pluralistic vision of Confucianism in East Asia. So the editors of a recent collection of essays on civil religion and habits of the heart in East Asia contend that Robert Bellah's concept of civil religion is different from and cannot admit within its definition state religions such as Maoism, which is "unambiguously a self-conscious, state-sponsored, institutionalized set of beliefs and practices." Moreover, a civil religion is a set of ethical ideals and aspirations that transcend, or "stand apart from and look beyond any secular, institutionalized authority," and are not bound to any particular doctrine or ideology.[81] Excepting the fact that it appealed to rather than rejected tradition, the national morality Inoue and other early twentieth-century Japanese intellectuals and officials promoted certainly resembles such institutionalized, beliefs and doctrines, and it was most certainly tied to institutionalized authorities such as Japan's Ministry of Education and the imperial throne.

In his analysis of Inoue Tetsujirō's national morality, Winston Davis suggested a refinement on the definition of civil religion itself, distinguishing between civil religion *tout court* and the "civil theology" that he defines Inoue's national morality under. He reiterated Bellah's understanding of civil religion as transcending "specific religious communities and dogmas," with its constituents being the unreflectively accumulated "precipitates of traditional religious communities," rather than a conscious fabrication. In contrast, civil theology "is the articulation of civil religion by the elite," and civil theologians like Inoue occupy a fuzzy, indistinctly defined zone between "popular opinion (where civil religion has its home) and the explicit articulation of this sentiment as politics," and in this zone they contrive to make the latter appear as an organic outgrowth of the former.[82]

Even admitting such conceptual refinements to the concept of civil religion, it remains in some respects difficult to segregate off from the notion of state religion or theology as Davis defines it. The ambivalent boundary between the two reflects the divided intellectual ancestry of the concept of civil religion itself, in Rousseau's and de Tocqueville's thought and also in the twentieth-century Japanese theorists Robert Bellah read before he came to his own understanding of the concept.

So there is Rousseau's recommendation for a "civil profession of faith," its "content . . . fixed by the sovereign—not exactly as religious dogmas, but as social sentiments that are needed to be a good citizen and a faithful subject" that may banish those who do not subscribe to this faith, and that tolerates particular religious faiths so long as they refrain from theological intolerance or sectarianism.[83] Then there is Alexis de Tocqueville's concept of an organic, nonsectarian American Christianity, a "democratic and republican religion" that historically made an immense contribution to the "establishment of a republic and of a democracy in public affairs," combining "the notions of Christianity and of liberty so intimately in (American) minds," and which had acquired the voluntary adherence of all Christian sects.[84]

A number of scholars have also drawn attention to some affinities between Bellah's concept of civil religion and the somewhat divergent understandings of national morality and *Kokutai* ideology formulated by Inoue[85] and his former student Watsuji Tetsujirō, one of the authors of the 1937 propaganda tract *The Principles of the National Polity*. Indeed, Amy Borovoy has recently argued for a direct line of influence between Watsuji's political philosophy and Bellah's concept of civil religion, especially in light of Bellah's ambivalent treatment of Watsuji's thought in a landmark essay published in 1965 in the *Journal of Asian Studies*.[86] Space here is insufficient to follow the details of Borovoy's investigation. Still, it is striking that Bellah severely criticized Watsuji's concept of the state as the "highest ethical structure," realized in a Japanese community united through selfless reverence for the emperor, arguing that this ideal afforded no place for individual dissent, nor for any "transcendental standard relative to which individual or social action can be judged."[87] Yet Bellah's comparative analysis of American and

Japanese civil religion in his 1982 book *Varieties of Civil Religion* paralleled the anti-individualist critique of American society he attributed to Watsuji in his 1965 essay. Bellah asserted that as the public morality and transcendental values of America's civil religion lost their persuasiveness for a "cognitive elite" in late twentieth-century America, American society became what Watsuji had described in the 1940s: a Hobbesian order in which atomized individuals are barely held together in their contractual assent to moral rules "for the protection of their common interests."[88] In contrast, Bellah idealized a Japanese public ethic "that encouraged a kind of moral heroism among the common people."[89]

In any case, Bellah described the twentieth-century "emperor system" "of which state *Shintō* was a constituent part" as the "modern Japanese civil religion," though its "hierarchical" character differentiated it from American civil religion, which is distinguished by its "equality."[90] Yet if Japan's civil religion is (or was) "self-conscious, state-sponsored (and) institutionalized," some aspects of Bellah's definition of American civil religion also incorporates these elements, further blurring the line between civil religion and state religion. Bellah recognized the appearance of a new language and symbolism of death, rebirth, and sacrifice for nation in American civil religion following the Battle of Gettysburg, and in the aftermath of the Civil War. President Lincoln is shown as giving the first major (elite) articulation to this language in his Gettysburg Address. The "physical and ritual" expressions to this new symbolism that Bellah lists are all at least in part the products of state sponsorship and institutionalization—the national cemeteries and memorials for the war dead, and memorial days for their ritual remembrance.[91] Through such explicit state sponsorship and the acts of institutional authority, and through the spontaneous participation of American citizens themselves, "the theme of sacrifice was indelibly written into the American civil religion."[92]

A final juncture where the line between civil religion and state religion or theology blurs is where there is a weakening influence of the transcendental principles of the former—that is, a weakening of the "subordination of the nation to ethical principles that transcend it in terms of which it should be judged."[93] This transcendentalism ought to distinguish American civil religion from the state religion or theology of early twentieth-century Japan. For as I have made clear regarding Inoue's national morality, loyalty and filial piety are not ethical principles that transcend the nation-state, for the objects of these principles are the sacralized constituents of the *Kokutai* itself, including first of all the emperor and his ancestors. Thus employed, these principles do not permit adverse judgment or dissent against *Kokutai* doctrine, as the historians who spoke for a more scientific approach to the *Nanbuko-cho* historical problem learned in 1911–1912, and as the Christian writer and teacher Uchimura Kanzo learned when he provoked Inoue's ire by failing to bow before an image of the *Imperial Rescript on Education* at Tokyo High Middle School, in the famous *Lese Majeste* affair of January 1891. In a manner reminiscent of Rousseau, Inoue denounced the conscience-based dissent of Christians like Uchimura as instances of sectarian intolerance, directed at other religions, and against the sacred imperial cults and institutions of the *Kokutai*.[94]

Yet, as some commentators have pointed out, a certain theocratic dogmatism can also be detected in the practices Bellah associated with American civil religion, even if it has not established for itself the coercive political consensus of Meiji era Japan.[95] In American civil religion as Bellah interpreted it, ancestral figures such as the Founding Fathers or the war dead, and "scriptures" such as the Declaration of Independence and the Constitution, are themselves sacred.[96] Transcendental principles such as liberty and freedom of speech are supposed in principle to permit dissent or criticism against these sacred figures and texts, in distinction from the inviolable sacred constituents of the *Kokutai*. In practice, however, in American "culture war" controversies surrounding these sacred figures and texts, there is a vehemence in public denunciation of such dissent and criticism suggestive of state religion dogmatism. So long as such denunciation is confined to public-sphere exchange and free speech protections remain intact, it may be a moot point to speak of the "weakening" of such transcendental principles. Still, such bitter controversy reminds us again of the fuzzy line distinguishing civil from state religion.

The conceptual fuzziness and ambivalent intellectual history of the concept of civil religion does not rule decisively against its use. The lesson we can take from the dénouement of Inoue Tetsujirō's Confucianized national morality is that care must be taken in upholding the ideal of a Confucian civil religion in today's diverse East Asia—of upholding it in an atmosphere of competing nationalisms preoccupied with past victimhood and present cultural survival, which might co-opt this ideal. In today's geopolitical conditions, there is no gainsaying that the "precipitates" of Confucian tradition may yet again be refashioned in a potent, illiberal ideal of unified loyalty and filial piety to nation, projected outward in reactive, even hegemonic self-assertion. For today's advocates of a concept of civil religion who believe it is compatible with the actually existing pluralism within and between East Asian societies, the better option would be to recognize it as an "amalgam of traditions," including Confucianism.[97] Its definition would be guided not by felt needs for reactive self-definition against other nations, or against "Western" or "globalized" imports such as Christianity or individualism, but by inclusiveness of the actually existing diverse *and* shared ideals, aspirations, traditions, and collective memories of citizens within particular East Asian nations. The next two chapters, however, will consider political philosophical proposals for Confucian democracy in which Confucian norms and sentiments are assumed to play a rather more central role in the quotidian ethical lives of East Asians.

CHAPTER 6

Epistemic Elitism, Paternalism, and Confucian Democracy

The Diversity of Confucian Democracy Proposals

An interesting feature of English language discussion of Confucian thought is the range of arguments it has fielded for the compatibility between Confucianism and democracy. Some philosophers are trying to convince English-speaking audiences of this compatibility with blueprints for nonliberal democratic institutions that are adapted to the Confucian, communitarian traditions of East Asian countries. Others argue for a synthesis of pragmatist and Confucian political thought, which can yield democratic practices and values that are viable alternatives to liberal individualist concepts of democracy. Representative of the former group is Daniel Bell's suggestion for a representative democracy "with Confucian characteristics" in China, featuring an upper house of unelected officials of demonstrated moral and intellectual merit.[1] Representative of the latter group are thinkers such as David Hall, Roger Ames, and Tan Soor-hoon, who see common cause between classical Confucian ideals of moral cultivation in governance, and the democratic ideas of Western pragmatist philosophers such as John Dewey.[2]

Taking inspiration from Thomas Metzger,[3] I propose in this chapter to develop a fresh, *epistemic* critical perspective on arguments for Confucian democracy. This perspective highlights the epistemically elitist and paternalistic division of labor that pre-Qin Confucianism posits for governance: between leaders whose moral and intellectual cultivation qualifies them both to rule and to *know* the good of those whom they rule, and the masses who are ruled by them. Insofar as some contemporary Confucians reject or modify this division of labor in forging an alliance with Deweyan political philosophy, it must be asked whether the resulting philosophical syncretism retains recognizably Confucian or Deweyan partners. Insofar as this division of labor is accepted in other proposals for Confucian democracy, serious questions arise over their potential legitimacy in contemporary East Asia.

Epistemic Elitism and Paternalism in Pre-Qin Confucian Thought

A common thread running through English language discussion of Confucian political philosophy over the past twenty-five years is this: Economic and social modernization are advancing rapidly in East Asian societies, and their most important moral tradition, Confucianism, has been under attack for over a century by Eastern and Western critics, who have seen it as an obstacle to modernization. However, as we saw in chapter 1, contemporary Confucian philosophers such as Tu Weiming argue that this same tradition has helped shepherd East Asian modernization while ameliorating its negative effects, including egoism and materialism, income inequality, social injustice, and neglect of the vulnerable and the aged. The difficult task is to identify which aspects of Confucian tradition can be, or already have been, successfully adapted to manage modernizing conditions in East Asian societies, while at the same time being compatible with the growing democratic sensibilities of East Asians.

One path for developing a Confucian democratic philosophy taken by a recent generation of Confucian scholars writing in English such as Daniel Bell, David Hall, Roger Ames, and Tan Sor-hoon is to return to the pre-Qin era Confucian texts of Confucius and Mencius, which are untainted by later, legalist interpellations and by the state ideology that Confucianism became during the Han and later dynasties. The emphasis these works place on the importance of minimally coercive, mutually beneficial human relations as schools of moral cultivation, and on cultivated humaneness and merit (rather than birthright or might) as sources of legitimacy in governance, suggests some compatibility with democratic practices. Here, however, I am interested in whether extant notions of "Confucian-inspired" democracy are politically viable in contemporary East Asia and philosophically persuasive. In order to test for that viability and persuasiveness, I will first reconstruct three principles for elitist and paternalistic governance from Mencius and

Epistemic Elitism, Paternalism, and Confucian Democracy   165

then evaluate how much they are accommodated by different advocates of Confucian democracy today.

Book 3 of the *Mencius* famously refutes a contemporary thinker with Mencius, Xu Xing, who argued that rulers share in the physical labor of their subjects—and that there be no division of labor between rulers and ruled. Mencius invoked the precedents of past exemplary rulers and their ministers to justify a division of labor in political activity that had already been hinted at by Confucius:

> In the time of Yao, the Empire was not yet settled. The Flood still raged unchecked, inundating the Empire; plants grew thickly, birds and beasts multiplied; the five grains did not open; birds and beasts encroached on men. . . . The lot fell to Yao to worry about this situation. He raised Shun to a position of authority to deal with it. Shun put Yi in charge of fire. Yi set the mountains and valleys alight and burnt them, and the birds and beasts went into hiding. Yu dredged the Nine rivers, cleared the courses of the Chi and the T'a to channel the water into the Sea, deepened the beds of the Ju and the Han, and raised the dykes of the Huai and the Ssu to empty them into the River. Only then were the people of the Central Kingdoms able to find food for themselves.[4]

After noting how improved methods of cultivation introduced by the minister Hou Chi led to increased population and inadvertently to degeneracy and idleness, Mencius added that Yao "appointed Hsieh as Minister of Education whose responsibility was to teach the people human relationships: love between father and son, duty between ruler and subject, distinction between husband and wife, precedence of the old over the young, and faith between friends."[5]

In this passage Mencius asserts the legitimacy of rule by a morally and intellectually cultivated elite—a legitimacy grounded in their ability to master and engineer physical nature for the human good, and in their ability to rectify human nature through inculcation of the five human relationships (*wulun* 五伦) and their associated obligations and virtues.

We can note in passing the sophisticated argument by analogy behind the claim "that those who use their minds . . . rule" and "those who use their muscles . . . are ruled." Xu Xing's doctrine of individual self-sufficiency in the production of goods required the "wise ruler to share the work of tilling the land with his people." Against this, Mencius observed both that it was practically impossible for anyone, including Xu Xing, to be entirely self-sufficient in producing goods for their own needs. There is greater efficiency in the production and distribution of goods in a society where there is a division of labor between specialists in crafts and specialists in agriculture, who trade their products with one another. If everyone followed Xu Xing's doctrines, "the Empire (would) be led along the path of incessant toil."[6] Just as efficiency in the production and distribution of goods is made possible by a division of labor and specialization, so also the efficient rule of empires requires a class of morally and intellectually cultivated specialists who rule, separate from those "who are ruled" and who support the rulers with their labor.

Mencius's argument for elite governance complements Confucius's earlier assertion that those who "hold no rank in a state do not discuss its policies."[7] Confucius justified his exclusion of commoners from political deliberation through appeal to the ideals of social stability and centralization in governance, in accordance with the heavenly mandate (*tianming* 天命) for rulers: "When the way prevails under heaven, policy is not decided by Ministers; when the way prevails under heaven, commoners (*shuren* 庶人) do not discuss public affairs."[8] Confucius made ominously clear what would happen if the wrong people usurped the policymaking powers that properly belong to the rulers of a centralized state. In such circumstances, "the way does not prevail," the mandate of Heaven is withdrawn, and both dynasties and usurpers soon fall.

This raises the awkward question of how itinerant scholars like Confucius or Mencius could claim for themselves the privilege of speaking out on public affairs in the times when they were not holding any political office and were, in effect, commoners. Perhaps their argument would be that in times when the way *does not* prevail (and Confucius and Mencius certainly thought it did not prevail in their times), morally and intellectually cultivated commoners such as exemplary persons (*junzi*) not only can, but also must, speak out on public affairs in urging its restoration. They are therefore to be distinguished from those commoners who also comprise the masses (*min* 小人)—the masses are those who do not cultivate themselves morally or intellectually, and who are therefore never qualified at any time to speak out on public affairs.

We can summarize the principle for Confucian Elite Governance (CEG) thus: Governance is most efficient, most able to preserve social order and in accordance with the Mandate of Heaven, where there is a division of labor between those who, through demonstrated moral and intellectual excellence, are qualified to deliberate and rule for the public good, and those who are not qualified, and who are ruled.

CEG grounds what can be termed a strongly *perfectionist* conception of governance, in which it is the duty of rulers to promote the moral good of citizens or subjects. However, CEG does not make clear by itself what justification there is for believing that morally and intellectually excellent elite deliberators can *know* the public good and therefore deliberate effectively for it without much informational input from those whom they rule over—who, after all, have little or no say in public affairs. It does not furnish the epistemic grounds for thinking that such a division in intellectual labor in governance will be effective.

We should also note also that this perfectionism, at least in early Confucian thought, promotes a *comprehensive* doctrine of the good. It is comprehensive in John Rawls's sense of the word because it seeks, with the aid of a tradition of thought teaching the five primary relationships, the authoritative pronouncements of sages and the practice of rites, to rank and prescribe coherently the goods and virtues to be upheld in all spheres of human life.[9] It is comprehensive in the additional sense that its goal is the conformity of all citizens to "the way" exemplarily demonstrated by sage rulers and exemplary persons, and because it is intolerant of rival doctrines that teach different conceptions of the way.[10] Knowledge of the tradition that so comprehensively ranks moral goods and virtues and knowledge of how to uphold them in context-sensitive ways is no easy achievement.

Thomas Metzger[11] has pointed to a traditional "epistemic optimism" in Chinese society regarding the capacity of suitably cultivated elite deliberators to know the good of those on whose behalf they are deliberating, and to know the most effective means for exemplifying that good—and about the efficacy of meritocratic methods (such as rigorous public service examinations) for identifying such intellectually and morally excellent deliberators. Yet he is highly skeptical about the capacity of such elites to live up to this epistemic optimism in actual governance.[12]

In an analysis of status conflict in postwar Japanese society, political scientist Susan Pharr argues that in certain types of cultural circumstances elite deliberators may be capable of knowing and securing the good of the masses subject to their rule (as that good is understood by both), *without requiring much of their informational input.* Pharr writes the following about the governing methods of Japan's bureaucratic managers, business and political leaders in the post-1960 era of economic prosperity:

> [T]he cultural homogeneity of Japan is an important asset to authorities in carrying out their mandate. In a society where elites are not expected to be directly responsive to the public and where the direct articulation of grievances by social subordinates is discouraged, this homogeneity enables elites to understand and anticipate the needs of those subject to their authority.[13]

On this argument, the capacity of elite governments and bureaucracies to rule effectively without *much* informational input from their subordinates relies on—is contingent on—cultural homogeneity in values. Such homogeneity limits the range of needs, discontents, and expectations that superiors could conceivably have to know and anticipate from subordinates in well-functioning, stable hierarchical relationships.

Mencius's description of the benevolent ruler who knows intimately the "business of the people" and the agricultural, taxation, and educational policies needed to ensure their constancy provides an ancient precedent for the epistemic elitism Pharr describes above.[14] However, he did admit the need for wider consultation in more difficult circumstances, such as when a ruler deems it prudent to hear a wide range of opinions, including from commoners, before choosing advisors from lower social ranks or before deciding whether a death sentence is justified.[15]

In light of this, CEG can be supplemented with a more implicit, epistemic principle for Elite Governance Efficacy (EGE), a principle that is *not* specific to Confucian ideals of benevolent governance: In conditions of cultural homogeneity in values and conceptions of the good shared between elite rulers and their subordinates, the former can be reasonably expected to know, and deliberate effectively for, the latter's good without relying (much) on the latters' informational input.

However, this principle only justifies self-imposed restrictions on bottom-up information flow from the masses under elite governance. What of top-down information flow? In European, American, and East Asian liberal democracies, at least since the latter half of the twentieth century, an important component in governmental legitimacy is a willingness (making allowance for national security considerations) to be transparent about decision-making processes and the information lying behind them, to facilitate informed judgments by citizens on government decisions. This duty to "come clean," enforced by a vigilant press and civil society, has its counterpart in an important epistemic principle described by Alvin Goldman, which he describes as a corollary of the "requirement of total evidence" principle in inquiry:

If agent X is going to make a doxastic decision concerning question Q, and agent Y has control over the evidence that is provided to X, then, from a purely epistemic point of view, Y should make available to X all of the evidence relevant to Q that is (at negligible cost) within Y's control.[16]

However attractive this principle is, Goldman finds sound epistemic reasons for believing that in some instances Y is *not* under an obligation to divulge "all available evidence" to X, such as in legal settings where judges may exercise discretion on what evidence to release to jurors to help them decide the truth of a case. When Y "substitutes [his or her] wisdom for that of [X] in determining on epistemic grounds what, if any, evidence relevant to Q may be divulged to X, Y is practicing *epistemic paternalism*."[17] We could go further than Goldman and state that there is a *strong* variant of epistemic paternalism that extends to Y's determination, again on epistemic grounds, that X is not competent to "make a doxastic decision regarding question Q," and from which it follows that Y is not under an obligation to reveal to X any evidence relevant to the resolution of question Q.

Epistemic paternalism is obviously very relevant to a consideration of information transfer between rulers and ruled in early Confucian ideas of governance. Suppose we take at face value the epistemic optimism Confucianism traditionally entertains regarding "the capacity of elite deliberators to know the good of those on whose behalf they are deliberating, and to know the most effective means for achieving that good." Suppose we also take at face value Mencius's conviction that the masses are insufficiently cultivated to reflect morally on what they practice and Confucius's claim that they "are only able to follow the way rather than to understand it."[18] These convictions point to a presumption in favor of *strong* epistemic paternalism in Confucian governance. This presumption is hardly unique to Confucianism. But given the strength of epistemic optimism within Confucian thought and the political practice it influences, the presumption is not as contested as it has been in European political thought and practice since the late eighteenth century. We can state this principle for strong Epistemic Paternalism in Governance (EPG) thus: Insofar as elite rulers alone are morally and intellectually qualified to know and deliberate for the good of those whom they rule, they are not obliged to reveal to the latter information relevant to deliberating for that good.

Inasmuch as we accept that there are residual Confucian values in East Asia's developmentalist, bureaucrat-guided representative democracies (and this point is up for debate), we could say they are instances of democratic polities that tacitly "implement Confucian values"[19] and accommodate CEG, EGE, and (less often) EPG in moderate form. To that extent, the "Confucianism and democracy" compatibility argument can be settled.

What will be at issue here is not so much the overall compatibility of democracy and Confucianism as the persuasiveness and potential legitimacy of particular proposals for Confucian democracy. I will first evaluate proposals by Roger Ames and David Hall and Tan Sor-hoon that modify or reject the ideas connected with CEG, EGE, and EPG in favor of a Deweyan-Confucian democratic ideal. I will then consider one proposal for Confucian representative democracy by Daniel Bell that is more accommodating of CEG.

Confucian Role Ethics, Pragmatism, and Confucian Democracy

Proposals for a participatory Confucian/Deweyan democracy often incorporate the Confucian role ethics approach discussed in chapter 2, of which the roles in Mencius's five relations (*wulun*) are representative. Recall Mencius's descriptions of those five relations: of "love between father and son, duty between ruler and subject, distinction between husband and wife, precedence of the old over the young, and faith between friends." Each of them requires particular exercises of other-regarding conduct from their participants. In each of these relationships (excepting friendships) lower-ranked participants—sons, subjects, wives, and the young—will be disposed to respect the authority of the higher-ranked participants in return for the humaneness and beneficence of the latter. The filial obedience in sons' love for fathers and the fraternal obedience of younger for older brothers also provides a general pattern for morally correct behavior in subordinates toward their social superiors. In these relations, the practice of ritually prescribed duties in other-directed roles also provides the basis for moral self-cultivation.

However, for early Confucian thought there is also an arguably asymmetrical evaluation of the epistemic capacities of partners in these relations to know and deliberate for their own and others' good. In line with virtue epistemologists, I would argue that epistemic evaluation goes beyond verification of individual propositions to include what Lorraine Code has called "credibility-discerning and -establishing activities" of the epistemic characters of their agents.[20] In other words, we are more likely to trust as veridical the beliefs coming from agents we believe to be epistemically competent in the relevant field or domain. Applying the EGE and EPG principles in the context of Mencian ethics, we will find that it is the ruling partner in four of the five relationships—the father, husband, older brother, or prince who is best qualified, who in principle possesses "credible epistemic character" sufficient to be trusted to know the good of his dependents and deliberate for it. There seems little need for the deliberators in such relationships to pass on to their subordinates information that could help them to determine their own good, or (in the case of princes, say) to acquaint themselves respectfully with the dissenting beliefs of their ministers, let alone that the latter would feel entitled to offer them. On the face of it, this does not sit well with the more egalitarian commitments of John Dewey's political thought.

Many Confucian scholars will object to this reduction of the five relationships to relations of power, uncritical obedience, and epistemic deference—and to the suggestion that Mencius's division of labor between elite rulers and the ruled replicates such relations. Tu Weiming has argued that critics of Confucianism often focus their ire on the *three* relationships (*san gang* 三綱) between ministers and kings, husbands and wives, and sons and fathers that Confucianism promoted as a state ideology during the Han Dynasty. Those critics then erroneously represent the three relationships as *the* Confucian conception of morally rectified social relations. The politicised Confucian representation of these three relationships aimed at maintaining social stability rather than "the well-being of individual persons in these dyadic relationships," and emphasised power, hierarchy, and "one-way obedience." Mencius's earlier emphasis on the duty of superiors to subordinates and his "spirit of mutuality" in the five relationships was obscured in this state ideology.[21]

In Tu's idea of "the self as the centre of relationships," the five relationships permit mutual moral cultivation for all their members through the practice of filial piety, humaneness, justice, and ritual propriety in fulfilling their duties to other members, and at different times of their lives people may assume both subordinate or leadership roles in relation to others. Criticisms of Confucianism often highlight how it has reduced women to domestic servitude. Yet the *Tao Yao* (桃夭) poem in the *Book of Poetry* provides a more flexible understanding of their domestic roles, emphasizing both a bride's fertility and her aptness for household management: "The peach tree is young and elegant; / Abundant will be its fruits. / This young lady is going to her future home, / And will order well her house and chamber."[22]

It is incorrect, then, to claim that people are locked into immoveable, hierarchical relations in these roles, and that evaluations of their epistemic character will be impervious to their growing experience in comprehending and acting for the good of others. Even if CEG, EGE, and EPG justify inequality in deliberative roles in these relationships, anyone who lives a reasonably full life will get his or her chance to acquire knowledge of, and act beneficently for, the good of others across different relationships. This point will hold for both men and for women in any kind of role in which they deliberate for the good of others, such as younger siblings or their children. An exemplary person or sage such as Confucius or Mencius would stand out, however, in her cultivated abilities as parent, scholar, teacher, or minister to realize the widest range of moral and material goods for others.

For his part, Tu acknowledges that no sharp division exists between the mutuality embodied in Mencius's concept of the five relationships and the authoritarian three bonds later Confucianism promoted. He pleads merely that critics not "misinterpret the five relationships" in light of the historically well-attested, oppressive consequences of the three bonds embodied in traditional Chinese social practices.[23]

Some contemporary critics of Confucianism, such as Ci Jiwei, have not been impressed by such subtle distinctions between the three bonds and the five relationships, noting that for *both* the familial practice of filial piety "serves as the training ground for loyal obedience (*zhong*) in the hierarchical relation between the ruler and his subjects."[24] There is indeed a good deal of tolerance for "one-way obedience" even in Mencius's treatment of filial relations. Thus while "love between father and son" implies a degree of mutual affection, as we have already seen, Mencius also stressed the importance of filial obedience in the face of parental violence, holding up Shun's forbearance for his filicide-inclined father as an example. For his part, Confucius famously emphasized the character-forming benefits of such obedience for loyal subjects in states.

Contemporary Confucians claim that the practice of remonstrance by social inferiors to their superiors is a means for blocking the degeneration of the five relationships into "one-way obedience." As an ideal, it provided valuable models for ministers or itinerant scholars trying to rein in the avarice and militarism of princes, and for humbleness in superiors trying to better themselves by heeding their subordinates' exhortations. Yet the way early Confucianism hems in remonstrance with mollifying ritual gestures—to the point where a parent threatening his neighbors is free to beat the son who entreats him not to do so until he draws blood—suggests how fragile this barrier to one-way obedience is.[25]

Another key vulnerability for Tu's distinction between the five and three relationships lies in the husband-wife relation, which is characterized by mutuality in his Mencian interpretation.[26] Unfortunately for Tu's progressive views on marital relations, Mencius's own understanding of the wife's duty to her husband leaves little to distinguish their relation from the manner in which it is conceived in the three bonds, as a fixed, hierarchical relationship that permits its subordinate party only limited powers of deliberation and a limited sphere to exercise them in—namely, the household chambers mentioned in the *Tao Yao* poem: "'When you go to your new home, be respectful and circumspect. Do not disobey your husband.' It is the way of the wife or concubine to consider obedience and docility the norm."[27]

What basis is there for a philosophical alliance between this ethics and Dewey's democratic political and moral philosophy? It seems that Dewey's apparent antipathy for liberal individualism and his invocation of terms like "Great Community" makes that alliance possible. Not only are liberal ideals of individual rights and personal autonomy absent from the ancient Confucian texts, those ideals are also explicitly criticized in most modern reconstructions of Confucian ethics as a role ethics. However, the common run of liberal opinion in the West is that individualism, autonomy, and democracy are conceptually interdependent. Without individualism or autonomy, democracy becomes impossible. For different advocates of Confucian democracy, these conceptual connections are dissoluble. Some contemporary Confucians will point to those successful democracies in East Asia that have supposedly incorporated Confucian values of paternalism and elitism into governance, promoted the continuance of communitarian values, and discouraged individualistic conduct. But for those Confucians who reject paternalism and who are sympathetic to Dewey's thought there is a different point to make. They will argue that Western liberals typically forget that in Western philosophical traditions there are advocates of democracy like John Dewey who are critical of liberal individualism.

For Dewey's Confucian sympathizers such as Tan Soor-hoon, Dewey's ideal of participatory democracy as a "Great Community," in which citizens are educated to participate in co-operative inquiry into the problems thrown up by communal living in a large-scale society, also provides a modern home for Confucian moral cultivation.[28]

The epistemically egalitarian, participatory conception of democracy that Dewey developed does pose some difficulties for this democratic Confucian-pragmatist alliance. Dewey's 1927 book *The Public and Its Problems* is a key work of political philosophy for Confucians attracted to his thought. Dewey makes an *egalitarian* argument for articulate, public involvement in inquiry into social affairs affecting its welfare, stating his opposition to "rule by those intellectually qualified, by expert intellectuals."[29] Perhaps this is a position that his Confucian admirers can live with. Most important for them is that *The Public and Its Problems* criticizes a liberalism that conceptualizes individuals as possessed of natural rights in separation from and in tension with associational life, and that fixates on an artificial argument over the struggle for the liberties of the "individual" against "collectivity."[30]

Yet it is going too far to claim, as Roger Ames does, that "[t]here is an absence in both Confucianism and Dewey of many of the prerequisites for liberal democracy . . ." and that in Dewey's communitarian democratic ideal "the greatest guarantees of human liberty are not the entitlements guaranteed by rights-talk, but a flourishing community, and where liberty is not the absence of constraint, but full participation in self-governance."[31] To see why he is going too far, we need only consider what Dewey says about his key concept of *publicity*. Dewey defined publicity in *The Public and Its Problems* as "freedom of social inquiry and of distribution of its conclusions . . . in respect to all consequences which concern (the public)"[32] Publicity was, for Dewey, the precondition for "articulate publics," publics with a "common interest in the consequences of social transactions" that are informed by freely conducted social inquiry and deliberate over applying its conclusions to the problems of community life.[33]

Dewey thought that one of the great prerequisites for publicity is the rather liberal-looking "freedom of expression."[34] Dewey would have been comfortable terming this a *right* to be held by all mentally competent persons, even if he disagreed with classical liberal conceptualizations of this right. Dewey embraced both the ideals of a "flourishing community"[35] *and* a reconstructed conception of "entitlements guaranteed by rights-talk" as mutually reinforcing prerequisites for freedom. So in a later book, *Freedom and Culture*, he proposed to update Jeffersonian ideals of *natural* law and rights as the *moral* values and rights of democracy. Rights would be the outcome of concerted intellectual and political effort rather than being the antecedent properties of individuals.[36] It is true that he also objected to a merely negative freedom, involving removal of "formal limitations" on speech, since it is insufficient for full freedom of expression. Positive freedom involves—to the fullest extent possible—active public participation in deliberation over public affairs, through which its members can develop "the ability to judge of the bearing of the knowledge supplied by (expert inquirers) on common concerns."[37] Still, negative freedom remained for Dewey a necessary component for securing *full* freedom of expression, even if by itself it is not sufficient.

Dewey believed that stable community associations, beginning with the family, are the nurturers of intellectual skill for participating in dialogue over public affairs.[38] There is a resemblance with the Confucian ethical idea of family relations as the loci for moral cultivation. Yet there are also profound differences with pre-Qin Confucianism over the freedoms required by Deweyan publicity that cannot be ignored. For Deweyan freedom of expression would admit the equal opportunity of *all* mentally competent adults to participate in public policy deliberation: the uninformed, the morally uncultivated, and those who erroneously think themselves the intellectual equals of all others, alongside those who are expert, informed, and morally cultivated. It holds out the (perhaps forlorn) hope that the latter can exercise an educative influence on the former. This is the ethical individualist kernel in the Deweyan ideal of publicity. It protects freedom of expression for all rationally competent adults, as a necessary condition for their participation in public deliberation, and does not exclude them from participation on the basis of comprehensive doctrines that identify only certain morally or intellectually qualified individuals as competent to deliberate for the public good.

Deweyan publicity, together with its egalitarian prerequisite of freedom of expression, is clearly opposed to the CEG, EGE, and EPG principles. Against CEG it asserts the entitlement of ordinary members of the public to participate in deliberation over policy affecting their affairs; against EGE it asserts that governance is *not* efficient without informational and evaluative input from the public into public policy formation and application; and against EPG it requires transparency in the distribution to the public of data relevant to deliberation over public policy.

Dewey did not advocate an ideal of public participation in which everyone is equally expert, however. Genuine experts such as scientists, scholars, and bureaucratic policymakers have a role to play in identifying problems, initiating inquiries into them, and publishing their findings and proposals.[39] But Dewey's idea of an "articulate public" also places epistemically demanding expectations on ordinary citizens to comprehend those findings and proposals (once they have been conveyed to the public in more generally comprehensible means by the mass media) and evaluate their applicability in resolving complex political, social, and economic problems.

Ames's conception of Confucian democracy would be ambivalent about a full rejection of CEG, EGE, and EPG. This ambivalence is revealed in his considerations of the role the exemplary person plays in a "ritualized living" that he thinks can enrich the Deweyan ideal of community. In such ritualized living, "from the family expanding outward . . . (exemplary) persons . . . emerge as objects of profound communal, cultural, and ultimately religious deference."[40] Now in pre-Qin Confucianism, it is exemplary persons who are best qualified to cultivate knowledge of moral values and the capacity to deliberate from them, cultivating the good on behalf of themselves, family dependents, and subjects of the state. Confucians such as Ames find repugnant the liberal individualism that envisages *all* citizens, whatever their moral or intellectual cultivation, enjoying personal liberties to live out their own conceptions of the good life, without any deference to the exemplary person's own claims to know and deliberate for it. It is true that Dewey despaired of liberal individualism too, observing how out of kilter it is with the vast, impersonal institutional forces that govern actual people's lives, hemming in their exercise of liberties and preferences and keeping them in the grip of "inertia, prejudices and emotional partisanship."[41]

Nevertheless, a Deweyan democrat would recoil at the elevated place that Ames assigns to the exemplary person in a reformed community life. For Ames, the ideal intellectual marketplace resembles a *gemeinschaft* bound by ritual norms in which the relatively uncultivated know (without being coerced) to listen deferentially "to those in society possessed of true excellence."[42] However, the practice of ritualized deference he advocates must surely count as a dampener on publicity and on public deliberation over expert inquiry, and is at odds with the *symmetrical* model of argumentative deference ritual outlined in chapter 3. In particular, it is hard to see how persons immersed in deferential, ritualized relations with exemplary persons can attain to that occasional divesting of and critical examination of intellectual habits and beliefs that Dewey thought essential for "intelligent furthering of culture."[43] For such a process of reflection would require intellectual detachment of the individual from the primary experience of ritually governed roles in asymmetrical deference relationships, where a sense of cultivated spontaneity rather than calculating reflection is dominant. In short, ritualized reverence and "profound deference" to the exemplary person *does not* find a comfortable place within the Deweyan great community, in which ordinary citizens critically and robustly evaluate different expert policy proposals for resolving problems in community life.

For her part, Tan Sor-hoon has much more unambiguously repudiated the ideas associated with CEG, EGE, and EPG, arguing that the elitist, paternalistic and sexist practices and attitudes attributed to Confucianism by its critics are not integral to it. Thus, Confucianism can emancipate itself from an exclusionary, elitist conception of *who* should govern.[44]

Tan's vision is for a flexible, adaptive form of Confucianism in which values such as filial piety or loyalty actualize themselves flexibly in context-sensitive ways, and are treated as derivative of more fundamental Confucian notions of "*ren, li* and *yi*."[45] So in modernized social, contexts, out-of-date conceptions of filial piety will be revised, losing the patriarchal and paternalistic trappings it once had. Tan is wary of political perfectionism, however, and her pluralism in the identification and ranking of Confucian values is combined with the conviction that government and citizens can jointly realize a common good in "free discussions."[46]

This notion of a positive if not perfectionist governmental role in fostering the good life, and the view that liberal individualism, in placing "the isolated individual above the community" and encouraging an "ethos and ethic of aggressive self-assertions,"[47] is not at home in Asian cultural contexts disposes Tan to be sympathetic to communitarian "internal critiques" of liberalism. However, her goal is ultimately a balance between liberal and communitarian views of the individual and society.[48]

It should not be forgotten, though, that an "ethic of aggressive self-assertions" that puts the defiant individual at odds with the community has proven attractive to East Asian intellectuals. The Chinese writers of the May the 4th Movement come readily to mind in this respect. We have also seen how the Japanese bluestockings of *Seitō* journal had shaken Japanese society with their impassioned arguments for women's intellectual and creative freedoms, their practice of free love, and their increasingly politicized attacks on the modernized patriarchal family system, embodied in the ideal of *ryōsai kenbo*, or "good wife and wise mother." As I argued in chapter 2, Confucianism perfectionism might construe these feminists' rejection of filial obedience and their attempts to overturn "traditional" gender roles as an unreasonable attack on the moral goods of the family.

Supporters of a moderate, non-elitist Confucianism like Tan might try to incorporate this feminism into their reconstructed Confucian/Deweyan vision. For them, such feminists would represent a *junzi*-like ideal of self-cultivation put at the service of a feminist reconstruction of morality. A feminist *junzi*'s self-cultivation can authoritatively establish a *feminist* community, developing moral ideas at odds with those of wider society. However, rather than isolating themselves in individualistic defiance of social convention, such feminists can end up establishing a transformative relation to it. In cultivating themselves in innovative ways, they experience constraint by their social environment, and are provoked to reform it.⁴⁹ Perhaps in this way the disencumbered self discussed in chapter 2 can, as it were, return to the fold with a vision for more just relations between men and women.

Hiratsuka Raichō could be viewed as representing this vision. In her 1913 manifesto "The New Woman" *Atarashii Onna* 新しい女, published in defiance of growing public censure of the *Seitō* 青鞜 women, she appropriated for her "New Woman" ideal a famous proverb on self-cultivation from section six of the Confucian classic *The Great Learning (Da Xue* 大學): "An ancient Chinese emperor's motto says: 'if just one day you can renew yourself, then day by day renew yourself, you will renew yourself every day.'"

But then, in a vehement denunciation of this same tradition, which takes the sage kings of the past as its models for exemplary conduct, Hiratsuka added:

> The New Woman brings down a curse on "yesterday." The New Woman will not endure to be someone who silently walks the way of the oppressed, old fashioned woman (*furui onna* 古い女). The New Woman is not satisfied with a feminine existence reduced to ignorance, to slavery, to being a mere slab of meat for the sake of male egoism. The New Woman hopes to destroy the old morals and laws (*furuki dōtoku, hōritsu* 古き道徳、法律) created for the sake of male convenience . . . day by day (she) . . . strives to create a new kingdom, with a new creed, a new morality and a new law.⁵⁰

Hiratsuka's iconoclasm is representative of the uncompromising rejection by early East Asian feminists of the remnants of familial Confucian morality in their time, and of state ideologies such as *ryōsai kenbo* that cherry-picked Confucian ideas and incorporated them into modernized gender roles. Deweyan pragmatism can embrace their standpoint, as an instance of that individual agency that is the origin of "[e]very *new* idea, every conception of things differing from that offered authorized by current belief," reconstructing "accepted beliefs" even as it faces the threat of suppression in "a society governed by custom."⁵¹

But can a reconstructed Confucianism embrace the personal autonomy that Hiratsuka and other early Asian feminists fought for, which is now unreflectively taken for granted in the individualized life choices of many young, educated East Asian women, and remain recognizably Confucian? For this concept of autonomy, all mentally competent women are in principle capable, through deliberation, of coming to *know* and act reflectively for their own good.

I think that it would want to, but this would be reason to doubt its Confucian credentials. For the central problem here is that the exclusion of paternalism and elitism from Tan's Confucian/Deweyan democratic ideal—the rejection of CEG, EGE, and EPG—would eliminate the politically perfectionist rationale of a classical Confucian ethics of self-cultivation centered on the exemplary person, who acts for the good of his own family as a father and for the good of the subjects of a state as a minister: the "gentleman (*junzi*) cultivates in himself the capacity to be diligent in his tasks . . . He cultivates in himself the capacity to ease the lot of other people . . . He cultivates in himself the capacity to ease the lot of the whole populace."[52]

Hiratsuka's New Woman individualism stands squarely in opposition to this rationale for the Confucian exemplary person—in seeking to know and deliberate for her own good, she rejects the paternalistic beneficence of others who would define and act for her good on her behalf within the five relationships, as parents, older male siblings, husbands, parents-in-law, or the ministers of a state. This rejection, we might feel, is based on a correct assessment of the rottenness of the familial morality and state gender ideology of *that time*, which cloaked male egoism and a patriarchal modernizing agenda with Confucian platitudes. Tan's more pluralistic, reformed Confucian morality would also share in this rejection. But to the extent that elitism and paternalism themselves are also rejected, the result will be a reformed (and undoubtedly attractive) morality, a morality with undoubted Confucian inspirations, that is no longer recognizably Confucian.

Neither Dewey's conception of an "articulate public," nor Hiratsuka's New Woman ideal could accept this elitism and paternalism. Nor would Tan accept it. Her arguments for an alliance between Deweyan democratic philosophy and a reconstructed, egalitarian, and broadly feminist friendly Confucianism are unpersuasive to the extent that the latter loses its distinctive Confucian character in being thus reconstructed.[53]

Confucian Elite Governance and Democracy "With Confucian Characteristics"

Daniel Bell's proposal for a bicameral political system that limits non-elite participation in politics retains something of classical Confucianism's ideal of governance by persons of demonstrated moral and intellectual virtue, remaining in this sense true to the *telos* of classical Confucian ethical cultivation. In contrast to Ames and Tan, Bell proposes a more definitive blueprint for Confucian democratic institutions. This blueprint draws some inspiration from elite bureaucrat-led forms of government in East Asia, as well as from Western economic and judicial institutions staffed by unelected, expert officials.[54]

Bell's proposal for a "democracy with Confucian characteristics" for China combines an electoral system for the selection of political leadership in a lower parliamentary house with a rigorous exam-based system for the selection of morally and intellectually cultivated members for an upper house of policy review, which has veto power over legislative proposals by the lower house. He has variously referred to the upper house as a "House of Scholars" and as a *Xianshiyuan* (賢士院). He has also suggested an alternative role for the *xianshiyuan* as the dominant decision-making body, with the lower, democratically elected house restricting itself to the transmission of the "people's (relatively uninformed) preferences" to the upper house. Bell thinks a proposal like his own has a reasonable chance of uptake in a country such as China, where ordinary people still hold to "the idea of respect for rule by an educated elite."[55] However, recently Bell has distanced himself from this proposal, arguing instead for a "vertical model" of governance, with democracy practiced at the local government level, while meritocratic political institutions are responsible for central government.[56] Unlike his earlier bicameral model, Bell thinks that this model does align to some degree with an actually existing, if still evolving, vertical system of governance in China, and that it does not suffer the potential legitimacy problems Bell now acknowledges in his bicameral proposal.[57] Nevertheless, given its affinities with some liberal arguments for meritocratic political institutions and my own interest in assessing the contribution of Confucian ideas to liberal political philosophy, I will give more consideration to Bell's earlier bicameral model here.

Bell's is not the only proposal for a multicameral democratic political system incorporating Confucian characteristics. Joseph Chan has outlined a similar bicameral system for a representative democracy, but distrusts an examination method that would select "political beginners" whose capacities for virtue are relatively untested and unknown by their peers. Chan opts instead for a selection process by which "seasoned participants in public service" in the courts, legislatures, civil service, administrative service, and diplomacy would be chosen by their peers and possibly by other distinguished people who work with them. Chan's upper house would have powers of legislative review in relation to the lower, popularly elected house, though the extent of its powers would vary according to the "level of virtue and competence of the citizenry."[58]

The Chinese Confucian scholar Jiang Qing's proposal for a tricameral Confucian political system has also lately been translated into English. Jiang proposes a House of Scholars (*Tongru Yuan* 通儒院) much like Bell's, though composed of *Confucian* scholars; a democratically elected "House of the People" (*Shumin Yuan* 庶民院); and a "House of the Nation" (*Guoti Yuan* 国体院) standing for the cultural continuity of China, led in hereditary fashion by a descendant of Confucius, and containing descendants of great Chinese leaders, retired officials, other worthy people, and representatives of the main religions in China.[59]

In this system, Confucianism would be a state religion. However, Jiang does not identify his proposed political system as democratic.[60] Such a lack of identification puts his proposal largely beyond the critical purview of this chapter, though I will return to it occasionally in the following discussion. Also, since Chan's model differs only in its selection methods from Bell's, and Bell has offered more detailed descriptions of his proposed upper house across different publications, I will focus more on Bell's model from this point.

One more thing does need to be said about the "Confucian" characteristics of these diverse proposals. Stephen Angle has stated that "putting virtuous and talented people into positions of power is a Confucian goal,"[61] but it has also been a goal for some liberal thinkers. So Joseph Chan has identified an affinity between his version of an unelected upper chamber of legislative review, its virtuous deliberators chosen by peer recommendation in accordance with "Confucian ideas of selection," and John Stuart Mill's nineteenth-century proposal for a House of Statesmen.[62]

Bell has also recognized affinities between proposals for meritocratic political institutions in liberal thought and his Confucian-based proposal for such an institution. As he notes, in the 1980s the classical liberal economist Friedrich Hayek presented a model for a parliamentary upper house to conduct legislative and administrative rule oversight, composed of people "who have proved themselves in the ordinary business of life" chosen to serve fifteen-year periods, at the age of forty-five, by regional caucuses of their age peers.[63] A common denominator in these proposals, Confucian or liberal, is a fear of the despotism of the unchecked, ill-informed "ascendency of the majority" in electoral politics.[64] From Bell's or Chan's point of view, this could be seen as one of those happy coincidences where a proposed ideal or policy, far from reflecting the parochial views of one "comprehensive doctrine," is in fact compatible with "a great many such doctrines," liberal or not.[65] This coincidence in opinion should also serve as a reminder that, contrary to contemporary belief, liberalism and democracy are not always easy partners. There is also something more than a coincidence of opinion between liberals and Confucians urging a meritocratic system for selecting government officials. The use of examinations in the selection of public officials in Western European nations commenced only in the nineteenth century, following the recommendations of eighteenth- and nineteenth-century scholars who had studied the Chinese *keju* system.[66] The discussion and criticisms that follow will be applied to Confucian-inspired proposals for a multicameral parliament like Chan's and Bell's, but they can be applied to liberal versions of such proposals as well.

Bell talks up the democratic credentials of his proposal by stating that external monitoring of the *xianshiyuan* can take place through mass media investigation and scrutiny, and through the public raising of grievances. The deliberations of the *xianshiyuan* would be broadcast on television and the internet to facilitate public understanding and scrutiny.[67] Bell's proposal would involve acceptance of CEG, preserving the ideal that governance is most effective when the intellectually and morally cultivated govern on behalf of the less cultivated. Still, its acceptance of a need for transparency of the *xianshiyuan*'s deliberations to media and civil society scrutiny, and of bottom-up transference of the public's preferences via the elected representatives of a lower house, suggests a partial rejection of EGE and EPG.

Serious questions must be raised, however, about the legitimacy of CEG in a contemporary East Asian context. CEG relies for its legitimacy on elite deliberators demonstrating that they possess sufficient moral and epistemic excellence in knowing, deliberating for, and securing the public good to justify the public's epistemic-moral optimism (in other words, its faith) in their governance. The important question in increasingly pluralistic societies is whether such deliberators *can* know enough to deliberate effectively for the public good. More particularly in East Asian societies with a Confucian history, there is the further question of whether attributions of intellectual and moral virtue to those deliberators can survive scrutiny by increasingly educated and media savvy citizens.

For one thing, the homogeneous value commitments identified in EGE as supporting elite knowledge of and efficacy in securing the good of subordinates are fading away in East Asia. Growing value pluralism is the product of changed social conditions and prosperity fostered by the very modernizing economic policies that East Asian political elites have pursued since 1945. In Japan, Taiwan, and South Korea, where postwar developmental goals have been substantially achieved, the relative homogeneity in values between elite bureaucrats, business organizations, and deferential citizens that make EGE practicable can no longer be counted on. Alternately intimidated or attracted by the prospects of economic globalization, different interest groups are now articulating sharply divergent needs and grievances that complicate national policy formation.[68] Feminist and environmentalist movements have emerged to express protests that conservative bureaucratic and political leaders seem ill-equipped to anticipate, let alone accommodate. Government exhortations to citizens to maintain traditional filial piety practices, and laws penalizing unfilial behavior, face opposition from young people and elderly welfare groups who oppose such government interference.[69]

At a deeper level, a number of national crises have exposed the limits of the top-down, bureaucracy-guided national policymaking characteristic of the East Asian developmental model, a model that scholars such as Tu Weiming and Daniel Bell see as the legatee of Confucian ideals of good governance. Tu has written of an "ever-expanding network of human-relatedness" fostered by particularistic Confucian values such as loyalty and deference, allowing East Asian elites to rally citizens behind developmental policies that achieved substantial economic and welfare goods. He has also praised the "internal cohesion" that relegates "to the background" the obstructive, adversarial relationships associated with American civil society.[70]

Following the Fukushima Daiichi nuclear power plant meltdowns after Japan's 2011 earthquake and tsunami, independent investigations revealed the darker side of an "ever-expanding network of human-relatedness" cultivated in Japan's bureaucracy-led nuclear power policy: bureaucrats, government ministers, industry leaders, electricity utility management, scientists, the mass media, and the rural communities hosting nuclear power plants were implicated in a deeply insular system of collusion and patronage, nicknamed "The Nuclear Village" (*Genshiryoku mura* 原子力村). This system enabled regulatory capture, incompetent observation of safety standards, and deceptive reporting of safety lapses. At the same time, dissenting scientific, activist, and media voices who could have encouraged stricter regulatory oversight and infrastructure improvements were "relegated to the background" by "internally cohesive," epistemically insular networks of bureaucrats, power utility management, and the scientists and engineers in their pay.[71]

What implications do these failures have for Bell's proposal for an unelected, meritocratic *xianshiyuan* in China? In the modernized Confucian ideal of societal harmony in the pursuit of a national good determined by a highly educated, unelected elite, that elite can no longer carry the burden of exemplary virtue that Confucians would expect of it. In the conditions of increasing publicity in democratic East Asia, both in conventional media and social network services, and even in the limited conditions for such publicity in China, epistemic and moral failures in governmental responses to national crises are now rapidly exposed and investigated, and the results of such investigation are widely publicized.

The lesson is that the political perfectionism in paternalistic, elite governance is vulnerable to falsification. In the Confucian classics, the exemplary persons and sages are either the rare ministers and sage kings of the past who knew and acted for the good of their kingdoms, or the itinerant scholar-officials such as Confucius, the lonely possessors of humaneness continually frustrated by its absence in the society they saw around them. Yet if, after all, the moral and intellectual cultivation of an exemplary person is a difficult attainment, leaving a majority of superiors and rulers falling short in knowing the good of their subordinates, and if modern conditions of publicity render rulers' epistemic and moral failings so much more transparent to the public than in the past, we can expect a growth in epistemic pessimism that makes the legitimacy of elitist and paternalistic rule harder to sustain. In fact, support for paternalistic governance is in decline in *democratizing* East Asian societies.[72]

Indeed, some of the optimistic predictions Bell and Jiang make about the epistemic and moral excellence of the House of Scholars' appointees do not stand up well to scrutiny. Both hold that democratically leaders, bound by limited electoral terms and the preferences of electoral majorities, have incentives to promote short-term economic gain over electorally unpopular environmental protection policies, and to neglect protection of unpopular minorities as well as the interests of future generations.[73] Appointees to Bell's *xianshiyuan* or Jiang's House of Scholars, possessed of proven intellectual and moral merit and immune to electoral pressure, will have the leeway to propose robust environmental policies and protect the interests of minorities and of future generations.

Given the lack of precedents for a *xianshiyuan* or House of Scholars, these arguments are rather difficult to evaluate. Still, claims about the *xianshiyuan* members' environmentalist acumen do seem discordant both with the traditional Confucian literature and with the environmental protection record of premodern scholar-ministers and Asian developmental state bureaucracies. Jiang holds that environmental protection is a moral value connected with the transcendent, "sacred legitimacy" of the Way of Heaven, which opposes a popular democratic will seeking domination of the natural environment.[74]

However, Mencius was quite explicit in praising rulers who could *master* physical nature with land clearance and infrastructure programs to provide food and economic security for their subjects.[75] By the eighteenth century, the scholar-ministers of imperial China had become very successful in living up to this ideal. But their dam, irrigation, and agricultural improvement projects also left a legacy of disastrous environmental degradation for the twentieth century. This suggests that they possessed no greater foresight, nor sensitivity, to ecological issues than the democratically elected European and American governments that presided over tremendous environmental despoliation in the course of late nineteenth- and twentieth-century industrialization.[76]

I would add that in the developmental states of post-1945 East Asia, environmental protection was hardly on the minds of elite bureaucrats and politicians until civil society groups emerged in the 1980s to bring the environmental consequences of rapid economic modernization to public notice.[77] Both Bell and Jiang practically ignore the historical record of civil society movements in both East Asian and European representative democracies that have educated and mobilized the public on issues such as environmental conservation and minority rights.

Doubts must be raised about the legitimacy of a modified application of CEG even in China's case. As noted, Bell thinks China has more fertile ground for acceptance of a democracy guided by unelected, meritocratically selected officials, and "[i]n East Asian societies with a Confucian heritage, where the good of the family has been regarded as the key to the good life for two millennia . . . [m]ost people have devoted their time and energy to family and other 'local' obligations, with political decision-making left to an educated, public-spirited elite."[78]

This claim has been disproven by the explosive development of democratization and "public-spirited" civil society movements in South Korea, Taiwan, and Hong Kong between the early 1970s and the 1990s. In the civil society sectors of these countries we can see a foreshadowing of likely challenges to the legitimacy of a *xianshiyuan* if it is ever implemented in China, alongside the press freedoms and institutionally mandated transparency that Bell recommends. Hong Kong is an instructive example. Bell himself has acknowledged the lack of legitimacy in its less than democratic political system.[79] But he underestimates both the degree of popular sentiment for a full franchise and evidence of increasing public demands for participation in public policy deliberation.[80] In all likelihood, most Hong Kong citizens would not be satisfied with a bicameral system in which only one house is directly elected.

But why in the end does Bell want to meld democratic rule with rule by "Confucian exemplary persons" if he is so pessimistic about the deliberative capacities of ordinary citizens? He gives two reasons: First, democratic practices of transparency and accountability for public officials are needed because of documented failures in bureaucracies insulated from public oversight. Second, regimes that do not give to citizens "the symbolic ritual of free and fair elections" have trouble maintaining their legitimacy.[81]

Bell only barely acknowledges one more legitimating reason—that democracy *in theory* facilitates civil society forums for citizen participation, to express, exchange, and modify their views about public policymaking and to deliberate over alternative policy measures. Acknowledging this third reason, however, sets up a potential conflict with the *xianshiyuan* members' own exercise of their deliberative prerogatives, and the same could be said for Joseph Chan's proposed upper house of virtuous, exemplary veterans of public service. What if civil society groups and ordinary citizens not only criticize their decisions, but also question their authority and relevance, and actively compete with them in policy deliberation? One option for cutting off these sorts of tactics would be to regulate dissent, discouraging ill-informed or antiauthority expression directed against the *xianshiyuan* or upper house. Jiang Qing seems to favor these measures.[82] Such measures would involve some coercive realization of EGE and EPG—certain disharmonious, morally uncultivated, or uninformed agents would be excluded from public policy discussion, and the *xianshiyuan* or upper house would be allowed some discretion in what aspects of its deliberations, and the policy inquiries lying behind them, should be released to the public.

In this way the *xianshiyuan*'s or upper house's control of public policy deliberation could be maintained, and those unqualified to deliberate marginalized. Bell opposes these sorts of restrictions, understanding that the *xianshiyuan*'s legitimacy would be undermined if it too often opposed the majority will,[83] and I am pretty sure that Chan would oppose such restrictions too. But then the dilemma for their constitutional proposals is this: they can either minimize the deliberative participation of the masses, remaining true to CEG, EGE, and EPG but risk undermining the legitimacy of the upper house or *xianshiyuan*, or they can accept the legitimacy of citizen participation and deliberation in politics, in which case both the legitimacy and relevance of the upper house or *xianshiyuan* will be open to contestation. Indeed, Bell has lately acknowledged that the legitimacy of his proposed unelected meritocratic chamber would be progressively undermined in any political system where at least some political leaders are chosen by "one person, one vote,"[84] and this motivated the change of mind that led him to advocate a "vertical" model of governance.

An Epistemically Elitist and Paternalist Counterargument

I am aware that many of the arguments I have marshalled so far against CPG, EGE, and EPG are partially or wholly empirical in character. To the extent that we can demonstrate, historically or through political scientific analysis, that elitist, paternalistic, and perfectionist governance is failing or has failed, the above-mentioned epistemic pessimism is warranted, and support for nonpaternalistic, non-elitist, and possibly nonperfectionist governance can be advocated as more suitable for pluralistic societies.

However, advocates of mixed Confucian or liberal constitutional government incorporating epistemic elitist and paternalist principles could still flexibly adjust their arguments to these empirically-based arguments. They could grant that citizens of postindustrial societies may be more diverse in their creeds, better educated, demanding nonpaternalistic respect and restraint from authority-holding officials. Consciousness of the moral and epistemic fallibility of such officials may also be higher in such societies, as stated above. More strongly paternalistic, perfectionist governance may well fail to acquire or sustain legitimacy in such circumstances.

Confucian or liberal advocates of a meritocratic upper house may then adjust their expectations about the powers that its officials can exercise in more pluralistic societies with more highly-educated citizens. Their powers in these kinds of societies may, by custom or by law, be limited to a power of remonstrance, with veto powers exercised only against legislative proposals that would violate constitutional powers and rights, attack minorities, threaten catastrophic environmental damage, or interfere with the decision-making powers of other unelected officials in (most) liberal democratic states, such as courts of law, central banks, and so forth. These rights of remonstrance and veto can be legitimated on strongly intuitive epistemic, *evidentialist* grounds.[85] Where a belief among the members of an upper house that elected officials and majorities of voters are disastrously acting against their own and the common good—whether through lack of sufficient knowledge of that good, willful defiance, or *akrasia*—is sufficiently supported by evidence for such failure, there are grounds for the upper house to intervene through remonstrance (by subjecting legislation proposals to strong criticism) and ultimately through its power of veto. If that power is exercised improperly or without sufficient regard for countervailing evidence, its members can be held to account and suffer damage to their moral authority. In the worst cases they may be dismissed from their positions or even prosecuted, if they acted under the influence of corrupt inducements.

This hybrid Confucian-liberal counterargument is potentially powerful in being applicable to liberal democracies or to prospective Confucian democracies. It preserves certain central insights of CPG, EGE, and EPG—indeed, the deliberations of an upper house in some such cases may justifiably not be made public when information bearing on national security is concerned. It preserves certain central Confucian insights about the meritocratic role of the *junzi* in governance—to advise rulers based on their own superior moral and intellectual excellence and sometimes to act decisively to curtail them when they act against their own good or the good of their subjects. In a liberal democratic society, or in a hybrid illiberal democracy such as Bell proposes, the role of such *junzi* is to remonstrate with both the electorate and their elected representatives.

Consider this example that would, by analogy, provide justification for Joseph Raz's "service conception of authority"[86] and also moral justification for accepting paternalistic, perfectionist intervention by the upper house as described above. A disaster has just occurred—a nuclear power plant only ten kilometers from my home has gone into meltdown (such as happened to Fukushima Daiichi Nuclear Power Plant immediately following the March 2011 Tsunami), though this has not yet been broadcast on the news. Members of the defense force arrive at my front door to ask me to evacuate immediately with my family, and have buses on standby to transport us out. Suppose I quibble with the soldiers and tell them that I need to know exactly what is going on before making up my mind to go with them, or that I and my family need more time to prepare for evacuation. Their response will be "sorry, orders are orders. We are only allowed to tell you—and we know this to be a fact—that you and your family's health will be in great danger if you remain. You must evacuate immediately." They may scold me if I continue to demand more information from them, or show signs of indecision, urging me to trust them that they know what they are doing and that it is "for my own good"—and in the end, they will order me and my family to board the bus for evacuation.

This scenario addresses in miniature the theoretical and normative questions of legitimacy in authority that Joseph Raz has famously sought to answer: How can one person's "say-so" constitute a reason for me to obey that person, as a duty? And how can we say that we have a duty to subject our will to another in this fashion? His "service conception of authority" states that the conditions for fulfilling the normative question are fulfilled when (1) I would be better able to follow right reasons for acting—reasons that apply to me anyway—by intending to submit to an authority's directives to do so, than when I do intend to do so; and (2) when, regarding the situation in which (1) arises, it is better for me to follow such reasons than to decide matters for myself, without such authority.[87] In the scenario above, the "reasons for acting" apply to securing my and my family's good in a most immediate sense—to the protection of our health, and possibly our lives, and those reasons hold irrespective of the say-so of the official directing me to act. There is then a perfectionist motivation at issue here: depending on how I and my family act, some of our most important goods are at stake, and the defense force members are there to ensure we act in accordance with the right decision—which they will in the last resort make for us. Their conduct is paternalistic, depending at least on a doubt that we can act for our own good by ourselves unaided by their authority.[88] This doubt arises from the conviction that we lack relevant knowledge that they or the agency they represent possess (and which they may have the right not to divulge to us), or because, even possessing that knowledge, we will be *akratic* or defiantly disobedient in our response to the emergency.

An epistemically paternalistic scenario in which we act under the direction of someone with *de facto* political authority, where there is also wider background of shared norms legitimating that authority, helps build a convincing analogy with the remonstration and veto powers of an upper house of *junzi*. Some of those norms will be the normative reasons grounded in a "service conception of authority" that fulfills perfectionist aims—to help us, even to direct us as citizens to realize our good and to avoid disastrously harming it, based on the evidentially based judgment that sometimes we do not know our individual and collective good as well as we should, or that we may act willfully or akratically against it.

This amended argument for paternalistic, perfectionist governance looks attractive and powerful, allowing for an integration of Confucian and non-Confucian/liberal intuitions about epistemic elitism and paternalism in a politically perfectionist, service conception of authority. It could act as another constitutional check on majoritarian abuses of power, and both customary and judicial restraints would prevent the upper house from engaging in "mission creep" with their remonstrative and veto powers. How might those sceptical of politically perfectionist paternalism like myself reply?

One objection arises from Jonathan Quong's criticism of political perfectionism, proceeding from his own "justice-based conception of authority," which functions analogically to, but in opposition to, Raz's service conception of authority. Quong's conception provides normative justification for a duty to obey authority because that is the best way to comply with our duty to render justice to others. For a justice-based conception of authority, however, it is not a duty of justice to "promote distinctive perfectionist policies." But Quong's most fundamental objection to the service conception of authority is itself quite simple: from the fact that I ought to do what someone else tells me to do, for instance because it will help me realize my interests or goods (which hold for me whether I am told to follow them or not), there is no prima facie reason that the person has a "moral right" to state and enforce that order. On Quong's view, there are also two presumptive wrongs with judgmental paternalistic motivations for a perfectionist, service conception of authority. First, in making a negative judgment about another's lack of ability or will to do the right thing, the paternalizer (such as a government agent) puts that person in an inferior position in relation to himself, violating a liberal democratic norm that all citizens be treated as free and equal citizens. Second, when directed against a sane adult, such a negative judgment involves treating her like a child, incapable of formulating, pursuing, or revising her good for herself. In this way, her dignity and moral status as a citizen is diminished.[89]

This objection, then, can disable the analogy between the mandatory evacuation thought experiment and the veto powers of an upper house of *junzi* by putting into question the paternalistic, perfectionist motivations supposedly central to both. The self-defense personnel who arrive on my doorstep to urge me to evacuate need not be motivated (and should not be motivated) by their conviction that I may be less aware of my own good than they are, or possibly unlikely or unwilling to act on such knowledge even if I possess it. Alternatively, on a justice-based conception of authority, they should be motivated by considerations of justice, if we accept "life and safety" as among Rawlsian primary goods that justice is supposed to secure—"the things which it is supposed that a rational man wants, whatever else he wants" and which are means to fulfilling the goods of whatever life he has chosen for himself, such as "rights and liberties, opportunities and powers, income and wealth."⁹⁰ It is their duty to inform me of all that I need to know to make an informed decision about securing the most basic of goods for myself and my children, to provide (if necessary) the means for evacuation and a place of emergency shelter for us, but not coercively to enforce our evacuation. In extreme cases there may be public safety grounds for coercively enforcing an evacuation order, but these are again potentially defensible (and legitimated by) appeal to a justice-based criterion, rather than to paternalistic considerations of my "own good." Similarly, where a Supreme Court overrides the legislative proposals of an elected legislature, the motivation will lie more plausibly with considerations of justice—of protecting a minority from unconstitutional persecution, for instance—than with a paternalistic conviction that the legislature, and those citizens who voted for it, "do not know their own good," or have through their intemperate passions become temporarily unwilling or incapable of acting for it.

This objection unifies moral objections to both interpersonal and institutional paternalism, and is an advance on other objections to epistemic elitism and paternalism in governance. However, as David Enoch has recently pointed out, such an argument sidesteps, but does not disarm, the central *epistemic* basis of paternalism, and indeed of the Confucian paternalism and perfectionism at issue in this chapter.⁹¹ The justice-based conception of authority may serve as one possible alternative to a service-based perfectionist conception that Confucians are more likely to be sympathetic with. But it yields no distinctive epistemic grounds for rejecting the argument for legitimating authority on a perfectionist version of the service conception. There are, in interpersonal and nonpolitical institutional relations, situations where one party is able to judge, on ample evidential grounds, that another party is not capable of acting for her own good or for some collective good she is a participant in, and in which intuitively we consider it morally remiss that the first party (or institutional agent) does not intervene, even coercively, on the basis of such knowledge. In chapter 4 I considered the case where a psychologically exhausted or cognitively impaired elderly parent may request adult children to act paternalistically on her behalf in medical care decisions. Or, in a case where mental impairment is temporary, I would be remiss if, knowing the state that a binge-drinking friend can get into when he drinks beyond a certain point, I did not intervene to stop him drinking when he appears unable to judge when he should stop. Similarly, in the institutional case a *junzi* holding veto powers may be faced with a legislative proposal displaying evidence that its draftees are ignorant of constitutional considerations that disqualify it, or that they drafted it in the grip of majoritarian partisan or sectarian passions that regards such considerations as irrelevant to them, though those considerations *are* relevant to their own and the collective good. It would be remiss, then, for the *junzi* not to act on such knowledge to remonstrate with and ultimately wield a power of veto over the draftees out of a conviction that she is acting for their own good and the good of the state.

Against Jonathan Quong[92] on this view, given the brute fact that I have reason to do something, or to refrain from doing it, there *is* reason to think that affects what moral rights another has toward me. If as a result of temporary or permanent mental impairment, or ignorance or *akrasia*, I am likely to act against my good, and another person has good evidence to believe this to be the case, it *can* intuitively follow that this person can (indeed ought to) claim a moral right to intervene and act for my own good. Thus, as I suggested in chapter 4, part of what it means to "be a filial son or daughter" extends to competent management of the affairs of an elderly parent no longer willing or able to manage them. Part of what it means to "be an exemplary person" or *junzi* as a member of an upper house is to exercise a power of remonstrance or veto when she knows that legislators and voters are clearly acting in ignorance of, or willfully or akratically acting contrary to, their own and the collective societal good. None of these epistemic considerations exclude a justice-based conception of authority, however. The two conceptions may be complementary to each other, and conceivably could be in perfectionist liberal or Confucian democratic constitutional orders.

Perhaps the strongest philosophical objection that remains against epistemic elitism and paternalism in governance involves first conceding the strength of the epistemic grounds for the argument for paternalism and perfectionism outlined above. We should concede that in certain domains of our interpersonal and institutional lives it is reasonable to act for others' good when we know they are not capable of doing so (or not willing to), or where it is most reasonable to submit to the authority of those who act for our good. We should also concede that people are free to commit themselves to comprehensive doctrines, to forms of the good life, where they voluntarily submit to traditionalist, paternalistic authority within families, organizations or small-scale communities (and, as stated in chapter 2, we should support robust exit rights for those who no longer wish to live such lives). But from public reason considerations that will be stated below, such paternalistic, perfectionist considerations should be excluded from those reasons that it would be admissible for agents of government to justify acting on in exercising coercive influence over the lives of private citizens. The argument, then, is that only justice-based conceptions of authority justifiable to people pursuing diverse varieties of the good life provide legitimate reasons for coercive interference in citizens' lives, or—if we are talking about policy formulation by legislators—for an upper house to veto policy proposals.

What is needed to justify this public reason-based rejection is a normative conception of citizens that supports, on public reason grounds, excluding epistemically paternalistic and perfectionist reasons for state coercion, a normative conception that could be expected to itself be the subject of consensus among citizens qua *citizens* themselves, irrespective of their diverse pursuits of the good life. One recommendation, offered by David Enoch, is a conception of citizens as *autonomous*.[93] Under this conception, if citizens are understood as being (or as if they are) rational adults capable of developing and living their own idea of the good life, it is impermissible to intervene in their lives to help them realize their good, or to prevent them from failing to realize it—or to realize some other conception of the good that the state considers better for them.

Instead, coercion would be justified only on a "justice-based conception" where it is the "best way" to ensure that citizens comply with the duties of justice they owe to others,[94] including when they act in an official capacity as agents of the state or as legislators. This would mean that they be directed not to coercively interfere with other citizens' access to or exercise of, or be directed to fulfill a duty to ensure their access to, Rawlsian primary goods.

Alternatively, on the capabilities approach favored in this book, a public reason-based justice conception of authority would justify the use of coercion or directive power only to the extent that it protects citizens' ability to exercise basic *capabilities* for health, education, and freedom of choice and expression and protects their access to resources needed for actualizing them, irrespective of whatever idea of the good life those capabilities are to realize themselves as functions within.[95] In this domain of political justice, and whether what is at stake are primary goods or capabilities, agencies of state would be required on what I call a subjunctive principle to act *as if* citizens are equally reasonable and autonomous, even if in particular instances evidentialist grounds exist for believing that they are not acting for their own good. Knowledge that others are acting, or will act, against their good (in whatever way that is conceived) may give reason to intervene "for their own good" in many domains of life—but public reason considerations of respect for autonomy, it would be argued, exclude these reasons as authority-legitimating reasons in the domain of governance. These public reason considerations would supplement the other, more empirically based reasons for scepticism about the efficacy of epistemic elitism and paternalism in governance of postindustrial, pluralistic societies that I outlined earlier in this chapter.

If this argument holds, its limitations need to be made clear. It does not on principle exclude the idea of an upper house selected on meritocratic criteria with remonstrative and veto powers over legislatures. A justice conception of authority *could* accept the legitimacy of such an upper house, so long as it acted only in accordance with the justice conception of authority and accepted customary and legal limitations on its veto powers. This perspective may concede that meritocratic criteria are important for selecting people best qualified—by their judicial and constitutional knowledge or political experience—to serve in this role. However, it would not in principle rule out other methods of selection, by lottery among all registered voters, by selection of mixed groupings of ordinary citizens and experts to engage in Deweyan democratic deliberation, or by conventional elections. But it would rule out the epistemically paternalistic, perfectionist grounds for legitimating its authority that Confucians and some liberals are likely to favor in establishing such an upper house.

There are two problems in the final position outlined above that need to be dealt with before concluding this chapter. The first is that the norm of personal autonomy is too conceptually implicated in comprehensive liberal conceptions of the good life—such as Kantianism—to serve as a *public reason* norm for excluding epistemic paternalism and perfectionism.[96] Since public reason liberalism is sometimes accused of itself being a political perfectionist doctrine that collapses into comprehensive liberalism, this problem merits serious consideration. Notions such as a "general capability for practical reason" suggested by Martha Nussbaum, or the kind of "deliberative freedom" I discussed in chapter 4, might work as substitute norms for personal autonomy, while doing analogous conceptual labor. These substitutes signify no more than recognition of reasonable adults' ability to decide for themselves and competently live what their valued way of life is, *even if* it involves voluntary submission to paternal or patriarchal authority in families, religious communities, or private associations of a type that would be disparaged by, say, comprehensive Kantian or Millian liberal doctrines, or by perfectionist feminisms. Such adults, concerned to protect their ways of life from perfectionist government interference—or from persecution by fellow citizens—would have moral reasons consistent with their own comprehensive conceptions of the good life to assent to this norm. In more common-sensical terms, such people may not prize autonomy, but they do prize being *left alone* to decide for themselves how best to live their lives, within the limits of laws protecting civil, political, and property rights.[97]

A second problem is that the public reason norms of which the justice-based conception of authority is a constituent part are still *liberal* norms, and no amount of semantic sleights of hand changing "autonomy" into "deliberative freedom" will alter this. On such a view, these liberal norms have developed organically in societies whose citizens traditionally adhere to them through sustaining a stably intergenerational, overlapping political consensus, even as they pursue more comprehensive doctrines in other domains of their lives. The problem is how such a liberal public reason could apply in societies where there is already tacit, widespread commitment to different traditions of values that would arguably ground a different public reason—for instance, a *Confucian* public reason. This problem will be subject matter for the next chapter.

CHAPTER 7

Perverse Doctrines and One Hundred Schools: Confucianism's Place in Modern Pluralistic Societies

*The Unexpected Rise of
Animal Welfare Consciousness in China Today*

In 2010, Canada appeared on the verge of signing a trade agreement that would save its seal products industry, enabling exports of seal fur, oil, and meat products to China. Canadian politicians and industry insiders were upbeat about the prospects for such a deal. Canada's *Globe and Mail* newspaper reported that, in contrast to Europe, the animal rights movement had not taken hold in China, where there is "a tradition of eating a wide variety of animals, including dogs." As one insider the newspaper spoke to said, "The Chinese eat anything."[1]

Unfortunately for the Canadian seal industry, Chinese animal welfare organizations the Canadians had never heard of got wind of the proposed agreement, and of the Canadian press statements about Chinese "culinary culture" and attitudes to animal welfare. A coalition of fifty such organizations denounced the cruelty of seal-hunting practices and mobilized public anger against the racism and cultural imperialism implicit in Canadian claims about Chinese eating habits.

In the face of this concerted opposition, the Chinese government backed away from consent to the proposal, and the Canadian government conceded defeat in 2014.[2] Canadian fisheries officials and industry lobby groups learned a lesson that needs to be understood more widely: that alongside other East Asian nations, China is a rapidly changing, increasingly diverse society, where stereotypically "Chinese" culinary habits such as the consumption of dog meat or of endangered animal products have become increasingly contested.[3]

What does this anecdote about animal welfare activism in China have to do with the question of Confucianism and its prospects in China, East Asia, and the West? Quite a lot. Alongside other cultural transformations in Chinese and other East Asian societies, it first raises definitional questions about the substantive, or categorical, identity attributions claimed for those societies, the very sorts of questions raised in chapter 1. In a society where ethical values about animal welfare are taking hold among urban elites, where Christian faith is spreading at an explosive rate and other Chinese religions are reviving, and in which there are now enormous inequalities in income distribution following thirty years of promarket reform, doubts must arise over claims that this society can meaningfully be categorized under an atheist, Communist collective identity or even a more tacit Confucian identity. Second, it raises questions about the sort of political order best able to cope with and provide stable means for achieving the public goods of increasingly diverse citizens in populous industrialized and postindustrial states, whether they are currently democracies or not.

The purpose of this chapter is threefold. The first is to urge greater recognition of the actual cultural, religious, and political diversity in East Asian societies, which puts into question claims for their tacit "Confucian" character. Recognition of such diversity would require political philosophers to confront the above-mentioned question of what political order is more capable of stably and justly securing public goods in such diversified societies. The answer, I shall argue, lies in the record for stable, pluralistic social order set by democratic societies in Europe, East Asia, Oceania, and North America, which all fit a minimal definition for liberal democracy: an electoral political order that grants to all of its citizens equal political rights, property rights, and civil rights.[4]

The chapter's second purpose is to provide a justification for liberal democracy conceived in a less comprehensive and least *morally taxing* sense, offered with due acknowledgment of the diverse and sometimes illiberal personal and corporate lives of its citizens, and of the diverse moral and cultural values that condition the constitutional priorities of different liberal democracies, *including* in East Asia. However, it may be difficult in light of recent critical discussions of John Rawls's political liberalism to assert plausibly that such a justification is free of prior commitments to some variety of liberalism as a comprehensive doctrine. Take for instance William Galston's criticism of Rawls's concepts of justice and right as *free standing* for the purposes of delimiting the role of liberal political philosophy. According to Rawls, political philosophy must present political conceptions of justice and right as if they are independent of and not consequences of religious, moral, and metaphysical comprehensive doctrines, and *even if* their historical derivation from such doctrines could be demonstrated. Galston's rejoinder is that, first, we are not in practice able to justify to ourselves and to others conceptions of right and justice without also appealing to various religious, moral, and metaphysical comprehensive doctrines, especially in times of political crisis when those concepts are challenged or subjected to conflicting interpretations. Second, Galston charges Rawls with presenting a truncated understanding of the role of political philosophy. This understanding takes for granted the legitimacy of a freestanding conception of justice and right, and rules out the invocation of comprehensive liberal or republican doctrines (for instance) in defending these conceptions, and defending the very idea of a liberal constitutional order, in argumentation against illiberal or undemocratic political doctrines.[5]

My own response to this disagreement is to try and have it both ways—to accept that there should be some conception of a freestanding conception of right and justice available for political philosophical argument, if only as a heuristic device, but to acknowledge that there is, and always will be, leakage from comprehensive doctrines in the wider public sphere into political liberal conceptions of justice. The important point is to show that in spite of such leakage these conceptions still place minimally taxing burdens on the consciences and liberties of those otherwise pursuing diverse goods and ways of life, while giving them scope to justify these conceptions to themselves with the conceptual resources provided by their own doctrines.

The chapter's third, and related, purpose is to show that this understanding of justice and right is at least a less morally taxing justification even in an East Asian context, leaving adherents of different ways of life and different doctrines to practice them, and to some extent to practice them unreasonably, so long as they also adhere to principles of justice and the associated political, civil, and property rights recognized under political liberalism, and can find the resources within their respective traditions and ways of life to justify to themselves why they do so. I hope to show what motivations citizens in East Asian societies would have to defend this liberal pluralism. Ultimately, what is at stake in this analysis is the welfare of individuals, to associate in ways of life, practices, and communities that they value, or to depart from them freely when they no longer value them, and to receive some degree of state support (financial, educational, and medical) to mitigate the socially destabilizing effects of market relations—and market failure—on associational life in liberal democratic societies. In part, this attempted accommodation between political liberalism and pluralism is motivated by the ethical individualist concern underlying this work—both the promotion of capabilities *and* their diverse functionings in preferred or customary ways of life, and to provide for robust evaluation of social and political institutions according to their capacity to enhance or impede those capabilities. In part, it is motivated by a desire to honor the actually existing diversity of spiritual, moral, and political life of East Asians.

This leaves the question of what place Confucianism realistically could (or does) have in the liberal pluralism envisaged here. In the last part of this chapter I will suggest that in the diverse forms it takes in moral practices of religious movements, civil society organizations, and conviction politics Confucianism can make rich contributions to the spiritual, cultural, intellectual, and political life of societies inside and beyond East Asia.

Ethical Diversity in East Asia and the Liberalism of Fear

In *Moral China in the Age of Reform*, Ci Jiwei outlines an argument for freedom in connection with a renovated conception of the good in a future postcommunist China. This argument for freedom differs from its more typical justification in liberal democracies—as a norm for justifying individuals' pursuit of their diverse, valued ways of life without coercive interference from other citizens or the state. Ci's discussion of freedom and of the good in China is worthy of consideration, since it provides a rather different justification for the establishment of a liberal political constitution in China, responding not to moral pluralism but to a hollowing out of the moral life itself.

According to Ci, in Western societies the concept of negative liberty arose in reaction against the lethal consequences of "intense and belligerent attachment to one conception or another of the good," manifested in sectarian conflicts in Europe from the sixteenth century onward. Contemporary China faces a very different predicament following the early twentieth-century collapse of the Qing Dynasty, and the late twentieth-century dissipation of Communist orthodoxy. There has consequently been "a hollowing out of what used to be a shared conception of the good and of the type of self embedded in it." The task, then, for China is not to establish freedom in a position of independence from and priority over the good, so that a higher regulatory regime can be established to regulate people's diverse pursuits of the good. Instead, a way must be found, first, to get freedom to help reconstitute "the capacity for seeking the good and making it one's own and ultimately the capacity for self-formation."[6]

The moral crisis Ci speaks of in his book, which he paraphrases as "the corruption of an entire people," involves massive, and increasingly normalized, breaches of "everyday norms of coexistence and cooperation" occurring at all reaches of society after three decades of industrialization and market reform. These breaches are so serious because, unlike in the West, there is no distinction between the right and the good by which a moral crisis can be compartmentalized and quarantined from politics. The Communist Party had supplied the Communist or socialist *telos* in relation to which morally good or bad actions could be defined and have their standards set.[7] This *telos* has lost credibility in the redevelopment of China as a protoliberal, market society.

With the hollowing out of this good, and disenchantment with its associated modes of moral exemplification which had once shaped moral agency, a *de facto* freedom permitted by market reform—without a well-developed rule of law—has spontaneously evolved in this vacated moral space. Such freedom has the potential to serve as a "vehicle for nihilism," or indeed is already doing so, manifested in rampant consumerism, egoism, corruption, and dishonesty at all levels of society, along with cynical, passive acquiescence of the people. All of this is facilitated by the patronage networks of the conspicuously enriched elites of the Communist Party itself, the biggest beneficiary of decades of market reforms. Before talk of freedom as the guarantor for the safe pursuit of diverse goods can begin, another task must be fulfilled, according to Ci. That is, to reevaluate freedom, "as the condition for a new moral subject and a new moral culture" and to ensure that it stands in the right relation to the good.[8]

I do not want to question Ci's analysis here, and certainly I feel ill-qualified to do so. But I wonder if, along with some other political philosophers, Ci has underestimated the impact of the rapid growth of Christianity and the more modest growth in postmaterialist values in China, with the latter manifested in participation in and support for environmentalism and animal welfare campaigns. In the empty core left by the evacuation of the Communist conception of the good, the rise of Christianity, revivals of Buddhism and Chinese folk religions, and the emergence of animal welfare or environmentalist movements are insinuating different conceptions of the good into public life, predicated on ideals of transcendental human relations with the divine, or on ideals of nonexploitative, humane relations with nonhuman nature.

It is likely that, so far, environmentalist and animal welfare consciousness are the preoccupations of a youthful, relatively wealthy urban minority. Christianity presents a different case: estimates of China's combined official and "house church" Christian congregations at upward of 150 million, increasing at a rate of perhaps 10 percent per year, are starting to make the minority label a little outdated.[9] Conceding this minority status should not blind us to the disproportionate social influence middle-class adherents of these movements and religious communities wield. Often possessing social capital indicators such as wealth, higher education, access to Communist Party patronage, and social media acumen, they are having a public impact out of all proportion to their numbers. They are able to broadcast their message, and their conceptions of the good, through nonconventional and conventional media and social networks, to recruit members through these channels, to author the narrative of their movements against nativist or nationalist opponents, and sometimes even to co-opt Communist Party collaboration.

In setting the problem for this chapter, I want to supplement Ci Jiwei's account of a moral crisis in China attending the hollowing out of a shared conception of the good and the spread of de facto freedom. I would suggest that two trends are at work, and interacting with each other in sometimes destabilizing ways: on the one hand, the hollowing out of the good Ci speaks of, and moral crisis, and on the other, in reaction to this, amidst ample evidence of egoism, anomie, and environmental degradation, a seeking of refuge in alternative conceptions of the good.

This is not to say that the latter developments provide an organic, spontaneous evolution out of the moral crisis as Ci conceptualizes it. There are many equally unhappy scenarios to consider in a future under an increasingly autocratic Communist Party regime. Interest groups and rival religious communities and organizations may try and co-opt regime support to legitimate their own activities and suppress organizations and groups they oppose. Alternatively, there are prospects for interest groups and religious communities to fall victim to arbitrary government repression. This has been the fate of Falun Gong and of Muslim minorities today.

Perhaps, then, contemporary China is not such a deviation from the "Western standard" of an industrialized society facing growing pluralism in the creeds and ways of life of its citizens, though its pluralism remains heavily policed. For evidence suggests growing religiosity, and among both educated, urban elites and migrant working-class people exposed to rapid modernization and globalization, an increasing embrace of Christian faith as both traditional religions and communist ideology no longer appear capable of giving spiritual meaning to life amidst such changes.[10] China too faces the problem of how to ensure that the resulting pluralism in religious belief remains *reasonable*, which is to say, characterized by mutual tolerance, reciprocity, and stable coexistence, and not so fraught with "belligerent and intense attachments" that adherents of different religions or factions would be drawn into sectarian strife with one another, or would try to co-opt the coercive powers of state to act on their behalf against others.

It may be that even given these facts of pluralism, by no means limited to "Western" societies, there is no *prima facie* reason that liberalism offers the best constitutional arrangement for the peaceful, co-operative coexistence of different ways of life. Autocratic or illiberal democratic polities may ground their legitimacy on their ability to manage such pluralism by outlawing or heavily regulating interest groups, religions, or lifestyles they deem to be morally or politically destabilizing. This indeed is the strategy of the present-day Communist Party government in China. Further, it may be argued that a political liberalism that attributes to its citizens certain fundamental moral capacities such as a sense of justice, recognition of the equality of others in the political sphere, and an ability to formulate, revise, or alter their conceptions of the good still imposes a comprehensive, morally taxing notion of liberal moral personhood upon nonliberal groups living in a liberal society.[11]

One potent counterargument the advocate of political liberalism has to this response derives from what Judith Shklar called a "liberalism of fear," grounded in vivid memory of past repressions and cruelties. It is a memory of how past governments (or, though Shklar did not emphasize this, powerful past factions), acting as the agent of one comprehensive conception of the good, and without the constitutional limits on their powers secured by political and civil rights, have exercised vast and cruel coercive powers over the defenseless, the weak, and the less powerful minorities. The liberalism of fear motivates people who might otherwise be inclined to quarrel over values, including the value of justice itself, to agree to recognize as publically justified a minimal set of political principles through which they can stably and consensually coexist. It proceeds not *toward* a *summum bonum*, a greatest good to which all citizens must be directed to strive for, but *from* shared knowledge of a *summum malum*[12]—the greatest of evils, which arises when sectarianism and absolutism take hold in governance. Ethical individualism and its refined version in the capabilities approach enjoins this liberalism to focus on the suppressive and exploitative power of the state—and of powerful factions or institutions—on the lives of vulnerable individuals. Here the focus of concern is on exercises of power that revile and eliminate their preferred or customary ways of life, eliminate *them* as the reviled practitioners of those ways of life, or which degrade them to a mere means for the economic ends of others.

Memory of the bloody religious wars and massacres of Reformation-era Europe, and of the twentieth-century genocides, provides the paradigmatic "Western" foundation for this liberalism of fear. Yet in East Asia, subject matter for such a liberalism is abundant. In Japan, memory remains of the early twentieth-century mutation of a conservative, nominally sectarian constitutional regime into the vehemently intolerant hypernationalism of the 1930s and '40s, as documented in chapter 4, which crushed internal dissent, wreaked havoc on the rest of Asia, and eventually brought catastrophic defeat upon itself. In South Korea and Taiwan subsist the memory of the traumatic repressions inflicted by autocratic regimes upon dissidents—of the Guangju Massacre, suppressions of organized labor, and the mass incarcerations and killings during the "White Terror." China, meanwhile, retains the marginalized or suppressed memory of the multiple economic, political, and cultural disasters the Mao regime visited on its own people, and of repressions against dissidents and minorities, some of which continue to the present day.

A distinguishing feature of a liberalism of fear is that it makes less morally taxing demands as a condition for adherence to its central principles in comparison to other liberalisms that Shklar describes, such as the liberalism of natural rights or a liberalism of personal development and autonomy—the liberalisms respectively of Locke and Mill.[13] One need not subscribe to liberal conceptions of personhood and of personal autonomy to have an affinity for a liberalism of fear. Christians, Muslims, Buddhists, and religious Confucians alike may cleave to illiberal, paternalistic, or patriarchal beliefs within the spheres of their own lives and require such adherence from fellow practitioners as a condition for continued membership in their associations, communities, or congregations. Within their communal lives, they may legitimately have little truck with the liberal conception of personhood, beyond respect for the freedom of association of their members, including their entitlements to exit with their personal possessions and property. Yet they have reason to fear governments that act as agents of one comprehensive conception of the good or one comprehensive moral code, or which align themselves with or represent the interests and good of the most powerful factions in a society in order to suppress weaker minorities and dissenting individuals. For they all have institutional memories of being such minorities.

Of course, fear of arbitrary power exercised by others against one's own sect or valued way of life need not be expressed as a *liberalism* of fear, recognizing political liberalism as the best remedy for that fear. An alternative, one might say historically classic, mode of both articulating and neutralizing fear of such repression is through sectarianism. Existential security for the sectarian is dependent on the widest possible writ for his sect's valued way of life and comprehensive moral code; the sources of existential insecurity are identified in rival, heretical sects and in dissenting individuals that it is the role of sect authorities to somehow keep at bay, exclude, and if possible repress, lest they grow powerful enough to threaten the sect, its truths, and its ritual normativity. A hard-won wisdom—a part of the wisdom cultivated in a liberalism of fear—in societies where pluralism is emerging (such as early modern Europe) is that the odds of a complete victory, through the suppression of rival sects and dissenters, are lower than those of defeat and subsequent suppression of one's own sect, under government power monopolized or co-opted by a rival sect. Harder won is the insight that victory and the imposition on society of the orthodoxy of one's own sect may become an unstable source of security. Its defeat and overthrow by a rival sect can lead to even more calamitous persecutions, of sect leaders convicted of crimes against rival sects when they held the reins of government, and the delegitimation of one's sect's beliefs and desertions of adherents that follow from such total political defeat.[14] Perhaps the hardest won insight is into the instability of the sort of compromise that can result when there is mutual understanding that such victories are beyond reach—a *modus vivendi* without a common understanding of justice equally binding on all sects and their adherents. For the toleration established by that *modus vivendi* is contingent on an equality of strength between rival sects, which is susceptible to break down if one sect becomes numerically and politically more powerful than the other, and is then in a position to suppress its rival.[15]

These insights provide moral psychological reasons for understanding why liberal democracy, as the liberalism of fear understands it, is a rare and fragile undertaking—in East Asia perhaps, but also in Europe, North America, and Oceania. It cuts against the grain of categorical identity affiliations (sectarian, ethnic, or national) that found their existential security on a maximally expansive writ for their creed or ethnos, staking out their entitlement to seek their goods or to impose their moral code at the expense of other weaker, minority creeds, ethnic groups, or affiliations. The lessons from past repressions enjoined by a liberalism of fear can be trivialized or forgotten in the face of the powerful psychological pull exerted by categorical affiliations—beginning with the existential security promised in a way of life inclusive of those who share the same fundamental beliefs, habits, rituals, loyalties, or ethnic descent. But these lessons also provide a moral psychological understanding of the *reasonableness* of the mutual moral recognition and respect shared memory of past repressions can push members of rival affiliations and creeds toward, with no presumption of substantive commitment to liberalism within their own conceptions of the good. This liberalism calls on adherents of these creeds and affiliations to acknowledge their common vulnerability to repression from sectarian or ethnic conflict, and to find within their own doctrines the premises with which they can proceed to recognize people following different conceptions of the good as fellow citizens in equal standing before the law, as moral persons who are bearers of political and civil rights. In this respect, these doctrines become reasonable.

Liberalism also calls on adherents to adjust (but not censor) the moral language of their creed or sect for participation in intercreedal and intercommunity inquiry within a "public political forum" over the application of laws and enforcement of political and civil rights, using reasons that are comprehensible and noncoercively persuasive to all. This is of course the language of John Rawls's "public reason."[16] These are morally taxing requirements that, as I said, cut against powerful sectarian and morally particularist impulses, but they are minimally taxing compared to the alternatives. In the next section, in the course of fleshing out the arguments for this conception of political liberalism, I will show that, in relation to one Confucian conception of public reason advanced by Sungmoon Kim,[17] the pluralistic variety of liberalism I advocate does make the more minimal, morally taxing demands.

Public Reason and Liberal Pluralism

I will propose here an ideal type of liberal pluralism, applicable in cross-cultural contexts that could help to manage, and help render articulate, relations between the communities or publics in which different conceptions of the good are followed, which recognizes wider possibilities for exchange between them than are stipulated by the more austere conditions of a public reason in a public political forum focused on the questions of how to interpret and justify principles of justice. Yet if my proposal is persuasive, such a liberal pluralism also encompasses and does not conflict with the public reason of Rawls's political liberalism. Acknowledging a wider realm of public discourse in which diverse goods are affirmed and contested enables a clearer picture to arise of the pluralism not only within but also between liberal democratic societies.

The following analysis will draw its inspiration from a variety of thinkers such as Isaiah Berlin and John Dewey who have written on pluralism about the good and ethical values.[18] Focusing on such values, this analysis proceeds from these principles:

1. The objectivity of values. Values include the thick ethical concepts and social facts of the sort described in chapter 1; they are specifiable, and stably specifiable, independent of individual whim or preference. This holds as well for essentially contested value concepts; even if irreducibly polysemantic, they are stably specifiable according to linguistic and evaluative standards relative to the group within which they are accepted as action-guiding. In other words, once virtue-concepts, norms, political and ethical ideals, and exemplars enter a world of public discourse and become the subject of a common understanding, allegiance or disagreement sufficient to be action-guiding for those who live by them and to be at least understandable as action-guiding by those who do not,[19] they are already specifiable as values as opposed to preferences alterable by the subjective whim of those who hold them.

2. The finitude of values. Distinguished from more inchoate, almost innumerable individual preferences, I take it from Isaiah Berlin[20] that there are at any one time in a society—or today, in more globalized ethical and political discourse—a limited set of values in circulation, reflecting politically and culturally conditioned felt needs, desires, and anxieties that are themselves responsive to and constrained by certain universal moral psychological facts and, indeed, human capabilities—even if those facts and capabilities are not themselves articulated and known. This principle by itself does not mandate evaluative ranking of values. It merely limits the range of values that can be plausibly held at any one time.

3. Values are for the most part susceptible to objective evaluation and ranking, but can also be incommensurable. This is to say that, through inquiry into values in relation to more contingent enabling or disabling social conditions for their realization, and to moral psychological facts and human capabilities, we can often evaluate values as more or less realistic in their prospects for action-guiding conduct, and as more or less good or bad, and be in a position at the termination of inquiry to know (to have warrant) that they are so. But there are limits to our capacity to rank goods; in the flurried diversity of different comprehensive doctrines and ways of life, some goods may obdurately resist comparative ranking that either establishes their equality and compatibility, or justifies the evaluative subordination of one to the other, at least in a way that is susceptible to an overlapping consensus.

How might this ranking work, or fail to work? On this matter Dewey was more illuminating than Berlin. We can take as our example a value prized by sectarians: the value of exclusivity in matters of truth and ritual practice. For doctrinal exclusivity, not only are the beliefs and practices of one's sect infallibly true and correct, but also, the rival truth claims and nonconforming practices of dissenters or rival sects are not tolerated, for being inconsistent with the desired uniformity of belief and practice demanded by exclusivity. Within a sect, exclusivity is a desired end attained by policing of adherents' beliefs, and punishment or expulsion of nonconformists. But as we saw, sectarians may regard exclusivism about the truths and practices of their sect as something that an entire society must live under.

Supposing, then, that members of a sect regard the diversity of doctrines and ritual practices in their surrounding society as a problem to be solved, a lack to be made up for—exclusivity will become a desired outcome and anticipated result, an "end in view" which, acted on, will resolve the problem and attain their desired outcome.[21] From the perspective of this end in view, various courses of action will themselves be evaluated, selected, and put into effect to achieve the outcome of exclusivity in doctrine and practice—a campaign of proselytizing on behalf of one's sect and of public denunciations of rival sects' beliefs, harassment of their members, attempts to co-opt government support in suppressing them, or direct efforts to gain political power in order to use the coercive powers of state more thoroughly to suppress rival sects. Suppose, then, that historical inquiry or experience reveals that the results of such actions are incessant controversy with rival sects and dissenters, communal violence, preemptive co-option, or capture of government executive powers by rival sects to suppress one's own sect, tit-for-tat ethnoreligious cleansing, and warfare with results as potentially devastating for one's own sect, for their lives, wealth, and property, as it is for others. In such circumstances, the historically recorded, experienced outcomes diverge from those desired and anticipated by ends in view, and so "the valuation of ends in view is tested by consequences that actually ensue." The failure in agreement between hoped for and experienced or historically demonstrated outcomes provides means for revaluing desires, ends in view, and the means originally intended for achieving them.[22] The bitter wisdom reaped from such experience, or the settled conclusion of historical inquiries, may be, at least in *political* relations outside of one's sect, to rank exclusivism lower as a value than tolerance or respect.

Still, wisdom extends to recognizing the limits of such ranking, when it encounters value incommensurability. One expression of sectarianism more difficult to regulate in liberal democratic societies is the public expression of contempt and denigration for another sect's or ethnic group's beliefs and practices, which falls short of libel, threats, intimidation, and incitements to violence typically covered by criminal and civil law protections. On the one hand, as advocates of hate speech law point out, once such public expressions accumulate they can negatively impinge on the value of equality, particularly the entitlement of all to equal respect for their dignity as human beings and as fellow citizens. According to these advocates, such impingement can be worst for those belonging to vulnerable religious or ethnic minorities; it inflicts moral harms on them and damages their fragile standing as citizens entitled to equal respect, even when it does not involve libel, or physical violence.[23]

On the other hand, on the Deweyan value inquiry outlined above, state intervention to criminalize hate speech could have grievous unintended consequences on the value of liberty, particularly on freedom of speech. Yet refraining from formulating and enforcing such regulation gives an appearance of state (and also wider civil societal) tolerance for accumulating expressions of hatred that generate fear and insecurity for members of vulnerable minorities, who are otherwise supposed to be afforded equal protection under civil rights law. In such circumstances it may prove difficult either to rank liberty and civic equality as of equal value, with legislative compromises that equally satisfy the claims of both values, or to rank one over the other in a manner that is susceptible to an overlapping consensus.

4. Moral evaluation and ranking of values, and consequent knowledge of what values are realistic or unrealistic, beneficial or harmful, is fallible and susceptible to revision. Such fallibility follows from recognition or honest acknowledgment of value incommensurability in particular cases. This insight is also the gift of long experience, as values or systems of values have collapsed under their own incoherencies or have been recognized as sources of enormous human suffering, even if they had initially passed some sort of objective, indeed "scientific," evaluation, or were the settled legacies of a long-held tacit "know-how" or traditional knowledge. Two corollaries follow from this. The first is that there can be no finally definitive, comprehensive ranking of values, by which some can be established on context-independent grounds to be paramount or more fundamental than others. The second is that no person or class of persons has infallible access to objective moral insight into or knowledge of the value of values. This latter conclusion is consonant with the epistemically pessimistic attitude to the epistemic elitism and paternalism discussed in chapter 6.

Moral and epistemic fallibilism about values rules out value monism, in the form of a comprehensive, infallible, context-independent ranking of values, including the elevation of one set of values over others as the "summum bonum" of a society.[24] Knowing that moral evaluation of values, no matter how objective, is susceptible to error, that knowledge *that* certain values are realizable or unrealizable, right or wrong, better or worse is also not infallible, mandates a minimal tolerance for values and conceptions of the good life that we cannot be sure, according to currently observed standards of evaluation and inquiry, are unrealistic, harmful, or wrong. Nevertheless, this principled opposition to monism does not rule out attempting to root out, or even, as Berlin put it, "going to war against" certain values or systems of values which, on that same level of evaluation and inquiry, are shown to be destructive to other valued ways of life.[25]

These principles ideally govern conduct in a public domain of association and exchange that Hannah Arendt called the "social sphere,"[26] or what Rawls called the "background culture," distinguished on the one hand from the "public political forum," the realm of political conceptions of justice and right and of the rights interpreted in light of those conceptions, and on the other hand from the private sphere of the home, family, and intimate fraternity, characterized by exclusivity in relations with family members, friends, and sexual partners. In the social sphere, people associate and separate themselves from each other by differentiating standards and preferences, work at their life projects and enterprises, and find their sense of identity and belonging in communities and organizations governed by comprehensive doctrines of the good life, moral codes, and membership criteria that exclude many other fellow citizens—all in perfect consistency with their civil rights.

In this social sphere of most actually existing liberal democracies, people do not just live by the particular values of their organizations, associations, or communities. Adherents and spokespeople of different traditions, ways of life, communities, and religions also come into dialogue or even doctrinal conflict with one another in a marketplace of values that comprises part of this social sphere. In such interaction and dialogue they are not morally bound by the strictures of public reason to condition their public arguments and assertions with a "shared common knowledge" and with logical, epistemic, and moral standards of rationality deemed amenable to all citizens, or are at least they may only feel prudentially or strategically bound to condition their language in such a manner. Perhaps a weakness in Rawls's conception of public reason is that it is occasionally unclear how much its injunctions to reasonableness also require comprehensive doctrines themselves to be rational in the social (as opposed to public political) sphere. Must their adherents present themselves reasonably in their interactions with adherents of other comprehensive doctrines, in public discourse *outside* of the rarefied discussion in the public political forum of the applications of norms of justice and equality, and of civil rights? In the face of such a lack of clarity, the question arises whether it is reasonable to expect representatives of a particular, valued way of life to practice the Rawlsian virtue of reasonableness in articulating, defending, and promoting its particular truth and value in competition with others.[27]

Yet in actually existing liberal democracies (at least until recently) people have been free to exhort, declaim, criticize, and denounce in particularistic language, unapologetically, as Christians, Muslims, Confucians, or as atheists, conservatives, or progressives, as patriots of various stripes or as sceptics about patriotism, to assert the values of their creeds in order to police the orthodoxy of their adherents, to try to win over converts and engage in controversy with adherents of other creeds and communities. They are free to do so consistent with minimally reasonable respect for others' civil rights, including their entitlements to disencumber themselves of commitments to a particular creed, community, or relationship and exit from it, or to refuse to be bound by its moral codes and conceptions of the good in the first place.

In this social sphere of contemporary liberal democracies, creeds and associations that fall short of a minimal definition of "reasonableness," out of their intolerance of other's liberties or of the overall liberal constitutional order based on justice and equality, have historically been permitted to a certain extent. Fundamentalist religious groups, revolutionary political organizations, or chauvinistic nationalists are permitted, on Rawlsian grounds that, given the commitment of all citizens to uphold justice for one another in a liberal social order, no prima facie grounds exist to abrogate liberties for particular citizens or associations merely because they might be disposed to "act unjustly" and are in no position to complain when others do not tolerate them. More varied, circumstantial considerations arise as triggers for limiting the liberties of such groups and individuals when they actually do violate the liberties of others, or when they threaten the overall security of society and the "institution of liberty" itself.[28] In line with the third and fourth principles of value pluralism outlined above—that values can be objectively ranked as a consequence of moral inquiry, and also that such rankings can be fallible and susceptible to revision—citizens can trust in the organic educative influences of a constitutional regime grounded in principles of justice and equality, and in the more particular educative influences of freely conducted dialogue and inquiry, to encourage intolerant groups to give up the more unreasonable and potentially unjust aspects of their creeds and moral codes.

Nevertheless, controversies and confrontations even between "more reasonable" creeds and organizations in the social sphere can and do sometimes threaten civil rights, especially when one faction or creed tries to co-opt or capture legislative power to issue laws enforcing its conceptions of the good. Moreover, the value commitments pursued by people within different associations and communities—which sometimes enjoin a discriminatory or contemptuous attitude toward nonmembers or toward people who do not subscribe to its goods or its moral codes—can themselves be pulled into the domain of the public political forum and made the objects for possible applications of principles of justice by legislators or judiciaries. Hate speech has been proscribed in postwar European liberal democracies conscious of the effects of racial and religious hatred in the lead-up to World War II. Yet, as noted above, dilemmas have arisen over whether hate speech does, or does not, constitute a violation of civil rights to the extent that the liberty to engage in it must be legislatively proscribed, and these dilemmas are felt just as keenly in East Asian countries like Japan or South Korea as they are in "Western" liberal nations like the United States.[29] Dilemmas also arise when, for instance, values such as freedom of religious conscience clash with the value of equality. Are Christian bakers or photographers violating the civil rights of gay and lesbian couples when they invoke Christian conscience and refuse to bake wedding cakes for them or to take photographs at their weddings?[30] It is here that public reason dialogue and ultimately judicial agents must step in, and citizens and political and judicial officials alike are called on to do the difficult work of prescinding from more particular value commitments and moral codes to comprehend whether or how civil rights must be enforced in particular cases such as these.

Once we consider this social sphere with its diverse but also limited universe of values and the ways of life and association they guide, we are in a better position to appreciate not only the internal value diversity of liberal democratic societies, but also the value diversity between them—in ways that are conducive, or not so conducive, to fostering the capabilities and rights of their citizens. It was in this social sphere, in its embryonic form, that the values of civil and political rights, justice, civic equality, and franchise rights first arose and the conception of a public political sphere elaborating liberal rights and conceptions of justice was first formulated. The differential privileging of certain constellations of values in different liberal democratic societies, in accordance with the diverse influences of comprehensive moral and political doctrines within their political cultures, has led to differential emphases in interpretations of the political, civil, and property rights that otherwise distinguish these societies as constitutional liberal democracies.

So in the more social democratic political cultures of Northern Europe, greater attention is given to Rawlsian primary goods of bodily health, educational attainment, and wealth, or to the effects of "capability deprivation"[31] when poverty denies individuals access to health care, education, and incomes needed for their fully human functioning. In these societies, where there is greater consensus on an understanding of justice as securing equal access to such goods, or to securing provision for the appropriate exercise of capabilities, there is more support for redistributive taxation to fund, for example, universal health care and education. In the United States, where comprehensive doctrines of minimal government have been ascendant for four decades, such values are highly contested, and little consensus exists to justify universal health care, while government spending on public education and welfare is stagnating. These developments, coupled with growing income inequality and the intergenerational entrenchment of wealth and educational attainment among the highest income holders, now appear conducive to a drift away from liberal democracy to illiberal oligarchy.[32] In East Asian liberal democracies, with recent histories of economically interventionist, developmental statism, there is greater (if now declining) public tolerance for paternalism or perfectionism in governmental industrial and social policy than in the United States or Oceanic democracies.

In all these societies, however, there is a minimum (if sometimes fraying) consensus on the provision of welfare safety nets for the unemployed, the mentally and physically impaired, and the elderly, though those nets vary in extent and efficacy. Moreover, labor laws in practically all liberal democratic societies protect workplace freedoms of association, acknowledging the rights of employees to formally associate in trade unions and to petition and protest for wages and against exploitative treatment that reduces them (more or less) to a means to the economic ends of others. When, in November 1970, the Korean trade unionist Chun Tae-il self-immolated in protest against the exploitation of Seoul's garment factory workers, his last words were "Comply with labour laws. We are not machines!"[33] The powerful impact his protest had on South Korea's human rights and labor movements highlights the potential universal appeal of liberal ideals of equal respect for human dignity as a component of justice, beyond the bounds of so-called "Western liberal" societies.

Liberal Pluralism and Nationalism

The liberal pluralism outlined here is compatible with Yuli Tamir's liberal nationalism for which "the liberal tradition, with its respect for personal autonomy, reflection, and choice, and the national tradition, with its emphasis on belonging, loyalty, and solidarity . . . can indeed accommodate one another."[34] Such accommodation rests on the assumption that the social sphere is also the domain of values and customs of national belonging sustained through common, voluntary participation in national rituals, in civic society groups, in the creation, consumption, and discussion of national literature, music, film, and television dramatizing national stories, right down to quotidian or bureaucratic language tacitly affirming a sense of collective belonging—the language of "banal nationalism." It is the domain in which values of solidarity, loyalty, and identity can be articulated, interpreted, evaluated, and argued over regarding the appropriate forms they should take for the citizens of a particular nation.

Liberal nationalism of this sort prizes freedom of choice, conscience, religion, and association for individuals to criticize, or to participate or not in practices associated with the fostering of civic belonging, loyalty, and solidarity, and indeed to immigrate to another society. It is thus compatible with the ethical individualism upheld in this book. If there is a danger that liberal nationalism as I am stating it here poses for liberal pluralism, it arises from the following concern: that the ideals of civic belonging, loyalty, and solidarity might become subsumed under an overriding categorical "singular attribution"[35] of political, moral, or religious societal identity, under which, as Tamir puts it, the "identity of individuals is totally constituted by their national membership."[36] In Chapter 5, we have already considered an instance of this in the hybrid Confucian national morality of pre-1945 Japan.

A more contemporary instance of this is a society defined substantively, say, by its political leadership or by powerful civic groups as "Christian" in view of its presumed majoritarian, traditional senses of belonging and identity, upholding a "Christian" way of life while practicing a liberal-Christian "tolerance" of other ways of life that minorities might practice. In such a case, the liberal and nationalist components of liberal nationalism threaten to come apart, *if* what is being proposed is a rather precarious *modus vivendi* stated from the point of view of a dominant categorical identity, that remains open to being enforced in sectarian terms. A Christian political doctrine (however the state chooses to define it) begins to look like a comprehensive doctrine of the good life for an entire society. The rights of religious minorities to follow their creeds may then be regarded as special dispensations granted by the majority, which may or may not stably hold depending on their whim, rather than as a principled stable outcome justified by public reasons legitimate for all—the sort of outcome based on an overlapping consensus.

This concern can be aroused in attempts to articulate the particular culture of a society as a particularist morality of ideals to be defended against "foreign" ideas that threaten to transform, and thus endanger, that cultural particularity. This sort of argument, common as we have seen in early twentieth-century Japan, has become common again in national and civilizational identity politics arguments against globalization and modernization, where "Western" liberal ideals, doctrines, and practices are seen as a source of such threat. The danger here is twofold. First is the potential for conflict between presumed "indigenous" cultural or national ideals to which adherence is required, as a condition for preserving the integrity of indigenous culture and national identity, and "Western" liberal values of freedom of speech, conscience, and association that also claim widespread allegiance. Second is a danger of an outright abrogation, or rejection, of these liberal values inasmuch as they are viewed as threats to cultural integrity and national identity. In this chapter, which focuses for the most part on actually existing East Asian democracies where these liberal freedoms are taken for granted, it is the first danger that I shall consider here.

This focus goes to the heart of claims about the "Confucian" identity of East Asian societies. In a work dedicated to critical evaluation of contemporary arguments for a Confucian politics or morality, it is obvious that principles three and four in the liberal value pluralism described above are incompatible with the state establishment of Confucianism as a strongly comprehensive doctrine, with its hierarchy of goods and values established by an infallible moral knowledge accessible to a class of morally and intellectually cultivated persons. However, these principles can accommodate the existence of different reasonable comprehensive doctrines—when their advocates are capable of practicing minimal tolerance for rival doctrines. Principles one to four at minimum require a political order with institutions and laws that protect freedom of conscience, freedom of speech, and freedom of association, though as a range of thinkers from Kant to Berlin note, it is at least conceivable that a mild autocracy might secure these freedoms. Liberal pluralism does not entail liberal democracy. There are a number of empirical arguments pointing to liberal democracy as its most favorable and stable home, providing for peaceful transitions in power and the peaceful removal of governments that a citizenry deems to be incompetent, under a constitutional framework ensuring that citizens and government respect political, property, and civil rights.

Evaluating the Case for a Confucian Public Reason

In the sheer variety of Confucian political philosophies in circulation today are some that do acknowledge the facts of value pluralism, while seeking to justify the instituting of a Confucian democratic order that can accommodate them. Kim Sungmoon, for instance, argues for a *Confucian* public reason, for which Confucian habits of the heart and sentiments, suitably reinterpreted for public and political rather than moral deliberation, "broadly constitute" that reason. In stating this acknowledgment, Kim is more realistic than those Confucian philosophers who rather glibly assume a value homogeneity in the public spheres in East Asian societies, at least in the matter of adherence to Confucian values. Kim's public reason, unlike that advocated by Rawls or other "deontological liberals," is presented as an organic outgrowth of the background civic cultures of East Asian societies. It dispenses with Rawls's freestanding conception of justice insulated from such civic culture. It also differs from the more limited, institutional scope of some political liberal understandings of public reason. Kim's concept of public reason extends beyond the public political sphere deliberations of legislative, executive, and judicial authorities over constitutional principles of justice to incorporate deliberations over policy questions by ordinary citizens in the public sphere.[37] Given the strength of Kim's arguments in support of this Confucian public reason, and its differences with the non-Confucian liberal pluralism I have argued for, it is important to evaluate his arguments in some detail.

Kim's public reason, or 'reasons," is ultimately grounded in culturally particular Confucian sentiments and passions—grouped together in what Kim calls a "critical familial affection."[38] These sentiments and passions provide adequate motivation for "concerns about things (all citizens) care about," and ensure that public reason does not just consist of "rational considerations" accessible to all and that are partly justified from within their own conceptions of the good life.[39] This is also a public reason *perfectionism* because it recognizes that (1) there is a "valuable Confucian way of life" shared and valued by the citizens of a "Confucian society" and (2) that the state may permissibly encourage or discourage activities that connect with the standing of key Confucian values, reinterpreted as public values that all citizens may follow, irrespective of their own diverse conceptions of the good: filial piety, ancestor worship, ritual propriety, and social harmony.[40] Though Kim seems to think that this Confucian public reason is at least partly approximated in the political institutions and practices of contemporary East Asian representative democracies, he also presents it as a "regulative ideal" against which those institutions and practices can be evaluated and criticized.[41] Some clear disagreements between Kim's understanding of public reason and mine are implicit in this brief sketch. Before attending to them, I want to consider Kim's motivations for regarding culturally particular Confucian sentiments and habits of the heart as the constituents of a public reason that is also attuned to liberal democratic institutions and practices.[42]

Kim is writing from a perspective that tries to balance (1) the claims of national cultural particularism, asserting the value of a nation's particular ways of life and the entitlement of its citizens to protect and cherish them through exercise of national self-determination,[43] with (2) the universalist claims of a political philosophy that identifies cross-cultural criteria for the better types of political constitution by which people can stably practice such valued ways of life. This perspective has a respectable, if neglected, pedigree in European liberal thought, extending from Johann Herder through Isaiah Berlin to the liberal nationalism of Yael Tamir.[44] Herder, for instance, favored liberalism and republicanism as better forms of government and upheld liberal principles of "free investigation" "as the sole antidote against delusion and error." Yet he also believed that, in accordance with their own entitlement to cultural self-determination, "[t]he roses for the wreath of freedom must be picked by a people's own hands and grow happily out of its own needs."[45]

Kim's analysis and justification for a Confucian public reason is another instance of such a balancing perspective. As we have already noted in chapter 1, Herder worried about the culturally homogenizing forces unleashed by French rationalist Enlightenment thought on the diverse folk cultures of Europe, and on the cultures of peoples outside of Europe. Kim for his part is concerned about the onslaughts of a "global monism of liberal democracy." Non-Western peoples wishing to democratize their societies are in this instance confronted with dominant, comprehensive liberal discourses that also require them to give up their distinctive, culturally nonliberal ways of life and adopt a *liberal* public reason as a condition of "successful" democratization.[46]

What Kim has in mind is not a Confucian democracy distinguished agonistically from "liberal democracy," but a proposal to "Confucianize partially liberal and democratic regimes that currently exist" in East Asia.

He claims that "liberal discourse and liberal-democratic institutions are not socially relevant in East Asian societies, where citizens are soaked in Confucian habits and mores, often without self-awareness."[47] This remark might seem suggestive of a cultural incompatibilist argument against liberal democracy even in East Asia's representative democracies where, Kim claims, there is "discord between the more or less liberal-democratic institutional-political hardware and the social-cultural software that should operate it."[48] Yet Kim makes it clear that he still wants to see liberal-democratic institutions fully operative in East Asian societies, given their proven track record in checking abuses by power holders and protecting the "public freedoms" and rights of citizens. The compromise between "liberal" hardware and "Confucian" software that Kim proposes, then, is that the former be adapted to the Confucian "habits and mores" of East Asian citizens. This can be brought about through the translation of the language of liberal rights into Confucian idioms and "their reappropriation with reference to public reason" conceived, as we have seen, in Confucian terms.[49]

A concern may arise at this point that Kim's public reason Confucianism inclines toward an overriding categorical and monist conception of citizenship identity as Confucian, to the detriment of other identities and conceptions of the good that citizens of East Asian societies may want to pursue, as liberals, Buddhists, Taoists, Christians, secularists, and so forth. This is clearly not Kim's intent, as is made clear in his statement of the principles for Confucian public reason in his book *Public Reason Confucianism: A Reconstruction*, which I reproduce in full below:

P1: The valuable Confucian way of life refers to the collective way of living widely shared and cherished by citizens in a Confucian society.

P2: Citizens in a Confucian society are still saturated with Confucian habits, mores, and moral sentiments, despite their subscriptions to various comprehensive doctrines, and even though they may not hold Confucianism as their self-consciously chosen personal value system.

P3: In a Confucian society, all citizens are equal to one another qua public citizens and together they exercise popular sovereignty.

P4: The Confucian (democratic) state respects constitutional rights held by its citizens, among others, the rights to religious freedom, freedom of conscience, freedom of expression, and freedom of association; thus the state has no desire either to suppress value plurality in civil society or to elevate Confucianism as the state religion.

P5: Confucian public reason refers to the reason of the democratic citizens in a Confucian society and it is rooted in Confucian mores, habits, and moral sentiments such as, but not limited to, filial piety and ritual propriety; it delineates the legitimate boundary of state action and provides moral content (which is open for public contestation) for basic rights, duties, and liberties.

P6: A subscription to Confucian public reason (as stipulated in P5) on the part of voluntary immigrants and cultural associations formed by them is the inevitable price for the fair terms of integration into the Confucian society (such as the equal right to freedom of association). While Confucian public reason must be justifiable to *all* citizens in a Confucian society, including immigrants, immigrated citizens must strive to negotiate their religious or nonreligious comprehensive doctrines with Confucian public reason in order to fully exercise their constitutional rights and liberties.[50]

P1 and P2 state the culturally particularist aspects of Kim's public reason argument, and P3 and P4 the universalist elements, guaranteeing to all citizens the equal rights and liberties of a typical constitutional liberal democracy. P5 and P6 set out the obligations that adherents of diverse comprehensive doctrines and ways of life in a pluralistic society have to engage in an overlapping consensus that ensures their ways of life and doctrines comport with this public reason. Intriguingly, from the point of view of Kim's Confucian political perfectionism, even traditional Korean clans practicing a comprehensive Confucian morality may be legally directed to abandon sexually discriminatory practices, because they do not comport with Confucian *public* reason norms that uphold women's equal rights to participate in Confucian ritual life.[51]

Kim's is a sophisticated, well-worked-out argument for a culturally distinctive public reason that can nevertheless embed liberal democratic institutions and practices in East Asian societies. There are nonetheless two queries that I want to raise. The first concerns his analysis of two moral psychological traits—*chong* (정), or "familial affectionate sentiment," and *uri* (우리), or "we-ness," that are, in their interaction, the "uniquely Korean-Confucian" constituents for the South Korean variety of Confucian public reason.[52] I argue that these may just as plausibly be construed as essentially contested concepts open to being claimed for different Korean cultural and ethnic nationalist as well as Confucian interpretations. The second query regards the potential for public reason Confucian perfectionism as Kim conceives it to impose morally taxing, unreasonable burdens on the consciences of adherents of different ways of life that may not conform with certain Confucian *public* norms—including South Korea's large population of Protestant Christians.

In chapter 1 I raised some doubts about the attribution of Confucian collective identities to modern East Asian societies, and about claims for Confucian habits of the heart as the underlying unreflective ethical values of East Asian people. These doubts affect the plausibility of P1 and P2 of Kim's public reason Confucianism quoted above, as principles for a Confucian public reason. Suffice it to say that irrespective of those doubts, I do not consider Kim to be imposing a categorical, singular affiliation-based conception of Confucian identity on East Asian societies—he is no Confucian monist. He makes it clear that citizens of those societies do have "subscriptions to comprehensive doctrines" through which they can pursue multiple affiliations and acquire multiple religious and political identities compatible with citizenship in a society with a Confucian constitutional order.

Kim's social psychological analysis of *uri* and *chong* proceeds from observations of the intensely felt collective belonging among contemporary Koreans, and the moral emotions associated with it, including accountability and shame for actions that are not the personal responsibility of individual citizens. By itself, the social psychological aspect of Korean collective identity is susceptible to criticism in that it swallows up the individual, preventing the emergence of autonomous selves. However, Kim argues that there is in addition a politically constituted *uri*-consciousness among Korean citizens in Korean democratic society, within which individual identities are cultivated and developed and have their agency enhanced through interaction with "other, interdependent selves" forming a "unique group dynamic" rarely found in Western societies.[53] *Uri* in this form is analogous to a Rousseauan "general will" that generates a collective political interest as well as a deeply shared sense of political responsibility that is "uniquely Korean-Confucian."[54]

The phenomenon of *uri* is intended to explain the sustained vitality of Korean civil society, which has retained high levels of mass participation and protest mobilization well after the establishment of liberal democracy, while other postdictatorship democracies have seen that civil society energy dissipate. It also explains the collectively felt shame and responsibility Koreans have been observed to express, by taking responsibility for and mobilizing against what they see as the corrupted state of their political representatives in mass protest campaigns.

The familial affectionate sentiment of *chong* shapes *uri* into a politically responsible civic virtue, preventing it from taking shape in a more sinister, amoral, and antidemocratic mass mobilization. *Chong* is often claimed to be difficult to explain to non-Koreans, but Kim interprets it as an "emotional glue" enabling the formation of a politically responsible Korean "we-ness." It is an "affectionate relationality" and emotion turning the Korean self into an interdependent self by "constantly situating the self in *uri*-relationships" with their own highly particularized moral and cultural codes. *Chong* affection has its basis in and is at first cultivated in Korean familial relations, encompassing both positive and negative, and critical feelings, including not only affection and loyalty for but also deep resentment against and shame on behalf of loved ones. These emotions are then sublimated into and give expression in the civic virtue of *uri*-responsibility.[55] The identification of *chong* and *uri* as familial sentiments constitutive of civic belonging and collective responsibility underwrites Kim's argument that these are also Confucian-based sentiments. For he argues that a democratic Confucian politics such as the one he infers from Korean democratic civic life does incorporate a modernized idea of the Mencian idea of "the political as familial," of a society in which citizens relate to each other, and their political representatives, as if they were members of a larger family.[56]

Chong and *uri* are social facts of the sort described under my first principle of liberal pluralism, and are constituents in South Koreans' moral psychological and civic self-imaginings *as* Koreans. My question is whether they are essentially contested concepts, thereby falling short of the third criterion for identifying thick ethical concepts as *Confucian* ethical concepts, as explained in chapter 1. Now *chong* would seem to be an obvious candidate for consideration as a Confucian moral sentiment, and not only because of its familial orientation. The Chinese character for what Koreans define as *chong*—情—has its roots in the Confucian tradition, where 情 (*qing*) denotes a variety of meanings. In the *Mencius* it refers to what is essential or proper to something's nature, such as human nature and the moral feelings that grow out of it.[57] In the *Book of Rites*, *qing* can also be translated as "feelings," and the Liyun chapter refers to the "seven emotions"

(七情 *qiqing*) of human beings: joy, anger, sadness, fear, love, disliking, and liking.[58] Sixteenth-century Korean Neo-Confucian scholars famously debated these "seven feelings" or emotions and their connection to Mencius's "four beginnings."[59] There would appear, then, to be historical continuity between the *chong* of Korean Neo-Confucians and the *chong* of contemporary Korean familial sentiments.

Yet the appearance of continuity between classical *qing* and contemporary *chong* could also be plausibly explained as an artefact of modern Japanese scholarly translation applied to modern European psychological concepts, subsequently translated into Korean. Reconceptualized as a modern, psychological term, *chong* entered the Korean language in the early twentieth century from Japanese, through the influential literary essays and novels of Yi Kwangsu, one of Korea's pioneering nationalist intellectuals. It did so in an explicitly anti-Confucian form. Yi, who received a modern education in Japan and graduated from Waseda University, acquiring from his studies a tripartite understanding of human psychological faculties divided into intellect, feeling, and will (知情意 *chijōi/chichongui*).[60] This tripartite understanding was introduced into Japanese with Nishi Amane's pioneering translation of a Western psychological work in 1875–1876, Joseph Haven's *Mental Philosophy: Including the Intellect, Sensibilities and Will*. In this book Nishi translated sensibility or feeling using the classical Chinese character 情.[61] Haven himself was working with the rich eighteenth-century tradition of psychological theorizing running through Christian Wolff to Immanuel Kant, in which feeling or sensibility (*gefühl*) came to be recognized as a separate mental faculty from knowing, with its own distinct subject matters in aesthetics.[62]

As I pointed out in chapter 1, Nishi and other Japanese scholars who used classical Chinese characters and neologisms in translating European philosophical and psychological terms were hugely influential for later Korean and Chinese scholarship and literature, which assimilated this vast new translated corpus.[63] Yet such a linguistic indigenization of originally foreign ideas may serve to obscure their foreign origins.

In any case, in Yi's 1916 essay "What is Literature?" there is an expressly anti-Confucian conceptualization of *chong* that is quite at odds with Kim's Confucian-familial understanding of the term. He believed, in fact, that the influence of Chinese culture and Confucianism had *prevented* the development of *chong* among Koreans. Coupled with his recognition that the emotions have their own psychological faculty independent of knowledge and will, Yi argued that the literary and visual arts are the independent fields in which human emotions are expressed and "find fulfillment" and they should not be subordinated to science or morality.⁶⁴ *Chong* had been realized in this manner in the European arts since the Renaissance. Yet under the influence of Chinese culture and Confucian morality during the Chosun Dynasty, Koreans were "enslaved by a strict standard of morality" that prevented them from developing visual and literary arts that gave independent expression to emotions.⁶⁵ In Korea's pre-Confucian dynasties, literary and visual arts had embodied "Korean thoughts and emotions," but these arts had been lost or suppressed through the brute intrusion of Chinese culture. Yi hoped that the influx of Western culture would help Koreans to build a new "spiritual civilization," including a new literature that authentically embodied their thoughts and emotions.⁶⁶ Yi went further in his short stories and in his first and most famous novel, *Heartless* (무정 *Mujong*) to show how the influence of Confucian morality and its patriarchal customs had prevented the full development of *chong* between Korean men and women and in the national life of Koreans.⁶⁷

Kim's interpretation of *chong* ties it to Confucian famialism; but Yi's cultural nationalist interpretation required the repudiation of Confucian morality, as a condition for Koreans to realize interpersonal and national *chong*. Contemporary Korean self-imaginings of *chong* might well seem to fulfill Yi's hopes for such a realization, but he would have rejected any proposed Confucian genealogy for this sentiment. *Uri* also emerges as an essentially contested concept in light of Yi's and later Korean nationalists' treatment of this concept. Shin Gi-Wook has argued that, like other prominent Korean intellectuals of the period, Yi made a transition from cultural to ethnic nationalism by the early 1930s. By then he had repudiated his earlier individualism for a racialized collectivism, characterized by doctrines of "we-ism" (*uri-chuui*) as well as groupism and totalitarianism. Shin adds that Yi's theory of Korean ethnic nationalism was influential for post-1945 conceptions of the Korean nation in both North and South Korea.⁶⁸ Some scholars today are detecting the emergence of a Korean "globalized cultural" nationalism expressed in the slogan "our nation" (우리나라 *uri nara*) in place of older ethnic nationalist slogans such as "our nation/people" (우리민족 *uri minjok*), which rejects ethnic- and affiliation-based arguments for unification with North Korea.⁶⁹ This globalized cultural nationalism bears some comparison to Kim's conceptualization of *uri*-responsibility, but attributions to it of a Confucian heritage are disputable.

Key components of Kim's Confucian public reason including the moral psychological and civic sentiments of *chong* and *uri* appear to have a contested conceptual character in twentieth-century Korean nationalist and intellectual history. Kim's Confucian-Korean famialist interpretation of these concepts' conflicts with cultural and ethnic nationalist framings of these same concepts in Korean literary and political thought, which were non- or anti-Confucian, and hostile to Chinese cultural influence in Korea. From this point of view there might still be culturally particular public reasons operating in Korean life, grounded in sentiments such as *chong* and *uri*, embedding and conditioning liberal political institutions and practices much as Kim argues. But the notion that these are distinctly and historically *Confucian* sentiments is open to dispute by rival Korean intellectual traditions that also have a claim on them.

Yet as P5 of Kim's principles for Confucian public reason make clear, there is more to Confucian moral sentiments than the Korean sentiments of *chong* and *uri*. Other relevant moral sentiments include those found throughout East Asian societies with a Confucian heritage, such as ritual propriety, filial piety, and ancestor worship. P6 requires, as we have seen, an effort by citizens committed to diverse conceptions of the good to also engage in an overlapping consensus on these public reason sentiments as civic virtues. In his 2014 book, *Confucian Democracy in East Asia*, Kim argues that citizens in a Confucian democracy are "*morally* required to vigorously and voluntarily embody the Confucian mores and habits that sustain and reproduce their public way of life," because their public reasons are anchored in Confucian habits and mores, and also because, as citizens of such a Confucian democracy, they should not reject what they have in common in civic life in spite of their own pluralistic commitments to diverse goods, especially when their society is confronted with the "ethically and culturally monistic force of globalization."[70]

My concern here is that this political perfectionist aspect of Kim's democratic Confucianism risks imposing morally taxing burdens on citizens committed to diverse conceptions of the good life—burdens more taxing than those imposed by a more minimal nonperfectionist liberal constitution of the sort that I am arguing for. It is important, though, to understand why Kim gives such prominence to Confucian sentiments such as ritual propriety in his account of Confucian public reason. He conceptualizes a shared Confucian civility as a "bridging social capital that aims at social integration across cultural, ethnic and religious difference."[71] This bridging capital, as a central function of the Confucian "public culture" Kim identifies in East Asian societies, is based on adherence to core perfectionist Confucian values such as filiality, harmony, respect for the elderly, and deference, "which are respected as public virtues" independently of the private value and religious choices or orientations of their citizens. Kim adds that "it is through the continued practice of *li* that these public virtues are socially available in those increasingly pluralist societies." The rituals that embody these virtues can bond together citizens with otherwise different value orientations. They serve to facilitate civil communication between citizens through a self-imposed restraint enacted in (ideally) smooth ritual performance, and "mutual reciprocity"—"the capacity to seek fair terms for co-operation for its own sake."[72] This is roughly in accordance with the socially "thin" conception of rites I argued for in chapter 3, and so Kim's version of it in his proposed Confucian civil society deserves further consideration.

What Korean public rituals, or *li*, based on these supposedly shared virtues could claim such a shared allegiance? One example would be *Jesa* (제사)—memorial rites performed for departed family members and ancestors. *Jesa* rites are held on the anniversaries of the deaths of individual departed family members and traditionally performed in the homes of the eldest sons of families. They involve elaborate ceremonial settings and offerings of food and drink on specially prepared altar tables. There are also *Jesa* rites venerating family ancestors performed on public holidays such as *Chuseok*, the Korean Thanksgiving holiday. During that time many families return to home towns or rural districts where ancestral graves are located to participate in communal family activities, meals, and ritual food offerings to ancestors and to visit and bow before ancestral graves.

If we do recognize *Jesa* as a Confucian practice, we are in a position to identify it as one of the constituent elements of a public, Confucian bridging capital, of filial sentiments expressed in *li* that bring together in family settings people of otherwise diverse professions and faiths, horizontally binding "individuals who are socially and culturally diverse" as citizens of a Confucian democratic culture. Moreover, participation in *Jesa* requires no thoroughgoing commitment to Confucianism as a comprehensive doctrine; it rather resembles an interdenominational service. Early twenty-first-century surveys have indicated that strong public participation in *Jesa* support this view, with over 78 percent of South Koreans across denominational lines reported as participating in it.[73] Thus it is an element of a "Confucian public culture" "which any Korean, regardless of her private value system, can empathetically resonate with" while still possessing "a right to contest its public nature."[74]

This latter point is an important concession, because *Jesa* is mostly prohibited within Korea's large Protestant Christian communities, which constitute 20 percent of the Korean population. Such prohibitions on individual participation in *Jesa* are a source of well-documented discord within some Korean families with diverse values and religious faiths,[75] and also of discord within Korean Protestant congregations. Surveys have shown individual Protestant Christians to be almost evenly split about whether or not to participate in *Jesa*, in spite of official Protestant prohibitions on their practice.[76] Protestant congregations have developed compromise Christian memorial rites which constitute a partial adaptation to traditional ancestral rites. However, they omit key aspects of the *Jesa* ceremony, and there is little consensus within congregations over their practice.[77]

The partial or complete refusal of many Korean Protestants, or of other nonconformists to participate in *Jesa* rites, *could* be construed as an *unreasonable* refusal to subscribe to the norms and sentiments of Confucian public reason, especially in view of the "bridging capital" value such norms and sentiments have for binding citizens of diverse creeds and affiliations in a public life as citizens of a Confucian democracy. What would be the response of an advocate of Confucian public reason to this unreasonableness? One option is to argue that Korean Protestant Christians are also "*morally* required to vigorously and voluntarily embody" Confucian mores and habits, by observing these rites syncretically much as people of other denominations such as Buddhists and Catholics do.

It is hard, however, to see how such "requirement" could not darken into a mobilization of sectarian sentiments against Protestant Christians who refuse to comply, especially if their beliefs come to be seen as one aspect of a culturally deracinating, global "ethical monism," as an uncompromising foreign religion negatively impacting on the indigenous Confucian mores and habits of Korean society. Confucian political perfectionism in this instance need not exercise a coercive power; it could be exhortative, with governments sponsoring educational campaigns and advertising on the social and moral benefits of *jesa*; or politicians and other officials could issue direct appeals to, or criticisms of, those who refuse to participate in it. In a society with a strong sense of national, collective belonging such as South Korea, a negative mobilization of public sentiments from such public exhortations and criticisms is not inconceivable. While there would in this instance be no direct exercise of government coercive power, the "indirect" coercion exercised by government agencies encouraging civic mobilization against members of dissenting creeds can be highly effective in inhibiting their personal liberties and associational freedoms. This is what transpired in the aftermath of the *Lese Majeste* affair involving the dissenting Japanese Christian Uchimura Kanzo in 1891. The Meiji-era constitution of the time protected religious freedoms. But Christians such as Uchimura who were hounded out of their jobs and subjected to extremely negative publicity and public harassment still experienced something like "combined capability deprivation." Formally, under law they had the right to practice their faith conscientiously, but requirements for Christian teachers and pupils in schools to bow before copies of the *Imperial Rescript*, and fierce public, media, and official condemnation of those who did not, severely limited the "substantial freedoms" that the law otherwise granted them for religious liberty, freedom of conscience, and freedom of association. Kim certainly is supportive of Christian freedoms of association and expression,[78] so what I am concerned with here is one potential unintended, negative application of his proposed public reason norms.

A perfectionist Confucian public reason could end up imposing morally taxing burdens on the lives of people pursuing diverse conceptions of the good in different associations and communities—more morally taxing than the burdens a nonperfectionist public reason would impose, with more austere, Rawlsian understandings of justice and the limits of its enforcement in the social sphere. This is not to say that, from the ethical individualist perspective favored in this book, and from a variety of other liberal or Confucian perspectives, the exclusionary or sectarian practices of Protestant congregations are not above criticism and reform. Being able to express love and veneration for departed family members and ancestors in a culturally valued way is an important capability potentially thwarted by Protestant prohibitions upon *Jesa* rite practices.

However, the liberalism of fear that underlies this chapter's liberal pluralism enjoins caution about direct or indirect state interference in the affairs of such associations, beyond enforcement of exit rights, property rights, and rights to life and freedom of expression. Its characteristic suspicion is that even well-intended perfectionist objectives may unduly burden the religious and associational freedoms of individuals within those organizations, and generate precedents for "mission creep" in increasingly intrusive interventions in associational life. For a more restricted liberalism there are safer options for relief for the thwarted interests of dissenting members within particular creeds and associations. For instance, Protestant congregants who wish to practice *Jesa* rites may also mobilize public support or criticism on their behalf to make the moral case for doctrinal flexibility within their denomination, leave to join a more inclusive congregation, or leave and set up their own congregation.

In the end, my disagreements with Kim's public reason Confucianism are something of a family quarrel, since we both recognize the legitimacy of the current pluralistic liberal democratic order in East Asia's constitutional democracies, and both recognize the importance of sustaining valued ways of life, cultural affiliations, and national belonging that can also shape the constitutional value priorities of liberal institutions and practices. Our differences lie in (1) my own doubts that Confucianism continues to constitute a deep, unreflective matrix for East Asian civic belonging and identity; (2) my argument that claims for its centrality in sentiments of civic belonging and identity are in any case contestable in the diversified twentieth-century political, religious, and cultural heritages of East Asian societies such as South Korea; and (3) my conviction that political perfectionism is a less desirable means for securing a stable, pluralistic society in which diverse individuals, associations, and sects can pursue their valued ways of life in peace.

The Prospects for Confucianism: A More Modest Assessment

I conclude this chapter, and this book, by revisiting its main theme: the prospects for Confucianism. The first prospect is the capacity of diverse Confucian doctrines to contribute new themes, concepts, and argumentative perspectives to global philosophical conversations in moral and political philosophy. Having spent the greater part of this book exploring that thesis, I will not develop it further here.

The other prospects, as I see them, are these: First, that Confucianism can contribute both inspiration and doctrinal content to NPOs and religious organizations practicing varieties of Confucian "comprehensive doctrines" that can expand the marketplace of ideas and ethical practices in East Asian civil societies, or in civil societies beyond East Asia; and second, that Confucianism can be a source of inspiration for a type of conviction politics in representative democratic polities, articulating high standards of ethical conduct for elected officials.

On the one hand there is scope for advocacy and social capital building by Confucian NPOs that attends to the practice of filial piety norms in contemporary East Asian society. The rapid undermining of the material and demographic conditions for filial piety practices in East Asian family life, evidenced by individualization, defamiliation, and the rise of impoverished, lonely elderly households is a matter of great concern for Confucians today. While the focus of much advocacy has been on the rights elderly parents have to emotional and financial support from adult children, there needs to be a frank acknowledgment about when such care can no longer be reasonably expected, where no such adult children exist (and this scenario is likely to increase as the proportion of childless, single adults in the population grows as a whole), or where the health care and support needs of longer-lived and frail elderly place unbearable care and financial burdens on adult children on lower incomes and in precarious employment sectors. More robust state welfare and income provisions for elderly people are not incompatible with statements in *The Book of Rites* and *The Mencius* that call for public welfare provisions for elderly people who cannot be supported by adult children.

Confucian NPO's potential advocacy for greater state involvement in providing professional care, income, and capability-enhancing lifestyle opportunities for elderly people could proceed alongside advocacy for the protection of the elderly from financial exploitation, and also fraud and physical or emotional abuse from carers. NPOs could also advocate for tax incentives, family support allowances, family care leave, and subsidized professional home care services to encourage coresidency between parents and adult children, relieve care burdens, and mitigate the socially atomizing effects of market relations on family life. Finally, Confucian NPOs could provide volunteer as well as professionally staffed services offering companionship, prepared food, medical support, and participation in community and educational activities to the lonely elderly, with participation in such volunteer work providing ample opportunities for the cultivation of Confucian virtues through filial-like relations of care, love, and service for the elderly.

The role of new Confucian religions in East Asian civil societies is cause for some ambivalence. On the one hand there is scope for them to enrich the religious lives of East Asians by providing the chance to participate in a way of life that claims a deep connection with the premodern past of East Asian societies, and such claims can be an important source of solace, spiritual identity, and life meaning for those disoriented by the pace and scope of modernization. On the other hand, some Confucian religious organizations' "Confucian Heritage"–based claims to legitimacy as state religions in Chinese society presents problems for a liberal normative or indeed Confucian public reason perspective on pluralism in East Asia liberal democracies today.

Two instances of new Confucian religions are the Hong Kong–based Confucian Academy, founded in 1930, and the much smaller Halls of the Sage Confucius Project, based in the Mainland China city of Shenzhen and founded in 2009 by Zhou Beichen, a follower of the philosopher Jiang Qing, whose political philosophy I discussed in the previous chapter.[79] The proselytizing ambitions of these new religions, their promotion of ritual activities, private education, volunteerism, and philanthropic activities such as the establishment of hospitals and Confucian Halls and temples, and even their cultural heritage claims to special legitimacy in East Asian societies pose no reason for anxiety for liberal pluralists or for Confucian public reason advocates. They are in competition with each other and other religions such as Christianity to offer spiritual and social services to attract followers and legitimate their claims to special spiritual status and authority. Even in today's heavily policed marketplace of ideas in China, citizens are free to embrace, dispute, or ignore their claims to a special cultural heritage and legitimacy.

Of greater concern are the claims made on behalf of some of these new Confucian religions to state religion status, on the basis of their alleged continuity with the practices and doctrines of premodern state-sanctioned Confucianism. Scholars have noted that the publically stated ambitions of the Confucian Academy to reassert Confucianism as central to China's "spiritual civilization" and to strengthen "unity and national cohesion" are consonant with the cultural nationalist ideology of the Communist Party government, and intended to gain favor from it.[80] Zhou Beichen is far more ambitious in making claims for a Confucian state religion in China, and as we saw in the previous chapter, Jiang Qing's proposed tricameral system of parliament premised on a Confucian cosmology and theology would go a long way toward instituting it. The familiar problems of accommodating pluralism in religious belief—and of capability deprivation through limitations on religious freedoms and conscience—arise in the implementation of such a scheme.

The use of state agencies to socially engineer commitment to state Confucian doctrine through mass education, the institution of state rituals, and the punishment and marginalization of religious dissenters or nonconformists cannot be discounted, as I stated in chapter 5. In the present-day conditions of limited pluralism and individualization in Chinese society, with the Communist Party divided over residual allegiance to Communist doctrine and indifferent or hostile to the idea of Confucianism as a successor state doctrine, the prospects for a Confucian state religion might seem rather limited in China. However, as the Communist Party transforms under personalized autocratic rule, Confucianism may be appropriated more aggressively to shore up regime legitimacy, and aspirations to regional hegemony.

There is, finally, the contribution that a self-conscious Confucian sensibility, as a morality of ideals, can make to a conviction-based politics in East Asian representative democracies. The late South Korean president

Kim Dae Jung provides one pattern for such a politics. I define conviction politics as the conduct of political campaigns, policy, and an overall political career in accordance with deeply held principles and values, rather than in response to a perceived consensus or majoritarian sentiment (though these latter responses may contextually be allowed a subordinate role in the conviction politician's conduct). By itself, this definition could also encompass the Confucian conviction politics of autocratic statesmen such as Lee Kuan Yew and Park Chung-Hee. What distinguishes Kim Dae-Jung's conduct as an elected official and president, I would argue, was a sense of his being a democratically representative official whose legitimacy rested on his responsibility to the will of the people who elected him, *and* also to the law which limited his executive power. For Kim, such representation and legitimacy could be conceptualized in liberal democratic and Confucian terms.[81]

Kim's conviction politics was revealed in a life of political activism and service consistent with his professed Catholic Christian and Confucian ideals, and in his published statements on the role of Confucianism in contemporary political and ethical life. In his life's work as a dissident and as a president, he held to the Christian value of forgiveness, which lay behind his decision to pardon two former Korean presidents implicated in the Kwangju Massacre in 1980.[82] His opposition to successive autocratic regimes in the 1970s and 1980s finds its echoes in Confucian traditions of remonstrance against unjust authority, and in Christian theological dissent against temporal power that violates natural law. Welfare reforms in the first year of his presidency in 1997–98, including the expansion of employment insurance for the unemployed and the introduction of a universal, redistributive public pension system, are consonant with the social-justice orientation to retiree and elderly welfare that can be associated with progressive liberal and Confucian thought. In his ethical ideals, Kim did not embody some deep Confucian habits overlaid by Westernized ethical accretions; rather, and in the pluralistic spirit expressed in this chapter, Confucian, Catholic, and liberal doctrines contributed side by side to his ethical stance.

Kim's 1994 *Foreign Affairs* article "Is Culture Destiny?" famously rebutted Lee Kuan Yew's invocation of Confucian values on behalf of autocratic governance.[83] Kim argued against Lee that democracy is not alien to East Asian cultural traditions, that justifications for democracy are multiple and can also be found in Asia's "rich heritage of democracy-oriented philosophies and traditions." Buddhism and the late nineteenth-century Korean *Tonghhak* rebellion supplied non-Confucian sources for such a heritage. Kim pointed to Mencius's concept of the Mandate of Heaven, of "the people's right to rise up and overthrow" sovereigns who had lost that mandate, to the ancient Confucian adage that "the will of the people is the will of Heaven" and to historical Confucian institutions such as the Boards of censors that curbed the misrule of emperors and ministers to argue that "the fundamental ideas and traditions necessary for democracy (historically) existed in both Europe and Asia."[84] Scholars may question the anachronism in Kim attributing "democratic traditions" and rule of law institutions to China's and Korea's dynastic states. However, arguments like this do contribute to interlocking, pluralistic justifications for responsible representative governance, to an overlapping consensus inventively drawing on traditional beliefs and moralities, which can defuse anxieties about the dissolution of indigenous traditions by Westernization.

Kim's legacy as a statesman is not unblemished, and this is not the place to engage in hagiography. My modest argument is that, insofar as he consistently, and without sectarian intent, embodied in his conduct as an activist, politician, and president Confucian, Christian, and liberal ideals, his is a pattern worth following for other East Asian politicians interested in innovatively reappropriating Confucian ideals for democratic and civic life. This pattern does not hold the diverse peoples of East Asian nations to a vision of their unity in a shared, even tacit Confucian heritage, which many would not be inclined to consent to. Rather, it identifies Confucianism as one among many sources of ideals, exemplars, and stories for fashioning collective senses of belonging, identity, and national purpose in diverse societies.

Notes

Preface

1. See my "Toward a Comparative Metaphysics in Pragmatist and Confucian Thought," *Humanitas Asiatica* (2000), 1, 1: 95–115; and "Democracy and Confucian Values," *Philosophy East and West* (2003), 53, 1: 39–63.

Introduction

1. Shinozaki Mamoru, *Syonan: My Story* (Singapore: Marshall Cavendish, 2011), p. 75. Shinozaki was also known as the "Japanese Schindler" for saving thousands of ethnic Chinese lives during the Sook Ching Massacres committed by Japan's occupation forces in February–March 1942.

2. See for example Mark Schuman, *Confucius: And the World He Created* (New York: Basic Books, 2015), pp. 209–210; Jack Barbalet, "Confucian Values and East Asian Capitalism: A Variable Weberian Trajectory," in *Routledge Handbook of Religions in Asia*, edited by B. Turner and O. Salemink (London: Routledge), pp. 315–327; Terence Chong, "Asian Values and Confucian Ethics: Malay Singaporeans' Dilemma," *Journal of Contemporary Asia*, 32.3 (2002): 394–406; and Neil Englehart, "Rights and Culture in the Asian Values Argument: The Rise and Fall of Confucian Ethics in Singapore," *Human Rights Quarterly*, 22.2 (2000): 548–568.

3. Michael R Phillips, Xianyun Li, and Yanping Zhang, "Suicide Rates in China, 1995–99," *The Lancet*, 359.9309 (2002): 835–840.

4. Wang Chong-Wen, Cecilia L.W. Chan, and Paul S.F. Yip, "Suicide Rates in China from 2002 to 2011: An Update," *Social Psychiatry and Psychiatric Epidemiology*, 49.6 (2014): 929–941.

5. Sun Jiandong, Xiaolei Guo, Jiyu Zhang, Cunxian Jia, and Aiqiang Xu, "Suicide Rates in Shandong, China, 1991–2010: Rapid Decrease in Rural Rates and Steady Increase in Male–Female Ratio," *Journal of Affective Disorders*, 146.3 (2013): 361–368.

6. Phillips et al., "Suicide Rates in China," 835–840.

7. For a definitive account of working conditions and labor-organizing activism in South Korea's textiles industry in the 1970s, see Chun Soonok, *They Are Not Machines: Korean Women Workers and their Fight for Democratic Trade Unionism in the 1970s* (Burlington, VT: Ashgate 2003).

8. Jie Zhang, Xiao Shuiyuan, and Zhou Liang, "Mental Disorders and Suicide among Young Rural Chinese: A Case-Control Psychological Autopsy Study," *American Journal of Psychiatry*, 167.7 (2010): 773.

9. Martha Nussbaum, "Capabilities as Fundamental Entitlements: Sen and Social Justice," *Feminist Economics*, 9.2–3 (2003): 40–42.

10. Martha Nussbaum, *Women and Human Development: The Capabilities Approach* (Cambridge: Cambridge University Press: 2000), pp. 71–73.

11. Natsume Sōseki, *My Individualism* (私の個人主義 *Watashi no Kojinshugi*). Translated by J. Rubin. *Monumenta Nipponica*, 34.1 (2011): 38, 41.

12. Martha Nussbaum, *Creating Capabilities* (Cambridge, Mass.: Belknap Press, 2011), pp. 20–24.

Chapter 1

1. John Newman, *A Letter Addressed to the Duke of Norfolk on Occasion of Mr. Gladstone's Recent Expostulation* (London: D.M. Pickering, 1875), p. 61.

2. See Lionel Jensen, *Manufacturing Confucianism: Chinese Traditions and Universal Civilization* (Durham, NC: Duke University Press, 1997), pp. 8–9, 33–34; and Anna Sun, *Confucianism as a World Religion: Contested Histories and Contemporary Realities* (Princeton, NJ: Princeton University Press, 2013).

3. See Donald Sutton, "Ritual, Cultural Standardization and Orthopraxy in China: Reconsidering James L. Watson's Ideas," *Modern China*, 33.7 (2007): 3–21.

4. Gan Chunsong, "The Decline of China's Examination System and the Disintegration of Institutionalized Confucianism." *China Review.* www.china-review.com/sao.asp?id=2083. Accessed October 5, 2015.

5. James Grayson, *Korea: A Religious History* (London: Routledge, 2002) p. 136.

6. Sun, *Confucianism as a World Religion*, p. 157.

7. Kim Kwang-ok, "The Reproduction of Confucian Culture in Contemporary Korea: An Anthropological Study," in *Confucian Traditions in East Asian Modernity*, edited by W. Tu (Cambridge, Mass: Harvard University Press, 1996), pp. 202–228.

8. The distinction between discursive and intellectual Confucianism was suggested to me by Callum Brown's analysis of late nineteenth- and twentieth-century British Christianity in *The Death of Christian Britain* (Abingdon, Oxfordshire: Routledge, 2009).

9. See John Lie, *Han Unbound: The Political Economy of South Korea* (Stanford, Calif.: Stanford University Press, 1998), pp. 15–17; and Andrew Walder,

China Under Mao: A Revolution Derailed (Cambridge, Mass.: Harvard University Press, 2015), pp. 48–51.

10. Benjamin Elman, *Examinations in Late Imperial China* (Berkeley: University of California Press, 2000), pp. 261–280.

11. Cao Xueqin, *The Dream of the Red Chamber* (*Hóng lóu Mèng* 紅樓夢), translated by F. and I. McHugh (New York: Pantheon 1958), p. 29.

12. Elman, *Examinations in Late Imperial China*, pp. 194–195.

13. These stories are anthologized in *Selected Stories of Lu Hsun*, translated by H. and G. Yang (Peking: Foreign Languages Press, 1960).

14. Qtd. In Somerset Maugham, *On a Chinese Screen: Sketches of Life in China* (London: Heinemann, 1922), p. 153.

15. Gan, "The Decline of China's Examination System."

16. Tongdong Bai, "An Old Mandate for a New State. On Jiang Qing's political Confucianism," in Jiang, Q., *A Confucian Constitutional Order: How China's Ancient Past Can Shape Its Political Future*, edited by D. Bell (Princeton, NJ: Princeton University Press, 2012), pp. 113–129.

17. See Chan Serina, *The Thought of Mou Zongsan* (Leiden: Brill, 2011), pp. 74–78.

18. Jensen, *Manufacturing Confucianism*, pp. 64–70.

19. Yu Pung Kwang, "Confucianism," in *The World's Parliament of Religions*, Vol. I, edited by J. Barrows (Chicago: The Parliament Publishing Company, 1893), pp. 378–379.

20. Wolfgang Lippert, "Language in the Modernization Process: The Integration of Western Concepts and Terms into Chinese and Japanese in the Nineteenth Century," in *New Terms for New Ideas: Western Knowledge and Lexical Change in Late Imperial China*, edited by M. Lackner, I. Amelung, and J. Kurtz (Leiden: Brill, 2001), pp. 59–63. The transmission of this translated knowledge from Japan to the rest of East Asia was rapid. Ten thousand Chinese students are on record as studying in Japan just in the years 1906–1907, including one of the founders of China's "modern literary world," Lu Xun. See Cheng Ching-mao, "The Impact of Japanese Literary Trends on Chinese Writers," in *Modern Chinese Literature in the May Fourth Era*, edited by M. Goldeman (Cambridge, Mass.: Harvard University Press, 1977), pp. 64–66.

21. Shirai Masato, "The Rediscovery of Chinese Thought as 'Philosophy' in the Japanese Meiji Period." *Journal of International Philosophy* (国際哲学研究 *Kokusai Tetsugaku Kenkyū*), 5 (2016): 321.

22. Inoue qtd. in Okita Yukuji, "Concerning Inoue Tetsujirō and *Cosmos Journal*" (『六合雑誌』における井上哲次郎 *Rikugo Zashi ni okeru Inoue Tetsujirō*). *Studies in the Social Problems of Christianity* (キリスト教社会問題研究 *Kirisutokyō Shakai Mondai Kenkyū*), 30 (1982): 202.

23. Kiri Paramore, *Japanese Confucianism* (Cambridge: Cambridge University Press, 2016), p. 150. In the 1884 edition of his philosophical dictionary, Inoue translated Confucianism as 孔教 (*Kōkyō*) "Confucian Religion" and as 儒學 (*jugaku*). See *Philosophical Dictionary* (哲學字彙 *Tetsugaku Jii*) (Tokyo: Tōyōkan, 1884), p. 23.

24. Inoue Tetsujirō, *The Philosophy of the Japanese Wang Yangming School* (日本陽明學派之 哲學*Nihon Yōmei Gakuha no Tetsugaku*) (Tokyo: Fuzanbō, 1900), pp. 2, 3–4.

25. See Paramore, *Japanese Confucianism*, p. 150; and Sang Bing, "Japan and Liang Qichao's Research in the Field of National Learning," translated by M. Hu, *ChinaJapan.Org*, 2012, pp. 5–24. chinajapan.org/articles/12.1/12.1sang5-24.pdf. Accessed May 19, 2018.

26. Chun-chieh Huang and John Tucker. "Introduction," in *Dao Companion to Japanese Confucian Philosophy*, edited by C. Huang and J. Tucker (Dordrecht: Springer, 2014), pp. 6–8; and Kiri Paramore, "'Civil Religion' and Confucianism: Japan's Past, China's Present, and the Current Boom in Scholarship on Confucianism," *The Journal of Asian Studies*, 74.2 (2015): 269–282.

27. See Gene Blocker and Christopher Starling, *Japanese Philosophy* (New York: State University of New York Press, 2010), pp. 3–4.

28. Stephen Angle, *Contemporary Confucian Political Philosophy* (Cambridge: Polity Press, 2012), p. 139.

29. Inoue Tetsujirō, *Philosophical Dictionary* (哲学字彙 *Tetsugaku Jii*) (Tokyo: Maruzen, 1912), p. 171.

30. Chan Serina, *The Thought of Mou Zongsan*, pp. 68–75; and David Elstein, *Democracy in Contemporary Confucian Philosophy* (London: Routledge, 2014), pp. 52–53. For a rather revealing discussion of the Qing Dynasty's apparently ruinous effects on China's national culture, see Mou Zongsan, "The Rise of Buddhist Learning in the Northern and Southern Dynasties, Sui and Tang," in *Late Works of Mou Zongsan*, translated by J. Clower (Leiden: Brill, 2014), pp. 181–182.

31. Robert Bellah, *Tokugawa Religion* (New York: Free Press, 1985), p. 3.

32. Tu Weiming, "Cultural China: The Periphery as the Center," *Daedalus* 120.2 (1991): 1–32; and "Multiple Modernities: A Preliminary Inquiry into the Implications of East Asian Modernity," in *Culture Matters: How Values Shape Human Progress*, edited by L. Harrison and S. Huntingdon (New York: Basic Books, 2000), pp. 256–266; and Peter Berger, "An East Asian Development Model?" in *In Search of an East Asian Development Model*, edited by P. Berger and H.M. Hsiao (New Brunswick, NJ: Transaction Books 1988), pp. 3–11.

33. Ezra Vogel, *The Four Little Dragons: The Spread of Industrialization in East Asia* (Cambridge, Mass.: Harvard University Press, 1991), pp. 83–84, 91–102; and Morishima Michio, *Why Has Japan Succeeded? Western Technology and the Japanese Ethos* (Cambridge: Cambridge University Press, 1984).

34. Tu Weiming, "The Confucian Dimension in the East Asian Developmental Model," *Kasarinlan* (1990): 61.

35. Ibid.

36. See for instance Gu Hongming, *The Spirit of the Chinese People* (Beijing: The Peking Daily News, 1915), pp. 154–155.

37. Zhang Junmai, Tang Junyi, and Mou Zongsan, "Manifesto for a Reappraisal of Sinology and the Reconstruction of Chinese Culture," in *Sources of Chinese Tradition*, Vol 2., edited by W. De Bary and R. Lufrano (New York: Columbia University Press), pp. 550–555.

38. See Zheng Yongnian, *Discovering Chinese Nationalism in China* (Cambridge: Cambridge University Press, 1999), pp. 77–78.

39. For a discussion of postcolonial theory influence in contemporary intellectual debates over cultural identity and nationalism in China, see Yingjie Guo, *Cultural Nationalism in Contemporary China* (Routledge Curzon: London, 2003), pp. 114–117; on the appropriation of postcolonial and postmodern concepts by Hindu nationalists in India, see Meera Nanda, *Prophets Facing Backwards: Postmodern Critiques of Science and Hindu Nationalism in India* (New Brunswick, NJ: Rutgers University Press, 2003).

40. See Royce's approving discussion of the loyalty embodied in Japan's *Bushidō* code, derived from Nitobe Inazo's 1900 book *Bushido: The Soul of Japan*, in *Loyalty* (New York: Macmillan, 1908), pp. 71–77; for a more recent example, see Henry Rosemont, "Whose Democracy, Which Rights? A Confucian Critique of Modern Western Liberalism," in *Confucian Ethics: A Comparative Study of Self, Autonomy, and Community*, edited by K. Shun and D. Wong (Cambridge: Cambridge University Press, 2004), pp. 49–71.

41. Aamir Mufti, "Why I Am Not a Post-secularist," *Boundary 2*, 40.1 (2013): 7–19.

42. Roger Ames and Henry Rosemont, "Were the Early Confucians Virtuous?" in *Ethics in Early China*, edited by C. Fraser, D. Robins, and T. O'Leary (Hong Kong: University of Hong Kong Press, 2011), p. 22.

43. Johann Herder, "History of the Asian States in General," in *Johann Gottfried Herder on World History: An Anthology*, translated by E. Menze and M. Palma (London: Routledge 1997), pp. 247–248.

44. Johann Herder, *Outlines of a Philosophy of the History of Man*, translated by T. Churchill (New York: Bergmann, 1966), pp. 227–228.

45. Henry Rosemont. "Rights-Bearing Individuals and Role-bearing Persons," in *Rules, Rituals and Responsibility: Essays Dedicated to Herbert Fingarette*, edited by M. Bockover (La Salle, IL: Open Court, 1991), p. 73.

46. Bhikhu Parekh, *Rethinking Multiculturalism: Cultural Diversity and Political Theory* (Cambridge, Mass.: Harvard University Press 2002), p. 137.

47. Ruiping Fan, *Reconstructionist Confucianism: Rethinking Morality after the West* (Dordrecht: Springer, 2003), p. 57.

48. Tan Sor-hoon, *Confucian Democracy: A Deweyan Reconstruction* (Albany: State University of New York Press 2003), p. 201.

49. Daniel Bell, *Beyond Liberal Democracy: Political Thinking for an East Asian Context* (Princeton, NJ: Princeton University Press, 2009), pp. 19, 9.

50. David Hall and Roger Ames, *Democracy of the Dead* (La Salle, IL: Open Court, 1999), 11, 204.

51. Such critics include Amartya Sen, "Democracy as a Universal Value," *Journal of Democracy*, 10.3 (1999): 3–17; Jun Sang-in, "No (logical) Place for Asian Values in East Asia's Economic Development," *Development and Society*, 28.2 (1999): 191–204; Michael Hill, "Asian Values as Reverse Orientalism: Singapore," *Asia Pacific Viewpoint*, 41.2 (2000): 177–190; and Inoue Tatsuo, "Liberal Democracy and Asian Orientalism," in *The East Asian Challenge for Human Rights*, edited by J. Bauer and D. Bell (Cambridge: Cambridge University Press 1999), pp. 27–59.

52. John Makeham, *Lost Soul: "Confucianism" in Contemporary Chinese Academic Discourse* (Cambridge, Mass.: Harvard University Press, 2008).

53. Ai Jiawen, "The Refunctioning of Confucianism: The Mainland Chinese Intellectual Response to Confucianism since the 1980s," *Issues and Studies*, 44.2 (2008): 29–78; and Heike Holbig and Bruce Gilley, "Reclaiming Legitimacy in China," *Politics & Policy*, 38.3 (2010): 395–422.

54. Hillary Putnam, *The Collapse of the Fact-Value Dichotomy* (Cambridge, Mass.: Harvard University Press 2004), p. 39.

55. Bernard Williams, *Ethics and the Limits of Philosophy* (London: Fontana, 1985), pp. 140–141.

56. Emile Durkheim, *The Rules of the Sociological Method*, translated by W.D. Halls (New York: Free Press, 1982), pp. 50–51. I am grateful to Phillip Ivanhoe for bringing this work to my attention.

57. Paramore, "'Civil Religion' and Confucianism," 278.

58. Cao Xueqin, *The Dream of the Red Chamber*, pp. 118–119.

59. Uma Narayan, "Essence of Culture and a Sense of History: A Feminist Critique of Cultural Essentialism," *Hypatia*, 13.2 (1998): 88.

60. A bilingual copy of the *Rescript* can be found on the website of the Meiji Jingu Shrine. "The Imperial Rescript on Education," *About Meiji Jingu*. www.meijijingu.or.jp/english/about/6.html. Accessed February 24, 2017.

61. Yosano Akiko, "O Brother, Do Not Die" (君死にたもうこと勿れ *Kimi Shinitamō Koto Nakare*) in *Collected Poetical Works* (詩歌集 *Shiikashu*), edited by Shinbo Kōtarō (Tokyo: Hakuhōsha, 1987), pp. 34–35. I am grateful to Janine Beichman for sharing with me her translation of this poem, which I have drawn on here.

62. Chieko Mulhern, "Yosano Akiko," in *Japanese Women Writers: A Bio-critical Sourcebook* (Westport, Conn: Greenwood, 1994), p. 490.

63. Robert Bellah, Richard Madson, William Sullivan, Anne Swidler, Steven Tipton, *Habits of the Heart* (Berkeley: University of California Press, 2008), p. 334.

64. Intriguingly, in his own studies of middle-class Korean family life under compressed modernity, sociologist Chang Kyung-sup detects not one but four competing ideologies: a still dominant (and modernized) Confucian ideology ceding influence to rival ideologies of instrumental, affectionate, and individualist famialism. See Chang, "The State and Families in South Korea's Compressed Fertility Transition: A Time for Policy Reversal?" *Journal of Population and Social Security*, 1: (2003): 596–610.

65. Doh Chull Shin, *Confucianism and Democratization in East Asia* (Cambridge: Cambridge University Press, 2012), p. 320.
66. See OECD, "Poverty Rate" (indicator) (2014). DOI: dx.doi.org/10.1787/0fe1315d-en Accessed February 24, 2017.
67. Charlotte Ikels, "Introduction," in *Filial piety: Practice and Discourse in Contemporary East Asia* (Stanford, Calif.: Stanford University Press, 2004), pp. 14–15.
68. See Chang, "The State and Families in South Korea's Compressed Fertility Transition," 598–599; and Yamashita Junko, Soma Naoko, and Raymond Chan, "Re-examining Family-Centered Care Arrangements in East Asia," in *Handbook on East Asian Social Policy*, edited by M. Izuhara (Cheltenham: Edward Elgar, 2013), pp. 472–491.
69. Daniel Bell and Hahm Chiahark, "Introduction: The Politics of Affective Relations in East Asia," in *The Politics of Affective Relations: East Asia and Beyond*, edited by D. Bell and H. Chiahark (Oxford: Lexington, 2004), p. 2.
70. For a more historically nuanced anthropological analysis of *guanxi* that eschews reductionist assumptions about its "Confucian heritage," see Yao Souchou, *Confucian Capitalism: Discourse, Practice and the Myth of Chinese Enterprise* (London: Routledge, 2002), pp. 101–121.
71. Joseph Chan, *Confucian Perfectionism: A Political Philosophy for Modern Times* (Princeton, NJ: Princeton University Press, 2014), pp. xii–xiii.
72. Chad Hansen, *A Daoist Theory of Chinese Thought* (Oxford: Oxford University Press, 1992), pp. 5–6.
73. See Chunmei Du, *Gu Hongming and the Re-invention of Chinese Civilization*. PhD thesis, Princeton University: Proquest Dissertations Publishing, 2009; and Gotelind Muller, *Gu Hongming (1857–1928) and China's Defence against the Occident*. Unpublished manuscript (Heidelberg: University of Heidelberg, 2013) archiv.ub.uni-heidelberg.de/volltextserver/15423/1/Gu%20Hongming%20englisch.pdf. Accessed February 24, 2017.
74. Gu, *The Spirit of the Chinese People*, pp. 71, 72–73.

Chapter 2

1. Michael Sandel, *Democracy's Discontent* (Cambridge, Mass: Harvard University Press, 1998), pp. 6, 70.
2. Alasdair Macintyre, *After Virtue* (Duckworth: London, 1982), p. 59.
3. Jeremy Waldron, "When Justice Replaces Affection: The Need for Rights," in *Liberal Rights: Collected Papers 1981–1991* (Cambridge: Cambridge University Press, 1993), pp. 374–375. My thanks are due to one anonymous reviewer for drawing my attention to this article.
4. Edmund Gosse, *Henrik Ibsen* (New York: Charles Scribner's Sons, 1908), p. 146.

5. Henrik Ibsen, *A Doll's House*, translated by William Archer (Boston: William Baker, 1890), p. 119.

6. Henry Rosemont, *Against Individualism: A Confucian Rethinking of the Foundations of Morality* (Lanham, MD: Lexington, 2015), p. 64.

7. Charles Taylor, *The Ethics of Authenticity* (Cambridge: Cambridge University Press, 1991), p. 17.

8. This position is derived from Ingrid Robeyns, "Sen's Capability Approach and Gender Inequality: Selecting Relevant Capabilities," *Feminist Economics*, 9.2–3 (2003): 61–92; and Martha Nussbaum, *Women and Human Development: The Capabilities Approach* (Cambridge: Cambridge University Press, 2000), pp. 73–74.

9. For a discussion of this facet of ethical individualism see Steven Lukes, *Individualism* (Colchester: ECPR Press 2006), p. 88.

10. Nussbaum, *Women and Human Development*, p. 40.

11. Ibsen, *A Doll's House*, p. 117.

12. Lukes, *Individualism*, p. 88.

13. See Kristie Dotson, "A Cautionary Tale: On Limiting Epistemic Oppression," *Frontiers*, 33.1 (2012): 31. The quoted descriptions about adaptive preferences are taken from Amartya Sen, 1995. "Gender Inequality and Theories of Justice," in *Women, Culture and Development: A Study of Human Capabilities*, edited by M. Nussbaum and J. Glover (Oxford: Oxford University Press, 1995), pp. 262–263.

14. Miranda Fricker, *Epistemic Injustice: Power and the Ethics of Knowing* (Oxford: Oxford University Press, 2007), pp. 9–30.

15. Dotson, "A Cautionary Tale," p. 32.

16. Henry Rosemont, "Two Loci of Authority: Autonomous Individuals and Relational Persons," in *Confucian Cultures of Authority*, edited by R. Ames and P. Hershock (Albany: State University of New York Press, 2006), p. 10.

17. David Hall and Roger Ames, *Democracy of the Dead*; and Henry Rosemont and Roger Ames, "Were the Early Confucians Virtuous?" in *Ethics in Early China*, edited by S. Fraser, D. Robins, and T. O'Leary (Hong Kong: HKU Press), pp. 17–41.

18. Macintyre, *After Virtue*, p. 55.

19. Rosemont, *Against Individualism*, pp. 36–37.

20. For discussion of these types of properties, see Epstein, "Ontological Individualism Reconsidered," *Synthese*, 166.1 (2009): 187–213.

21. Hall and Ames, *Democracy of the Dead*, p. 197.

22. Rosemont and Ames, "Were the Early Confucians Virtuous?" p. 22.

23. Ibid., pp. 25–26.

24. Ibsen, *A Doll's House*, p. 122.

25. Sandel, *Democracy's Discontent*, pp. 292–293.

26. Epstein, "Ontological Individualism Reconsidered," p. 207.

27. Rosemont, "Two Loci of Authority," p. 26.

28. Michael Sandel, "Religious Liberty-Freedom of Conscience or Freedom of Choice?" *Utah Law Review*, 3 (1989): 611–612.

29. Sandel, *Democracy's Discontent*, pp. 114–115.
30. Macintyre, *After Virtue*, p. 35.
31. Rosemont, "Two Loci of Authority," p. 26.
32. Sandel, "Religious Liberty-Freedom of Conscience or Freedom of Choice?" pp. 610–611.
33. William James, *The Varieties of Religious Experience* (London: Longman, Green and Co., 1916), pp. 176–177.
34. Gosse, *Henrik Ibsen*, p. 146.
35. Marie-Louise Roberts, *Disruptive Acts: The New Woman in Fin-de-Siecle France* (Chicago: University of Chicago Press, 2002), pp. 22–26.
36. See Somdatta Mandal, "Was Tagore a Feminist? Re-evaluating Selected Fiction and their Film Adaptations," in *Boundaries of the Self: Gender, Culture and Spaces*, edited by D. Banerjee (Newcastle on Tyne: Cambridge Publishers, 2014), pp. 71–74. Martha Nussbaum also discusses Tagore's Mrinal in *Women and Human Development*, pp. 44–45.
37. Though by 1920 some *Ryōsai Kenbo* advocates supported entry of women into the workforce, so long as it did not conflict with their domestic duties. See Koyama Shizuko, *Ryosai Kenbo: The Educational Ideal of 'Good Wife and Wise Mother' in Modern Japan*, translated by Stephen Filler (Boston and Leiden: Brill, 2012), pp. 122–125.
38. Ibid., p. 49.
39. Ibid., pp. 50–51.
40. Qtd. in Hiratsuka Raichō, *In The Beginning, Woman was the Sun*, translated by T. Craig (New York: Columbia University Press, 2006), pp. 218–219.
41. Tomida Hiroko. *Hiratsuka Raichō and Japanese Feminism* (Leiden: Brill, 2004), p. 165.
42. Kato Midori, "A Doll's House" (人形の家 *Ningyō no Ie*), in *Seitō: Collected Essays on Women's Liberation* ("*Seitō*": *Josei Kaiho Ronshū*「青鞜」女性解放論集), edited by Kiyoko Horiba (Tokyo: Iwanami Bunko), p. 52.
43. Ueno Yoko, "From 'A Doll's House' to the Woman Problem" (人形の家より女性の問題へ' *Ningyo no Ie' yori Josei no Mondai e*) in Ibid., p. 46.
44. Ueda Kimi, "Reading 'A Doll's House'" (人形の家を読む *Ningyo no Ie wo Yomu*) in Ibid., pp. 60–61.
45. Joan Templeton, "The Doll House Backlash: Criticism, Feminism and Ibsen" *PMLA*, 4.1 (1989): 32.
46. Kato, "A Doll's House," p. 55.
47. Hiratsuka Raichō, *Collected Works: Vol. 1: Seitō* (著作集 [1]):「青鞜」*Chosakushū [1]: Seitō*) (Tokyo: Otsuki Shoten, 1983), pp. 217–218.
48. Ibid., 219–221.
49. Stanley Cavell, *Cities of Words* (Cambridge, Mass.: Harvard University Press, 2005), p. 255.
50. Nussbaum, *Women and Human Development*, p. 220.

51. Ibid., pp. 232–233.
52. Hiratsuka, *Collected Works*, p. 221.
53. Kato, "A Doll's House," p. 54.
54. Yosano Akiko, "Rambling Talk" (そぞろごと *Sozorogoto*) in *Seito: Collected Essays on Women's Liberation* (*"Seitō": Josei Kaiho Ronshū*「青鞜」女性解放論集), edited by Kiyoko Horiba (Tokyo: Iwanami Bunko), p. 12.
55. *Book of Rites* (Tan Gong II: 113).
56. See Mencius (3B2).
57. Joseph Chan, "Moral Autonomy, Civil Liberties, and Confucianism," *Philosophy East and West*, 52.3 (2002): 281–310.
58. Ibid., p. 301.
59. Mencius (IVA17).
60. Ibid. (VB2).
61. Ibid. (VB1).
62. Chan, "Moral Autonomy, Civil Liberties, and Confucianism," p. 289.
63. Mencius (VII A 33).
64. Chan, "Moral Autonomy, Civil Liberties, and Confucianism," p. 299.
65. Ibid., p. 291.
66. Ibid., p. 300.
67. Ibid., p. 293.
68. Ibid., p. 301.
69. Liberal perfectionists, on the other hand, *may* consider it acceptable for the state to interfere coercively, or noncoercively, to discourage patriarchal family relations or other patriarchal associations, out of a conviction that such ways of life are less valuable than those characterized by sexual egalitarianism. In this chapter and in chapters 6 and 7 I take the view that such relations and associations should be left alone, to the extent that their members' civil rights (including rights of exit) and property rights are not violated.

Chapter 3

1. Oscar Wilde, *The Complete Works of Oscar Wilde Volume 2: De Profundis*, "Epistola: In Carcera et Vinculus," edited by I. Small (Oxford: Oxford University Press, 2000), p. 160.
2. For definitions of asymmetrical deference, see Goffman, "The Nature of Deference and Demeanor," *American Anthropologist*, 58.3 (1956): 477–479; and Randall Collins, *Interaction Ritual Chains* (Princeton and Oxford: Princeton University Press, 2004), p. 278.
3. Michael David Ing, *The Dysfunction of Ritual in Early Confucianism* (Oxford: Oxford University Press, 2012), pp. 45, 152–167.
4. Ibid., pp. 46–47.

5. *Analects*, 3:1.
6. Kenko Yoshida, *Essays in Idleness* (徒然草 *Tsurezuregusa*), translated by D. Keene (Tokyo: Tuttle, 1997), p. 106.
7. Mozi. *Mozi: Basic Writings*, translated by B. Watson (New York: Colombia University Press, 2003), p. 70.
8. I am following Phillip Ivanhoe's definition of Mohism here. See *Confucian Self-Cultivation* (Indianapolis/Cambridge: Hackett Publishing, 2000), p. 15.
9. Mozi, *Basic Writings*, p. 79.
10. Herbert Fingarette, *Confucius: The Secular as Sacred* (San Francisco: Harper Collins 1972), p. 4.
11. *Analects*, 10:16.
12. Mozi, *Basic Writings*, p. 132.
13. For an extended discussion of the "subjunctive reality" generated by ritual interaction, see Adam Seligman, Robert Weller, Michael Puett, and Simon Bennett, *Ritual and its Consequences* (Oxford: Oxford University Press 2008), pp. 7–8, 17–43.
14. *Analects*, 10:4.
15. See Fingarette, *Confucius: The Secular as Sacred*, p. 3.
16. Ibid., pp. 8, 12.
17. Xunzi, *Basic Writings*, translated by B. Watson (New York: Colombia Press, 2003), p. 93.
18. *Book of Rites*, Qu Li, p. 9.
19. Fingarette, *Confucius: The Secular as Sacred*, p. 7.
20. Xunzi, *Basic Writings*, p. 104.
21. Ibid., p. 93.
22. Ibid., p. 38.
23. Mozi, *Basic Writings*, pp. 35–36.
24. Xunzi, *Basic Writings*, p. 48.
25. Ibid., p. 123.
26. Erving Goffman, "The Nature of Deference and Demeanor," *American Anthropologist*, 58.3 (1956): 477–479.
27. Bertram Doyle, *The Etiquette of Race Relations in the South: An Essay on Social Control* (Chicago: The University of Chicago Press, 1937), p. 142.
28. Susan Pharr, *Losing Face: Status Politics in Japan* (Berkeley: University of California Press, 1990), pp. 65, 67.
29. Michael Schulz, *The Rural Face of White Supremacy: Beyond Jim Crow* (Urbana and Chicago: University of Illinois Press, 2005), pp. 5, 130, 151.
30. Pharr, *Losing Face*, p. 67.
31. Doyle, *The Etiquette of Race Relations*, p. 158.
32. Ibid., p. 142.
33. Pharr, *Losing Face*, p. 68.
34. Stephen Angle, *Contemporary Confucian Political Philosophy* (Cambridge: Polity Press, 2012), pp. 131–132.

35. Richard Wright, *Uncle Tom's Children* (New York: Harper Collins, 1938), p. 15.

36. Pharr, *Losing Face*, p. 67.

37. Angle, *Contemporary Confucian Political Philosophy*, p. 137.

38. Ogasawara Yuko, *Office Ladies and Salaried Men: Power, Gender and Work in Japanese Companies* (Chapel Hill: University of North Carolina Press, 1998), p. 42.

39. Pharr, *Losing Face*, p. 59.

40. Ibid., p. 72.

41. Angle, *Contemporary Confucian Political Philosophy*, p. 131.

42. See Goffman, "The Nature of Deference and Demeanor," 479. I derive the term "categorical-based" esteem and deference from Collins, *Interaction Ritual Chains*, pp. 276–277.

43. See Collins's discussion of ritual in patrimonial households in *Interaction Ritual Chains*, pp. 289–290.

44. Erving Goffman, "On Facework: An Analysis of Ritual Elements in Social Interaction," in *Language, Culture and Society*, edited by B. Blount (Long Grove, IL: Waveland Press), p. 222.

45. Collins, *Interaction Ritual Chains*, p. 269.

Angle, Stephen. 2012. *Contemporary Confucian Political Philosophy*. Cambridge: Polity Press.

46. Wright, *Uncle Tom's Children*, p. 15.

47. For instance, a young person of privileged wealth and background walking through or spending time in a "tough" working-class neighborhood will find him- or herself having to reinterpret and express his face in a very different way in relation to any physically strong, assertive young men he encounters, whose own status group self-definition is based on the capacity for intimidation and physical violence.

48. Lilian Smith, *Killers of the Dream* (New York: Norton, 1949), p. 96.

49. Daniel Bell, *China's New Confucianism* (Princeton, NJ: Princeton University Press 2008); and Aaron Stalnaker, "Confucianism, Democracy and the Virtue of Deference," *Dao*, 12.4 (2008): 441–459. The pagination for Stalnaker's paper is taken from indiana.edu/~relstud/assets/docs/Stalnaker_Confucianism%20Democracy%20 and%20Deference.pdf. Accessed March 7, 2017.

50. Bell, *China's New Confucianism*, pp. 38–39.

51. Ibid., p. 45.

52. Ibid., p. 45.

53. Ibid., pp. 45–50.

54. These data are derived from "OECD Income Distribution Database (IDD): Gini, Poverty, Income, Methods and Concepts" (2016). *OECD*, Organization for Economic Co-operation and Development. www.oecd.org/social/income-distribution-database-h. Accessed January 3, 2017.

55. This data is taken from "Gender Wage Gap" (2016), *OECD*. Organization for Economic Co-operation and Development. www.oecd.org/gender/data/genderwagegap.htm. Accessed January 3, 2017.

56. Stalnaker, "Confucianism, Democracy and the Virtue of Deference," pp. 1–2.
57. Ibid., p. 8.
58. Ibid., p. 22.
59. Ibid., p. 10.
60. Ibid., pp. 11–13.
61. Ibid., p. 14.
62. Ibid., p. 16.
63. Ibid., p. 19.
64. Ibid., p. 24.
65. Ibid., p. 26.
66. Macintyre, *After Virtue*, pp. 187–193.
67. Ibid., p. 190.
68. Ibid., p. 241.
69. Collins, *Interaction Ritual Chains*, p. 292. See also Maruyama Masao, *Japanese Thought* (日本の思想 *Nihon no Shisō*) (Tokyo: Iwanami Shoten, 1961), pp. 169–199.
70. Ibid., p. 292. I once had the honor of meeting the Prime Minister of Japan, while working as a disaster relief volunteer following the Kumamoto Earthquake in 2016. In hindsight, my deferential gesture—of doffing my helmet as he approached to shake my hand—must have seemed rather anachronistic by modern Japanese standards.
71. Callum Brown, *The Death of Christian Britain*, pp. 174–180.
72. Collins, *Interaction Ritual Chains*, p. 292.
73. Differences over such criteria for excellence in character divide along different faultlines, including the secular and the religious, and also, with increasing prominence in recent years, between ethical and economic globalists and "parochial" nationalists. The secular globalist may wonder whether there is any moral excellence or capacity worth deferring to in a small-town Christian minister who denounces homosexual and transgender lifestyles. The parochial nationalist may think the same about the irreligious urban activist who advocates for sexual minorities. See Jonathan Haidt, "The Ethics of Globalism, Nationalism and Patriotism" (2015) www.humansandnature.org/the-ethics-of-globalism-nationalism-and-patriotism. Accessed January 26, 2017.
74. Collins, *Interaction Ritual Chains*, pp. 290, 296.
75. Sungmoon Kim, *Confucian Democracy in East Asia: Theory and Practice* (New York: Cambridge University Press, 2014), pp. 59–60.
76. *Book of Rites*, Tan Gong, 1: 53. For a fascinating discussion of blood feuds and the "ritual regulation of vengeance" set forth in Pre-Qin and Han texts like the *Liji* see Anne Cheng, "Filial Piety with a Vengence: The Tension between Rites and Law in the Han" in *Filial Piety in Chinese Thought and History*, edited by A.K. Chan and S. Tan (London: Routledge, 2004), pp. 29–44.
77. Tan, *Confucian Democracy: A Deweyan Reconstruction*, p. 84.

78. Erving Goffman, "Deference and Demeanor," pp. 478–479.
79. Wilde, *The Complete Works of Oscar Wilde, Volume II*, p. 160.
80. Isaiah Berlin, "The Bent Twig: A Note on Nationalism," *Foreign Affairs*, 51.1 (1972): 11–30.
81. Stephen Angle, *Contemporary Confucian Political Philosophy*, p. 130.
82. Jurgen Habermas, *Justification and Application*, translated by C. Cronin (Cambridge, Mass.: Harvard University Press, 1996), p. 31.
83. Ibid., p. 56.

Chapter 4

1. Hsieh Yuwei, "Filial Piety and Chinese Society," in *The Chinese Mind: Essentials of Chinese Philosophy and Culture*, edited by C.A. Moore (Honolulu: University of Hawaii Press, 1967), p. 183.
2. Li Chenyang, "Shifting Perspectives: Filial Morality Revisited," *Philosophy East and West*, 47.2 (1997): 218–219.
3. Doh Chull Shin, *Confucianism and Democratization in East Asia*, p. 181.
4. Fan, *Reconstructionist Confucianism*, p. 73.
5. Henry Rosemont and Roger Ames, "Translators' Preface." In *The Chinese Classic of Family Reverence: A Philosophical Translation of the* Xiaojing, translated by H. Rosemont and R. Ames (Honolulu: University of Hawaii Press 2009), pp. xi–xii.
6. Henry Rosemont and Roger Ames, "Family Reverence (*xiao* 孝) as the Source of Comsummatory Conduct (*ren* 仁)," *Dao*, 7.1 (2008): 10.
7. Alan Chan and Tan Sor-hoon, "Introduction." In *Filial Piety in Chinese Thought and History*, pp. 2–3.
8. To his credit, Sungmoon Kim also regrets these trends that oppose "communal" Confucian family values to the "individualism" of liberalism. He argues instead that Confucians need to develop more sophisticated criticisms of liberalism in light of contemporary liberal theory's preoccupations with civic virtue "connecting the individual and society" and also because classical liberal thinkers such as Locke *did* give substantial consideration to the family as "an important ethical space" for the cultivation of liberal virtues, and of self-mastery over narcissistic passions. See Kim, "Self-transformation and Civil Society: Lockean vs. Confucian," *Dao*, 8 (2009): 384.
9. Henry Rosemont and Roger Ames, *Confucian Role Ethics: A Vision for the 21st Century?* (Taipei: University of Taiwan Press, 2016), p. 109.
10. Phillip Ivanhoe, "The Shade of Confucius: Social Roles, Ethical Theory and the Self." In *Polishing the Chinese Mirror: Essays in Honor of Henry Rosemont Jr.*, edited by M. Chandler and R. Littlejohn (New York: Global Scholarly Publications, 2007), pp. 37–38.
11. Macintyre, *After Virtue*, pp. 57–59.
12. Ivanhoe, "The Shade of Confucius," pp. 39–40.

13. Liu Liangjian, "Virtue Ethics and Confucianism: A Methodological Reflection," in *Virtue Ethics and Confucianism*, edited by S. Angle and M. Slote (London: Routledge, 2013), pp. 68–69.

14. See Li Chenyang, "Shifting Perspectives," pp. 218–219.

15. *Analects*, 1:2.

16. Phillip Ivanhoe, "Filial Piety as a Virtue," In *Working Virtue and Contemporary Moral Problems*, edited by R. Walker and P. Ivanhoe (Oxford: Oxford University Press, 2007), p. 298.

17. Ibid., p. 302.

18. Ibid., p. 304.

19. Ibid., p. 304; see also Li, "Shifting Perspectives," pp. 225–227.

20. Ivanhoe, "Filial Piety as a Virtue," p. 305.

21. Li, "Shifting perspectives," p. 221.

22. *Analects*, 1:2.

23. See *Book of Rites* (Ji Yi: 4).

24. Ivanhoe, "Filial Piety as a Virtue," p. 307; see also Li, "Shifting Perspectives," pp. 223–225.

25. Brian Outhwaite *Clandestine Marriage in England, 1500–1850* (London: Hambledon Press, 1995.), pp. 52–54.

26. William Fleetwood, *Relative Duties of Parents and Children, Husbands and Wives, Master and Servant* (London: C. Harper 1705), p. 1.

27. Ibid., pp. 4–5.

28. Ibid., 8.

29. Ibid., p. 16.

30. Ibid., p. 1.

31. Patrick Delaney, *Fifteen Sermons Upon Social Duties* (London: J. Rivington, 1738), p. 141.

32. Ibid., p. 141.

33. Ibid., pp. 161–162.

34. Ibid., p. 165.

35. Ibid., p. 145.

36. Ibid., p. 152.

37. Ibid., p. 150.

38. Ibid., pp. 120, 128, 150–151, 159, 169, 295.

39. Fleetwood, *Relative Duties*, p. 24.

40. Ibid., p. 30.

41. Delaney, *Fifteen Sermons*, pp. 152–153.

42. Fleetwood, *Relative Duties*, pp. 6–7.

43. Delaney, *Fifteen Sermons*, p. 140.

44. Ibid., p. 142.

45. Hester Chapone, Letter to Samuel Richardson, *The Posthumous Works of Mrs. Chapone* (London: John Murray, 1807), p. 93.

46. Fleetwood, *Relative Duties*, p. 36.
47. Ibid., pp. 38–39.
48. Ibid., p. 44.
49. Ibid., p. 43.
50. Ibid., pp. 44–45.
51. Delaney, *Fifteen Sermons*, p. 153.
52. Ibid., pp. 155–156.
53. John Locke, *The Works of John Locke, Volume II* (London: Awsham Churchill, 1722), p. 174.
54. Tom Keymer, *Richardson's Clarissa and the 18th Century Reader* (Cambridge: Cambridge University Press, 2004), pp. 98–99.
55. Samuel Richardson, Letter to Miss Highmore, *The Correspondence of Samuel Richardson*, p. 217; this discussion draws on Keymer, *Richardson's Clarissa*, p. 122.
56. Richardson, *Clarissa, or the History of a Young Lady, Volume VIII* (London: J. and F. Rivington, 1774), p. 377.
57. Chapone, *The Posthumous Works of Mrs. Chapone*, p. 32.
58. Mary Wollstonecraft, *A Vindication of the Rights of Men and a Vindication of the Rights of Women*, edited by S. Tomaselli (Cambridge: Cambridge University Press, 2009), p. 248.
59. "Introduction," in *The Posthumous Works of Mrs. Chapone*, p. VII.
60. Carole Pateman, *The Sexual Contract* (Cambridge: Wiley, 1988), pp. 168–169.
61. *Women and Wisdom of Japan*, translated by S. Takaishi (London: John Murray, 1905), p. 37.
62. Takahashi, "Introduction," in Ibid., p. 27.
63. Remarkably, Hiratsuka chose to announce her elopement in *Seitō*, in a public letter addressed to her parents, which provoked much public criticism of her actions. See "To My Parents, about My Becoming Independent" (独立するについて両親に *Dokoritsu suru ni tsuite Ryōshin ni*), *Collected Works: Vol. 1: Seitō*, p. 293; and *In the Beginning, Woman was the Sun*, pp. 241–244.
64. Tanizaki Junichirō, *The Makioka Sisters*, translated by E. Seidensticker (London: Vintage Books, 1983), pp. 429–437, 528–529.
65. Ibid., p. 530.
66. Elizabeth Anscombe, "Modern Moral Philosophy," *Journal of Philosophy*, 33.124 (1959): 4–5.
67. Christina Hoff Sommers, "Filial Morality," *The Journal of Philosophy*, 83.8 (1986): 336.
68. Ibid. Sommers opposes her concept of "differential pull" to the more impartial "ethical pull" proposed by utilitarians and Kantians.
69. Ibid., p. 337.
70. Li, "Shifting Perspectives," pp. 215–217.
71. Samuel Richardson, *Clarissa, or the History of a Young Lady, Volume II* (London: J. and F. Rivington, 1748), p. 33.

72. Sommers, "Filial Morality," p. 334.
73. Simon Keller "Four Theories of Filial Duty," *The Philosophical Quarterly*, 56.223 (2006): 266.
74. Amartya Sen, *The Idea of Justice* (London: Penguin, 2012), pp. 260–262.
75. Keller, "Four Theories," pp. 269–270.
76. See Nancy Jecker, "Taking Care of One's Own: Justice and Family Caregiving," *Theoretical Medicine*, 23 (2002): 121–123 and Maria Stuifbergen and Johannes Van Delden, "Filial Obligations to Elderly Parents: A Duty to Care?" *Medical Health Care and Philosophy* (2011), 14: 70.
77. See Gerald Dworkin, *The Theory and Practice of Autonomy* (Cambridge: Cambridge University Press, 1988), pp. 48, 15.
78. I take this definition of autonomy competence from John Christman, "Relational Autonomy, Liberal Individualism and the Social Constitution of Selves," *Philosophical Studies*, 117 (2004): 155.
79. See Catriona Mackenzie, "Relational Autonomy, Normative Authority and Perfectionism," *Journal of Social Philosophy*, 39.4 (2008): 512–533; and "The Importance of Relational Autonomy and Capabilities for an Ethics of Vulnerability," in *Vulnerability: New Essays in Ethics and Feminist Philosophy*, edited by C. MacKenzie, W. Rogers, and C. Dodds (Oxford: Oxford University Press), pp. 33–60.
80. For a definition of the substantivist understanding of autonomy, see Christman, "Relational Autonomy, Liberal Individualism," p. 148.
81. Mackenzie, "Relational Autonomy, Normative Authority," pp. 514, 527.
82. Ibid., pp. 528–529, 522.
83. For an argument along similar lines, see Christman, "Relational Autonomy, Liberal Individualism," pp. 154–159.
84. Jonathon Quong, *Liberalism Without Perfectionism* (Oxford: Oxford University Press, 2011), p. 80.
85. See Charles Foster, 2010. "Autonomy Should Chair, Not Rule," *The Lancet*, 375. 9712 (2010): 368–369.
86. See Ruiping Fan, *Reconstructionist Confucianism* (Dordrecht: Springer, 2010), p. 13.
87. For a nuanced discussion of relational autonomy limitations in aged care settings, see Susan Sherwin and Meghan Winsby, "A Relational Perspective on Autonomy for Older Adults Residing in Aged Care Homes," *Health Expectations*, 14.2 (2011): 182–190.
88. *Encyclopedia of Korean Folk Literature*, edited by M. Chung, T. Kim, H. Ahn, and H. Cho (Seoul: The National Folk Museum of Korea, 2014), p. 249.

Chapter 5

1. Lu Xun, *Selected Works of Lu Xun*, translated by H. Yang and G. Yang (Beijing: Foreign Languages Press, 1957), pp. 86–90.

2. See especially Kiri Paramore, "Civil Religion and Confucianism," pp. 269–282.

3. Norman Kutcher, *Mourning in Late Imperial China: Filial Piety and the State* (Cambridge: Cambridge University Press, 1999), pp. 2–3.

4. Mencius (5A4).

5. Ibid. (5A3).

6. See Miranda Brown, *The Politics of Mourning in Early China* (New York: State University of New York Press, 2007), pp. 37–38.

7. Han Feizi, *Han Feizi: Basic Writings*, translated by B. Watson (New York: University of Columbia Press, 2003), pp. 106–107.

8. *Classic of Filial Piety*, 1.

9. Ibid., 5.

10. Bob Wakabayashi, "Aizawa and His New Theses," in *Anti-foreignism and Western Learning in Japan: The New Theses of 1825*, translated by B. Wakabayashi (Cambridge, Mass.: Harvard University Press), pp. 121–122. Discussions of the Kingly Way can be found in early Confucian classics such as the *Mencius* and the *Xunzi*. According to Inoue, the "Kingly Way" principle is also expounded in the *Great Learning* and in the "Great Plan" (洪範 *Hong Fan*) chapter of the *Book of Documents* (書經 *Shujing*). See Inoue, *Eastern Culture and the Future of China* (東洋文化と支那の将来 *Tōyō Bunka to Shina no Shōrai*) (Tokyo: Risosha, 1939), p. 110.

11. Aizawa Seishisai, "New Theses," in Ibid., p. 153.

12. Ibid., pp. 157–158.

13. Ibid., p. 158.

14. For further discussion of the issue of continuity between early and late nineteenth-century Japanese formulations of *Kokutai* ideology, see Kiri Paramore "Anti-Christian Ideas and National Ideology: Inoue Enryo and Inoue Tetsujirō's Mobilization of Sectarian History in Meiji Japan," *Sungkyun Journal of East Asian Studies*, 9.1 (2009): 107–144.

15. Maruyama Masao, *Studies in Intellectual History of Tokugawa Japan*, translated by M. Hane (Princeton, NJ: Princeton University Press 1974), pp. xix–xx.

16. Eshima Kenichi, "An Application of Confucianism in the Formative Process of "Kokumin-doutokuron" (「国民道徳論」の形成過程における儒教の応用 *Kokumin Dōtokuron no Keisei Katei ni okeru Jyukyō no Ōyō*) *Studies in Sociology, Psychology and Education: Inquiries into Humans and Society* (社会学心理学教育学：人間と社会の探究 *Shakai Gaku Shinri Gaku Kyōiku Gaku: Ningen to Shakai no Tankyū*), 65 (2007): 113.

17. Elie Kedourie, *Nationalism* (London: Hutchinson University Library, 1961), pp. 13–43.

18. Ibid., p. 23.

19. Ibid., pp. 39–41; for an intriguing discussion of the early twentieth-century convergences between European-educated Japanese and Indonesian nationalists' organic, famialist imaginings of their respective national identities in distinction

from the "individualism" of the West, see David Bourchier, *Illiberal Democracy in Indonesia: The Ideology of the Family State* (London: Routledge, 2015), pp. 43–60.

20. Ernst Gellner, *Nations and Nationalism* (Ithaca, NY: Cornell University Press, 2006), pp. 124–128.

21. Max Weber, "The Social Psychology of the World Religions," in *From Max Weber: Essays in Sociology*, translated by H. Gewirth and C. Mills (New York: Oxford University Press, 1946), p. 279.

22. Nishibe Susumu, "The Morality of the Nation" (国民の道徳 *Kokumin no Dōtoku*) (Tokyo: Sankei Shimbun News Service 2000), p. 67.

23. "Imperial Rescript," *About Meiji Jingu*. Meiji Jingu. www.meijijingu.or.jp/english/about/6.html. Accessed February 18, 2017.

24. Paramore," Anti-Christian Ideas and National Ideology," p. 119.

25. Inoue Tetsujirō, *Commentary on the Rescript, Vol. 1* (勅語衍義 *Chokugo Engi*) (Tokyo: Inoue Sokichi, 1891), p. 5.

26. See Mencius (1A5).

27. Inoue, *Commentary, Vol. 1*, pp. 30–31.

28. Qtd. in Eshima Kenichi (my translation), "The Formative Process of Inoue Testujiro's Kokumin-Doutokuron in the Meiji Era" (明治期における井上鉄次郎の「国民道徳論」の形成過程に聞する-考察 *Meijiki ni okeru Inoue Testujirō no Kokumin Dōtokuron no Keisei Katei ni kan suru Kōsatsu*). *Studies in Sociology, Psychology and Education: Inquiries into Humans and Society (*社会学心理学教育学：人間と社会の探究 (*Shakai Gaku Shinri Gaku Kyōiku Gaku: Ningen to Shakai no Tankyū*) 67: 22.

29. Ibid.

30. Inoue Tetsujirō, *Outline of a National Morality* (国民道徳概論) (*Kokumin Dōtokugairon*) (Tokyo: Sanseidō, 1921), pp. i–ii.

31. Winston Davis, "The Civil Theology of Inoue Tetsujirō," *Japanese Journal of Religious Studies*, 3.1 (1976): 17–18.

32. See Isomae Junichi, *Religious Discourse in Modern Japan: Religion, State and Shintō* (Leiden: Brill, 2014), pp. 173–174.

33. Inoue, *Outline*, p. 4.

34. Ibid., p. 6.

35. Georg Hegel, *Lectures on the Philosophy of World History*, translated by J. Hoffmeister (Cambridge: Cambridge University Press, 1975), pp. 96–97.

36. Ibid., 102–103.

37. Kenjō Teiji, "Inoue Tetsujirō's Revision to *Introduction to National Morality*" (井上哲次郎による『国民道徳概論』改訂作業とその意味 *Inoue Tetsujirō ni yoru 'Kokumin Dōtoku Gairon' Kaitei Sagyo to sono Imi*), *Chiba University Studies in the Humanities* (千葉大学人文研究 *Chiba Daigaku Jinbun Kenkyū*), 37 (2008): 162; and Inoue, *Outline of a National Morality*, p. 11.

38. Inoue, *Outline*, p. 176.

39. Ibid., p. 183.

40. Ibid., p. 8.

41. Ibid., p. 9; see also Kenjō, "Inoue Tetsujirō's Revision," p. 162, on Inoue's deep ambivalence about the influence of Western ideas on Japan's morality.
42. Gellner, *Nations and Nationalism*, pp. 16–17.
43. Wakabayashi, "Aizawa and his New Theses," p. 125.
44. Inoue, *Outline*, p. 176.
45. Ibid., pp. 276–277.
46. Ibid., pp. 277–278.
47. Ibid., pp. 280–281.
48. Ibid., pp. 286–287.
49. Ibid., p. 281.
50. Ibid., pp. 282–283.
51. Ibid., p. 277.
52. Ibid., p. 280.
53. Ibid., pp. 287–288.
54. Ibid., pp. 288–289.
55. Ibid., p. 286.
56. Ibid., p. 287.
57. Ibid., Appendix, p. 7.
58. Ibid., Appendix, p. 9.
59. Ibid., Appendix p. 2; for further discussion of this controversy, see John Brownlee, *Japanese Historians and the National Myths, 1600–1945* (Vancouver: UBC Press, 1999), p. 122; and Isomae, *Religious Discourse in Modern Japan*, pp. 172–174.
60. Eshima, "An Application of Confucianism in the Formative Process of "Kokumin-doutokuron," p. 113.
61. Maruyama, "Introduction," p. xviii.
62. See Roger Brown, "Visions of a Virtuous Manifest Destiny: Yasuoka Masahiro and Japan's Kingly Way," in *Pan-Asianism in Modern Japanese History: Colonialism, Regionalism and Borders*, edited by S. Saaler and J. Koschmann (London: Routledge, 2007), pp. 133–151.
63. *Principles of the National Polity* (國體の本義 *Kokutai no Hongi*) (Tokyo: Ministry of Education, 1937), p. 42.
64. Inoue, *Outline*, p. 277; *Principles of the National Polity*, pp. 148–149.
65. *Principles of the National Polity*, p. 149.
66. Ibid., p. 370.
67. *The Way of Subjects* (臣民の道 *Shinmin no Michi*) (Tokyo: Ministry of Education, 1941), p. 57.
68. Ibid.
69. See Yamamuro Shin'ichi, *Manchuria under Japanese Domination*, translated by J. Fogel (Philadelphia: University of Pennsylvania Press, 2006), pp. 74–80.
70. Inoue Tetsujirō, *Eastern Culture and the Future of China*, pp. 30–31.
71. Ibid., pp. 105–106.
72. See John Boyle, *China and Japan at War, 1937–1945: The Politics of Collaboration* (Stanford, Calif.: Stanford University Press, 1972), p. 94.

73. Inoue, *Eastern Culture and the Future of China*, p. 105.
74. Ibid., p. 106.
75. Ibid., pp. 107–110. On Yasuoka's interpretation of the Imperial Way, see Brown, "Visions of a Manifest Virtuous Destiny," pp. 141–142.
76. Boyle, *China and Japan at War*, pp. 95–96.
77. Rabindranath Tagore, *Selected Letters of Rabindranath Tagore*, edited by K. Dutta and A. Robinson (Cambridge: Cambridge University Press, 1997), p. 497.
78. Nishibe, *The Morality of the Nation*, pp. 6, 69.
79. Robert Bellah, "Civil Religion in America," *Daedalus* (Fall 2005): 45.
80. See Kiri Paramore, "'Civil Religion' and Confucianism," pp. 275–276; and Nakajima Takahiro, "The Restoration of Confucianism in China and Japan: A New Source of Morality and 13 Religion," in *Facing the 21st Century*, edited by W. Lam and C. Cheng (Tokyo: Nanzan Institute for Religion & Culture 2009), pp. 45–49. Sebastian Billioud and Joel Thoraval provide further, anthropological grounds for skepticism about the prospects of a Confucian civil religion in *The Sage and the People: The Confucian Revival in China* (Oxford: Oxford University Press, 2015), pp. 168–169.
81. Kim Sungmoon and Phillip Ivanhoe, "Introduction," in *Confucianism, A Habit of the Heart: Bellah, Civil Religion, and East Asia*, edited by S. Kim and P. Ivanhoe (Albany: State University of New York Press), pp. 5–6.
82. Davis, "The Civil Theology of Inoue Tetsujirō," pp. 5, 36.
83. Jean Jacques Rousseau, *The Social Contract, or Principles of Political Right*, translated by Henry Tozer (London: Swan Sonnenschein, 1895), pp. 227–229.
84. Alexis De Tocqueville, *Democracy in America*, translated by H. Reeve (London: Longmans, Greene & co, 1889), pp. 238–239.
85. Paramore, *Japanese Confucianism*, p. 275.
86. Amy Borovy, "Robert Bellah's Search for Community and Ethical Modernity in Japan Studies," *The Journal of Asian Studies*, 75.2 (2016): 467–494; and Robert Bellah, "Japan's Cultural Identity: Some Reflections on the Work of Watsuji Tetsuro," *The Journal of Asian Studies*, 24.4 (1965): 573–594.
87. Bellah, "Japan's Cultural Identity," pp. 589–590.
88. Bellah, Ibid., pp. 581–582; see also Robert Bellah and Phillip Hammond, *Varieties of Civil Religion* (Eugene, OR: Wipf and Stock, 1982), pp. 35–36; and Borovoy, "Robert Bellah's Search for Community," p. 487.
89. Bellah and Hammond, *Varieties of Civil Religion*, p. 37.
90. Ibid., p. 31.
91. Bellah, "Civil Religion in America," pp. 46–47.
92. Ibid., p. 48.
93. Robert Bellah, *Beyond Belief: Essays on Religion in a Post-Traditionalist World* (Berkeley: University of California Press, 1991), p. 168.
94. *The Conflict between Education and Religion* (教育と宗教の衝突 *Kyōiku to Shūkyō no Shōtotsu*). (Tokyo: Keigyo Shato 1893), pp. 8–9.

95. Okuyama Michiaki, "Civil Religion in Japan? Rethinking the Arguments and their Implications," *Religious Studies in Japan*, 1 (2009): 66.
96. Bellah, "Civil Religion in America," p. 47.
97. Kim and Ivanhoe, "Introduction," p. 6.

Chapter 6

1. See for example Daniel Bell, "Democracy with Chinese Characteristics: A Political Proposal for the Post-Communist Era," *Philosophy East and West*, 49.4 (1999): 451–493; and *Beyond Liberal Democracy: Political Thinking for an East Asian Context* (Princeton, NJ: Princeton University Press, 2006).
2. David Hall and Roger Ames, *Democracy of the Dead*; Roger Ames, "Confucianism and Deweyan Pragmatism: A Dialogue," *Journal of Chinese Philosophy*, 30.3-4 (2003): 1–26; and Tan Soor-hoon, *Confucian Democracy: A Deweyan Reconstruction* (Albany: State University of New York Press, 2003).
3. Thomas Metzger, *A Cloud Across the Pacific: Essays on the Clash between Chinese and Western Political Philosophies Today* (Hong Kong: The Chinese University Press, 2005), p. 31.
4. Mencius (3A4); see also *Analects* (4.11).
5. Mencius, Ibid.
6. Ibid.
7. *Analects* (8.14).
8. *Analects* (16.2).
9. John Rawls, *A Theory of Justice* (Cambridge, Mass.: Harvard University Press 1996), pp. 12–13, 59; see also Joseph Chan, "Legitimacy, Unanimity, and Perfectionism," *Philosophy & Public Affairs*, 29.1 (2000): 13, 17.
10. Rawls, *A Theory of Justice*, p. 37; see also Joseph Chan, "Moral Autonomy, Civil Liberties, and Confucianism," *Philosophy East and West*, 52.3 (2002): 295.
11. Metzger, *A Cloud across the Pacific*, pp. 21–31.
12. Thomas Metzger, *The Western Concept of a Civil Society in the Context of Chinese History* (Stanford, Calif.: Hoover Institute, 1998), p. 15.
13. Susan Pharr, *Losing Face: Status Politics in Japan*, p. 222.
14. Mencius (3A3).
15. Ibid. (1B7).
16. Alvin Goldman, *Liasons: Philosophy Meets the Cognitive and Social Sciences* (Cambridge, Mass.: MIT Press, 1992), p. 209.
17. Ibid., p. 214.
18. Mencius (7A5) and *Analects* (8.9).
19. David Elstein, "Why Early Confucianism Cannot Generate Democracy." *Dao: A Journal of Comparative Philosophy* (2011) 9.4: 431–432.

20. Lorraine Code, *What Can She Know? Feminist Theory and the Construction of Knowledge* (Ithaca, New York: Cornell University Press, 1991), pp. 7, 182, 224.

21. Tu Weiming, "Probing the 'Three Bonds' and 'Five Relationships' in Confucian Humanism," in *Confucianism and the Family*, edited by W. Slote and G. De Vos (Albany: State University of New York Press 1998), pp. 122–123.

22. *Book of Poetry* (詩 *Shi*) I.1:6.

23. Tu, "Probing the Three Bonds," p. 130.

24. Ci Jiwei, "The Confucian Relational Concept of the Person and its Modern Predicament," in *Personhood and Health Care*, edited by D. Thomasma and C. Weisstub (Dordrecht: Kluwer, 2001), p. 155.

25. *Book of Rites* (12.18).

26. Tu, "Probing the Three Bonds," pp. 132–133.

27. Mencius (3B2).

28. Tan Soor-hoon, "Democracy in Confucianism," *Philosophy Compass*, 7.5 (2012): 299–300.

29. John Dewey, *The Public and Its Problems*, in *John Dewey, The Later Works: 1925–1953*, Vol. II, edited by J. Boydston (Carbondale: Southern Illinois University Press, 1990), p. 362. Unless otherwise specified, all references to Dewey's thought will be to the *Later Works* (*LW*) edition, together with volume and page number.

30. Dewey (*LW*2, p. 358).

31. Roger Ames, "Confucianism and Deweyan Pragmatism: A Dialogue," p. 26.

32. Dewey (*LW*2, p. 339).

33. Ibid., p. 320.

34. Ibid., p. 339.

35. Dewey, *Freedom and Culture* (*LW*13, pp. 176–177).

36. Dewey, Ibid., pp. 173–174.

37. Dewey, *The Public and Its Problems* (*LW*2, p. 365).

38. Ibid., pp. 370–372.

39. Ibid., pp. 364–365.

40. Ames, "Confucianism and Deweyan Pragmatism: A Dialogue," p. 25.

41. Dewey, *The Public and Its Problems* (*LW*2, pp. 294, 340).

42. David Hall and Roger Ames, *Thinking Through Confucius* (Albany: State University of New York Press, 1986), p. 155.

43. John Dewey, *Experience and Nature* (*LW*1, p. 40).

44. Tan, *Confucian Democracy*, p. 111; and "Democracy in Confucianism," pp. 295–296, 299.

45. Tan, *Confucian Democracy*, p. 7.

46. Ibid., pp. 162, 12.

47. Parekh cited in Ibid., p. 9.

48. Ibid., p. 17.

49. Ibid., pp. 32–33.

50. Raichō, *Collected Works: Vol. 1*, pp. 257–258.
51. John Dewey, *Democracy and Education* (New York: Free Press, 1916), p. 346.
52. *Analects* (14.45, 6.28).
53. However, a "paternalistic" and elitist form of feminism would be compatible with pre-Qin Confucianism, inasmuch as it demands equal opportunity for suitably cultivated women to join the ranks of exemplary persons and ministers of state. See, for instance, Sin Yee Chan, "Gender and Relationship Roles in the *Analects* and the *Mencius*," *Asian Philosophy*, 10.2 (2000): 115–132.
54. Daniel Bell, "Democracy with Confucian Characteristics," p. 453, and *Beyond Liberal Democracy*, p. 158.
55. Bell, *Beyond Liberal Democracy*, pp. 176, 166.
56. Daniel Bell, *The China Model: Political Meritocracy and the Limits of Democracy* (Princeton, NJ: Princeton University Press, 2015), p. 162.
57. Ibid., pp. 167–169.
58. Joseph Chan, *Confucian Perfectionism: A Political Philosophy for Modern Times* (Princeton, NJ: Princeton University Press, 2014), pp. 105–111.
59. Jiang Qing, *A Confucian Constitutional Order: How China's Ancient Past Can Shape its Political Future*, translated by E. Ryden, edited by D. Bell and R. Fan (Princeton, NJ: Princeton University Press, 2012), p. 41.
60. Ibid., pp. 63–64, 27, 31–35, 37.
61. Stephen Angle, *Contemporary Confucian Political Philosophy*, p. 55.
62. See Chan, *Confucian Perfectionism*, p. 107; and John Stuart Mill, *Representative Government* (Kitchener, Ontario: Batoche, 2001), pp. 147–154.
63. Friedrich Hayek, *Law, Legislation and Liberty Volume 3: The Political Order of a Free People* (London: Routledge and Keegan Paul, 1982), pp. 112–116; see also Bell, *The China Model*, pp. 160–161.
64. Mill, *Representative Government*, p. 150.
65. Chan, *Confucian Perfectionism*, p. 203.
66. Teng Ssu-yu, "Chinese Influence on the Western Examination System: I. Introduction," *Harvard Journal of Asian Studies*, 7.4 (1943): 267–312.
67. Daniel Bell, "Toward Meritocratic Rule in China? A Response to Professors Dallmayr, Li and Tan," *Philosophy East and West* 59.4 (2009): 555.
68. The bitterly divided responses of Korean and Japanese peak agricultural and business interest groups to free-trade negotiations are a case in point. Such interest groups had previously enjoyed fairly harmonious relations in the corporatist, developmental postwar states in Korea and Japan.
69. See Eun Ki-soo, "Changing Roles of the Family and State for Elderly Care: A Confucian Perspective," in *Aging and Challenges to Families*, edited by V. Bengston and A. Lowenstein (New York: Walter de Gruyter, 2003), pp. 253–234.
70. Tu Weiming, "The Confucian Dimension in the East Asian Development Model," pp. 65, 67.
71. Ishibashi Katsuhiko, "Naturally, It's a Nuclear Earthquake Disaster" (まさに原発震災だ *Masa ni Genpatsu Shinsai da*) *Sekai* (世界) (May 2011): 126–133.

72. Doh Chull Shin *Confucianism and Democracy in East Asia*, p. 125.
73. Daniel Bell, *Beyond Liberal Democracy*, pp. 157–160, 176–178; Jiang, *A Confucian Constitutional Order*, p. 35.
74. Jiang, *A Confucian Constitutional Order*, p. 35.
75. Mencius (3A4).
76. See Elizabeth Economy, *The River Runs Black: The Environmental Challenge to China's Future* (Ithaca, NY: Cornell University Press, 2010); and Lilian Lee, *Fighting Famine in North China: State, Market, and Environmental Decline, 1690s–1990s* (Palo Alto, Calif.: Stanford University Press, 2007), pp. 2–10.
77. See for instance Kim Sunhyuk, "Democratization and Environmentalism: South Korea and Taiwan in Comparative Perspective," *Journal of Asian and African Studies*, 35.3 (2000): 287–302.
78. Daniel Bell, *Beyond Liberal Democracy*, p. 150.
79. Ibid., pp. 161–162.
80. Ma Ngok, *Political Development in Hong Kong: State, Political Society and Civil Society* (Hong Kong: University of Hong Kong Press, 2007), pp. 224–225; and Eliza Lee et al., *Public Policymaking in Hong Kong: Civic Engagement and State-society Relations in a Semi-democracy* (Vol. 13) (New York: Routledge, 2013), pp. 8–9.
81. Bell, *Beyond Liberal Democracy*, pp. 172–173.
82. Jiang, *A Confucian Constitutional Order*, pp. 64, 220.
83. Bell, *Beyond Liberal Democracy*, p. 178.
84. Bell, *The China Model*, p. 167.
85. For a definition of evidentialism, see David Enoch, "What's Wrong with Paternalism: Autonomy, Belief and Action." *Proceedings of the Aristotelian Society*, 137th Session (2016) (draft paper), p. 9.
86. Joseph Raz, "The Problem of Authority: Revisiting the Service Conception," *Minnesota Law Review*, 90 (2006): 1003–1044.
87. Ibid., pp. 1012–1014.
88. I am following Jonathon Quong's definition of paternalism here; see his *Liberalism without Perfection* (Oxford: Oxford University Press, 2012), p. 80.
89. Jonathon Quong, "*Liberalism without Perfection*: Replies to Gaus, Colburn, Chan 30 and Bocchiola." *Philosophy and Public Issues*, 2.1 (2012): 67–68; and *Liberalism without Perfectionism*, pp. 100–101.
90. Rawls, *A Theory of Justice*, p. 92.
91. Enoch, "What's Wrong with Paternalism," p. 6.
92. See Quong, *Liberalism without Perfectionism*, p. 115.
93. Enoch, "What's Wrong with Paternalism," pp. 29–30.
94. Quong, "*Liberalism without Perfection*: Replies," p. 67.
95. Amartya Sen, *The Idea of Justice* (Cambridge, Mass.: Harvard University Press 2009), pp. 231–235.
96. John Rawls, "The Idea of an Overlapping Consensus," *Oxford Journal of Legal Studies*, 7.1 (1987): 6.

97. Martha Nussbaum, "Political Soul-making and the Imminent Demise of Liberal Education." *Journal of Social Philosophy*, 37.2 (2006): 305–306.

Chapter 7

1. Campbell Clark, "Facing Backlash in Europe, Canada Hunts for New Seal Market in China," *Globe and Mail* (January 12, 2010) beta.theglobeandmail.com/news/politics/facing-backlash-in-europe-canada-hunts-for-new-seal-market-in-china/article4351652. Accessed March 3, 2017.

2. Michael McDonald, "Sale of Seal Meat to China Thwarted by Anti-hunt Activists: Fisheries Minister," *CTV News* (April 14, 2014) www.ctvnews.ca/mobile/canada/sale-of-seal-meat-to-china-thwarted-by-anti-hunt-activists-fisheries-minister-1.1774111. Accessed March 3, 2017.

3. For an up-to-date analysis of developments in animal welfare consciousness and activism in China, see Peter Li and Gareth Davey, "Culture, Politics and Future Directions: A Review of China's Animal Protection Challenge," *Society and Animals*, 21 (2013): 34–53.

4. I am following the definition of liberal democracy given by Sharun Mukand and Dani Rodrik in "The political Economy of Liberal Democracy." Unpublished Working Paper. Coventry: University of Warwick. Department of Economics (2015). Warwick economics research papers series (WERPS) (107).

5. See William Galston, *Liberal Pluralism: The Implications of Value Pluralism for Political Theory* (Cambridge: Cambridge University Press, 2002).

6. Ci Jiwei, *Moral China in an Age of Reform* (Cambridge: Cambridge University Press, 2014), pp. 184–185.

7. Ibid., pp. 15, 17.

8. Ibid., p. 185.

9. Rodney Stark and Wang Xiuhua, *A Star in the East: The Rise of Christianity in China* (West Conshohocken, Penn.: Templeton Press, 2015).

10. Ibid., p. 1058.

11. See John Rawls, "Justice as Fairness: Political not Metaphysical," *Philosophy & Public Affairs*, 14.3 (1985): 233; and Parekh, *Rethinking Multiculturalism*, pp. 86–87.

12. Judith Shklar, "The Liberalism of Fear," in *Liberalism and the Moral Life*, edited by Nancy Rosenblum (Cambridge, Mass.: Harvard University Press), p. 29.

13. Ibid. pp. 26–27.

14. The devastating overthrow of the Muslim Brotherhood government in Egypt in 2013 provides the most recent instance of this, though this faction practices a nonviolent variety of comprehensive political Islam.

15. Rawls, "The Idea of an Overlapping Consensus," pp. 12–13.

16. Ibid., pp. 8–9; see also John Rawls, *The Law of Peoples with "The Idea of Public Reason Revisited"* (Cambridge, Mass.: Harvard University Press, 2000), pp. 133–134.

17. See Kim Sungmoon, *Confucian Democracy in East Asia*.

18. See Isaiah Berlin, *The Power of Ideas*, edited by H. Hardy (Princeton, NJ: Princeton University Press, 2013) pp. 1–29; and John Dewey, *Theory of Valuation* (Chicago: University of Chicago Press, 1939).

19. See Isaiah Berlin, *The Crooked Timber of Humanity*, edited by H. Hardy (London: John Murray, 1990), pp. 11–12.

20. Ibid., p. 12.

21. Dewey, *Theory of Valuation*, p. 34.

22. Ibid., pp. 52–53.

23. Jeremy Waldron, "Why Call Hate Speech Group Libel?" *2009 Holmes Lectures, Harvard Law School* (Cambridge, Mass.: Harvard University, 2009). www.law.nyu.edu/sites/default/files/ECM_PRO_063312.pdf. Accessed June 3, 2018.

24. See William Galston, *Liberal Pluralism*, pp. 31–32.

25. Isaiah Berlin, *The Power of Ideas*, p. 15.

26. Hannah Arendt, "Reflections on Little Rock," *Dissent*, 6 (1959): 50–51.

27. See for example Parekh, *Rethinking Multiculturalism*, pp. 88–90. Some of Rawls's clearest statements on the requirement of reasonableness in the public political forum—and the lack of requirement for *public* reasons in the "background culture"—can be found in *The Law of Peoples*, pp. 133–134, 149–156.

28. Rawls, *A Theory of Justice*, pp. 218–220.

29. See Joo Young-Lee, "Hate Speech in South Korea," *Focus* (2017): 87 www.hurights.or.jp/archives/focus/section3/2017/03/hate-speech-in-south-korea.html. Accessed June 3, 2018; and for a discussion of hate speech in Japan, Shaun O'Dwyer, "Perfectionism & Hate Speech Law," *Philosophy Now*, 123 (2017): 8–10.

30. The difficulty in adjudicating such cases arises in establishing principled grounds for showing that the goods or services refused for reasons of religious conscience are *public* goods or services "in the public domain where all men are equal," as Hannah Arendt once put it, such as hotels in business districts or real estate agencies, where people's civil rights would be burdened if either a private or public organization or company invokes a discriminatory justification for not serving them. See Arendt, "Reflections on Little Rock," p. 52.

31. On the concept of capability deprivation, see Sen, *The Idea of Justice*, pp. 254–257.

32. See Thomas Piketty, *Capital in the 21st Century*, translated by A. Goldhammer (Cambridge, Mass.: Belnap Press, 2017), pp. 661–662.

33. Chun Soonok, *They Are Not Machines*, pp. 142–143.

34. Yuli Tamir, *Liberal Nationalism* (Princeton, NJ: Princeton University Press, 1993), p. 6.

35. I take my definition of "singular attribution" concepts of identity from Amartya Sen, *Identity and Violence* (New York: W.W. Norton 2006), pp. 1–17; see also Tamir, *Liberal Nationalism*, p. 79.

36. Yuli Tamir, *Liberal Nationalism*, p. 36.

37. Kim, *Confucian Democracy in East Asia*, p. 128.

38. Ibid., p. 137.

39. Ibid., pp. 131, 135.

40. Kim Sungmoon, *Public Reason Confucianism: Democratic Perfectionism and Constitutionalism in East Asia* (New York: Cambridge University Press, 2016), p. 87.

41. Ibid., pp. 28–29.

42. Kim, *Confucian Democracy in East Asia*, pp. 10, 23.

43. Ibid., 5–6; and *Public Reason Confucianism*, p. 69.

44. Tamir, *Liberal Nationalism*, pp. lix–x, 79.

45. Johann Herder, *Philosophical Writings*, edited by M. Forster (Cambridge: Cambridge University Press, 2004), pp. 370, 413.

46. Kim, *Public Reason Confucianism*, p. 70.

47. Kim, *Confucian Democracy*, p. 10.

48. Ibid.

49. Ibid., p. 11.

50. Kim, *Public Reason Confucianism*, pp. 87–88.

51. Ibid., pp. 141–162, 172.

52. Kim, *Confucian Democracy*, pp. 216, 222.

53. Ibid., pp. 213–214.

54. Ibid., pp. 218–220.

55. Ibid., pp. 217–219.

56. Ibid., pp. 147, 170.

57. Mencius (6A8).

58. *Book of Rites* (Liyun, p. 18).

59. See Edward Chung, *The Korean Neo-Confucianism of Yi T'oegye and Yi Yulgok* (Albany: State University of New York Press 1995), pp. 39–61.

60. Yi Kwangsu, "The Value of Literature (Munhak ŭi Kachi)," translated by J. Rhee, *Azalea: Journal of Korean Literature and Culture*, 7 (2011): 288; and Yi Kwangsu, "What is Literature? (Munhak Iran Hao)," translated by J. Rhee, in Ibid., p. 295. In this section I develop a line of argument initially sketched by Sheila Miyoshi-Jagger in *Narratives of Nation-building in Korea: A Genealogy of Patriotism* (London: Routledge, 1994), pp. 23–24. I am also grateful for her helpful comments and suggestions.

61. See Takahashi Koizumi, "Joseph Haven's 'Mental Philosophy' and Nishi Amane's Theory of Human Nature" (西周訳『奚般氏心理学』と西の人間性論 *Nishi Amane Yaku 'Heiban shi Shinrigaku' to Nishi no Ningensei Ron*), *Philosophy* (哲学 *Tetsugaku*), 58 (1971): 172–173. The 1912 edition of Inoue Tetsujirō's *Philosophical Dictionary*, p. 53, gives *Kanjō* (感情) as one rendering for feeling or *gefühl*, and this is how the term is often translated in modern Japanese.

62. Joseph Haven, *Mental Philosophy: Including the Intellect, Sensibilities and Will* (Boston: Gould & Lincoln, 1872), pp. 29–31, 428–430.

63. See Lippert, "Language in the Modernization Process," pp. 59–64.

64. Yi, "What is Literature?" pp. 296–297.

65. Ibid., pp. 298.
66. Ibid., pp. 302.
67. Miyoshi-Jagger, *Narratives of Nation Building in Korea*, pp. 34–40.
68. Shin Gi-Wook, *Ethnic Nationalism in Korea: Geneology, Politics and Legacy* (Stanford, Calif.: Stanford University Press, 2006), pp. 47–49.
69. See Emma Campbell, *South Korea's New Nationalism: The End of 'One Korea'?* (Boulder, CO: First Forum Press, 2015).
70. Kim, *Confucian Democracy in East Asia*, p. 136.
71. Ibid., p. 268.
72. Ibid., pp. 90–91.
73. Park Chang-Won, *Death Rites in Korea: The Confucian-Christian Interplay* (Unpublished PhD Thesis, Durham, NC: Department of Theology and Religion, Durham University, 2008), p. 234.
74. Kim, *Confucian Democracy in East Asia*, p. 284.
75. Park, *Death Rites in Korea*, pp. 243–248.
76. Ibid., pp. 234–235.
77. Ibid., p. 190.
78. Kim, *Confucian Democracy in East Asia*, pp. 238–239.
79. For anthropological discussion of these two religious organizations upon which my discussion is substantially based, see Billioud and Thoraval, *The Sage and the People*, pp. 147–152, 152–164.
80. Ibid., p. 151.
81. My thanks are due to Lee Kwanhu for making me think more deeply about what would distinguish Kim Dae-Jung's Confucian conviction politics from that of Park Chung-Hee. My brief discussion of the concepts of representation and legitimacy in both Confucian and liberal thought draws from Lee's *Political Legitimacy, Representation and Virtue* (Unpublished PhD thesis, London: University College, London, 2014), pp. 105–126.
82. Michael Breen, "Kim Dae-Jung, Korea's Greatest Democrat," *Korea Times* (24 August 2011). www.koreatimes.co.kr/www/common/printpreview.asp?categoryCode=363&newsIdx=93445. Accessed February 6, 2017.
83. Kim Dae-Jung, "Is Culture Destiny?" *Foreign Affairs*, 73.6 (1994): 190.
84. Ibid., pp. 191–192.

Index

Note: For terms that are translated from both Chinese and Japanese, the Chinese Pinyin romanization of the original term is given first, followed by the Japanese *Romaji* romanization.

Aizawa, Seishisai, 137–138, 139, 145–146, 147
Ames, Roger, 17, 19, 40–42, 98, 99, 163, 164, 170, 174, 176, 180
Adaptive preferences, 38, 39, 125
Amaterasu (Goddess and legendary founder of Japan's Imperial Line), 137, 141, 146, 154, 157
Angle, Stephen, 12, 77, 80, 89, 181
Animal welfare, 197–198, 201–202
Anscombe, Elizabeth, 116
Arendt, Hannah, 211, 261n30
Aristotle, xiii, 100
Arnold, Matthew, 32
Austen, Jane, 87
Autonomous individual, 19, 33, 40, 44, 46
Autonomy, 52, 119, 123–124, 173, 193–195, 204
  Confucian concepts of, 52–58
  Liberal concept of, 55, 204
  Moral, 52–56
  Personal, 52, 53–55, 56–58, 173, 178–179, 194, 204, 215

  Relational-perfectionist concept of, 124–127, 128
  Substantivist concept of, 125–127

Background culture/social sphere, 211–213, 215, 228 261n27
Bellah, Robert, 13, 14, 26, 159–161
Bell, Daniel, 19, 81–83, 84, 89, 164, 170, 180–187, 188
Berger, Peter, 13
Berlin, Isaiah, 92, 207–208, 211, 216, 218
Bluestockings
  British, 108–109, 112, 114
  Japanese, 35, 47–49, 58, 117
Boyle, John, 156
Buddhism, 4, 10, 13, 20, 138, 144, 145, 151, 152, 157, 201, 204, 219, 227, 232
Buddhist temples, 3
Bushidō, 145, 146

Capabilities, capabilities approach, xii–xiv, xv, xvi, 34–35, 36–39,

Capabilities, capabilities approach *(continued)*
    46, 50, 52, 55, 56, 57, 73, 76, 79, 103, 119–122, 123–125, 127, 193, 194, 200, 204, 207–208, 213, 214, 228, 230, 231, 261n31
Cao, Xueqin, 87
Cavell, Stanley, 50
Chan, Joseph, 29–30, 52–57, 180, 181, 186
Chapone, Hester, 108, 112, 114
Cheng, Hao, 149
Chinese Imperial Civil Service examinations (科舉制 *Keju zhi*), 1, 2–4, 5, 6, 182
Christianity, x, 2, 7, 9, 23, 26, 41, 43, 109, 111, 112, 137, 138, 159, 161, 162, 198, 201–202, 203, 204, 212, 213, 215, 219
    Catholicism, 1, 2, 3, 22, 227, 232
    Protestantism, 41, 221, 226–228
Chong (정 familial affectionate sentiment), 221–225
Chun, Tae-il, 214
Ci, Jiwei, 172, 200–202
Civil Religion, 13–14, 132, 139, 144, 160, 161–162
    American, 13, 160–161
    Confucian, 13–14, 17, 31, 132, 158, 161, 255n80
    Japanese, 139, 144, 158–161
Code, Lorraine, 170
Collins, Randall, 89
Communism, xii, 15, 29, 155, 198, 200, 201, 203, 231
    Chinese Communist Party, 4, 20, 201–203, 231
Communitarian, Communitarianism, vii, x, xii, xiv–xv, 15, 16, 19, 33–36, 40, 44, 52, 157, 163, 173–174, 177

Comprehensive doctrines, 58, 167, 182, 194–195, 199, 212, 215, 216, 218, 220, 221, 229
    Confucian, vii, xvi, 56, 58, 132, 167, 214, 220, 226, 229
    Liberal, 194, 199, 218
Confucian conviction politics, 231–233
Confucian democracy (*see* democracy)
Confucian heritage, ix, xiv, 3, 7–8, 29–30, 185, 224, 225, 230, 233, 241n70
Confucian meritocratic governance, 167, 180–183, 185, 187–188, 194
Confucian public reason (*see* public reason)
Confucian temples, 2–3, 6, 131, 231
Confucian role ethics, xv, 41–42, 45, 51, 53, 99, 170, 173
Confucian virtue ethics, xv, 99–101
Confucianism
    As civil religion (*see* civil religion)
    As a habit of the heart (*see* habits of the heart)
    As philosophy/thought, 2, 10–12, 33, 139
    As religion, 2, 10, 230–231, 237n23
    As state religion (*see* state religion)
    Discursive, 5–6
    Folk, 6–7
    Institutional, 2–3, 6
    Intellectual, 3–4, 6
    Progressive, 30, 75–78, 80, 83
Confucius, ix, xv, 2, 3, 9, 30, 41, 51, 53, 62–63, 66, 67–68, 92, 102, 103, 106, 107, 131, 135, 155, 164, 165, 166, 169, 172, 181, 184, 230
Cultural essentialism, 25, 28

Daoism, 4, 20, 92, 219
    Daoist temples, 3
Davis, Winston, 158–159

Delaney, Patrick, 101, 105–111, 116, 121
  On Chinese and Confucian filial piety, 106, 107, 110
Democracy
  Anti-capitalist, 154
  Confucian, vii, xvi, 19, 33, 26, 162, 163–165, 170, 173–179, 180–187, 188, 192, 218–229
  Deweyan, xvi, 19, 157, 170, 173–179, 194
  Illiberal, nonliberal, 163, 188, 203
  Liberal, vii, xiv, xvi, 13, 18, 87, 89, 157, 159, 173, 174, 181, 187–188, 190, 192, 198, 200, 205, 207, 209, 213–214, 216, 218, 219, 220, 222, 229, 232–233, 260n4
De Tocqueville, Alexis, 159
Dewey, John, xvi, 19, 90, 94, 157, 163, 164, 170, 171, 173–176, 177–179, 194, 207–208, 210
Discourse ethics, 94, 96
Doh, Chull Shin, 27, 97
Doyle, Bertram, 73, 75
Durkheim, Emile, 21, 70

Enlightenment, The, 14, 17, 18, 218
Enoch, David, 191, 193
Environmentalism, 183, 185, 201, 202
Epistemic character, 170, 171–172
Epistemic deference, 171
Epistemic elitism, xvi, 168, 179, 189, 191–192, 194, 210
Epistemic injustice, 37–38
Epistemic paternalism, xvi, 169, 179, 189, 191–193, 194, 210
Epistemology, xvi
  Evidentialist epistemology, 188, 193
  Feminist epistemology, 37–38
  Virtue epistemology, 170

Epistemological crisis, 10
Eshima, Kenichi, 142–143, 151
Exemplary person (君子 *junzi*), 41, 53, 54, 99, 133, 166, 167, 172, 176, 177, 179, 184, 186, 188–192

Fan, Ruiping, 19, 97
Feminism, feminists, xv, 25, 47, 49–51, 52, 56, 59, 113, 124, 126, 127, 177–179, 183, 194
  Confucian feminism, 177–179
  Feminist epistemology (*see* epistemology)
  Perfectionist feminism (*see* perfectionism)
Fichte, Johann, 140
Filial piety (孝 *xiao/kō*), ix, xi, xiv, xv, xvi, 7–8, 12, 13, 21, 23–24, 25, 27, 28, 51, 52, 57, 65, 71, 97–129, 132, 133–136, 137–138, 139, 140–142, 145, 146, 148, 151, 152–153, 156, 170, 172, 177, 183, 192, 218, 220, 225–228, 229–230, 240n64
  Oneness of loyalty and filial piety (忠孝一致 *chūkō icchi*), 138, 146, 153
  Rights-based concept of filial piety, 117–119
  Role-ethics concept of filial reverence, 98, 99, 101
  Unity of loyalty and filial piety (忠孝一本 *chūkō ippon*), 32, 135, 142–143, 146–149, 151, 152–154, 156, 161
  Virtue-ethics concept of filial piety, 98, 99–101, 102–103
Filmer, Robert, 106
Fingarette, Herbert, 61, 68, 69, 90
Fleetwood, William, 101, 105–111, 116

Fricker, Miranda, 38

Galston, William, 199
Gellner, Ernest, 140, 145
Gemeinschaft, 16, 176
Gesellschaft, xvi
Goffman, Erving, 73, 78, 90
Goldman, Alvin, 168–169
Good Wife and Wise Mother (良妻賢母 *ryōsai kenbo*), 47–49, 177, 178, 243n37
Gosse, Edmund, 35, 47
Guanxi (关系), 28–29
Gu, Hongming, 6, 32

Habermas, Jürgen, 94, 96
Habits of the Heart
  Confucian, 13, 17, 20, 26, 29, 31, 158, 217, 218, 221
  North American, 22, 26
Hall, David, 19, 40–41, 163, 164, 170
Han, Feizi, 135–136
Hanlin Academy, 3
Hansen, Chad, 31
Hate speech, 209–210, 213
Haven, Joseph, 223
Hayek, Friedrich, 181
Hegel, Georg, 10, 12, 144
Herder, Johann, 17–18, 218
Hinduism, Hindus, 8, 239n39
Hiratsuka, Raichō, 49–50, 51, 56, 57, 114, 178–179, 250n63
Hobbes, Thomas, 70
Hsieh, Yuwei, 97
Humaneness/benevolence (仁 *ren*), xv, 8, 52, 53, 62–67, 68, 72, 86, 91, 97, 99, 100, 103, 104, 171, 177
Huntingdon, Samuel, 15
Hu, Shih, 9

Ibsen, Henrik, xv, 34, 35, 42, 44, 47, 49, 58

Identity politics, x, 216
Imperial Way, The (皇道 *kōdō*), 155
Individualism
  Atomistic, 12, 16, 160
  Confucian, 153
  Ethical, xi–xiv, 18, 33, 35–39, 46, 50, 51, 54, 56, 58, 72, 79, 83, 98, 175, 200, 204, 215, 228, 242n9
  Feminist, 49–50, 177–179
  Metaphysical/ontological conception of, 40, 43–44, 46
  Possessive, 110
  Western liberal/rights-bearing, xv, 14, 15, 16, 19, 26, 30, 33, 34, 42, 43–44, 47, 52, 97, 132, 151, 154, 162, 163, 173, 176, 177, 248n8, 253n19
Individualization, xii, 229, 231
Ing, Michael Kualana, 62–63, 65
Inoue, Kowashi, 25, 141
Inoue, Tetsujirō, xvi, 10–11, 12, 132, 138–155, 158–159, 161, 237n23, 252n10, 262n61
Islam, Muslims, 8, 16, 204, 212, 260n14
Ivanhoe, Phillip, viii, 99–100, 102–104, 107, 116, 245n8

James, William, 45
Jesa (제사 Korean memorial rites), 226–228
Jesuits, 2, 9
Jiang, Qing, 157, 181, 184–185, 186, 230, 231
Judaism, 23
Justice (non-Confucian), 34, 87, 106, 125, 134, 135
  Free-standing concept of justice, 199, 217
  Political liberal concept of justice, 199, 203, 205, 207–208, 211, 212–214, 228
  Social justice, 129, 232

Justice-based conception of authority, 190–195

Kant, Immanuel, xiii, 10, 50, 85, 140, 194, 216, 223, 250n68
Kato, Midori, 48–49, 51
Kedourie, Elie, 140
Keller, Simon, 120
Kim, Dae Jung, 231–233
Kim, Sungmoon, viii, 89, 206, 217–226, 228–229, 248n8
Kingly Way, The (王道 ōdō), 137, 152, 154–156, 252n10
Koyama, Shizuko, 48

Lee, Kuan Yew, 232
Legalists, legalism, 19, 92, 133, 135–136, 148, 164
Liang, Qichao, 11
Liang, Shuming, 11
Liberalism, 14, 18, 19, 29, 34, 174, 177, 182, 204, 206, 218, 228, 248n8
  Comprehensive (see comprehensive doctrines)
  Economic, 18
  Neoliberalism, 12, 14, 16, 18, 82
  Of fear, 203–206, 228
  Political liberalism, 14, 26, 198–199, 200, 203, 205, 206, 207
  Public reason liberalism (see *public reason*)
Li, Chenyang, 97, 102, 103, 104, 108, 116, 118
Lincoln, Abraham, 160
Liu, Liangjian, 100
Locke, John, 104, 108, 110, 204
Loyalty (忠 zhong /chū), xv, 12, 13, 25, 50, 82, 107, 132, 133–138, 139–140, 141–142, 144, 146, 148–149, 151, 152–153, 160, 177, 183, 239n40
  The oneness of loyalty and filial piety (see filial piety)
  The unity of loyalty and filial piety (see filial piety)
Lu, Xun, 5–6, 131, 155, 237n20

Macintyre, Alasdair, 35, 40, 44, 46, 87, 100
Mackenzie, Catriona, 125
Maruyama, Masao, 88, 139
Marxism, xiii, 15, 18
Maugham, Somerset, 6, 32
Mencius, xv, 41, 51, 52–53, 83, 84, 133, 134–135, 142, 155, 164, 165–166, 172, 185, 222, 230, 252n10
Metzger, Thomas, 163, 167
Mill, John Stuart, 126, 181, 194, 204
Mito School, 132, 137, 142, 146, 153
Morishima, Michio, 13
Motoda, Nagazane, 25, 141
Mou, Zongsan, 8, 9, 12, 15
Mozi, Mohism, xv, 31, 62–69, 71
  State consequentialism of, 65, 72
Mufti, Aamir, 16

Narayan, Uma, 25
National Polity (國體 Kokutai), xvi, 137–138, 143, 150, 151, 152–154, 159, 160–161, 252n14
Nationalism, xv–xvi, 92, 132, 140, 239n39
  Banal, 215
  Confucian, 12
  Cultural, 9, 12–13, 15, 32, 139, 224
  Ethnic, 139, 152, 221, 224–225
  Hypernationalism, 15, 132, 140–141, 152–153, 156, 204
  Illiberal, 157
  Liberal, 215–216, 218
  Statist, 12, 25, 31, 132, 139, 140, 156, 157, 214

National morality (国民道徳 *kokumin dōtoku*), 11, 12, 131, 138, 139, 143–161, 215
Natural law, 54, 116, 174, 232
Newman, John Henry, 1
New Woman, The (新しい女 *atarashii onna*), 47, 50, 178–179
Nishibe, Susumu, 141, 157
Nishi, Amane, 10, 223
Noguchi, Yone, 156
Nussbaum, Martha, xii, 50, 194, 243n36

Ogasawara, Yuko, 76
Orientalism, 9, 16, 19, 28, 33

Paramore, Kiri, 11, 23
Parekh, Biku, 19
Park, Chung-hee, 232
Particularism
　Ethical and cultural, 34–35, 42, 51, 118, 183, 206, 212, 216, 218, 220
　National, 129, 151, 157, 218
Pateman, Carol, 113
Perfectionism, 30
　Confucian, 39, 55–59, 179, 184, 189, 220–221
　Ethical, 39, 125
　Feminist, 125–127, 194
　Liberal, 192, 244n22
　Political, 39, 55–59, 125–127, 167, 177, 179, 184, 187–194, 214, 217, 220–221, 225, 227–228, 229
Pharr, Susan, 75, 76–77, 167, 168
Plato, 100
Pluralism, x, xv, xvi, 1, 34, 39, 56, 57, 62, 85–86, 92, 158, 161, 177, 179, 182, 187, 194, 198–200, 202–203, 205, 206, 207–216, 217, 220, 222, 225–226, 228, 229, 230, 231, 232–233

Postcolonial theory, 15, 16, 99, 239n39
Pragmatism, xvi, 19, 157, 163, 173, 178
Primary goods, 190–191, 193, 214
Properties, 40
　Membership, 41, 43
　Relational, 41, 43
Private sphere, 113, 144, 211
Public Reason, 192, 193–195
　Confucian, 195, 206, 217–228, 230, 231
　Rawlsian, 206–207, 211, 212–213, 216, 217, 230, 261n27
Public political forum, 206, 211–213, 261n27
Putnam, Hillary, 20

Quong, Jonathon, 126, 190, 192

Rawls, John, 167, 190, 193, 198–199, 206, 207, 211–212, 214, 217, 228
Raz, Joseph, 189
Republicanism, 155, 159, 218
　Republican liberalism, 34, 199
Richardson, Samuel, 87, 101, 108–109, 111–113, 116, 118
Rights, 19, 34, 40, 43, 44, 87, 88, 94, 111, 118, 119, 129, 173, 185, 187, 190, 192, 211, 214, 219–220, 228, 229
　Animal, 197
　Civil, 29, 76, 195, 198, 199, 203, 206, 210, 211, 212–214, 216, 217
　Deontological, 117–119
　Human, 18, 19
　Natural, 174, 204
　Political, 195, 198, 199, 203, 206, 213, 214, 217
　Property, 110, 195, 198, 199, 214, 217, 228

Righteousness/Justice/Appropriateness (*yi* 義), xv, 62–63, 62–67, 67, 68, 72, 90–91, 97, 134, 171, 177
Ritual Deference, ix, xv, 62, 65, 67, 98, 108, 225
  Asymmetrical, 62, 70–71, 72, 73, 73–80, 82, 83–89, 118, 176, 183
  In Japanese workplace tea serving (お茶くみ *ochakumi*), 74–77, 83
  In the Jim Crow South, 73–77, 79–80
  Symmetrical, 62, 77, 90–96
Ritual propriety (*li* 禮), xv, 8, 61–97, 171, 177, 226
Rosemont, Henry, 17, 19, 35, 40–42, 44, 45, 56, 98, 99
Ross, Robbie, 61–62, 90–91
Rousseau, Jacques, 159, 161, 221
Royce, Josiah, 16, 239n41

Sage, 53, 54, 69, 71, 112, 133, 137, 138, 167, 172, 178, 184
Sandel, Michael, 35, 42, 44–46
Sectarianism, 159, 161, 192, 200, 203–206, 208–209, 215, 227–228, 233
Seitō Journal (青鞜), 47–49, 51, 56, 57, 177, 178, 250n63
Sen, Amartya, xii, 121
Service conception of authority, 188–191
Shin, Gi-wook, 224, 263n68
Shinozaki, Mamoru, ix, 235n1
Shintō, 11, 13, 137–138, 140, 141, 145, 157, 160
Shklar, Judith, 203–204
Shun (legendary sage king), 51, 133, 134–135, 165
Sima, Guang, 149
Smith, Adam, 109
Smith, Lilian, 80
Social facts, 21–24, 30, 207, 222
Social media, 92–93

Sommers, Christina Hoff, 101, 117–119, 250n68
Sōseki, Natsume, xiii
Stalnaker, Aaron, 81, 83–88, 89, 91, 96
State religion, 158, 159–161
  Confucian, 3, 139, 157, 181, 220, 230–231
Sun, Anna, 3
Sun, Yat Sen, 155

Tagore, Rabindranath, 47, 156, 243n36
Tamir, Yuli, 215, 218
Tang, Junyi, 15
Tanizaki, Junichirō, 115
Tan, Sor-hoon, 19, 90, 163, 164, 170, 173, 176–179, 180
Taylor, Charles, 35, 36
The self
  As disencumbered, xv, 33, 35, 45, 46, 51, 52, 58, 114, 178
  As encumbered, xv, 40, 44, 51, 54
  As unencumbered, xv, 33, 34–36, 40, 43–44, 46
  Substantial, 40–41, 42–43
Thick ethical concepts, 20–29, 30, 207, 222
Tomida, Hiroko, 48
Trade unions, xii, xiv, 214, 236n7
Tu, Weiming, 13–14, 164, 171–172, 183

Uchimura, Kanzo, 161, 227–228
Universalism, 11, 24, 145
  Ethical/moral universalism, 24, 34, 94, 98, 101, 118, 129
  Universalist political ideologies, 15
  Universalist political philosophy, 218, 220
Uri (우리 weness), 221–222, 224–225
  Uri minjok (우리민족 our nation/people), 224
  Uri nara (우리민족 our nation), 224

Utilitarianism, 11, 19, 26

Vogel, Ezra, 13
Volksgeist, 12, 144–146

Waldron, Jeremy, 34
Wan Chung (disciple of Mencius), 134–135
Wang, Yangming, 11, 152, 155
Watsuji, Tetsujirō, 152, 159–160
Weber, Max, 13, 79, 132, 141, 143, 151
Wilde, Oscar, 61–62, 90–91
Williams, Bernard, 20
Wollstonecraft, Mary, 113
Wordsworth, William, 32

Wright, Richard, 76, 79
Wu, Jingzi, 4

Xunzi, 62, 69–72, 74, 75, 81
Xu, Xing, 165–166

Yasuoka, Masahiro, 152, 154, 155
Yi, Kwangsu, 223–224
Yosano, Akiko, 25, 51
Yoshida, Kenkō, 63
Yoshida, Shōin, 146, 153
Yu, Pung Kwang, 10

Zhang, Junmai, 11, 15
Zhou, Beichen, 230
Zhu, Xi, 149

www.ingramcontent.com/pod-product-compliance
Lightning Source LLC
Chambersburg PA
CBHW020641230426
43665CB00008B/265